One-Day Adventures by Car

ONE-DAY ADVENTURES BY CAR

With Full Road Directions for Drives out of New York City

by **Lida Newberry**
Revised by Joy Johannessen

HASTINGS HOUSE · PUBLISHERS
New York

Hastings House, Publishers
New York, New York

Distributed to the trade by
Kampmann & Company, Inc.
New York, New York

Library of Congress Cataloging in Publication Data

Newberry, Lida.
  One-day adventures by car.

  Includes index.
  1. New Jersey–Description and travel–1951–Tours. 2. New York (State)–Description and travel–1951–Tours. 3. Connecticut–Description and travel–1951–Tours. 4. Automobiles–Road guides–New Jersey. 5. Automobiles–Road guides–New York (State) 6. Automobiles–Road guides–Connecticut. I. Title.
  ISBN 0-8038-9280-2   86-082711

Manufactured in the United States of America

10 9 8 7 6 5 4 3 2 1

Contents

INVITATION TO ADVENTURE

In all directions from New York City superb highways lead to a wonderland of scenic beauty and historical lore, to noble houses and spacious gardens, to villages cultivating the arts and crafts, and to an ever-changing shoreline. All these can be reached in motor-car drives usually within a 100-mile radius, inside of one day.

One day there and back—no overnight stay—and an exhilarating adventure of exploration and discovery, right on our doorstep.

Have a good day.

LIDA NEWBERRY

A NOTE ON THE FIFTH EDITION

Many of the attractions listed in earlier editions of *One-Day Adventures by Car* have since closed, many of those that remain have changed considerably, and many new ones have appeared. The book has been extensively revised, but I have tried to preserve the spirit of adventure and discovery that animated the late Lida Newberry.

I began this revision with the intention of thanking by name the many people who helped in it. It quickly became apparent that such a listing was impractical, so I will only say this. To work on a travel guide is to get to know America and Americans at their best—proud of their local traditions, working to preserve their natural, historical, and cultural heritage, eager to share their knowledge and experience of the places they call home. I thank them all.

J. J.

INTRODUCTION

The sites covered in this book lie mainly within a 100-mile radius of New York City, though there are some extension trips up to 150 miles away. With rare exceptions, restaurants and lodgings are not included. The territory is divided into eight adjoining areas beginning south along the Atlantic Coast and forming an arc that encompasses much of New Jersey, upstate New York, and western Connecticut, with occasional excursions across the Pennsylvania and Massachusetts borders. Finally we drive across Long Island and then return home for a brief look beyond the Empire State Building and Broadway to the attractions of Staten Island, the Bronx, Queens, and Brooklyn.

Most of the trips include several sites and list each separately, with full information on hours, fees, and facilities in italics, followed by a description of the site; detailed driving instructions appear at the end of the trip in "For the Driver." Some of the trips, particularly those to areas beyond the 100-mile radius, are arranged as drives, and various points of interest along the way are given in SMALL CAPITAL LETTERS, with capsule descriptions incorporated into the driving instructions. Small capitals are also used to call attention to sources of further information and to attractions nearby or on the way to featured sites.

Hours, Fees, and Facilities
The italicized material following the name, address, and telephone number of each site gives information on season, hours, admission fees (including senior citizens' and children's rates), facilities, and other applicable information (special events, pet policies, wheelchair access, etc.). Every effort has been made to insure the accuracy of this information. However, hours of operation and fees are subject to change without notice and often fluctuate from one year to the next.

The facilities or range of activities offered at a given site may also change. As this book was being updated, for example, certain beaches in the Palisades Interstate Park system, normally open all summer, were closed intermittently due to a shortage of lifeguards; federally operated parks and historic sites, facing possible budget cuts under the Gramm-Rudman Act, were unsure of hours, fees, and staff availability for the coming season; and many private operators of amusement parks and recreational facilities had temporarily discontinued, or were contemplating discontinuing, various rides and activities because of skyrocketing insurance costs. On the other hand, many sites were remodeling, expanding, and planning to increase their services.

To be absolutely certain that a given site will be open, affordable, and in full operation when you plan to visit it, call in advance.

Facilities for Handicapped Travelers

A special effort has been made to include information on wheelchair facilities, Braille Trails, fragrance gardens, tactile displays, and other features designed to increase a site's accessibility to all visitors. For easy reference, this information always appears at the end of the italicized material accompanying each entry. (See also "Special Passes to Federal and State Sites," below.)

A site described as "fully wheelchair-accessible" has reserved or unproblematic parking, at least one wide entrance, ramps and/or elevators, and specially equipped restrooms; "wheelchair-accessible" means that the site has wide doors and ramps designed for wheelchairs or that it is naturally barrier-free; "manageable for wheelchairs" means that hills, rough spots, low steps, or other impediments are negotiable. If a site "will accommodate wheelchairs," it has no special facilities and is difficult or impossible to manage unaided, but the staff will gladly assist you and show you as much of the site as possible; in these cases, it is helpful to call in advance.

Pets

Where applicable, this guide includes information about whether and under what conditions pets are allowed on the sites. Remember never to leave your pet in the car with the windows rolled up. *On a hot summer day, do not leave your pet in the car at all;* even with the windows down, the danger of dehydration and heat-stroke is very real.

Group Travel

If you're planning a group outing, *always* call ahead. Most sites require advance reservations and offer special discounts for groups, often at a substantial savings over the regular admission fee. Some sites will open specially or remain open beyond their scheduled hours to accommodate groups; some have tours, demonstrations, lectures, film showings, etc., available to groups but not to individual travelers; and some have facilities for rental to groups.

Distances and Tolls

The one-way distances given at the beginning of each trip are estimated from the George Washington Bridge (GWB) to the farthest point on the trip, unless otherwise noted. The speed indications immediately following are based on the route given in "For the Driver" at the end of each trip and assume light traffic.

General toll information for each area is given in the driving guidelines ("Traveling to Area A," etc.) that appear at the beginning of that area. New York City bridge and tunnel tolls (see p. xvi) are *not* included in the tolls given in "For the Driver," which are one-way highway tolls collected in both directions. If your route differs from the one suggested in "For the Driver," these tolls should be adjusted accordingly, and doubled if you take the same route going and coming back. Remember to add the bridge and tunnel tolls as appropriate.

Maps and Driving Instructions

Before setting forth on your one-day adventure, arm yourself with a good map, one that is detailed enough to be followed along with the directions in "For the Driver." The various state and local tourism organizations (see "Further Information," below) will happily supply you with all the free maps you can use.

The directions in "For the Driver" take you out of the city via a given exit point and then from the first to the last site on each trip. Many of the routes were chosen for their scenic appeal and leisurely pace and are not necessarily the most direct or the fastest. Of course the best route out of the city will depend on your place and time of departure, and you will want to choose the exit point most convenient for you. You may also want to take the fastest route rather than the most scenic, skip one or more sites on a trip, or combine trips. The book is designed to help you do this. At the beginning of each area is a page of general information ("Traveling to Area A," etc.) giving the relevant exit points, principal highways, and connections in that area. Using this information, you can plan the route that suits you best. Because a given trip generally picks up where the previous trip left off or contains cross-references to other trips and nearby sites, it's easy to create your own itinerary.

Any seasoned New York driver has his or her own bag of tricks for dealing with the ever-present specter of the New York City Traffic Jam, appearing predictably during rush hour and on most weekends, but equally capable of materializing suddenly out of nowhere, for no apparent reason, at any time. Use all the wiles at your disposal to keep the specter at bay: avoid rush hour when possible (though at least you'll be going out when the commuters are coming in, and vice versa), get an early start on weekends, check the newspapers or radio to see if there's any construction work in progress on your route—and bring a good book along in case your best efforts fail.

Finally, a word to the wise. Don't drink and drive; obey traffic regulations, and fasten your seatbelt.

The Great Outdoors

If you're going to spend a day outdoors, plan sensibly: be prepared for rain and dress appropriately, bearing in mind possible temperature differences in wilderness areas; in warm weather, bring insect repellent; be sure to obey applicable safety regulations for activities like swimming, boating, canoeing, skiing, and horseback riding; don't take pets into areas where they are prohibited, and keep them leashed as required; don't feed or otherwise disturb wildlife, don't pick or destroy flowers and plants; light fires only in designated areas and be sure to extinguish them carefully. If you're going fishing, find out whether state laws, seasons, and limits apply. If you're visiting a municipally run beach or other facility, inquire about nonresident permits and fees.

For further information about federal and state parks, preserves, recreation areas, historic sites, and other facilities, contact the following sources.

National Park Service
Room 1013
US Department of the
   Interior
18th and C Sts., NW
Washington, D.C. 20240

202-343-4917

National Forest Service
US Department of
   Agriculture
14th St. and Independence
   Ave., SW
South Agriculture Building
Washington, D.C. 20250

202-447-3760

New York State Office of
   Parks, Recreation, and
   Historic Preservation
Empire State Plaza
Albany, NY 12238

518-474-0456

New Jersey Department of
   Environmental Protection
Division of Parks, Forestry
   and Recreation
CN 404
Trenton, NJ 08625

609-292-2733

Connecticut Department of
   Environmental Protection
Parks and Recreation
   Division
165 Capitol Ave.
Hartford, CT 06106

203-566-2304

Pennsylvania Department of
   Environmental Resources
Office of Public Information
Harrisburg, PA 17120

717-787-2657

Massachusetts Department
   of Environmental
   Management
Division of Forests and Parks
Leverett Saltonstall
   Building
Government Center
100 Cambridge St.,
   19th Floor
Boston, MA 02202

617-727-3180

Special Passes to Federal and State Sites

There are three congressionally authorized passes for visitors to federal parks, historic sites, and other facilities administered by the National Park Service. The Golden Eagle Passport ($10), for persons under 62, is valid for one calendar year and is available by mail from National Park Service or Forest Service headquarters in Washington, D.C. (see above), or from their regional offices. The Golden Age Passport, for persons 62 and older, and the Golden Access Passport, for blind and disabled persons, are lifetime permits issued to citizens or permanent residents of the United States; both are available directly from the sites that accept them and need not be obtained in advance.

All three passports admit holders without charge to parks, monuments, historic sites, and recreation areas in the National Park Service system where entrance fees are imposed. They are valid for the passport holder and accompanying passengers in a private car or, where entry is not by private car, for the passport holder and immediate family. The Golden Eagle Passport is a worthwhile investment for travelers planning several visits to National Park Service sites that charge entrance fees; it does not cover use fees (e.g., for camping, boat launches, parking, etc.). In addition to free entry, the Golden Age and Golden Access Passports provide a 50% discount on use fees.

Most state park systems have comparable passports or permits available to state residents. For information about these, contact the state park departments listed above.

Sources of Further Information

All the states featured in this guide have tourism divisions that will assist you in planning a trip to the attractions within their borders and send you quantities of free information on request.

New York State Department of Commerce
Division of Tourism
1 Commerce Plaza
Albany, NY 12245

518-474-4116
800-CALL-NYS

New Jersey Department of Commerce and
    Economic Development
Division of Travel and Tourism
CN 286
Trenton, NJ 08625
609-292-2470

Connecticut Department of Economic Development
Tourism Division
210 Washington St.
Hartford, CT 06106

203-566-3385
800-243-1685
800-842-7492 (in CT)

Pennsylvania Department of Commerce
Bureau of Travel Development
416 Forum Building
Harrisburg, PA 17120

717-787-5453
800-VISIT-PA

Massachusetts Department of Commerce and Development
Division of Tourism
100 Cambridge St.
Boston, MA 02202

617-727-3201
800-343-9072

For Massachusetts and Connecticut, you can also contact the New
England Vacation Center, 630 Fifth Ave., New York, NY 10020
(212-307-5780).

Regional, county, and local tourism agencies tend to be staffed
with enthusiastic, knowledgeable, helpful people and are usually
gold mines of information on specific areas; these are listed in the
text where appropriate.

NEW YORK CITY BRIDGE AND TUNNEL TOLLS

Port Authority Crossings (New York-New Jersey)

GEORGE WASHINGTON
  BRIDGE
LINCOLN TUNNEL
HOLLAND TUNNEL
GOETHALS BRIDGE
BAYONNE BRIDGE
OUTERBRIDGE CROSSING

$2 collected inbound to city, no toll collected outbound

Interborough Crossings

BROOKLYN-BATTERY
  TUNNEL
QUEENS-MIDTOWN TUNNEL
TRIBOROUGH BRIDGE
BRONX-WHITESTONE BRIDGE
THROGS NECK BRIDGE

$2.00 collected in both directions

HENRY HUDSON BRIDGE

$1 collected in both directions

VERRAZANO-NARROWS
  BRIDGE

$4.00 collected from Brooklyn to Staten Island, no toll collected from Staten Island to Brooklyn*

*One-way toll collection on the Verrazano is being tried as an experiment; depending on the results, the bridge authority may reinstitute two-way collection, $2.00 each way.

New Jersey Shoreline and Colonial Trails

• *Our first trips unlock the treasure chest that lies close to New York City in New Jersey. Nature has been lavish with this shoreline, providing over 120 miles of white ocean sand, rolling breakers, and fresh, unpolluted air. Long Branch, Asbury Park, Atlantic City are on our route. Seaside amusement parks, marine museums, wildlife refuges, and pine barrens invite us. Turning inland, we follow historic trails that lead us to Revolutionary battlefields and white mansions preserved from colonial days. Eventually we cross the Delaware River into beautiful Bucks County in southeastern Pennsylvania.*

Exit Points
George Washington Bridge (GWB), Lincoln Tunnel, Holland Tunnel, Verrazano-Narrows Bridge, Goethals Bridge

Main Roads
Garden State Pkwy (GSP), New Jersey Tpk (NJT)

Connections
To reach GSP
  —from GWB, follow signs for I-80 and take it west about 10 mi to Exit 62;
  —from Lincoln Tunnel, follow signs for NJ 3 and take it west about 11 mi to signs for GSP;
  —from Holland Tunnel, follow signs for NJT and, depending on destination, take NJT south to Exit 11 and GSP, or north to Exit 16W to NJ 3 west to signs for GSP;
  —from Verrazano Bridge, take I-278 west across Staten Island to NY 440, following signs for Outerbridge Crossing and continuing on 440 briefly after Outerbridge to jct with GSP.
To reach NJT
  —from GWB, follow signs;
  —from Lincoln Tunnel, follow signs;
  —from Holland Tunnel, follow signs;
  —from Verrazano Bridge, take I-278 west across Staten Island, following signs for Goethals Bridge, then follow signs from Goethals Bridge to NJT.
To reach GWB
  —from GSP, use Exits 163 or 159 southbound, Exits 159 and 161 northbound;
  —from NJT, use Exits 18E/18W.
To reach Lincoln Tunnel
  —from GSP, use Exit 153 southbound, Exit 153A northbound;
  —from NJT, use Exit 16E.
To reach Holland Tunnel
  —from GSP, use Exit 141 southbound, Exits 129 or 140 northbound;
  —from NJT, use Exit 14C.
To reach Verrazano Bridge
  —from GSP, use Exits 137 or 129 southbound, Exits 127, 129, or 137 northbound;
  —from NJT, use Exit 13.

3

Tolls

One-way highway tolls (collected in both directions) are given in "For the Driver" at the end of each trip and are calculated from GWB unless otherwise indicated. To estimate tolls from other exit points: from Lincoln Tunnel, subtract 30¢ on NJT, 15¢ on GSP; from Holland Tunnel, subtract 20¢ on NJT, 25¢-35¢ on GSP; from Verrazano Bridge, subtract $1 on NJT, 75¢ on GSP.

For New York City bridge and tunnel tolls, see p xvi, remember to add these to the highway tolls as appropriate, depending on your route.

Sandy Beach and Highlands at New York's Doorstep

TRIP A-1

MOUNT MITCHILL, Atlantic Highlands

TWIN LIGHTS STATE HISTORIC SITE, Highlands

SANDY HOOK UNIT, Gateway National Recreation Area

DISTANCE: From GWB to farthest point, Sandy Hook, about 55 mi. Mainly fast speeds.

Mount Mitchill, Atlantic Highlands, NJ. The highest point along the Atlantic Coast from Maine to Florida (263 feet) offers views of distant New York, Sandy Hook, and the Atlantic Highlands Municipal Harbor. Mount Mitchill County Park is a nice place to stop and picnic while enjoying the sights. The ATLANTIC HIGHLANDS HISTORICAL SOCIETY, 27 Prospect Ave., Atlantic Highlands, NJ 07716 (201-291-2718), maintains a museum and library (open Sundays 1-4 from Memorial Day to Labor Day, free, wheelchair-accessible) in a restored 20-room Victorian mansion on the slope of Mount Mitchill. The town will celebrate its centennial in 1987; check for special events.

Twin Lights State Historic Site, Lighthouse Rd., Highlands, NJ 07732 (201-872-1814). *Grounds open daily all year 9-dusk; museum open daily all year 9-5; closed Thanksgiving, Christmas, New Year's. Free. Self-guided tour, audio stations, films and slide programs, picnic facilities and grills. Leashed pets only. Parking lot has ramp, and some exhibits are wheelchair-accessible; site being remodeled to further accommodate wheelchairs.*

Twin Lights, on the Navesink Highlands, has been the site of a lighthouse since 1756. The present structure was built in 1862 and became America's first electrically powered lighthouse in 1898. The next year Guglielmo Marconi conducted the first practical demonstration of wireless telegraphy by transmitting the America's Cup race results from Twin Lights to the *New York Herald* newspaper, some 15 miles away. The museum chronicles these and other significant chapters in the history of American seafaring; in addition to a working replica of Marconi's wireless, there are specimens of Jersey-built boats, a lighthouse lens exhibit, and the one remaining station of the old US Life Saving Service, which merged with the Revenue Cutter Service in 1915 to become the US Coast Guard. From the twin towers of the lighthouse we enjoy a panoramic view of the Atlantic and New York Harbor.

Sandy Hook Unit, Gateway National Recreation Area, PO Box 437, Highlands, NJ 07732 (201-872-0115). *Grounds open daily all year dawn-dusk; visitor center open daily all year 8:30-5; museum open all year Sat-Sun 1-5. Beach parking fee (per motorized vehicle) Memorial Day to Labor Day $2 weekdays, $3 weekends and holidays; other activities and parking free. Parking in designated areas only; 1-hr parking limit at visitor center. Ranger-led and self-guiding tours (history tour, beach and forest walks, old Dune Trail); swimming (Memorial Day to Labor Day) in lifeguard areas only during posted hours; picnicking, cooking, surfing, windsurfing, in designated areas only (check with ranger); fishing by permit (free); food, refreshments, restrooms, showers, beach supplies, phones, and first aid available at beaches. No walking on dunes, no biking on boardwalks, no pets at beaches, leashed pets only elsewhere. Ramps at visitor center and beach parking area, some wheelchair-accessible restrooms.*

Gateway National Recreation Area was created by Congress in 1972 as one of the nation's first major urban park areas. It opened in 1974 under the management of the National Park Service, which has spearheaded a vigorous effort to preserve the area and reverse the environmental degradation that has taken place over the centuries since the Algonquin Indians roamed these shores. It consists of four units: the Jamaica Bay, Breezy Point, and Staten Island Units in New York, and Sandy Hook in New Jersey. Together they serve as a refuge in the heart of the megalopolis for many species of flora and fauna, including *Homo sapiens*. For FURTHER INFORMATION and a biannual program guide to events at all four units, contact the Public Affairs Office, Gateway National Recreation Area, Building 69, Floyd Bennett Field, Brooklyn, NY 11234 (718-338-3687).

The Sandy Hook Unit extends over an arm of land that has had strategic importance in the defense of New York Harbor since colonial times. At the Spermaceti Cove Visitor Center there are exhibits describing the natural and cultural history of Sandy Hook, aquariums with local marine life, and a 14-minute slide program shown on request. From the Sandy Hook Museum in Fort Hancock's guardhouse and jail we can take guided tours through the fort and the great gun emplacements, Mortar Battery and Battery Potter. We can also visit the Sandy Hook Proving Ground, where US Army weapons were tested from 1876 to 1920 (report any bullets or projectiles to a ranger immediately; *do not handle*). Sandy Hook boasts the oldest operating lighthouse (1764) in the US, and the peninsula's fragile sand dune ecology shelters a great variety of plant and animal life. The famed holly forest is a perennial attraction, and over 300 species of birds have been sighted in the area, including the endangered osprey.

Sandy Hook is still under development, and the National Park Service is continually experimenting with new programs. It is wise to check hours and scheduling in advance if you are interested in a particular attraction or activity. Over two million people visited Sandy Hook last year; you may want to plan your trip for spring, fall, or winter, when the park is less crowded.

FOR THE DRIVER: Take GSP south to Exit 117 ($1.15) and pick up NJ 36 southeast through Keansburg, passing signs for KEANSBURG AMUSEMENT PARK (201-495-1400). A few mi after, exit at sign to Atlantic Highlands Business District. At Mount Ave (Borough Hall and police station on corner) turn right and go up hill to Prospect Ave and Atlantic Highlands Historical Society Museum, on right. To reach Mount Mitchill County Park, go back down hill to road you came into town on and continue toward municipal harbor. Just before harbor, turn right on Ocean Blvd and go about 1½ mi to top of Mount Mitchill and park. (You can get there from the museum, but it's tricky. Ask directions at museum if you want to try.)

Continue on Ocean Blvd and rejoin NJ 36 southeast to Highlands. Just before Highlands Bridge, turn right on Portland Rd and take an immediate right onto Highland Ave. Proceed up hill to Twin Lights entrance, on left. Access road is steep and narrow, so exercise caution.

Go back to NJ 36, turn right, cross Highlands Bridge, and turn left into Sandy Hook Unit, Gateway National Recreation Area. At entrance to Sandy Hook, you are about 5 mi north of Long Branch, first stop on Trip A-2, and about 10 mi east of Marlpit Hall, one of the sites on Trip A-9.

Where Presidents Sought Sea Breezes

TRIP A-2

 LONG BRANCH

 ASBURY PARK

DISTANCE: From GWB to Long Branch, about 60 mi; to Asbury Park, about 65 mi. Mainly fast speeds.

Long Branch. *Tourist season Memorial Day to Labor Day; beach season weekends Memorial Day to mid-June, daily mid-June to Labor Day. Beach fees: weekdays $2 adults, $1.50 students; weekends and holidays $3 adults, $2 students; senior citizens free. Swimming, fishing pier, boardwalk activities. No pets on beaches, no pets or bikes on boardwalk. Boardwalk wheelchair-accessible. For further information, contact the Greater Long Branch Chamber of Commerce, 494 Broadway, Long Branch, NJ 07740 (201-222-0400).*

From the Civil War to the First World War, well before the word "lifestyles" was coined, this popular resort town played host to the nation's rich and famous. Presidents Grant, Garfield, Arthur, McKinley, Hayes, Harrison, and Wilson worshiped at the Episcopal church, which is known today as the Church of the Presidents and houses the LONG BRANCH HISTORICAL MUSEUM (201-229-0600), open to the public by appointment. Also open to the public is WOODROW WILSON HALL (201-222-6600) in nearby West Long Branch. Now the administration building of Monmouth College, this lavish 130-room mansion was built as a private residence at a cost of $10.5 million just before the Crash of '29. More recently it appeared as Daddy Warbucks' mansion in the 1982 movie *Annie.*

Long Branch's fine beaches still draw thousands of visitors, and the town is currently building a new oceanfront promenade. One of the latest attractions is KID'S WORLD (201-222-0005), an educational amusement park with water slides, playgrounds, clowns, animals, computers, picnic areas, and more, open from early May until early September.

Asbury Park. *Tourist season Memorial Day to Columbus Day; beach season Memorial Day to Labor Day. Beach fees: weekdays $5 adults, weekends and holidays $8 adults; children and senior citizens less (check for new rates going into effect in 1986). Swimming, fishing, surfing in designated areas, boardwalk activities. Free municipal band concerts on boardwalk Sun and Thurs July-Aug; year-round special events, including annual boat show, arts festival, bocce tournament, clown convention and festival. No pets on beaches, no pets or bikes on boardwalk. Boardwalk wheelchair-accessible. For further information contact the Greater Asbury Park Chamber of Commerce, PO Box 649, Asbury Park, NJ 07712 (201-775-7676).*

Asbury Park, another popular resort town, is famous for its boardwalk, Convention Hall, saltwater taffy, and Bruce Springsteen. It was founded in 1871 by New York brush manufacturer James A. Bradley as a vacation colony for temperance advocates. The town takes its name from Francis Asbury, the first American bishop of the Methodist Episcopal Church. It is studded with fine architecture in a wide variety of styles and in recent years has undertaken an ambitious waterfront and downtown redevelopment project. The indoor Palace Amusement Center offers activities rain or shine, and there's a lovely carousel nearby. In 1934 the luxury liner *SS Morro Castle* foundered a few hundred yards from Convention Hall, engulfed by a mysterious fire that claimed over 100 lives and burned for a week. It is said that the one-way street was invented in Asbury Park to handle the crowds that flocked to watch this grim spectacle.

FOR THE DRIVER: Take GSP south to Exit 105 ($1.25), then pick up NJ 36 east into Long Branch. On the way, you may want to detour south on Monmouth Rd to West Long Branch and Woodrow Wilson Hall, or north on Oceanport Ave to catch thoroughbred racing at MONMOUTH PARK (201-222-5100). Coming into Long Branch on 36, pass Ocean Blvd, turn right at Ocean Ave, and follow signs for Kid's World, at 65 Ocean Ave. The Church of the Presidents is further south, at 1260 Ocean Ave. From here, continue south on Ocean Ave about 3 mi to Asbury Park.

If skipping Long Branch or going to Asbury Park first, take GSP south to Exit 102 ($1.25), just past Asbury Park toll plaza. Follow Asbury Ave to traffic circle and follow signs into Asbury Park.

To a Restored Village and
a Religious Beach Resort

TRIP A-3

ALLAIRE STATE PARK, Farmingdale
ALLAIRE VILLAGE
PINE CREEK RAILROAD
OCEAN GROVE

DISTANCE: From GWB to Allaire, about 70 mi; from Allaire to Ocean Grove, about 10 mi. Mainly fast speeds.

Allaire State Park, PO Box 220, Farmingdale, NJ 07727 (201-938-2371). *Open daily all year, late Oct to mid-March 8-4:30, mid-March to Memorial Day 8-6, Memorial Day to 1st week of Sept 8-8, 2nd week of Sept to last week of Oct 8-6. Parking fee (Memorial Day to Labor Day only): cars $1 weekdays, $2 weekends and holidays; motorcycles $1. Picnic facilities, boating (canoe rentals), nature center (201-938-2003) staffed Memorial Day to Labor Day, fishing in season in Manasquan River (special Lower Mill Pond fishing area for children under 14), riding and hiking trails, campsites, 18-hole golf course (equipment rentals), cross-country skiing, sledding, refreshment stand. Leashed pets only in park, no pets in campsites. Most facilities not wheelchair-accessible; inquire about Braille Trail.*

In 1941 the family of newspaperman Arthur Brisbane deeded 1,200 acres of land to the people of New Jersey for use as a "historical center and forest park reservation." Since then the park has grown to cover over 3,000 acres of the New Jersey coastal plain.

Allaire Village, Allaire State Park (201-938-2253). *Open early May to Labor Day Mon-Sat 10-5, Sun 12-5; open some weekends in Mar-Apr, Sept-Dec (call in advance). Park admission fee includes village; check at visitor center for tour information and calendar of events (craft and antique shows, flea markets, concerts, annual St. Nicholas Day celebration). Chapel services Sun 9am end of June to end of August; general store open daily May-*

Oct, weekends April and Nov-Dec; wagon rides and pony rides daily May-Sept, weekends Sept-Dec. Buildings not wheelchair-accessible.

In the late 1700s Allaire was the site of a furnace and forge where iron was smelted from the "bog ore" produced by decaying vegetation. In 1822 James P. Allaire purchased the ironworks to supply his foundry in New York City and built a bustling industrial community of over 400 people. With the discovery of higher-grade Pennsylvania ore and the increasing use of coal, Allaire declined, and the ironworks shut down in 1848. Today the village has been restored, and we can visit a furnace, a carpenter's shop, a blacksmith's, a bakery, and many other original buildings.

Pine Creek Railroad, Allaire State Park (201-938-5524). *Operates 12-5 weekends and holidays Apr-June and Sept-Oct, 12-5 daily July-Aug, and for special Easter and Christmas events. Fare $1 per person. Not wheelchair-accessible.*

All aboard for a trip back in time on New Jersey's only live-steam narrow-gauge railroad. We'll ride in antique cars pulled by a coal-burning locomotive of the kind that was used to push back the frontiers of the American West.

Ocean Grove. *Tourist season Memorial Day to weekend after Labor Day. Beach fees (per person): adults $4 weekdays, $5 weekends and holidays; children under 12 free. Beach picnics (fires by permit), swimming, fishing, boardwalk activities. No pets on beaches. Boardwalks wheelchair-accessible. For further information and tours contact the Ocean Grove Camp Meeting Association, 54 Pitman Ave., Ocean Grove, NJ 07756 (201-775-0035).*

This attractive small town, noted for its Victorian architecture, serves as a setting for religious and cultural programs, Bible meetings, evangelical talks, recitals. A National and State Historic Site, it was founded in 1869 for Methodist camp meetings. The Ocean Grove Auditorium, New Jersey's largest, was designed according to biblical principles and is approached via the Pilgrim's Pathway, built without use of nails. Repentance of sinners is preached from the big stage, and surfside meetings are held on the boardwalk on Sundays during summer. In recent years, the resident orchestra has staged a summer Mozart festival.

FOR THE DRIVER: Take GSP south to Exit 98 ($1.40) and pick up I-195 west toward Trenton, or take NJT south to Exit 7A ($1.85) and pick up I-195 east. From I-195 take Exit 31B, Allaire State Park, make a right at 1st traffic light onto Rte 524, and follow signs into park.

Return to GSP and go north to Exit 100. Pick up NJ 33 east and take it about 4 mi to Ocean Grove.

A Safari in the Pine Barrens

TRIP A-4

SIX FLAGS GREAT ADVENTURE, Jackson

DISTANCE: From GWB, about 75 mi. Fast speeds.

Six Flags Great Adventure, PO Box 120, Jackson, NJ 08527 (201-928-3500). *Operating schedule varies each year; check in advance. Basic season is late Mar thru Sept: Mar to late May and after Labor Day 10-10 weekends and occasional weekdays; May-June 10-10 weekdays, 10-midnight weekends; July-Aug 10am-11pm weekdays, 10-midnight weekends; safari open 9-5, weather permitting, on days when park is open. Combination ticket (theme park and safari) $16.95 per person, theme park only $15.95, safari only $5.95; parking $3 per car; shows and arena concerts $2-$5. No pets in park; free kennels (owner provides food). No picnics in park, but picnic area adjoins parking lot; restaurants and snack bars. Limited number of rental strollers and free wheelchairs available at Guest Relations. Ramps to buildings and to all shows except arena; restrooms adapted for wheelchairs; plenty of benches and shade, level walks.*

Great Adventure, opened in 1974 on 1,500 acres of Pine Barrens, is two parks, an African safari and a theme park. Since every year brings new attractions and improvements, it is an annual affair for many visitors. The safari park is a maze of auto roads through 350 acres of simulated African plain harboring Bengal tigers, lions, rhinos, bears, llamas, giraffes, baboons, ostriches, and other wild animals. Three lanes provide stopping areas on either side; for those who don't want to drive or don't have cars, the park operates a safari bus ($2 per person). The animals take noontime siestas and are best viewed early or late in the day.

The theme park is alive with jousters, chariot racers, rodeo performers, clowns, dancing dolphins, and rides galore, including roller coasters, runaway trains, flying waves, two Great Flume rides, and the new Ultra Twister, a dizzying marvel of parabolic rail technology. Bugs Bunny and friends entertain in Looney Tunes Land, and Kiddie Kingdom gets the smallest fry into the act. There's an elaborate 19th-century carousel, and a 15-story ferris wheel in constant motion. We can shop at international bazaars and eat in an oversized Conestoga wagon, an emporium shaped like an ice cream sundae, a filigreed gazebo, or outdoors at an umbrella-shaded table.

FOR THE DRIVER: Take NJT south to Exit 7A ($1.85), then I-195 east about 12 mi to Exit 16, Mount Holly-Freehold, and follow signs to Great Adventure, about 3 mi southwest on Rte 537. Or take GSP south to Exit 98 ($1.40), pick up I-195 west about 15 mi to Exit 16, and proceed as above.

From Great Adventure you can easily reach ROVA FARMS (201-928-0928), a Russian resort community where you can visit an Orthodox church and dine at the local Russian restaurant (open Tues for lunch, Sat-Sun for lunch and dinner). Go northeast on Rte 537 just past jct with I-195, turn right on Rte 571, and go about 6 mi southeast to Rova Farms.

Sea Breezes and Sparkling Beaches

TRIP A-5

POINT PLEASANT BEACH

SEASIDE HEIGHTS and SEASIDE PARK

ISLAND BEACH STATE PARK, Seaside Park

DISTANCE: From GWB to Point Pleasant Beach, about 75 mi; to Seaside Heights, about 85 mi. Fast and average speeds.

Point Pleasant Beach. *Beach season Memorial Day to Labor Day. Boardwalk beach fees: adults $5 weekends and holidays, $4 weekdays; less for children and senior citizens, and for non-boardwalk beaches (fees vary). Swimming, deep-sea fishing, boat rentals, waterskiing, rides, amusements, boardwalk activities, special events. No pets on beaches. Boardwalk wheelchair-accessible. For further information contact Point Pleasant Beach Chamber of Commerce, 517A Arnold Ave., Point Pleasant Beach, NJ 08742 (201-899-2424).*

This Atlantic Ocean bungalow colony has 2 miles of white sandy beaches and a bustling boardwalk lined with arcades, rides, stores, and restaurants. The town is home port to a fleet of commercial fishing vessels, but folks out for pleasure rather than business will find plenty of action in these waters, either on their own or in numerous fishing tournaments throughout the season. The Walsh Off-Shore Grand Prix, one of the major powerboat races in the United States, attracts large crowds every July, and in September the Seafood Festival offers delicacies from the deep as well as an art show. Moonlight sailing is popular and provides good views of the Thursday night fireworks in summer.

Seaside Heights and **Seaside Park.** *Tourist season late May to mid-Sept. Beach fee: adults $1.25 weekdays, $2 weekends and holidays; children under 12 free. Some free parking on west side of town. Swimming, fishing, crabbing, surfboat rental, water skiing, jet skiing. Free entry to amusement park, fees per activity. No pets on beach. Beach has ramp for wheelchairs. For further information, contact Seaside Heights Visitor Information, Seaside Heights, NJ 08751 (201-793-8700), and Seaside Park Borough Hall, Seaside Park, NJ 08752 (201-793-0234).*

Fun and games for the whole family here on this beautiful 3-mile beachfront and mile-long boardwalk amusement park crammed with rides, wheels of chance, snack bars, restaurants, and shops. In late May Father Neptune opens the beaches for the season, and there are special events all summer, including fireworks on July 4th and every Wednesday night. There's an annual Mardi Gras celebration the weekend after Labor Day.

Island Beach State Park, PO Box 37, Seaside Park, NJ 08752 (201-793-0506). *Open daily all year, daylight hours; summer hours 8-8. Parking fee: Memorial Day to Labor Day $4 per car weekends and holidays, $3 weekdays; cars off-season and motorcycles all season $1; all vehicles 50¢ at Inlet Area control gate Memorial Day to Labor Day. Guided nature tours, swimming, surf fishing (24 hours a day by permit), picnicking and barbecuing (no facilities provided), surfing, beach strolling, scuba diving, beach buggies (for fishing only, by permit): all permitted in designated areas only. Lifeguards, bathhouses, storage lockers (25¢) available in*

some areas. No pets in swimming areas, leashed pets only else-
where. Some facilities wheelchair-accessible.

One of the few remaining natural barrier beaches, this narrow 10-mile strip of land is a lovely spot to picnic and enjoy the sights and sounds of the ocean. Two nature areas offer acres of dunes dotted with holly clumps and briar thickets, and there's a recreation area for more active pursuits. The southern tip of the park is just a stone's throw from Barnegat Light on Long Beach Island (Trip A-6). Remember that the dunes and beach grass are crucial to the island's fragile ecology; walk and drive only in designated areas.

FOR THE DRIVER: Take GSP south to Exit 98 ($1.40) and pick up NJ 34 southeast to jct with NJ 35. Continue southeast on 35 into Point Pleasant Beach. From here go south on 35 about 10 mi to Seaside Heights and Seaside Park. Entrance to Island Beach State Park is just south of Seaside Park as you go through town on Central Ave.

For a different return route, go back to Seaside Heights and pick up NJ 37 west towards Toms River. This will take you back to GSP north and GWB ($1.50) or lead you to several nearby attractions. From Hooper Ave exit north of 37, you can visit the OCEAN COUNTY COLLEGE PLANETARIUM (201-255-4144) on College Dr for daytime stargazing or evening concerts. Minutes away, on Fischer Blvd, is the CATTUS ISLAND PARK AND NATURE CENTER (201-270-6960), with a scenic bay view and abundant bird life. South off 37, in Toms River at 26 Hadley Ave, is the OCEAN COUNTY HISTORICAL SOCIETY MUSEUM (201-341-1880) and nearby Revolutionary War battle site in Huddy Park.

About 9 mi north of Toms River via US 9, 1 mi east of Lakewood on NJ 88, is OCEAN COUNTY PARK (201-370-7360), former Rockefeller estate and arboretum, offering swimming, a children's fishing lake, athletic fields, playgrounds, Slide City, shuffleboard, picnicking and grills, tennis, platform tennis, and canoeing.

For FURTHER INFORMATION about the many other attractions and recreational facilities in this area, contact the Toms River-Ocean County Chamber of Commerce, 48 Hyers, Toms River, NJ 08753 (201-349-0220).

A Day-Long Marine Drive

TRIP A-6

LONG BEACH ISLAND

DISTANCE: From GWB, about 115 mi to center of Long Beach Island. Mainly fast speeds.

We're now approaching an area beyond an average day's trip from New York City, but we'll take a few drives, get the lay of the land, and perhaps come back when we have more time.

Long Beach Island is an 18-mile-long barrier reef with bays and meadowlands on the inland side. Along with beautiful scenery, it offers a wide variety of recreational and cultural activities. Since our trip is planned primarily for the enjoyment of the drive, the directions are combined with brief descriptions of the principal attractions to be found along the way. If you plan to stop for a swim, apply to the nearest municipality for a beach badge (fees vary), required on all the island's beaches. For FURTHER INFORMATION about Long Beach Island, contact the Long Beach/Southern Ocean County Chamber of Commerce, 265 W. 9th St., Ship Bottom, NJ 08008 (609-494-7211), or the Ocean County Office of Tourism and Public Information, CN 291, Toms River, NJ 08753 (201-929-2138).

Take GSP south to Exit 63 ($1.75), then NJ 72 east to Long Beach Island. Cross the Causeway to Ship Bottom in the center of the island. Proceed a block or two and turn left (north) onto Long Beach Blvd., the main road that runs the length of the island. About 6 miles up, after passing through Surf City and Harvey Cedars, you will reach Loveladies, where you can stop in at the LONG BEACH ISLAND FOUNDATION OF ARTS AND SCIENCES (609-494-1241). Check here for information about exhibits, films, concerts, and lectures.

Continue on Long Beach Blvd. to Barnegat Light, near the tip of the island. Here, at 5th St. and Central Ave., is the BARNEGAT LIGHT MUSEUM (609-494-3407). Originally the island's one-room schoolhouse, the museum now houses a marine display including the French lens used in the original Barnegat Lighthouse crown, with 1,024 prisms forming 24 bull's-eye lens belts 15 feet high. Behind the museum are the Edith Duff Gwinn Gardens.

Just ahead, turn left to BARNEGAT LIGHTHOUSE STATE PARK (609-494-2016), with picnicking, fishing, and swimming. The main attraction is Old Barney, the famous lighthouse, commissioned in 1834 and in operation continuously for over 75 years thereafter. The long climb to the top offers a marvelous view.

Return along the main road to Ship Bottom and proceed south about 6 miles to Beach Haven. Here, among other activities, you can take the kids to THUNDERING SURF WATER SLIDE at 8th St. and Bay Ave. (609-492-0869) and FANTASY ISLAND AMUSEMENT PARK at 320 W. 7th St. (609-492-4000), visit the LONG BEACH IS-LAND HISTORICAL ASSOCIATION MUSEUM, Engleside and Beach Aves. (609-492-0700), or take in a show at the SURFLIGHT SUM-MER THEATER, 211 Engleside Ave. (609-492-9477).

Continue south as far as the road goes, to the HOLGATE WILD-LIFE REFUGE (609-652-1665), part of Brigantine National Wildlife Refuge (Trip A-7). This rather remote area is a nesting ground for skimmers, terns, and oystercatchers.

You have now completed your tip-to-tip tour of Long Beach Island. Go back to Ship Bottom for your return trip to New York.

More Adventures in the Pine Barrens

TRIP A-7

BASS RIVER STATE FOREST, New Gretna
BATSTO STATE HISTORIC SITE, Hammonton
TOWNE OF HISTORIC SMITHVILLE, Smithville
BRIGANTINE NATIONAL WILDLIFE REFUGE,
    Oceanville

DISTANCE: From GWB to New Gretna, about 125 mi. Mainly fast speeds.

Bass River State Forest, PO Box 118, New Gretna, NJ 08224 (609-296-1114). *Open daily all year, daylight hours. Parking fee Memorial Day to Labor Day $2 per car weekdays, $3 weekends and holidays; otherwise free. Swimming, picnic area and grills at beach, boating (free ramp), fishing, hiking and riding trails, camping, playground, nature area. No pets on beach, leashed pets only* *elsewhere. Wheelchair-accessible restrooms and beach at Lake Absegami.*

This large and beautiful woodland has good facilities and a lovely lake, Absegami. Horses can be rented from the nearby BASS RIVER RIDING RANCH (609-296-1755), just outside the park.

Batsto State Historic Site, RD 4, Hammonton, NJ 08037 (609-561-3262). *Grounds open daily all year; buildings open daily 10-5 Memorial Day to Labor Day. Parking fee weekends and holidays Memorial Day to Labor Day $2 per car; otherwise free. Free self-guided walking tour and nature tour, guided mansion tour ($1.50 adults, 75¢ children under 12), stagecoach rides (60¢). Visitor center and restrooms wheelchair-accessible; otherwise difficult for wheelchairs.*

The Dutch and Scandinavians called their steam baths *baatstoo,* a word the Indians adopted, which eventually turned into *batsto,* "bathing place." This historic village lies at the southern edge of WHARTON STATE FOREST (609-561-3262), a 108,000-acre tract of Pine Barrens offering picnicking, primitive camping, hiking, swimming, fishing, canoeing, and winter sports. On our self-guided tour we learn that nearly 1,000 people once lived and worked in 19th-century Batsto; we can visit the ironmaster's 36-room mansion, a carriage house, a blacksmith shop, some workers' homes, and the old bog iron furnace, which produced munitions used at Valley Forge. There is a feeling of mystery here; the great mansion rising out of nowhere should be in a thriving town, not among tall forest trees in the Pine Barrens. Batsto Nature Area, located just beyond the village, is always open during summer. It contains over 130 species of plants and many small animals.

Towne of Historic Smithville, Smithville, NJ 08201 (609-652-7775). *Open daily all year; shop hours vary with season. No admission fee, ample free parking. Annual Mayfest, Oktoberfest, tree-lighting ceremony, and other special events. Cobbled walk with curb, no wheelchair access to most buildings.*

The original Smithville Inn was established in 1787, and that era provides the flavor of the town reconstructed around it for our shopping and dining pleasure. Over 30 restored buildings are open for business, including several restaurants, antique shops, craft shops, a winery, and the Smithville Train, a miniature railroad offering seasonal rides through town.

Brigantine National Wildlife Refuge, PO Box 72, Oceanville, NJ 08231 (609-652-1665). *Open all year, daylight hours, weather permitting; office hours 8-4:30 weekdays. Free. Interpretive nature trails, fishing, crabbing, self-guided auto tour. Insect repellent recommended during summer months.*

Brigantine, established in 1939, is part of the Edwin B. Forsythe National Wildlife Refuge, over 34,000 acres of coastal wetlands vital to the protection of waterfowl and their habitat. The 8-mile auto tour includes 14 stops and lasts 1½ hours. Photographers with proper equipment may obtain permits to use the blinds. Over 250 species of birds have been sighted here and at the refuge's Holgate unit on Long Beach Island (Trip A-6), including the endangered peregrine falcon, piping plover, least tern, and black skimmer. The spring and fall migrations are spectacular (write or call in advance for a free calendar of wildlife events); the birds nest in Canada, winter in Florida, and regularly pass through here via the Atlantic Flyway. Besides these transients, over 150,000 waterfowl winter here. And all this with the long gray skyline of swinging Atlantic City a distant backdrop across the bay.

FOR THE DRIVER: Take GSP south to Exit 52 for New Gretna ($2). Turn right off ramp and go ¼ mi to sign for Bass River State Forest. Turn right here and go about 1 mi to entrance.

To continue to Batsto, follow signs from Bass River via back roads or return to jct with GSP and go past it about 1 mi to US 9. Go south about 1 mi on 9, through blinker light in New Gretna, to Rte 542. Turn right here and go 12½ mi to Batsto.

Return to jct of 542 and US 9 in New Gretna. Go south on 9, shortly rejoin GSP, then take Exit 48 (no toll) and continue south on 9 to Smithville.

From Smithville continue south about 1½ mi on US 9 to Oceanville. Watch for sign on left, just before Oceanville post office, to Brigantine, 1 mi east.

A Day in "The World's Playground"

TRIP A-8

ATLANTIC CITY

DISTANCE: From GWB, about 140 mi. Fast speeds.

Atlantic City, New Jersey's most famous resort town, has activities for almost every taste. In addition to the free public beaches and 6-mile boardwalk (America's first, built in 1870), there is a large selection of hotels offering casino gambling and top-flight entertainment year-round. In the northeast corner of the city is ABSECON LIGHTHOUSE (609-345-6328), built in 1857 and now a museum of coastal artifacts. A few blocks west is GARDNER'S BASIN (609-348-2880), a restored turn-of-the-century fishing village with a waterfront park, aquarium, marine mammal museum, and 18th-century clipper ship. Across from Gardner's Basin and Clam Creek, the FRANK S. FARLEY STATE MARINA (609-441-3600) has everything for the angler (surf and deep-sea fishing is excellent in these waters). Several blocks south of the lighthouse on Pennsylvania Ave. is GORDON'S ALLEY (609-344-5000), a pedestrian shopping mall. Among the attractions on the boardwalk, which is lined with shops and amusements, are the GARDEN PIER ARTS CENTER (609-347-5844), OCEAN ONE PIER (609-347-8082) for shopping and dining, and the famed CONVENTION HALL (609-348-7000), which hosts regular sports events and the annual Miss America Pageant. There's thoroughbred racing at the ATLANTIC CITY RACE COURSE (609-641-2190), Exit 12 off the Atlantic City Expressway.

For FURTHER INFORMATION about Atlantic City, contact the Atlantic City Convention and Visitors Bureau, 16 Central Pier, Atlantic City, NJ 08401 (609-345-7536), the Greater Atlantic City Chamber of Commerce, Central Pier, Atlantic City, NJ 08401 (609-345-5600), or the Atlantic City Public Relations Office, Convention Hall, 2310 Pacific Ave., Atlantic City, NJ 08401 (609-348-7044). For information about the Miss America Pageant, contact the Miss America Pageant Office, 1325 Boardwalk, Atlantic City, NJ 08401 (609-345-7571). Should you care to extend your stay in Atlantic City, you can call the central hotel reservation service toll-free at 800-524-1706.

FOR THE DRIVER: Take GSP south to Exit 38 ($2), then Atlantic City Expressway east directly to Atlantic City (25¢). On your way, you will pass exits for sites on Trip A-7.

Only a few miles south of Atlantic City, in Margate, is an attraction you may find hard to resist: LUCY THE MARGATE ELEPHANT (609-823-6519), a 6-story, 90-ton pachyderm made of wood and tin. This National Historic Landmark (open weekends 10-5 in spring and fall, daily 10-8:30 from June 15 to Labor Day; adults $1.50, children $1) was built in 1881 as a real estate promotion, then operated as a tourist attraction into the early 1960s. Facing demolition, Lucy was donated to the city of Margate and rescued by the Save Lucy Committee, a volunteer civic group that began restoring her in 1973. Today you can tour this Victorian architectural folly beginning at the rear legs and climbing up the spiral staircase to Lucy's howdah for a nice view of the surrounding seascape. If coming from Atlantic City, just go south out of town on Atlantic Ave; Lucy is at 9200 Atlantic. If traveling directly to Margate, task GSP south to Exit 36 ($2) and follow signs (or return to New York this way if going to Margate from Atlantic City).

To the Heart of Historic Monmouth County

TRIP A-9

MARLPIT HALL, Middletown

US ARMY COMMUNICATIONS-ELECTRONICS
   MUSEUM, Fort Monmouth

MONMOUTH COUNTY HISTORICAL ASSOCIATION,
   Freehold

NATIONAL BROADCASTERS HALL OF FAME, Freehold

COVENHOVEN HOUSE, Freehold

GARDEN STATE ARTS CENTER, Holmdel

CHEESEQUAKE STATE PARK, Matawan

DISTANCE: From GWB to first stop, Middletown, about 50 mi. Fast speeds, then average speeds on approx 45-mi loop to last stop, Cheesequake.

On our last few trips we have been traveling south along the Jersey shore, pushing to the outer limits of a day's journey from New York. Now we return to an area closer to the city and begin to move inland a bit to explore the natural, historical, and cultural attractions of Monmouth County. For FURTHER INFORMATION, contact the Monmouth County Department of Public Information and Tourism, Hall of Records Annex, Freehold, NJ 07728 (201-431-7310).

Marlpit Hall, 137 Kings Highway, Middletown, NJ 07748 (201-671-3237 or 462-1466). *Open April-Dec Tues 1-4, Thurs 1-4, Sat 10-4, Sun 1-4. Adults $1, senior citizens 75¢, children 6-18 50¢, under 6 free. First floor manageable for wheelchairs.*

Begun in 1685 by James Grover, Jr., as a one-room Dutch cottage, Marlpit was enlarged in the English style about 1740 by Tory merchant John Taylor. Today it is maintained as a museum by the Monmouth County Historical Association. The period furnishings reflect life in pre-Revolutionary Middletown.

US Army Communications-Electronics Museum, Building 275, Kaplan Hall, Fort Monmouth, NJ 07703 (201-532-2445). *Open all year Mon-Thurs 12-4; closed Fri-Sun and federal holidays. Free. Parking lot has ramp, and museum is wheelchair-accessible.*

Here we learn what a big role communications play in military campaigns, an aspect of warfare rarely seen by the civilian. We'll view quantities of apparatus of all kinds, from the signal flags of the Civil War to early satellite communications.

Monmouth County Historical Association, 70 Court St., Freehold, NJ 07728 (201-462-1466). *Museum open all year Tues-Sat 10-4, Sun 1-4; library open all year Wed-Sat 10-4. Adults $1, senior citizens 75¢, children 6-18 50¢, under 6 free. Difficult for wheelchairs.*

Founded in 1898, the Historical Association is dedicated to preserving and interpreting Monmouth County's heritage. Its headquarters, a beautiful three-story Georgian structure built in 1931, is the setting for one of the country's best regional museums. Fine examples of period furnishings and Americana are well displayed. The floor devoted to "attic artifacts" is especially popular with kids. The library is primarily for research and includes a genealogical and historical reference section. In addition to the museum, the association maintains four historic buildings in Monmouth County (Marlpit Hall, Covenhoven House, Allen House, Holmes-Hendrickson House).

National Broadcasters Hall of Fame, 22 Throckmorton St., Freehold, NJ 07728 (201-431-4656). *Open by appointment only. Adults $2, children $1. Difficult for wheelchairs, but will accommodate. May be moving to a new location, but plans uncertain as of this writing; call in advance.*

Here's a museum crammed with all things pertaining to radio broadcasting from its early years into the projected future. There are many fascinating mementoes of the industry, and actual programs can be heard in the small theater.

Covenhoven House, 150 W. Main St., Freehold, NJ 07728 (201-462-1466). *Open June-Oct, Tues 1-4, Thurs 1-4, Sat 10-4, Sun 1-4. Adults $1, senior citizens 75¢, children 6-18 50¢, under 6 free. First floor wheelchair-accessible.*

Maintained by the Monmouth County Historical Association, this Georgian house was built in the mid-18th century by William A. Covenhoven, a successful local farmer, and is furnished according to a 1790 inventory of his estate. In 1778, just before the Battle of Monmouth, the house served as headquarters for British general Henry Clinton.

Garden State Arts Center, Telegraph Hill Park, PO Box 116, Holmdel, NJ 07733 (201-442-9200). *Open all year daily. Grounds free, admission charged for performances. Most facilities wheelchair-accessible.*

Built and maintained by the New Jersey Highway Authority, this center for the performing and creative arts was designed by Edward Durrell Stone. It seats 5,100 in the amphitheater and another 4,000 on the adjacent lawn. There is a varied program of classical and pop concerts, musicals, ballets, ethnic heritage festivals, and special events for senior citizens, handicapped people, schoolchildren, and other groups.

Cheesequake State Park, Matawan, NJ 07747 (201-566-2161). *Open daily all year, daylight hours. Parking fee: Memorial Day to Labor Day $2 per car weekdays (Tues free), $4 weekends and holi-*

days; weekends May and Sept $2; other times free. Self-guided nature trails, hiking, jogging, cycling, swimming (lifeguards, bathhouses, concession stand during summer), picnic tables and grills, campsites, fishing and crabbing, playing fields, skating, sledding, cross-country skiing. Leashed pets only. Some areas and facilities wheelchair-accessible.

This 990-acre park only 40 miles from New York lies in the transition zone between New Jersey's northern and southern vegetation and thus has a unique diversity of plant and animal life. The whole park is a designated wildlife sanctuary. The name is a garbled English version of a Lenni Lenape Indian word meaning "quaking bog," and there is evidence that the area was inhabited as long as 6,000 years ago. There's a small display of Indian artifacts at the park office. The various hiking trails will take you through pine barrens, hardwood forests, marshlands, and swamps. Wildflowers abound in season, and a birdwatching checklist is available at the office.

FOR THE DRIVER: Take GSP south to Exit 114 ($1.15), then go east (left) on Red Hill Rd until it ends at Kings Hwy. Turn left and go about 1 mi to Marlpit Hall, on right.

From Marlpit Hall turn left and go east on Kings Highway to jct with NJ 35. Turn right on 35 and go south about 5 mi to Shrewsbury. At Sycamore Ave, on left, is OLD CHRIST CHURCH (201-741-2220), containing a rare copy of the Vinegar Bible, so called because "vineyard," in the parable, is misspelled. On right is ALLEN HOUSE, maintained by the Monmouth County Historical Association (201-462-1466). Built around 1750, it operated as the Blue Ball Tavern for many years and is today partially restored as a tavern, with gallery space for changing historical exhibits.

Continue south on NJ 35 briefly to jct with Rte 537. Turn left (east) to west gate of Fort Monmouth. Enter and go down Ave of Memories about 2 mi to sign for communications museum.

Go back to jct of NJ 35 and Rte 537. Proceed west on 537 about 10 mi to Freehold. At 1st light in town, 537 merges with NJ 79 to become Main St. Continue on Main past Hall of Records (Monmouth County Department of Public Information and Tourism is located in annex) to next light, Court St. Turn right and watch for Monmouth County Historical Association headquarters on left, across street from BATTLE MONUMENT.

Continue on Court St to next corner, Haley St, and turn left briefly to

Throckmorton St. Go 2 blocks on Throckmorton to Main, passing on left ST. PETER'S EPISCOPAL CHURCH (201-431-8383), used as a hospital by the British and later as a barracks by the Continental Army. Just across Main on Throckmorton is the National Broadcasters Hall of Fame.

Go back to Main St (go around block, since Throckmorton is one-way here) and go west (left) past jct with NJ 33. Here, en route to Covenhoven House, you can turn right and go west about 1 mi on 33 to FREEHOLD RACEWAY (201-462-3800), featuring harness racing, trotters, and pacers; just beyond is MONMOUTH BATTLEFIELD STATE PARK (201-462-9616), site of the longest battle of the Revolution, in which Molly Pitcher became legend by bringing water to her dying husband and going on to fight in his place. For Covenhoven House, don't turn on 33; continue past it on Main briefly to house, on left, just before Main meets US 9.

From Covenhoven House, turn right on Main St and go back into town to jct with NJ 79. Follow 79 north about 6 mi to Rte 520 and turn right (east) to jct with NJ 34. Turn left (north) on 34 and go about ½ mi to 1st right, Roberts Rd. Take this about 1½ mi to Longstreet Farm and Holmdel Park. Bear left here onto Longstreet Rd (Roberts goes off sharply to right) and watch for HOLMES-HENDRICKSON HOUSE, another building maintained by the Monmouth County Historical Association (201-462-1446), and a fine example of mid-18th-century local Dutch building traditions. From here, continue briefly on Longstreet Rd to Crawfords Corner Rd, turn right and make a quick left onto Holland Rd, take this under GSP, and turn left on Telegraph Hill Rd to Garden State Arts Center. If skipping Holmes-Hendrickson House, follow same directions out of Freehold but continue east on Rte 520 past jct with NJ 34 to GSP and take this north to Exit 116 (20¢) and arts center.

From arts center, continue north on GSP to Exit 120 (no toll) and follow signs for Cheesequake State Park. To return to New York from Cheesequake, follow signs in park to GSP and take it north back to GWB ($1).

Note that you can easily combine some of the stops on this trip with a visit to the shore sites in Trips A-1 and A-2.

To the Biggest Flea Market of Them All

TRIP A-10

ENGLISHTOWN AUCTION SALES, Englishtown

DISTANCE: From GWB, about 55 mi. Mainly fast speeds.

Englishtown Auction Sales, 90 Wilson Ave., Englishtown, NJ 07726 (201-446-9644). *Open all year Sat 7-5, Sun 9-5; also open 9-5 Mon* *of Labor Day weekend, Mon of Memorial Day weekend, Fri after Thanksgiving, Fri before Christmas; if phoning, call Fri-Mon 9-4. Free parking and entry. Wheelchair-accessible parking and restrooms.*

The mileage to Englishtown may look incongruous for a trip to a kind of glorified rummage sale, but not so to the avid auction buff, the antique enthusiast, the bargain sale fanatic. To tens of thousands of these, coming from as far away as upper New England, the Midwest, and the Deep South, this 50-acre flea market with over 700 vendors is a shopper's paradise. Described by the *New York Times* as "a glorious heap, with infinite possibilities," Englishtown Auction Sales was begun in 1929 by Steve and Katie Sobechko on land where the Battle of Monmouth once raged. It has survived two devastating fires and is still operated by the Sobechko family in the person of grandson Steve.

As you roam the streets and buildings, you can exchange your cash for evening dresses, army boots, cut-rate games, kitchen tables, ice cream molds, an elephant (so the story goes), and other treasures in untold categories. Concession stands dispense home-baked delicacies and foods of all kinds, and there are mountains of New Jersey produce. Arrive early to avoid parking problems and get a jump on the bargains.

FOR THE DRIVER: Take NJT south to Exit 9, New Brunswick ($1.50), then NJ 18 east about 4½ mi to Rte 527 (Englishtown-Old Bridge Rd). Turn right and go south about 8 mi to Englishtown, following signs for auction. Or take GSP south to Exit 123 (75¢), follow US 9 south for 7 mi to Texas Rd, turn right and go 2½ mi to Englishtown-Old Bridge Rd, at stop sign. Turn left and go 3 mi to Englishtown.

Englishtown is only about 5 mi from Freehold. If your flea market tolerance doesn't extend to a full day, you can easily combine this trip with parts of Trip A-9 or visit RACEWAY PARK (201-446-6331; taped message 446-6370), home of the National Hot Rod Association Summer Nationals, on Pension Rd off Rte 527 just north of the auction. It's open Wednesday evenings and Sundays from late March to late October, and for special events.

For a different route home and possibly an ocean dip after the dust of the battlefield, go south a few mi on Rte 527 to jct with NJ 33, then take 33 east about 20 mi past Monmouth Battlefield State Park (Trip A-9) to Asbury Park (Trip A-2).

Horticulture, Agriculture, and Culture

TRIP A-11

RUTGERS UNIVERSITY, New Brunswick
  RUTGERS DISPLAY GARDENS
  RUTGERS COLLEGE OF AGRICULTURE FARM
CORNELIUS LOW HOUSE, Piscataway
EAST JERSEY OLDE TOWNE, Piscataway

DISTANCE: From GWB, about 45 mi. Mainly fast speeds.

We are now in the heart of Middlesex County, land of the Lenni Lenape Indians, Thomas Edison, and Joyce Kilmer, among others. The county has a rich colonial and Revolutionary legacy and boasts an eclectic assortment of historical milestones, including the invention of the lightbulb and phonograph, the first printing press in New Jersey, the first medical society in the New World, the first snuff factory in the United States, the first canned food in the world (possibly the universe!), the first US black man to vote, the first intercollegiate football game, and the first US-made harmonicas. The dedicated and energetic organization that keeps track of such facts and anything else you may wish to know by way of FURTHER INFORMATION is the Middlesex County Cultural and Heritage Commission, 841 Georges Rd., North Brunswick, NJ 08902 (201-745-4489); the commission publishes a newsletter, a cultural calendar, and a very useful series of brochures outlining historic strolls through various towns in Middlesex County, including New Brunswick and East Brunswick.

Rutgers University, Van Nest Hall, New Brunswick, NJ 08903 (information 201-932-1766; campus tours 932-7799). *Free tours by arrangement. Most of campus wheelchair-accessible.*

Rutgers, the State University, was chartered in 1766 as Queens College and opened its doors in 1771. Today it serves a student population of over 47,000. Its libraries, art galleries, and museums are open to the public free of charge, and there are several theaters offering a varied program of plays and concerts. Of special interest are the JANE VOORHEES ZIMMERLI ART MUSEUM (201-932-7237), with an extensive permanent collection and changing exhibits, and the GEOLOGY MUSEUM (201-932-7243), with natural history exhibits, mineral and fossil displays, and Indian artifacts.

On our trip we are visiting two facilities administered by Cook College, the Rutgers college of agriculture and environmental sciences. For FURTHER INFORMATION contact Cook College Campus Tours, Waller Hall, PO Box 231, New Brunswick, NJ 08903 (201-932-8915).

Rutgers Display Gardens. *Open dawn to dusk daily; closed Dec. Free. Self-guided tour pamphlet available through Cook College Campus Tours. Grass paths over flat grounds; wheelchair-manageable with assistance.*

Here are the finest in ornamental plantings, including a nationally known holly orchard, an annual flower display, and a special lilac display in season. Nearby, in the northeast corner of Cook campus, is the Frank G. Helyar Woods, a mature hardwood forest with a nature trail winding through various woodland habitats.

Rutgers College of Agriculture Farm. *Open daily all year; barns closed at milking time. Free. No picnics. Some areas manageable for wheelchairs.*

We can wander about on our own here, observing cattle, pigs, sheep, horses, and the whole range of activities involved in operating this busy working farm. We may even be lucky enough to witness a birth or other special event such as shearing. Under no circumstances should we disturb the animals, pick plants, or litter the grounds.

Cornelius Low House/Middlesex County Museum, 1225 River Rd., Piscataway, NJ 08854 (201-745-4489 or -4177). *Open all year Tues-Sat 1-4; closed Mon and holidays; may be closed during installation of exhibits (call in advance). Free. Wheelchair-accessible parking, and museum will accommodate wheelchairs; call in advance.*

Administered as a museum by the Middlesex County Cultural and Heritage Commission, the Cornelius Low House was built in 1741 and is considered one of the finest examples of a Georgian manor house in the United States. The museum offers changing cultural, historical, and scientific exhibits and sponsors an ambitious program of workshops, concerts, and special events.

East Jersey Olde Towne, 1050 River Rd., Piscataway, NJ 08854 (201-463-9077). *Village open Apr-Oct on 3rd Sat of month 12-3; office and gift shop open more frequently (call for hours). Guided tours by appointment $1 per person. Annual July 4th celebration and Christmas candlelight dinner. Low steps into some buildings, partially manageable for wheelchairs; call in advance.*

This restored 18th-century village grew out of a successful campaign to save New Brunswick's historic Indian Queen Tavern (1686) from demolition. Under the leadership of Dr. Joseph H. Kler, East Jersey Olde Towne went on to mount similar rescue operations for other buildings threatened by the march of progress in the form of highway construction, traffic congestion, pollution, and McDonald's restaurants. All but 2 of the 20 buildings are original (Three Mile Run Church and the barracks are replicas), and most were dismantled stone by stone from threatened sites to be reassembled here on the banks of the Raritan. In addition to the tavern, the village includes a farmhouse (c. 1748), a schoolhouse (c. 1799), a doctor's office and residence (c. 1710), a blacksmith shop (c. 1760), and several homes and outbuildings. For an authentic glimpse of rural colonial life, it's hard to beat this model of painstaking preservation and restoration.

FOR THE DRIVER: Take GSP south to Exit 130 (75¢) to US 1 south, or NJT south to Exit 9 ($1.50) to NJ 18 towards New Brunswick to US 1 south. Just below jct of US 1 and NJ 18, pass a Sears shopping center and proceed to Ryders Lane, just beyond. Here take Milltown-East Brunswick exit in 2nd part of cloverleaf, then make an immediate left after divider at red sign for Rutgers Display Gardens. Sign is hard to spot, so stay alert for turn after divider ends.

Go back to Ryders Lane, turn right, go to end, and turn right again, following road through Sears parking lot back to US 1 south towards Trenton. Immediately on right is College Farm Rd, also easy to miss if you don't watch carefully. Turn here for farm.

Go back to US 1 and go north to jct with NJ 18. Take 18 northwest into New Brunswick and exit at sign for Highland Park, across Raritan River. As you come over bridge, keep left and proceed to stoplight at foot of bridge. Here make a sharp left turn onto River Rd. Continue on

River Rd to 2nd stoplight, turn right, and take 1st left into parking lot for Cornelius Low House. Gravel walkway through gate at end of parking lot leads to house. About 1 mi further on River Rd, at next stoplight, is East Jersey Olde Towne, on left in Johnson Park.

Also of interest is the METLAR/BODINE HOUSE (201-463-8363) at 1281 River Rd, just before the Low House on right. This colonial structure with Federal and Greek Revival additions features changing historical exhibits and a permanent collection of "Piscataway memorabilia."

To reach the main campus of Rutgers University from East Jersey Olde Towne, go back down River Rd to Low House. Opposite it is the historic LANDING LANE BRIDGE, originally erected in 1772, destroyed by fire in 1894, and replaced the following year by the present steel truss structure. Turn right at bridge and cross back over Raritan River into New Brunswick. Here, in Buccleugh Park, is the BUCCLEUGH MANSION (201-745-5094), a lovely Georgian house (1739) whose floorboards still bear the saber and spur marks left by the Enniskillen Guards of Northern Ireland, quartered there during the American Revolution. Continue on Landing Lane to Easton Ave, turn left, proceed to Hamilton St, and turn right. This takes you to information center at Van Nest Hall and puts you in easy walking distance of Zimmerli Museum and Geology Museum.

To return to New York City, go back to Easton Ave, turn right, and proceed to Albany St (NJ 27). A left turn here takes you back to NJ 18 and then to US 1 north or NJT north to New York. On your way, you may want to take a brief detour to the JOYCE KILMER BIRTHPLACE (201-745-5117) at 17 Joyce Kilmer Ave. Kilmer, author of the poem "Trees," and one of New Brunswick's most famous sons, was born in this modest Greek Revival home in 1886 and spent his early childhood here. Today it houses New Brunswick's Dial-a-Ride program for senior citizens but is open for tours by appointment. To reach it, turn right off Albany St onto George St before reaching jct with NJ 18. Go a few blocks down George to Bayard St and turn right to Joyce Kilmer Ave. Here turn left and go a block or so to Kilmer Birthplace.

A Historic Headquarters and an Ivy Tower

TRIP A-12

ROCKINGHAM STATE HISTORIC SITE, Rocky Hill
PRINCETON UNIVERSITY, Princeton

DISTANCE: From GWB, about 60 mi. Fast and average speeds.

Rockingham State Historic Site/Berrien Mansion, Box 22, Rocky Hill, NJ 08553 (609-921-8835). *Open all year Wed-Fri 9-12 and 1-6, Sat 10-12 and 1-6, Sun 1-6; closed Mon-Tues. Free. Not wheelchair-accessible.*

While waiting for the signing of the peace treaty with England, the Continental Congress convened at Princeton University. General Washington was invited to attend and made his headquarters at nearby Rockingham, using the Blue Room as his study. Here, in November 1783, he wrote his "Farewell Address to the Armies." We can visit his study and step out as he must have on the balcony, but we won't see the same terrain he saw, for the restored building has been moved from its original site.

Princeton University, Princeton, NJ 08544 (609-452-3603). *Orange Key Guide Service conducts free tours year-round Mon-Sat at 10, 11, 1:30, 3:30, Sun at 1:30, 3:30; Nassau Hall open weekdays 2-5, Sat 9-5, Sun 1-5. Most of campus wheelchair-accessible.*

Tours include Nassau Hall, which was the nation's capitol in 1783, Prospect Gardens, and the University Chapel. We may also take self-guided tours, first stopping at the information office for maps and directions. We may want to extend our campus tour by walking to Palmer Square for shopping. For interested parties, on advance notice, tours may be taken through the Art Museum, the Forrestal Scientific Research Center, and the Museum of Natural History. Theatergoers should check in advance on the program at Princeton's highly respected MCCARTER THEATRE (609-452-5200).

FOR THE DRIVER: Take NJT south to Exit 9, New Brunswick ($1.50), turn right towards New Brunswick on NJ 18 and shortly pick up US 1 south. Go several mi to sign for Franklin Park, turn right, go to end of road and turn left onto NJ 27 south. Go about 3 mi to jct with Rte 518 and continue on 518 (27 branches left) toward Rocky Hill. Shortly look for Rockingham on right.

Continue west on 518 several mi to jct with US 206. Take 206 south into Princeton. In town at jct with Rte 583, to your right is the BATTLE MONUMENT, and beyond it, MORVEN, home of the New Jersey Historical Society. To your left (NJ 27, Nassau St) is Princeton University. Guided tours start at Maclean House, the yellow building to the right of Nassau Hall.

Finding Outlets in Flemington

TRIP A-13

FLEMINGTON CUT GLASS
LIBERTY VILLAGE and TURNTABLE JUNCTION
BLACK RIVER & WESTERN RAILROAD
FLEMINGTON AGRICULTURAL FAIR AND
SPEEDWAY

DISTANCE: From GWB, about 65 mi. Fast and average speeds.

Flemington was settled in the mid-18th century on land originally owned by William Penn. In the late 1800s it became a center for the production of fine pottery and glassware, as it still is. Today it is the home of a formidable array of factory outlets, shops, and restaurants. Among the historic sites we can visit are FLEMING'S CASTLE (201-782-9824), built in 1756 by the innkeeper for whom the town is named; nearby KASE CEMETERY, containing tombstones of early settlers; and the COUNTY COURTHOUSE on Main St., a Greek Revival building where the Lindbergh kidnaping trial was held in 1935. For FURTHER INFORMATION on Flemington and environs, contact the Hunterdon County Chamber of Commerce, Tourism Division, 119 Main St., Flemington, NJ 08822 (201-782-5955), or the New Jersey Tourist Information Center in Liberty Village (201-788-5729).

Flemington Cut Glass, 156 Main St., Flemington, NJ 08822 (201-782-3017). *Open all year 10-5:30 daily except Easter, Thanksgiving, Christmas, New Year's. Ample free parking. Showrooms on ground floor can accommodate wheelchairs.*

A series of stores and houses contains a wide assortment of gifts, home decorations, and fixtures. There is an enormous selection of glassware as well as lamps.

Liberty Village and **Turntable Junction,** 1 Church St., Box 161, Flemington, NJ 08822 (201-782-8550). *Open all year 10-5:30 daily except Easter, Thanksgiving, Christmas, New Year's. Ample free parking. Shopper's Special Bus leaves daily from Port Authority*

Terminal in New York; $5.60 each way, free return with pur-
chases of $25 or more. Facilities laid out on one level and mostly
accessible to wheelchairs.

Liberty Village opened in 1972 as a working craft village and museum. Today it has been converted into a Colonial Shopping Plaza and, together with Turntable Junction, offers more than 80 different shops and restaurants housed in reproductions of historic buildings. We'll visit places like Old Tyme Favorites, The Village Artizan, Grandma's Curtains, Little Hobby's, and factory outlets for hosiery, designer clothing, glassware and crystal, handbags, clocks, furniture, shoes, and much more.

Black River & Western Railroad, PO Box 200, Ringoes, NJ 08551 (201-782-9600). *Trains operate mid-Apr to late Nov for 1½-hr round trip from Flemington to Ringoes; daily July-Aug, weekends and holidays Apr-June, Sept-Nov. Adults $5, children 5-12 $3, children 3-5 $1, under 3 free. Museum, picnic area, snack bar at Ringoes. Inquire about Sunday trips to Lambertville on the Delaware River. Will accommodate wheelchairs.*

We ride in coaches, some built in 1875, with oil-burning lamps, potbelly stoves, plush seats, all in perfect condition. This is a working passenger and freight standard-gauge steam railroad, not a miniature, and its colorful rolling stock attracts all buffs. But we don't have to be buffs to get a thrill out of our ride through the historic countryside.

Flemington Agricultural Fair and Speedway, PO Box 293, Flemington, NJ 08822 (201-782-2413). *Fair opens Tues before Labor Day and runs thru Labor Day; adults $3, children 6-12 $1.50, under 6 free; $1.50 parking fee on fairgrounds. Speedway open Apr-Nov for Sat night races.*

This annual event is a treat for all, and an especially good opportunity to show the youngsters what a typical small country fair is like. The speedway is located on the fairgrounds.

FOR THE DRIVER: Take NJT south to Exit 10, I-287 ($1.45), follow I-287 north about 15 mi to US 22 west (Exit 10, on left) to Somerville. Go about 3 mi on 22 and pick up US 202 south to Flemington; there are several exits for 202, so make sure you take the one marked for Flemington. In town, at traffic light just before Flemington Mall, turn right to Main St, just ahead. Turn right on Main and proceed a few blocks, crossing railroad tracks to Flemington Cut Glass.

Come back down Main St to Church St and turn right to Liberty Village and Turntable Junction. To reach Black River & Western Railroad office, continue down Church St to Central Ave, make a right on Central, and cross tracks to office, just beyond.

Formerly located on Mine St across from the south side of Turntable Junction was STANGL POTTERY, now the site of the PFALTZGRAFF STORE (201-782-2918), a large pottery outlet. Stangl is out of business, but those seeking the famed Stangl dinnerware and artware can find it at Popkorn Antiques on US 202 north of Flemington.

From Turntable Junction go back through town on Church St to NJ 31. The fairgrounds are 1½ mi north on 31.

Journeys in Bucks County, Pennsylvania

TRIP A-14

NEW HOPE
  PARRY MANSION
  MULE BARGE
  NEW HOPE STEAM RAILWAY AND MUSEUM
PEDDLER'S VILLAGE, Lahaska
DOYLESTOWN
  FONTHILL MUSEUM
  MORAVIAN POTTERY AND TILE WORKS
  MERCER MUSEUM and SPRUANCE LIBRARY
  NATIONAL SHRINE OF OUR LADY OF
    CZESTOCHOWA
  BUCKS COUNTY COVERED BRIDGES TOUR

DISTANCE: From GWB to New Hope, about 75 mi; to Doylestown, about 85 mi. Fast and average speeds

Bucks County is a large and historically important area. To do it justice, you really need more than a day, though we have tried to single out the more notable attractions, particularly in the eastern and south-central regions closest to New Jersey. For FURTHER

INFORMATION, contact the Bucks County Tourist Commission, 152 Swamp Rd., Doylestown, PA 18901 (215-345-4552).

New Hope began to flourish in the 1720s as a ferry town. It was known as Coryell's Ferry during the Revolutionary War, when the local people aided the Continental Army. The mills operated by Benjamin Parry in the late 18th century and the opening of the Delaware Canal in 1832 made the town a bustling commercial center for a time. In the early 1900s New Hope attracted many noted painters, and its reputation as an artists' colony was enhanced by the opening in 1939 of the Bucks County Playhouse, now the State Theatre of Pennsylvania. Annual New Hope events include the Auto Show (summer), the Antique Show (fall), and the Phillips Mill Art Exhibit (fall), a juried show of works by local artists. For FURTHER INFORMATION, contact the New Hope Information Center, S. Main & Mechanic Sts., New Hope, PA 18938 (215-862-5880).

Parry Mansion, S. Main & W. Ferry Sts., New Hope, PA 18938 (215-862-5652). *Open May thru Sept Fri-Sun 1-5. Donation $2 per person. Not wheelchair-accessible.*

This house was purchased by the New Hope Historical Society in 1966 from the descendants of Benjamin Parry, a wealthy lumbermill owner who built it in 1784. It has been restored to reflect the changes in interior decoration over time. We can see whitewash yield to wallpaper, candles to oil lamps, and the craze for Victoriana to more severe modern tastes.

Mule Barge, New Hope Barge Co., PO Box 164, New Hope, PA 18938 (215-862-2842). *Operates early Apr to mid-Nov, weather permitting; daily May to mid-Oct approx every hr 11:30-6; Wed, Sat, Sun in Apr approx every hr 1-4:30; Wed, Sat, Sun mid-Oct to mid-Nov approx every hr 11:30-4:30; open all holidays during season. Adults $4.95, over 65 $4.50, students with ID $4.25, children under 12 $2.75; free parking. Call for schedule and prices on evening dining barge (summer only). Well-behaved pets allowed. Barge is wheelchair-accessible.*

Here's a chance for a quiet, relaxing, hour-long ride on the historic Delaware Canal through New Hope and the surrounding countryside. During most of the season a barge musician and historian are aboard to entertain and inform us. Bring your camera, forget your problems.

New Hope Steam Railway and Museum, 32 W. Bridge St., New Hope, PA 18938 (215-862-2707). *Operates between New Hope and Buckingham May thru Oct, Sat and holidays 1:30 and 3:30, Sun 11:30, 1:30, 3:30. Adults $5, children $3; parking at station lot $3 in New Hope, free in Buckingham. Will accommodate wheelchairs.*

This 14-mile, 1½-hour round trip takes us from the restored New Hope Station (1891) across the trestle to which Pearl White was tied in the silent classic *The Perils of Pauline,* up Solebury Mountain, through Lahaska, and into Buckingham. We can also inspect the museum's extensive collection of antique cars and rolling stock. Traffic and parking can be a problem in New Hope during the height of the season, so we may want to drive to Buckingham, catch the early train from there to New Hope, spend a couple of hours sightseeing, and take the late train back, avoiding possible congestion and parking fees.

Peddler's Village, Rtes. 202 & 263, Lahaska, PA 18931 (215-794-7438). *Shops open all year: Jan-Mar daily 10-5, Fri until 9; Apr to Thanksgiving Mon-Thurs 10-5:30, Fri 10-9, Sat 10-6, Sun 12-5:30; Thanksgiving to Christmas Eve Mon-Sat 10-9, Sun 12-5:30, Christmas Eve 10-5. Ample free parking. Narrow brick walks, steps into buildings; difficult for wheelchairs.*

Located between New Hope and Doylestown, Lahaska (an Indian word meaning "place of much writing") is best known for its Peddler's Village. Originally a collection of barns and chicken coops, it is today an impressive reconstructed village with 42 shops grouped around a handsome common. Almost every kind of ware is found here, with an emphasis on crafts, antiques, and unusual items. The Peddler's Village Dinner Theatre (215-794-3460) offers concerts and Broadway shows during its winter and summer seasons. Annual events include the Festival of Flowers (June), the All-American Teddy Bear's Picnic (July), the Cabbage Patch Scarecrow Contest and Festival (late September to mid-October), and the Country Christmas Festival (December).

Doylestown, seat of Bucks County, is a picturesque country town best known for the works of its resident eccentric, Henry Chapman Mercer (1856-1930), a noted archeologist, antiquarian, and leader of the Arts and Crafts Movement. Annual events include the Mercer Museum Folk Fest in spring and the Village Fair, the Heart of Bucks Antique Auto Show, and the Antique Show, all in summer. For FURTHER INFORMATION contact the Bucks County Tourist Commission, 152 Swamp Rd., Doylestown, PA 18901 (215-345-4552).

Fonthill Museum, E. Court St., Doylestown, PA 18901 (215-348-9461). *Open all year daily 10-5; closed Thanksgiving, Christmas, New Year's. Adults $3, senior citizens $2.50, students $1.50. Guided tours only, last tour begins at 4; reservations advisable. Not wheelchair-accessible.*

Henry Chapman Mercer designed Fonthill, today a National Historic Landmark, as a home and showcase for his collection of tiles and prints from all over the world. The castlelike structure, begun in 1908, consists almost entirely of poured concrete—Mercer was an early proponent of concrete, well before it became popular as a building material. Each of the 30 rooms has a highly individual personality, with tiles sometimes depicting stories or historic events, and there are warrens, alcoves, and cubicles everywhere we turn on our fascinating tour of Fonthill.

Moravian Pottery and Tile Works, Swamp Rd., Doylestown, PA 18901 (215-345-6722). *Open Mar-Dec daily 10-5; closed Thanksgiving, Christmas, Easter. Adults $2, senior citizens $1.50, students $1; or $4.50 per family. Guided tours every 30 min, last tour begins at 4. Gift shop wheelchair-accessible; people in wheelchairs can manage part of tour and see some of tilemaking process.*

A National Historic Landmark, this Spanish Mission-style concrete tile works was built by Henry Mercer to revive the dying Pennsylvania-German art of tilemaking. Today it operates much as it did in Mercer's time, and tiles can be purchased at the gift shop. Over the years the tile works has furnished decoration for such notable installations as the John D. Rockefeller estate in New York, the casino at Monte Carlo, the Traymore Hotel in Atlantic City, and the Pennsylvania State Capitol.

Mercer Museum and Spruance Library, Pine St., Doylestown, PA 18901 (215-345-0210). *Museum open Mar-Dec Mon-Sat 10-5, Sun 1-5; closed Thanksgiving, Christmas. Library open all year Tues 1-9, Wed-Fri 10-5; closed July 4th, Thanksgiving, Christmas, New Year's. Admission (includes museum and library) $3 adults, $2.50 senior citizens, $1.50 students. Self-guided tours, gift shop. Annual Folk Fest on 2nd full weekend in May: adults $5, senior citizens $3, children 6-18 $2, under 6 free; or $12 per family. Museum has ramps and elevators; mostly wheelchair-accessible.*

Another imposing concrete structure and National Historic Landmark, the Mercer Museum houses the tools and products of more than 60 trades and crafts. It was established by Henry Mercer to display his collection of over 40,000 preindustrial tools and implements, from adzes to zithers, used to tame the frontier and build the nation. Fortunately for succeeding generations, Dr. Mercer saw these artifacts as the stuff of history rather than yard sales. Henry Ford, a man of strong opinions, called this 6-story treasure trove the only museum in the country worth visiting. Each year the museum hosts a Folk Fest featuring early American craft demonstrations, picnics, music, dancing, sheep shearing, quilting, wagon rides, and special children's events.

The Spruance Library is a gold mine of information on the nation's past. It contains special collections on Bucks County history and genealogy, and on early American technology, culture, and folk art; the Bucks County archives, dating back to 1682; and the Early American Industries Association Library. Both Spruance and the Mercer Museum are maintained by the Bucks County Historical Society.

National Shrine of Our Lady of Czestochowa, Ferry Rd., Beacon Hill, Doylestown, PA 18901 (215-345-0600). *Shrine and grounds open daily all year. Free. Masses: Sun 8am, 10, noon (Polish) and 9am, 11, 2:30, 5 (English); daily 7:30am (Polish) and 8am, 11:30, (English); Days of Obligation 7:30am (Polish) and 8am, 11-11:30, 5, 7 (English). Confession before masses or on request; devotions Sat 7pm, Sun after 2:30 mass; gift shop with items from Poland and devotional items; cafeteria (open Sun, closed Christmas, New Year's, Easter). Pets discouraged. Shrine and grounds largely wheelchair-accessible.*

Established in 1955 by the Pauline Fathers, the shrine is dedicated to Our Lady of Czestochowa (pronounced "Chen-sto-*ho*-va") in America. It houses a faithful reproduction of the Miraculous Painting of the Holy Mother, which is attributed to St. Luke and hangs in the Shrine of Czestochowa in Poland. The copy was blessed by Pope John XXIII on February 10, 1962.

Bucks County Covered Bridges Tour, Bucks County Tourist Commission, 152 Swamp Rd., Doylestown, PA 18901 (215-345-4552). *Call or write for detailed brochure on self-guided auto tour.*

This tour takes us to the remaining 13 of 36 covered bridges that once stood in Bucks County. Suggested point of departure is the Memorial Building and Visitor Center in Washington Crossing Historic Park (Trip A-16), but you can begin anywhere; the brochure offers very specific driving instructions and mileages so that you can go at your own pace. All told, it covers more than 100 miles, so be sure to leave plenty of time if you plan to complete the route. The bridges were constructed according to the lattice design developed by New Englander Ithiel Town in 1820. Among them are Erwinna Bridge, the county's shortest (56 feet), and South Perkasie Bridge (93 feet), which sports a sign reading "$5.00 fine for any person riding or driving over this bridge faster than a walk or smoking a segar on." The tour winds through most of Bucks County and can be combined with visits to other sites; contact the tourist commission for a Bucks County map and guide.

FOR THE DRIVER: Take NJT south to Exit 10, I-287 ($1.45), then follow I-287 north about 15 mi to US 22 west (Exit 10, on left) to Somerville. Go about 3 mi on 22 to exit for US 202 south to Flemington (make sure you take Flemington exit). Continue south on 202 across Delaware River (15¢) and pick up PA 32 south about 1 mi to New Hope. Continue south on 32 (Main St) across W Bridge St and go about a block to Parry Mansion, on corner of S Main and W Ferry Sts. On the way you pass CORYELL'S FERRY BOAT RIDES ON THE DELAWARE (215-862-2050), at 22 S Main. Opposite the mansion at 52 S Main is the GOLDEN DOOR GALLERY (215-862-5529), an attractive barn with graphics, sculpture, and crafts for sale, and next door to it, at 70 S Main, is the BUCKS COUNTY PLAYHOUSE (215-862-2041), famous for its lovely location and professional productions. The New Hope Information Center is a little south of the mansion, across Ingham Creek on the corner of S Main and W Mechanic Sts.

From here, continue south on Main to sign for New St. Turn right here, then right again to Mule Barge parking lot. For New Hope Steam Railroad, go back to S Main, turn left, and go north to W Bridge St (PA 179). Turn left here and go about a block, watching for distinctive witch's peak roof of station, on right.

Before leaving New Hope, the stout of heart may wish to take one of the GHOST TOURS arranged by psychic investigator Adi-Kent Thomas Jeffrey; call or write in advance, 912 Cherry Lane, Southampton, PA 18966 (215-355-7046 or 364-3915). Canoeing, rafting, and innertubing on the Delaware, and whitewater rafting on Tohickon Creek, are available about 7 mi north of New Hope on PA 32 at POINT PLEASANT CANOE OUTFITTERS (215-297-8181). On your way to Point Pleasant you'll pass the homes of some noted turn-of-the-century artists, the LUMBERVILLE COUNTRY STORE (dating from 1770), and, just across the river from Lumberville on the Jersey side (you can walk to it by footbridge), the BULL'S ISLAND SECTION (609-397-2949) of Delaware & Raritan Canal State Park, a haven for birds and birdwatchers. A few miles north of Point Pleasant is Erwinna, an old resort town near several of the stops on the Covered Bridges Tour.

To reach Lahaska from New Hope, go out of town on PA 179 south (W Bridge St) to jct with US 202 at 2nd light. Turn left here onto US 202 south. (The 10-mi stretch from New Hope through Lahaska to Doylestown has more antique shops than any other area in Bucks County.) About 3 mi south of New Hope on 202 is BUCKS COUNTRY VINEYARDS AND WINERY (in PA 800-523-2510, outside PA 800-362-0309), open daily for tours and wine-tasting. Continue south on 202 into Lahaska and Peddler's Village. At well-marked crossroads where you turn for village is THE YARD, a charming Victorian shopping center with 14 stores.

Continue on US 202 south from Lahaska to Doylestown. You will pass through Buckingham, where you can go south on PA 413 to visit the BUCKINGHAM VALLEY VINEYARDS AND WINERY (215-794-7188) or the WILMAR LAPIDARY MUSEUM (215-598-3572) in Pineville, one of the largest private collections of carved stones in the world.

Entering Doylestown on US 202 south, turn right at jct with PA 313 (Swamp Rd) and go about 1 mi to E Court St. Here you will find Fonthill Museum and adjacent Moravian Tile Works. Continue down E Court St to N Main St (Old Rte 611), turn left, go 3 blocks on N Main, and make next left onto Ashland St. At 1st corner, Ashland and Green, are Mercer Museum and Spruance Library.

Go back to E Court St, turn right, and return to PA 313. Make a left and proceed past jct with US 611 to 1st traffic light (Ferry Rd). Turn left and go 2 mi down Ferry Rd to Shrine of Our Lady of Czestochowa, on right. If you return to 313, turn left, go to 1st light, and turn left again on Maple Ave (becoming Dublin Rd), you can visit the PEARL S. BUCK HOME (215-249-0100 in PA, 800-523-5328 outside PA), containing memorabilia, Chinese artifacts, and the desk at which the author wrote *The Good Earth.*

Bert and Ernie and William Penn

TRIP A-15

SESAME PLACE, Langhorne

HISTORIC FALLSINGTON, Fallsington

PENNSBURY MANOR, Morrisville

DISTANCE: From GWB, about 80 mi. Fast and average speeds.

We are still in Bucks County, right on the outskirts of Philadelphia. Anyone wishing to sample the many attractions of the City of Brotherly Love can get FURTHER INFORMATION from the Philadelphia Convention and Visitors Bureau, 1525 John F. Kennedy Blvd., Philadelphia, PA 19102 (215-636-1666).

Sesame Place, PO Box 579, Langhorne, PA 19047 (215-757-1100 or 752-7070). *Open May-Oct: 10-5 daily May to mid-June, 9-8 daily mid-June thru Aug, 10-5 daily first week of Sept, 10-5 weekends mid-Sept to mid-Oct. Admission: May-June and Sept-Oct adults $8, children $10; July-Aug adults $9, children $11; plus 10% amusement tax and parking fee; children under 2 free. Many facilities and restrooms wheelchair-accessible.*

Sesame Place, designed primarily for children between 3 and 13, describes its philosophy as "magic and reason, fun and learning." We enter through the mouth of a large Big Bird model into the Water Court, featuring a maze, water slide, beach, and other activities. The Air Court offers more outdoor fun, including the Slippery Slope, the Zoom Flume, Grover's Rubber Band Bounce, and Rubber Duckie Rapids: parents can relax at the Adult Oasis and watch the fun. The Land Court has mazes, tunnels, mountains, nests, and tubes for climbing. Indoors there are plenty of hands-on science exhibits like the Zoetrope, the Anti-Gravity Mirror, the Gyrocycle, and a replica of the Sesame Street set. The Computer Gallery has games, graphics, and courses in computer use (call 215-752-4900 for course descriptions and prices). There's a Food Gallery, live shows with Bert, Ernie, and the Honkers, and the Sesame Place Animal Actors, featuring famous animals from various TV programs. At Mr. Hooper's Store you can buy Sesame Street products and souvenirs. The kids we know are crazy about Sesame Place, but they won't have to drag you there—you'll have a great time too (for $2 less!).

Historic Fallsington, 4 Yardley Ave., Fallsington, PA 19054 (215-295-6567). *Open mid-Mar to mid-Nov Wed-Sun 11-4. Adults $2, students under 18 $1, children under 12 50¢, under 6 free. Guided tours at regular intervals. Annual Historic Fallsington Day 2nd Sat in Oct. Wheelchair access to 1st floor of buildings.*

Fallsington, settled in the late 17th century by followers of William Penn, is an unspoiled village reflecting three centuries of American architectural history. Many of the houses are still occupied by descendants of the original settlers, and it's hard to believe that downtown Philadelphia is only minutes away. Four buildings have been restored and are open to the public: the Moon-Williamson House (c. 1685), a pioneer log building, one of the oldest in Pennsylvania; the Burges-Lippincott House, an elegant, beautifully decorated home built in four stages from 1700 to 1829; the Stage Coach Tavern, in continual operation from the 1790s until Prohibition; and the Gillingham Store, rebuilt in 1910, headquarters of Historic Fallsington, Inc., with a gift shop and an audiovisual program on Fallsington.

Pennsbury Manor, 400 Pennsbury Memorial Lane, Morrisville, PA 19067 (215-946-0400). *Open all year Tues-Sat 9-5, Sun 12-5; closed Mon and holidays except Memorial Day, July 4th, Labor Day. Adults $2.50, senior citizens $1.75, children 6-17 $1, under 6 free. Guided 1½-hr tours; last tour leaves at 3:30. Restrooms and tour wheelchair-accessible except for 2nd floor of manor.*

"The Country Life is to be preferr'd; for there we see the Works of God: but in Cities little else but the Works of Men," wrote

William Penn, Quaker, diplomat, and founder of Pennsylvania. No wonder he chose to live at Pennsbury, a beautifully restored manor house (1683) on the Delaware River, surrounded by 43 acres of gardens, orchards, and stately trees. The bake and brew house, the blacksmith's and joiner's shops, the replica of Penn's river barge, and the motley crew of farm animals give us a glimpse of the many activities that sustained the life of this country plantation. Inquire at Pennsbury about a package tour that includes BRISTOL and ANDALUSIA (two other historic sites further west along the Delaware), lunch at the King George II Inn in Bristol, refreshments, a slide program, and discounts at the museum shop.

FOR THE DRIVER: Take NJT to Exit 9, New Brunswick ($1.50), bear right after tollbooth onto NJ 18, and follow signs for US 1 south to Trenton. Remain on US 1 to jct with I-95, then take I-95 around Trenton and across the Delaware into Pennsylvania. Leave I-95 at Oxford Valley exit, turn right, and proceed to 2nd traffic light. Turn right to Sesame Place.

Go back to jct of I-95 and US 1. Go northeast on US 1 about 2 mi to Tyburn Rd. Turn right on Tyburn, then left at 2nd stoplight, and go ¼ mi to Meetinghouse Square in Fallsington.

Go back to Tyburn Rd, turn left (east), and continue on Tyburn across US 13 to New Ford Mill Rd. Turn right on New Ford and go to end, at Bordentown Ferry Rd. Turn right again on Bordentown and look for sign to Pennsbury Manor, shortly on left.

To return home, you can go back the way you came, or you can return to jct of Tyburn Rd and US 13, take 13 south a few mi to PA extension of NJT (25¢), and take NJT back to GWB ($2.30).

Across the Delaware with General Washington

TRIP A-16

WASHINGTON CROSSING STATE PARK, New Jersey
WASHINGTON CROSSING HISTORIC PARK,
   Pennsylvania

DISTANCE: From GWB, 75-80 mi. Mainly fast speeds.

We are a little northwest of Trenton, capital of New Jersey and site of the famous Revolutionary battle where Washington captured a Hessian garrison after crossing the icy Delaware River by night. There are numerous places of historical interest in Trenton, today a busy manufacturing town noted for its cable suspension bridges. Annual events include the Trenton Kennel Club Dog Show in early May and the Christmas Day reenactment of the crossing of the Delaware at Washington Crossing State Park, beginning on the Pennsylvania side. For FURTHER INFORMATION on Trenton and environs, contact the Mercer County Chamber of Commerce, 240 W. State St., Trenton, NJ 08608 (609-393-4143).

Washington Crossing State Park, Box 337-A, RD 1, Titusville, NJ 08560 (609-737-0623). *Grounds open daily all year, 8-8 Memorial Day to Labor Day, 8-dusk other times. Visitor center (609-737-9304) open daily Memorial Day to Labor Day 9-5, 9-4 Wed-Sun other times. Ferry House open Memorial Day to Labor Day Fri-Sat 10-4, Sun 1-4, and by appointment. Nelson House open Memorial Day to Labor Day Wed-Sat 10-4, Sun 1-4, and by appointment. Nature center (609-737-0609) open daily in summer, varied hours at other times; call for appointment. Parking fee weekends and holidays Memorial Day to Labor Day $1 per car; otherwise free. Open Air Theatre offers varied program during summer; check with box office (609-737-9721). Picnic facilities and grills, fishing areas. Leashed pets only. Visitor center and Ferry House wheelchair-accessible, some other facilities and parts of ground manageable for wheelchairs; Braille Trail at nature center.*

This park of over 800 acres contains the site where General Washington and his troops landed after crossing the Delaware on Christmas night, 1776. We can stroll along Continental Lane following the route the soldiers took in their march on Trenton. At the tavern in the Ferry House State Historic Site, Washington strategized with his generals while waiting for his army to complete the crossing. Nearby, an overlook gives us a view of the Delaware and the landing site, which can be reached by footbridge. We can also visit the remnants of the Nelson House, believed to have been the site of the original ferry station, and see various historical exhibits at the flag museum, nature center, and visitor center. Native New Jersey trees and shrubs are on display at the George Washington Memorial Arboretum, and seedlings thrive at the State Forest Nursery. In summer, the 1,000-seat theater provides an attractive natural setting for dramas and musical productions.

Washington Crossing Historic Park, Bucks County, PA 18977 (215-493-4076). *Grounds open all year daily 9-dusk. Buildings open all year daily, Mon-Sat 9-5, Sun 12-5. No admission fee for grounds; combination fee for buildings (except Bowman Hill Tower) adults $1.50, over 65 $1, children 6-17 50¢; Bowman Hill Tower $2 adults, $1.50 over 65, 50¢ children under 12. Leashed pets only. Visitor center, Durham Boat House, Thompson-Neely Barn, Wildflower Preserve and Trail, soldiers' graves, all picnic pavilions, and some restrooms wheelchair-accessible.*

We are lucky indeed to be able to view, after a few hours' drive, the tangible records of a great episode in American history, Washington's crossing of the Delaware on that stormy Christmas night in 1776. Here is the river, once filled with blocks of ice; here are the banks where the frostbitten Continentals embarked and landed; here are the houses they used for shelter; and here the heroic painting that has stirred our imaginations since school days.

Our tour begins at the Memorial Building and Visitor Center in the McConkey's Ferry Section of the park, near where the Continentals massed before their raid on the Hessian garrison in Trenton. Here, in Concentration Valley, the 2,400-odd patriots, beaten back in the disheartening campaigns of 1776, assembled to execute General Washington's bold strategy. At the Memorial Building, which houses the park offices, the Washington Crossing Library, galleries with changing exhibits, and an exact copy of Emanuel Leutze's *Washington Crossing the Delaware* (the original hangs in the Metropolitan Museum in New York), we can watch a color documentary on the crossing narrated by Chet Huntley.

Near the Memorial Building is the Point of Embarkation. Footpaths lead to a stone marker at the spot on the riverbank where the crossing began in 1776, and where the Christmas Day reenactment begins each year. Volunteers in uniform climb into a Durham boat with "General Washington" and paddle across, hopefully under conditions less hazardous than those of 1776. The full-scale reproduction used in the reenactment is on display at the Durham Boat House, which also has exhibits on Delaware River transportation history. Durham boats were flat-bottomed barges about 60 feet long used for hauling iron ore on the river. They were propelled by oars or sails.

Not far from the boat house is McConkey's Ferry Inn, where General Washington may have eaten his Christmas meal before starting across the river. The inn served as a guardpost for the ferry landing during the Continental Army's encampment. In the vicinity of the inn are the Taylorsville Store and several 19th-century houses, including Homewood, the completely restored residence of one of Taylorsville's founders.

Leaving the McConkey's Ferry Section of the park, we travel north to the Thompson's Mill Section and the Thompson-Neely House, headquarters during the crucial month of December 1776 for General Stirling, who commanded the troops stationed along the Delaware to prevent a British crossing. Nearby are a restored, operating watermill, a restored 18th-century barn, and the Revolutionary Soldiers' Graves. In this section of the park we also find Bowman's Hill Tower, erected in 1930 on the site where the Continental sentries kept watch for enemy activity. The 110-foot-high fieldstone tower has just undergone a $200,000 facelift, and visitors can now take an elevator to the top for a terrific view of the Delaware. Across Pidcock Creek from the tower is the Wildflower Preserve Building and Trail Area, where we can see Pennsylvania flora, a wildlife observatory, and changing exhibits. The peak season for blooms is April to June.

FOR THE DRIVER: This trip takes you very close to Princeton (Trip A-12), Bucks County (Trip A-14), and Sesame Place (Trip A-15). If coming from or combining with any of those trips, consult a map for the best route to the Pennsylvania or New Jersey sides of the Washington Crossing area.

If coming from New York, take NJT to Exit 9, New Brunswick ($1.50), bear right after tollbooth onto NJ 18, and follow signs for US 1 south to Trenton. Remain on US 1 to jct with I-95/295 and take I-95 west to last exit before Scudders Falls Bridge, NJ 29. Take 29 north about 4 mi to Washington Crossing State Park. Watch for stoplight at jct with Rte 546, turn right here, and go about 1 mi east to park headquarters.

Continue west across the Delaware on 546, which becomes PA 532. Just across river, turn right (north) on PA 32 and go a short distance to Washington Crossing Historic Park visitor center, on right, in Mc-

Conkey's Ferry Section of park. Continue north on 32 to Thompson's Mill Section.

When you leave Thompson's Mill Section, you are just a few mi south of New Hope. If you don't want to return the way you came, continue north on PA 32 to New Hope, pick up US 202 north to Somerville (15¢), then I-287 southeast to NJT and back on this ($1.45) to New York.

New Jersey from Edison Land to the Poconos

• *Here we begin by exploring the part of New Jersey closest to New York City. Unlike the trips in Area A, which follow one another in a fairly straight line, these come in clusters and are spread out across some of New Jersey's more populated regions. For the most part, the larger industrial cities are not included because of their heavy traffic. We gradually work our way westward across the Delaware River into the Poconos, where the extraordinary scenic beauty, the unhurried pace, and the great variety of recreational possibilities will beguile us for a day, a week, or as long as we care to stay.*

Exit Points, Main Roads, Connections
See "Traveling to Area A," p. 3. There are three additional main roads for Area B: I-80, I-78, and I-287.

Additional Connections
To reach I-80
   —from GWB, follow signs;
   —from exit points south of GWB for trips using, roughly, I-80 Exits 47 and up, take GSP Exit 159 or NJT Exits 18E/18W;
   —from exit points south of GWB for trips using, roughly, I-80 Exits 46 and down, take NJT Exit 15W to I-280 or GSP Exit 145 to I-280, then follow I-280 northwest to jct with I-80 near Parsippany.
To reach I-78 from any exit point
   —use NJT Exit 14 or GSP Exit 142. Note that a 5-mi stretch (Exit 48 to Exit 41) of I-78 west of Springfield, running through Watchung Reservation (Trip B-10), was recently completed and can be used instead of US 22.
To reach I-287
   —from GWB, take I-80 west off bridge to Exit 43;
   —from exit points south of GWB, depending on destination, take I-280 northwest to I-80 west to Exit 43, about 6 mi northeast of Morristown, or take I-78 west to Exit 30, about 4 mi north of Somerville.

Tolls
One-way highway tolls (collected in both directions) are given in "For the Driver" at the end of each trip and are calculated from GWB unless otherwise indicated. For New York City bridge and tunnel tolls, see p. xvi; remember to add these to the highway tolls as appropriate, depending on your route.

On the Other Side of the Golden Door

TRIP B-1

LIBERTY STATE PARK, Jersey City

DISTANCE: From GWB, about 20 mi. Average speeds.

Liberty State Park, Morris Pesin Drive, Jersey City, NJ 07304 (201-915-3400). *Open daily all year, 8-10 Memorial Day to Labor Day, 8-8 other times. No entry fee. Natural area with interpretive center (9-4 daily), trails, observation points; picnic area (no fires or grills allowed); fishing and crabbing; public swimming pool with lifeguards, bathhouses, concession stand (open Memorial Day to Labor Day: weekends $4 adults, $3 children under 12; weekdays $3 adults, $2 children under 12); public tennis courts (free), public boat launching ramp (open all year during daylight hours, no fee). Ferry to Statue of Liberty and Ellis Island (201-435-8509) May-Oct, adults $3.25, children under 12 $1.50. Concerts Tues evening and Sun afternoon in summer, special events all year. Leashed pets only. Barrier-free design gives full wheelchair accessibility to most park facilities and restrooms.*

Here is a glorious view we'll never forget. After our drive down State Flag Row (arranged in order of induction into the Union), we see just 1,750 feet ahead the Statue of Liberty, newly refurbished for her 100th birthday in 1986. To our left lies Ellis Island, and beyond, the confluence of the mighty Hudson and East Rivers. Between the two is all of lower Manhattan with its incomparable skyline. The Brooklyn Bridge is prominent, backed by the other bridges across the East River. To our right is the Verrazano Bridge linking Brooklyn with Staten Island. Finally, over the rooftops of Bayonne to the south, is the Bayonne Bridge, completing a giant arc linking three boroughs with New Jersey. The Staten Island Ferry and the popular sightseeing cruisers ply the waters of New York Harbor; tugs, cargo vessels, and, as an occasional bonus, one of the great ocean liners make a never-ending pageant on the waters.

Only 20 years ago this area of New Jersey was one of rotting docks, derelict boats, and marshlands. In the late 19th century it had been the site of a bustling commuter and freight rail terminal that handled tens of thousands of people each day, many of them immigrants who first set foot on the US mainland here after being processed at Ellis Island. But as truck and highway transport gained ground, these facilities became obsolete and were gradually abandoned. In 1964 the state of New Jersey established Liberty State Park and began a major cleanup of the harbor area. The first phase of development was completed in time for the nation's bicentennial, and the park got a new road, new lighting, flower gardens, and a general sprucing up for the Statue of Liberty centennial.

FOR THE DRIVER: Liberty State Park is only a few minutes from the Holland Tunnel via NJT extension south to Exit 14B (20¢). From exit ramp turn left onto Bayview Ave, becoming Morris Pesin Drive as you enter park.

From GWB take NJT south to Exit 14 to NJT extension to Bayonne and Jersey City. Get off at Exit 14B ($1.10) and proceed as above.

A Journey to Cherry Blossom Land

TRIP B-2

BRANCH BROOK PARK, Newark

DISTANCE: From GWB, about 20 mi. Mainly fast speeds.

Branch Brook Park, Lake St., Newark, NJ 07104 (201-482-4198). *Open daily all year. Free entry, nominal fees for tennis and skating. Playground and playing fields, cross-country trail, fitness course, jogging paths, fishing areas, skating rink, hard and clay tennis courts (some lighted), bocce court, cricket crease, horseshoe pitches, picnicking (no fires or grills allowed). Annual Cherry Blossom Festival, special events throughout the year. Leashed pets only. Largely wheelchair-accessible; inquire about SHAPE (Special Handicapped Activities Program of Essex). For further information contact Branch Brook or the Essex County Department of Parks, Recreation and Cultural Affairs, 115 Clifton Ave., Newark, NJ 07104 (201-482-6400).*

Every spring in April the cherry blossoms appear throughout the New Jersey park system. The most lavish of these displays, surpassing even the glories of the Tidal Basin in Washington, D.C., can be seen at Branch Brook Park, where almost 3,000 cherry trees in 28 varieties create a canopy of hues from white to rose to deep pink. The Branch Brook cherry blossoms made their first notable appearance in the early 1940s, some 13 years after a substantial gift from Caroline Bamberger Fuld, sister of department-store entrepreneur Louis Bamberger, enabled the Essex County Parks Commission to purchase 2,050 Japanese cherry trees. The trees came into their own as a tourist attraction after the anti-Japanese sentiment of World War II subsided, and they have been drawing people to Branch Brook in droves ever since.

The timing and duration of the blooming period depends upon the weather (cool, clement conditions produce the best results), but the flowers almost always appear by April 15, just in time for tax relief, and last for about 3 weeks. Some half a million people have come to view the trees each spring in recent years, and the 360-acre park is especially crowded on weekends. Don't expect to stroll in solitude, but go anyway. And no matter how tempting, DO NOT pick the blossoms, a gift from Mrs. Fuld and higher powers. Imagine your simple act of plucking multipled by 500,000 and consider the result.

Apart from the cherry trees, Branch Brook is an attraction at any time of year. It was laid out by Frederick Law Olmsted, designer of New York's Central Park, Washington's Capitol grounds, and many other beautiful parks and estates, and is maintained by the Essex County Department of Parks, Recreation and Cultural Affairs, which sponsors an ambitious program of outdoor activities and special events here and throughout its 5,600-acre park system.

FOR THE DRIVER: If you are going to Branch Brook for the cherry blossoms, consider driving or taking public transportation (bus, train, or PATH) to Penn Station in Newark. There's plenty of parking here, and easy access to the newly remodeled Newark City Subway, last stop Branch Brook; call NJ Transit (800-772-2222) for details.

If you are driving from GWB, take NJT south to Exit 16W (30¢), then NJ 3 east to NJ 21 south to Mill St exit, following signs into park. From Lincoln Tunnel get directly onto NJ 3 east and proceed as above.

Across from the southeast corner of the park is the CATHEDRAL OF

THE SACRED HEART (201-484-6400), the 5th-largest cathedral in the country, with a magnificent organ, beautiful stained glass, and fine architectural detail.

To the Laboratory of a Genius Who Changed Our Lives

TRIP B-3

EDISON NATIONAL HISTORIC SITE, West Orange

EAGLE ROCK RESERVATION, West Orange

DISTANCE: From GWB, about 25 mi. Mainly fast speeds.

Edison National Historic Site, Main St. & Lakeside Ave., West Orange, NJ 07052 (taped message 201-736-5050, further information 201-736-0550). *Open all year Wed-Sun 9-5; closed Thanksgiving, Christmas, New Year's. Admission 50¢ per person; under 16 and over 62 free. Guided 90-min tours begin at 9:30, last tour begins at 4. Fully wheelchair-accessible.*

Every American who can should make this pilgrimage to the laboratory of the man whose imagination and ingenuity dramatically changed our world. Thomas Alva Edison came to West Orange in 1887, after he had invented the lightbulb in Menlo Park. Here is the birthplace of the motion picture, the tape recorder, and many other inventions now taken for granted. We have an opportunity to come close to the man himself as we pass through his library and the old lab, where his coat hangs in its accustomed place and his tools lie ready at the workbench. In the theater we can watch Edwin S. Porter's *The Great Train Robbery* (1903), a landmark Edison production, and see informational films about Edison's life and times.

Near the lab is Glenmont, Edison's home, currently closed for restoration. Check at the lab on the progress of the work and the possibility of a tour. Edison bought this elegant house furnished but added many characteristic personal touches. He and his wife are buried here on the lovely grounds.

Eagle Rock Reservation, Eagle Rock Ave., West Orange, NJ 07052 (201-731-3000). *Open daily all year. Free. Wildlife preserve, picnic area, fireplaces, hiking trails, bridle paths, dressage training area.*

Leashed pets only. Roads and lookout points wheelchair-accessible.

This 400-acre park, administered by the Essex County Department of Parks, Recreation and Cultural Affairs, has two popular lookout points that afford a good view of the local landscape and the distant New York skyscrapers.

FOR THE DRIVER: Take GSP south to Exit 145 (60¢) or NJT south to Exit 15W (50¢) and pick up I-280 west. Watch for exit to Rte 508, Oranges and Montclair. Get off 280 here. Immediately is 508, Northfield Ave. Turn right to Main St, at traffic light just ahead. Turn left on Main past municipal buildings and continue several blocks to Edison National Historic Site, on right.

From here, continue on Main St briefly to Eagle Rock Ave, bear left on Eagle Rock, and follow it to top of hill and into park.

To return home, go south briefly on Prospect Ave (the western boundary of the park) to jct with I-280, then back as you came.

Art, History, and a President's Birthplace

TRIP B-4

ISRAEL CRANE HOUSE, Montclair

MONTCLAIR ART MUSEUM, Montclair

GROVER CLEVELAND BIRTHPLACE, Caldwell

DISTANCE: From GWB, about 25 mi. Mainly fast speeds.

Israel Crane House, 110 Orange Road, Montclair, NJ 07042 (201-744-1796). *Open Sept-June Sun 2-5 and by appointment; closed July-Aug except for special events. Free. Not wheelchair-accessible.*

Headquarters of the Montclair Historical Society, this handsome Federal mansion was built in 1796 by Israel Crane, a successful businessman and a descendant of the founding family of Montclair (originally called Cranetown). A civic group saved the house from demolition in 1965 and moved it from Old Road to the present site. It is beautifully furnished in the varying styles of the period 1740-1840, and there are lovely herb and pleasure gardens on the grounds. Visitors can watch and participate in open-hearth cooking and see a variety of craft demonstrations including weav-

ing, quilting, lacemaking, tinsmithing, blacksmithing, and bas-
ketry.

In the Victoriana House at 108 Orange Road are the Historical
Society office and a research library with materials on colonial
and local history. Israel Crane's general store has been recreated
in the Country Store Museum and Gift Shop, located in a house
built in 1818 by Nathaniel Crane. The ANTIQUES MARKET at 25
Depot Square (201-746-9337) supports the activities of the Montclair Historical Society.

Montclair Art Museum, South Mountain & Bloomfield Aves.,
Montclair, NJ 07042 (201-746-5555). *Open Sept-July Tues-Wed and
Fri-Sat 10-5, Thurs 2-9, Sun 2-5; closed Mon and during Aug.
Adults $2, senior citizens and students with ID $1, children under
18 free; free to all on Thurs. Main floor wheelchair-accessible.*

This is one of our finer small museums, with a permanent collection of over 6,000 works ranging from 19th-century portraiture
and landscape to abstract expressionism. The Hudson River School
is well represented, as are many noted Montclair artists (Charles
Parsons, Harry Fenn, George Inness, and others). The museum
also prides itself on its exhibits of Native American art, American
costumes, English and Irish silver, and Chinese snuff bottles.

Grover Cleveland Birthplace, 207 Bloomfield Ave., Caldwell, NJ
07006 (201-226-1810). *Open all year Wed-Fri 9-6, Sat 9-5,
Sun 1-6; closed occasionally when caretaker is away (call in advance). Free. Guided tour on request. Limited parking behind
house. Steps into house, but will accommodate wheelchairs.*

The Old Manse of the Caldwell First Presbyterian Church was
just 5 years old when Grover Cleveland was born there in 1837.
It's a homey place, furnished in late 19th-century style and maintained as a memorial to the only US president born in New Jersey, though he lived in it for only 4 years. Personal mementoes,
pictures, and letters from the famous are displayed in wall cases.

FOR THE DRIVER: Take GSP south to Exit 148, Bloomfield Ave (60¢),
and go right (northwest) on Bloomfield (Rte 506) to Montclair. Shortly,
at traffic light, turn left on Orange Rd and watch for Crane House, on
right.

From Crane House, continue down Orange Rd to Elm St, turn left, and go back to Bloomfield Ave. Turn left and go down Bloomfield past Orange Rd a block or so to art museum, on left.

From museum, continue northwest on Bloomfield about 3 mi to Caldwell. Shortly after you enter Caldwell, at Bloomfield and Arlington Aves, is the Cleveland birthplace.

On this trip you are very close to the stops on Trip B-3. You may wish to combine all or part of both trips. If you are coming from Eagle Rock Reservation, take Prospect Ave, at western edge of park, north about 2 mi to Bloomfield Ave. Turn right for art museum and Crane House, left for Cleveland birthplace.

Everything from Arboretum to Zoo

TRIP B-5

SOUTH MOUNTAIN RESERVATION, West Orange
TURTLE BACK ZOO
SOUTH MOUNTAIN ARENA
CORA HARTSHORN ARBORETUM AND BIRD
SANCTUARY, Short Hills

DISTANCE: From GWB, about 30 mi. Mainly fast speeds.

South Mountain Reservation, 560 Northfield Ave., West Orange, NJ 07052 (201-762-0408). *Open daily all year. Free. Wildlife preserve, picnicking and fireplaces, cross-country trail, hiking and interpretive trails, trout fishing at Diamond Mill Pond (609-292-9431), archery range, skating and zoo (see below). Leashed pets only. Some facilities wheelchair-accessible. For further information contact South Mountain or the Essex County Department of Parks, Recreation and Cultural Affairs, 115 Clifton Ave., Newark, NJ 07104 (201-482-6400).*

South Mountain comprises over 2,000 acres of beautiful woodlands bounded on east and west by two of New Jersey's three Watchung ridges (so named from the Lenni Lenape Indian word meaning "high hills"). General Washington and the Continental Army spent the hard winter of 1779-80 in nearby Morristown (Trip B-8) protected by these ridges, from which they could observe the British base on Staten Island and detect any troop movements. Today there are 8 lookout points in the park, including Washington Rock in the southeast corner.

The South Mountain area was heavily logged during colonial times and became the center of a papermill industry in the mid-1800s. In 1895, influenced by the ideas of Frederick Law Olmsted and in consultation with his firm, the Essex County Park Commission began purchasing land to create an integrated system of county parks and reservations. The commission undertook extensive reforestation of South Mountain and massive plantings of mountain laurel, wild azalea, and rhododendron. Today the reservation is a scenic jewel amidst the urban sprawl of metropolitan New York and New Jersey.

Turtle Back Zoo (201-731-5800). *Open daily all year; early Mar to late Oct Mon-Sat 10-5, Sun 11-6; other times 10-4:30 daily; closed Christmas Eve, Christmas Day, New Year's, Thanksgiving. Adults $3, senior citizens and children 3-12 $1.40, under 3 free. Stroller rental at main gate. Refreshment stands, picnic area (no fires allowed), miniature railroad, pony rides (85¢). Hilly in spots, but many walks are level, all are well paved, and restrooms are wheelchair-accessible; inquire about Friendship Festival Day for handicapped, held annually in May.*

Turtle Back, occupying 15 acres in the north end of South Mountain Reservation, is New Jersey's largest publicly supported zoo, with 500 animals of 200 different species. There's a children's zoo with special exhibits, and the kids will also enjoy the petting zoo, where they can rub elbows, noses, etc., with sheep and goats. The Education Center offers free presentations, films, and lectures. Turtle Back also sponsors research and breeding projects and is home to a number of endangered species: the South American tapir, Cereopsis goose, Laysan teal, bald eagle, Siberian tiger, spotted leopard, bog turtle, and corn snake.

South Mountain Arena (201-731-3829). *Open all year; public skating Tues and Thurs 10-noon, 9 pm-11pm; also Sun 2-4 Labor Day to mid-June. Adults $3.75, children under 17 $2.50, senior citizens $2.50 ($1 on Thurs); skate rental $1.50; chaperone 25¢; 15-min skating lesson $5 per person.*

There are two ice surfaces at this indoor rink, with plenty of room for the pros to sketch figure eights around those teetering on their blades or coasting on their ankles. The arena also hosts sporting events, concerts, and other special attractions.

Cora Hartshorn Arboretum and Bird Sanctuary, 324 Forest Drive South, Short Hills, NJ 07078 (201-376-3587). *Grounds open daily all year. Museum open all year Tues-Thurs 2:45-4:45, Sat 9:30-11:30. Free; donations accepted. No picnics, leashed pets only. No ramp into museum building; trails unpaved but wide and partly wheelchair-accessible.*

Three miles of wooded paths wind through this 17-acre arboretum. Fine specimens of flowering shrubs and wildflowers make it particularly attractive in spring. The museum exhibits change with the seasons, and there's a good natural science reference library.

FOR THE DRIVER: Take GSP south to Exit 145 (60¢) and pick up I-280 west to Exit 10, Northfield Ave. Go left on Northfield and head straight up mountain, watching for signs to South Mountain Reservation. As you drive through reservation on Northfield, South Mountain Arena is on right, opposite parking lot for Turtle Back Zoo.

Continue briefly on Northfield to Cherry Lane, turn left, and go south through reservation. At S Orange Ave, a left turn takes you to Crest Drive at eastern edge of reservation, where you can turn right and go up to Washington Rock Lookout. Proceeding straight across S Orange, Cherry Lane becomes Brookside Drive. Continue south on this, leaving South Mountain Reservation and passing PAPER MILL PLAYHOUSE (201-376-4343), the State Theatre of New Jersey, presenting quality dramas and musicals year-round. A little beyond playhouse, bear right to Hobart Ave, passing racket club and remaining on Hobart to Forest Drive. Turn left and go past underpass 1 block to next corner. Here is Cora Hartshorn Arboretum, just beyond old stone house.

Into the Heart of the Great Swamp

TRIP B-6

GREAT SWAMP NATIONAL WILDLIFE REFUGE,
   Basking Ridge

DISTANCE: From GWB, about 40 mi. Mainly fast speeds.

Great Swamp National Wildlife Refuge, RD 1, Box 152, Basking Ridge, NJ 07920 (201-647-1222). *Open all year daily dawn-dusk; headquarters open Mon-Fri 8-4:30. Free. Visitors allowed in designated public areas and on designated trails only; parking in designated areas only; no bicycles or horses on trails. No picnicking, no camping, no alcohol, no smoking except in parking areas, pets restricted to parking areas. Self-service information booth at Wildlife Observation Center, no scheduled tours. Waterproof shoes recommended, insect repellent and protective clothing advisable May-Sept. Not wheelchair-accessible once off main paved roads.*

About 25,000 years ago, the Wisconsin Glacier reached its southernmost point of advance, looked around, and retreated, leaving Great Swamp in its wake. In 1708 the Delaware Indians deeded a huge tract of land including Great Swamp to the English in exchange for a barrel of rum, 15 kettles, 4 pistols, 4 cutlasses, assorted goods and sundries, and 30 pounds sterling. Various attempts to log and farm the area proved unprofitable over the next two centuries. In 1959 an airport thought to settle where the glacier had feared to go, but the North American Wildlife Federation launched a successful campaign to block the project. The 3,000 acres purchased as a result of their efforts were donated to the Department of the Interior in 1960 and became the nucleus of today's 6,783-acre refuge.

Great Swamp is home to a great variety of flora and fauna, including swamp woodlands, hardwood stands, marshlands, over 200 species of birds, and numerous mammals, fish, reptiles and amphibians, among the latter the rare bog turtle and blue-spotted salamander. Since 1968 the eastern two-thirds of the refuge has been a designated wilderness area. Man-made structures and motorized equipment are prohibited, and the public is restricted to foot travel on more than 10 miles of trails. The western third is a wildlife management area regulated to maintain habitat and encourage breeding.

At the eastern end of Great Swamp, just outside the refuge boundary, is the GREAT SWAMP OUTDOOR EDUCATION CENTER (201-635-6629), operated by the Morris County Park Commission (201-829-0474). The center offers a varied program of weekend activities, guided tours, and workshops, and maintains a mile-long trail and boardwalk into the swamp. Outside the western boundary of the swamp is the SOMERSET COUNTY ENVIRONMEN- TAL EDUCATION CENTER (201-766-2489), a solar research station and park offering walking trails, field trips, and special programs.

FOR THE DRIVER: Take GSP south to Exit 142 (75¢) or NJT south to Exit 14 (70¢) and pick up I-78 west to Exit 48. Here take NJ 24 northwest to Chatham, about 4 mi. In Chatham turn left on Fairmount Ave at sign to Meyersville and go a little less than 2 mi to Southern Blvd. Turn right and go about ¾ mi to sign for Morris County Outdoor Education Center. Or, from Chatham, remain on Fairmount Ave and bear right onto Mey- ersville Rd. In Meyersville, turn right on New Vernon Rd and go almost 1 mi to White Bridge Rd. Turn left on White Bridge, go just over 1 mi to Pleasant Plains Rd, and turn right. Shortly watch for signs to south gate and refuge headquarters. For Somerset County Environmental Educa- tion Center, continue on White Bridge across Pleasant Plains Rd and watch for Lord Stirling Park and signs for center, just outside refuge boundary on right. To go directly from Meyersville to self-service infor- mation booth at Wildlife Observation Center, continue straight on New Vernon Rd across White Bridge Rd. New Vernon becomes Long Hill Rd and takes you to observation center, just under 1 mi on left.

Alternate route from GWB via interstate all the way: Take I-80 west off bridge to Exit 43, then I-287 south to Exit 26, N Maple Ave. Go south on N Maple about ¾ mi to Madisonville Rd, following signs for Great Swamp. At Madisonville turn left and go about ½ mi to Pleasant Plains Rd. Turn right here and pass through north gate to refuge headquarters.

On the Outskirts of the Great Swamp

TRIP B-7

MUSEUM OF EARLY TRADES AND CRAFTS, Madison

BASKING RIDGE

US GOLF ASSOCIATION GOLF HOUSE, Far Hills

US EQUESTRIAN TEAM HEADQUARTERS, Gladstone

DISTANCE: From GWB to farthest point, Gladstone, about 55 mi. Fast and average speeds.

Museum of Early Trades and Crafts, Main St. & Green Village Rd., Madison, NJ 07940 (201-377-2982). *Open all year Mon-Sat 10-5, Sun 2-5; closed major holidays. Suggested donation $1.*

Guided tours by appointment. No ramps, but will accommodate wheelchairs.

This eye-catching limestone building, almost a small castle, houses exhibits depicting New Jersey life from the 1600s to the 1800s. The exhibits include a schoolroom, a cobbler's shop, a kitchen, a general store, and an interesting array of period tools and the products they fashioned for the early New Jersey villagers. The building itself is a turn-of-the-century gem.

Basking Ridge is a small, historic town proud of its past and heedful of the present, making certain its appearance remains unchanged and attractive. On the way into town we pass Van Dorn Mill (1843), an architectural landmark and symbol of New Jersey farming. Markers along the main street tell of the earliest settlement here (1720), point out the site of the Widow White's tavern, where the treasonous General Charles Lee was ignominiously captured by the British (1776), and inform us that today's Presbyterian church supplanted a log church that had been erected under an old oak tree. In the adjoining cemetery this ancient tree, known as the Basking Ridge Oak, still stands. It is said to be second in size only to the Salem oak. For FURTHER INFORMATION, contact the Basking Ridge Association, Basking Ridge, NJ 07920 (201-647-6470).

US Golf Association Golf House, Liberty Corner Rd., Far Hills, NJ 07931 (201-234-2300). *Open all year Mon-Fri 9-5, Sat-Sun 10-4; closed major holidays. Free. A few steps into building, but displays and gift shop are all on main floor.*

In 1972 the United States Golf Association moved from New York into the red brick Georgian colonial estate once owned by the W. J. Sloane family of Far Hills. Part of the building is now a museum that charts the history of golf from its origins to the present day. Fascinating displays depict the evolution of golfing equipment, the rules of the game, and clothing worn on the links. We also see trophies, photographs, pictures of golf courses, and clubs and balls used by today's champions. There is a valuable golfing reference library, and the gift shop sells golf-related memorabilia and artwork.

US Equestrian Team Headquarters, Gladstone, NJ 07934 (201-234-1251). *Open all year Mon-Sat 9-1; closed major holidays. Free. Call in advance to make sure team is not on tour. Stables and some activities wheelchair-accessible.*

This is an extraordinary treat for horse lovers. Here we can watch the US riding teams train for the Pan American and Olympic games. The horses work out early in the morning, and rehearsals for the contests include dressage, show jumping, three-day eventing, and driving. The organization has a long record of major awards.

FOR THE DRIVER: Take GSP south to Exit 142 (75¢) or NJT south to Exit 14 (70¢) and pick up I-78 west to Exit 48. Here take NJ 24 northwest to Madison, about 6 mi. Go through downtown Madison on 24 (which becomes Main St) to jct with Green Village Rd. On left is Museum of Early Trades and Crafts.

Continue on 24 to Morristown (Trips B-8 and B-9). Go around Morristown Green to jct with US 202 and follow 202 south for 5 or 6 mi through an area of small towns and antique shops. Watch for Old Mill Inn on left, opposite Van Dorn Mill, on right. Here, at stoplight, turn left onto N Finley Ave and go about 1 mi to N Maple Ave. Here is the church and the cemetery where the Basking Ridge Oak stands. Drive or walk up the hill in front of the church for a good view of the center of town.

Return to US 202 and continue south about 6 mi to Far Hills and jct with Rte 512. Turn left on 512 and drive about 2 mi to Golf House, entrance on right.

Go back on 512 the way you came, continuing through Far Hills towards Pottersville. Near Peapack 512 veers left (watch for sign) to Gladstone. In Gladstone turn left on Pottersville Rd (still Rte 512), go through 1st light, then go about ½ mi to 3rd driveway on left, entrance to US Equestrian Team Headquarters.

The Continental Trail After Trenton, Before Yorktown

TRIP B-8

MORRISTOWN NATIONAL HISTORICAL PARK

DISTANCE: From GWB, about 45 mi. Fast and average speeds.

Morristown National Historical Park, Washington Place, Morristown, NJ 07960 (201-539-2085). *Grounds open all year daily dawndusk; buildings (visitor center, Ford Mansion, Historical Museum, Wick House) open Wed-Sun 9-5, closed Thanksgiving, Christmas, New Year's. No park entry fee; combination admission to Ford Mansion and museum 50¢ per person, under 16 and over 62 free. Free parking at museum and lots in Jockey Hollow. Brochures for self-guided auto tour of park and self-guided walking tour of Ford Mansion available at mansion and Visitor Center. Annual St. Patrick's Day weekend encampment with troop maneuvers, demonstrations of soldier life, Kiddie Corps for children. Leashed pets only. Visitor center and 1st floor of Ford Mansion and museum wheelchair-accessible.*

Created by Act of Congress in 1933, Morristown National Historical Park occupies some 1,600 acres that played a crucial role in the Revolutionary War. Twice, in 1777 and again in 1779-80, the Continental Army wintered here under conditions of extreme hardship. Washington chose Morristown because it is protected on the east by swamplands and by the Watchung ridges, which afforded an excellent vantage point for keeping watch on the large British force in New York City. But these strategic advantages were almost outweighed by bitter cold, chronic shortages of food and clothing, and outbreaks of disease—perhaps harsher enemies than the British. Though no decisive battles occurred at Morristown, the two winter encampments were in many ways the greatest test of Washington's leadership and the courage of his men.

Our tour begins at the Ford Mansion, built by Jacob Ford, Jr., between 1772 and 1774, and one of the grandest homes in Morristown at the time. When the Revolution began, Ford opened a gunpowder mill to supply the patriot army, in which he became a colonel. He took sick and died during the ill-fated New Jersey "Mud Rounds" campaign in the winter of 1776. Two years later his widow squeezed herself, her three children, and any belongings she valued (some of the patriots were prone to pilfering) into two rooms and offered the rest of the house to General Washington for use as his headquarters. Here he spent one of the worst winters of the 18th century, when no less than 28 blizzards blasted Morristown and compounded the miseries of his men; here he met with foreign dignitaries, including the young Marquis de Lafayette bringing welcome news of French support; here he fired off an endless stream of letters pleading provisions for the army from Congress and the states.

Behind the Ford Mansion is the Historical Museum, containing Washington memorabilia, period weapons, and a 104-pound link of the chain that was stretched across the Hudson from West Point to Constitution Island to block British warships (see Trip C-12). There are audiovisual programs on the events of the "Hard Winter" of 1779-80, dioramas depicting the Pennsylvania Line mutiny and Washington's meeting with Lafayette, and a Gilbert Stuart painting of Washington (not the one immortalized on the dollar bill).

Our next stop is Fort Nonsense, a hill that offers a commanding view of the surrounding countryside. Legend has it that Washington ordered the hill fortified to keep his troops occupied and take their minds off their troubles (which included a smallpox epidemic) during the first encampment of 1777. In fact the fort had great strategic value and was the site of a beacon that was part of an alarm system stretching all the way to the Hudson Highlands (see Madam Brett Homestead, Trip D-9). Today no trace remains of the earthworks and redoubt erected by Washington's men.

South of Fort Nonsense is Jockey Hollow, site of the 1779-80 encampment. Here Washington's troops felled some 900 acres of timber to build huts and keep themselves in firewood. Washington issued strict specifications for the construction of the huts, which were to be well drained and ventilated to avoid the outbreaks of disease that had decimated his troops at Valley Forge two years earlier. By January 1780, nearly 1,200 huts housed some 13,000 men, making Jockey Hollow temporarily the 6th-largest city in the United States. There are replicas of the soldiers' huts at Sugar Loaf Hill and markers throughout the hollow noting the locations of the various brigades. Sugar Loaf Hill, in particular, reminds us of the hardships of the Continental Army: in 1780 the troops of the Pennsylvania Line, stationed here, put down a mutiny by the 1st Connecticut Brigade; the following year they themselves mutinied, demanding back pay and redress of their many grievances. Captain Adam Bettin was killed during the mutiny and is buried in Jockey Hollow beside the Bettin Oak. Near Sugar Loaf Hill is the Grand Parade, a large field where the troops drilled when not confined to their huts by snowdrifts.

Also in Jockey Hollow is the Wick House, which served as headquarters for Major General Arthur Sinclair in 1779-80. This house was owned by Henry Wick, a prosperous farmer, and is very different from the Ford Mansion in its homey, comfortable air. Wick lived here with his daughter Tempe (short for Temperance), who distinguished herself, so the story goes, by hiding her horse in a closet when colonial troopers came to requisition it.

Apart from hiking trails at the Grand Parade, Morristown National Historical Park has no recreational facilities, but Jockey Hollow is adjacent to LEWIS MORRIS PARK (201-538-1947), a facility of the Morris County Parks Commission. Here there are picnic sites (fires permitted in designated areas), trails, campsites, playing fields, a Parcourse Fitness Circuit, and swimming, boating, and fishing at the Sunrise Lake Recreation Area. Winding through the park and into Jockey Hollow is a portion of PATRIOTS' PATH, a designated National Recreation Trail linking parklands and historic sites along the Whippany River. The path was conceived as a "linear park" and designed to prevent further degradation of the Whippany by promoting recreational activities compatible with the river environment. For FURTHER INFORMATION, contact the Morris County Parks Commission, 53 E. Hanover Ave., Morristown, NJ 07960 (201-829-0474), or Friends of Patriots' Path, 300 Mendham Rd., Morristown, NJ 07960 (201-539-7540).

FOR THE DRIVER: Take I-80 west off GWB to Exit 43, then I-287 south to Exit 32, Morristown. From exit ramp turn left on Ridgedale to Morris Ave, then left again on Morris Ave, crossing I-287 and passing Ford Mansion to Lafayette Ave. Here turn left and circle around on Lafayette to museum parking lot in back of mansion. The route is well marked with brown signs directing you to Washington's Headquarters. At mansion pick up brochure for self-guided tour through rest of park. Note that you are now within a short drive of the sites on Trips B-7 and B-9.

If you wish to begin your tour from the visitor center in Jockey Hollow, about 5 mi southwest of the Ford Mansion, remain on I-287 south past Morristown to Exit 26B, Bernardsville. Shortly after ramp pick up US 202 north to Tempe Wick Rd, turn left and proceed to Jockey Hollow, following signs for visitor center and parking. If you follow Jockey Hollow Rd north through the park and turn left, it will lead you into Lewis Morris Park.

More to See in Morristown

TRIP B-9

HISTORIC SPEEDWELL
SCHUYLER-HAMILTON HOUSE
ACORN HALL
FRELINGHUYSEN ARBORETUM
MORRIS MUSEUM

DISTANCE: From GWB, about 45 mi. Fast and average speeds.

Historic Speedwell, 333 Speedwell Ave., Morristown, NJ 07960 (201-540-0211). *Open early May to late Oct Thurs-Fri 12-4, Sat-Sun 1-5, and by appointment. Adults $2, senior citizens $1, children 50¢. Free parking at entrance, no cars allowed on site. No pets, no smoking or photographing inside buildings. Annual art show, crafts fair, folk festival, Christmas celebration, and other special events. Vail House wheelchair-accessible.*

Organized in 1966, Historic Speedwell preserves part of the Vail Homestead Farm, site of technological innovations that helped fuel America's Industrial Revolution. Judge Stephen Vail, self-made man and family patriarch, built the Speedwell Iron Works here along the Whippany River, and in 1818-19 the works cast most of the machinery for the *Savannah,* the first transatlantic steamship. In 1837 his son Alfred began a collaboration with Samuel F. B. Morse, and in January 1838 the first public demonstration of Morse's electromagnetic telegraph took place in the cotton factory (message: "A patient waiter is no loser," courtesy of Judge Vail).

A National Historic Site, Speedwell consists of 9 buildings, including the restored cotton factory, the Vail House, a water-powered wheelhouse, a granary, and 3 historic houses relocated from various parts of Morristown to avoid demolition. A detailed self-guided brochure is available from the Speedwell office, located in the Vail House, and there is a gift shop in L'Hommedieu House.

Schuyler-Hamilton House, 5 Olyphant Place, Morristown, NJ 07960 (201-267-4039). *Open all year 2-5 Tues, Sun, and Washington's* *birthday, other times by appointment; closed Christmas. Adults $1, children under 12 free. Many steps, difficult for wheelchairs.*

This colonial house was the setting for the courtship of Betsy Schuyler by Alexander Hamilton, then a colonel in the Continental Army, stationed in the nearby Ford Mansion (see Trip B-8) as part of General Washington's staff. The house has period furnishings and is maintained by the local chapter of the DAR.

Acorn Hall, 68 Morris Ave., Morristown, NJ 07960 (201-267-3465). *Open Mar-Dec Thurs 11-3, Sun 1:30-4; gardens open daily dawn-dusk; house and gardens closed Jan-Feb and major holidays. Adults $1, elementary and high school students 50¢. Guided tours, last tour begins ½ hr before closing. Annual Victorian Christmas decorations throughout Dec. Steps into house, interior difficult for wheelchairs.*

This excellently preserved Victorian house (1853) is the headquarters of the Morris County Historical Society. The scrollwork embellishments on the exterior are a good indication of what to expect inside. There are many priceless furnishings, including a Rococo Revival parlor set, a printed velvet rug identical to one displayed at London's Crystal Palace Exhibition in 1851-52, and some porcelains given to Commodore Perry, a relative of the second owner, when he opened Japan to Western trade in 1854. We are also welcome to browse in the Victorian reference library and the gift shop.

Acorn Hall takes its name from the majestic, centuries-old red oak that stands near the driveway. The Home Garden Club of Morristown has restored the grounds to recreate a period garden of extraordinary variety and beauty, well worth the trip in itself. There are sometimes docents available to give us a tour. If not, we can wander on our own using a detailed brochure that explains the plantings and describes the succession of bloom from early April to August.

Frelinghuysen Arboretum, 53 E. Hanover Ave., Morristown, NJ 07960 (201-829-0474). *Open mid-Mar to late Nov; grounds open 8-dusk; house open Mon-Fri 9-4:30, Sat-Sun 10-6 daylight savings and 9-5 standard time. Free. Hiking trails, nature programs, concerts, special events. No pets. Ramp into house; Red Trail and Braille Trail wheelchair-accessible.*

The Morris County Park Commission has its headquarters here in an 1891 country estate, a lovely specimen of Victorian architecture that also houses a fine horticultural library. Elaborate gardens, flowering shrubs, brilliant displays of roses and spring and fall bulbs, make the grounds worth visiting at almost any time of year. There are 127 acres of forest and gardens crisscrossed by well-marked trails. For $1 you can buy a trail guide that explains the various plantings and their special characteristics.

Morris Museum, 6 Normandy Heights Rd., Morristown, NJ 07960 (201-538-0454). *Open all year Tues-Sat 10-5, Wed until 8, Sun 1-5; closed Mon. Adults $1.50; children, students, senior citizens 50¢. Ramp into building, elevator for wheelchairs.*

This wonderful museum, in an imposing red-brick mansion, holds just about everything from fossils to live animals, art to archeology, old-time toys to computers. The museum sponsors a lively program of concerts, lectures, workshops, and special events, and there are lots of activities geared towards kids, including a special room for preschoolers.

FOR THE DRIVER: Take I-80 west off GWB to Exit 43, then I-287 south to Exit 35, NJ 10 and Whippany. Go west on 10 (away from Whippany) about 1½ mi to jct with US 202. Turn left and go south on 202 towards Morristown. Cross Hanover Ave and watch for Historic Speedwell, shortly on left (202 becomes Speedwell Ave).

Continue south on Speedwell to Spring St stoplight and turn left on Spring to Morris Ave, bypassing Morristown Green. Turn left on Morris Ave, continue to railroad trestle, then go 1 short block past it to Olyphant Place. Turn left here to Schuyler-Hamilton House, behind Texaco Station (not marked).

From here go back to Morris Ave, turn left, and continue across I-287 past Washington's Headquarters. Shortly come to 3-way split, with roads going left, straight, and right. Here, staying in righthand lane, you can go left around jughandle following sign for U-turn/hotel/Limdsley, then passing Governor Morris Inn to Acorn Hall, on right. However, it's easier to go on to the other sites and come back to Acorn Hall.

At 3-way split, bear right through stoplight onto Columbia Tpk, go uphill and turn left at 1st light onto Normandy Heights Rd, then make an immediate left to Morris Museum.

From museum turn left on Normandy Heights Rd and continue to Whippany Rd. Turn right on Whippany and proceed briefly to Hanover

Ave. Turn left on Hanover and go a short distance to Frelinghuysen Arboretum, on left, opposite Morris County Library.

Go back to Whippany, turn right, and return to 3-way split. Continue straight through stoplight past Governor Morris Inn to Acorn Hall driveway, on right. Just beyond, on right, is Lafayette St turnoff for Washington's Headquarters (Trip B-8).

From a Stage Coach Stop to the High Hills

TRIP B-10

STAGE HOUSE INN AND VILLAGE, Scotch Plains

TERRY LOU ZOO, Scotch Plains

WATCHUNG RESERVATION, Mountainside

TRAILSIDE NATURE AND SCIENCE CENTER,

Mountainside

DISTANCE: From GWB, about 40 mi. Mainly fast speeds.

Stage House Inn and Village, Front St. & Park Ave., Scotch Plains, NJ 07076 (201-322-4224). *Shops open all year Mon-Sat during business hours. Inn open daily 11:30-9:30, Fri-Sat until 10:30. Mostly wheelchair-accessible.*

This collection of restored 18th-century buildings holds a number of small shops surrounding a courtyard and offering early crafts, leatherwork, antiques, silverware, and more. The Stage House Inn, built in 1737, once served weary travelers taking the two-day trip between New York and Philadelphia on the Swift Sure Stage Line along the Old York Road. Across the street is the Cannon Ball Museum (open Sunday afternoons), hit by cannon fire during the Battle of Short Hills in 1777.

Terry Lou Zoo, 1451 Raritan Rd., Scotch Plains, NJ 07076 (201-322-7180). *Open daily all year, weekdays 10-4, weekends and holidays 10-6. Admission $3, children under 1 yr free; pony rides $1. Largely wheelchair-accessible.*

This privately owned zoo has an outstanding collection of tropical birds and game, including lions, tigers, hippos, elephants, and giraffes. The kids will enjoy the petting zoo and pony rides.

Watchung Reservation, Mountainside, NJ 07092. *Open all year daily. Free. Hiking trails, cross-country ski trails, picnic facilities and fireplaces, fishing and boating by permit at Lake Surprise, stables (fee) and bridle paths. Leashed pets only. Difficult for wheelchairs. For further information, contact the Union County Department of Parks and Recreation, Union County Administration Bldg., Elizabeth, NJ 07207 (201-527-4900).*

There's much to do in this scenic 2,000-acre preserve that stretches along the Watchung Ridges overlooking Blue Brook Valley. In season there's a wonderful rhododendron display, usually in peak bloom a little past mid-May. An observation tower 575 feet above sea level provides an excellent view and a good lookout for bird migrations. The 10-mile Sierra Loop and other marked hiking trails, the mile-long Lake Surprise, and the 30 miles of bridle paths are also popular attractions. Much of the reservation has been left in its natural state, and many Indian trails have been preserved. The name Watchung, meaning "high hills," was also left us by the Indians, and sometimes in these quiet woods you get the feeling they're not so far away from their old camping grounds.

Trailside Nature and Science Center, Coles Ave. & New Providence Rd., Mountainside, NJ 07092 (201-232-5930). *Visitor center and museum open 1-5 daily all year except New Year's, Easter, July 4th, Thanksgiving, Christmas. Planetarium open Tues, Thurs, occasionally Sun. Free except for planetarium shows (75¢). Museum and visitor center wheelchair-accessible.*

Trailside, located in Watchung Reservation, was New Jersey's first nature center. Designed by noted architect Michael Graves, it opened in 1941 and has been offering fascinating exhibits on animals, birds, plants, minerals, and other natural wonders ever since. The museum also features a Discovery Room for young children, with hands-on displays and live animals. At the visitor center there are permanent exhibits on the human and natural history of Watchung Reservation, changing art exhibits, a library, a gift shop, and gardens. The planetarium boasts a dome 18 feet in diameter, a Nova Star projector, and a Unitron telescope.

Trailside sometimes offers tours of another site in the reservation, Feltville, an old factory and mill town dating from 1841.

There's not much to see here if you go on your own (the buildings aren't open to the public), but it's worth a trip if you have a knowledgeable guide; inquire at the visitor center.

FOR THE DRIVER: Take GSP south to Exit 140A (75¢) or NJT south to Exit 14 (70¢). From either, pick up US 22 west and proceed past Somerville until 22 merges with I-78. Shortly take 2nd Clinton exit for Clinton-Pittstown (Exit 15), turn right from ramp onto W Main St (Rte 173), go about ¼ mi, and turn left to Old Red Mill and Clinton Historical Museum Village, just before bridge. From here cross Raritan to Hunterdon County Art Center, opposite museum on Center St.

Go back on Terrill to jct with US 22, turn right (east), and go back past Scotch Plains to Mountainside/New Providence Rd exit. Proceed on main road up mountain to Watchung Reservation. Turn right onto Tracy Drive, then take 3rd exit out of traffic circle. When road turns sharply left, turn right to Trailside parking lot.

George and Martha and Gardens of the World

TRIP B-11

WALLACE HOUSE STATE HISTORIC SITE, Somerville

OLD DUTCH PARSONAGE STATE HISTORIC SITE, Somerville

DUKE GARDENS FOUNDATION, Somerville

DISTANCE: From GWB, about 50 mi. Mainly fast speeds.

Wallace House State Historic Site, 38 Washington Place, Somerville, NJ 08876 (201-725-1015). *Open all year Wed-Fri 9-5, Sat 10-5, Sun 1-5; closed Thanksgiving, Christmas, New Year's. Free. Not wheelchair-accessible.*

This restored colonial house was probably one of the best of its kind when General Washington made it his headquarters in 1778, just after it was built. He and Mrs. Washington stayed here into the spring of 1779 while the Continental Army was camped at Middle Brook (now Somerville), experiencing remarkably moderate weather in contrast to the two brutal winters at Morristown (see Trip B-8). Our tour acquaints us with the military and social life of the house during the Revolution. The period furnishings are authentic, and the typical 18th-century kitchen has special interest.

Old Dutch Parsonage State Historic Site, 65 Washington Place, Somerville, NJ 08876 (201-725-1015). *Located across street from Wallace House, same information as above; check at Wallace House for caretaker.*

In this brick structure, built in 1751 and moved from its original site, the Reverend John Frelinghuysen established the first Dutch Reformed theological seminary in the New World. The seminary became Queens College and later Rutgers University (see Trip A-11). One of the occupants of the parsonage, the Reverend Jacob Hardenburgh, was a friend of Washington's. An interesting novelty is the smokehouse, usually built outdoors but here installed on the third floor, perhaps because of the constant wartime foraging.

Duke Gardens Foundation, PO Box 2030, Somerville, NJ 08876 (201-722-3700). *Open for guided tours Oct to early June daily 12-4 and Wed-Thurs evenings 8:30-10:30; closed Thanksgiving, Christmas, New Year's; advance reservations required. Adults $5, children 6-12 $2.50. No high heels, no cameras, no pets. Cobbled paths, narrow walks, some stairs; very difficult for wheelchairs.*

An acre of exquisite gardens in 11 different styles flourishes here under glass in carefully controlled temperatures. This truly memorable collection of international flora includes a lush tropical jungle, a starkly beautiful patch of Arizona desert, a formal French parterre garden, a Chinese grotto, an English summer garden, a Japanese garden, and an Indo-Persian display. Duke Gardens is one of the few attractions closed in summer and open in winter; it's a perfect escape from the city during those long gray months that never seem to end. Note again that advance reservations are required at all times.

FOR THE DRIVER: Take GSP south to Exit 140A (75¢) or NJT south to Exit 14 (70¢). From either, pick up US 22 west to Somerville. At jct with US 202/206, go south towards Princeton, staying on 206 when it branches off from 202 at Somerset Shopping Center. Shortly on 206, just beyond railroad overpass, is Somerset St, at light. Turn left for 1 block, then right at Middagh to the end. Turn left on Washington Place for Wallace House and Old Dutch Parsonage.

Go back to US 206 and continue south about 1 mi to Duke Gardens.

Shops and Houses out of America's Past

TRIP B-12

CLINTON HISTORICAL MUSEUM VILLAGE, Clinton
HUNTERDON ART CENTER, Clinton
MUSEUM AT NEW HAMPTON, Hampton

DISTANCE: From GWB to farthest point, New Hampton, about 75 mi. Mainly fast speeds.

Clinton Historical Museum Village, 56 Main St., Clinton, NJ 08809 (201-735-4101). *Open Apr thru Oct Tues-Sun 10-4. Adults $3, senior citizens $2, children 6-12 $1.50, under 6 free. Concerts and special events throughout season. Many wheelchair-accessible facilities and activities.*

You don't have to be an antiquarian to enjoy the Old Red Mill and reconstructed village set in a 10-acre park complete with waterfall and 150-foot limestone cliffs. Lifelike figures in costumes illustrate the uses of the period rooms in the mill, and the waterwheel still turns as it did in the days when grain, flaxseed, limestone, graphite, and talc were processed here. In addition to the mill we can visit a blacksmith shop, a turn-of-the-century general store and post office, an 1860 little red schoolhouse, a log cabin, old lime kilns, an herb garden, and the gift shop in the Educational and Cultural Center.

Hunterdon Art Center, 7 Center St., Clinton, NJ 08809 (201-735-8415). *Open all year Tues-Fri 12-4:30, Sat-Sun 1-5; closed major holidays. Suggested donation $1.50. Currently undergoing renovation to accommodate wheelchairs.*

This large, cool, barnlike gallery on the south branch of the Raritan River was once a gristmill (1837). Now it houses exhibits, a small theater, and displays of arts and crafts by prominent contemporary artists (some works are for sale). The center sponsors a variety of workshops and concerts throughout the year.

Museum at New Hampton, Musconetcong River Rd., Hampton, NJ 08827 (201-537-6464). *Open all year Tues 9-5, Thurs and Sat 1-5. Free. Workshops, craft classes, lectures, special events. Main floor wheelchair-accessible.*

Put on your pinafores, hitch up your suspenders, pack your McGuffey's Readers, and grab your slates—you don't want to be late for the Museum at New Hampton, a 19th-century school-house with a vintage, no-nonsense, Three-R's classroom featuring original books, old-style desks, and a potbellied stove. The building, constructed in 1823 as a one-room school, was enlarged in the 1870s, and the second floor is now used for changing exhibits of such esoterica as poison bottles, Hunterdon County milk bottles, and clothespin dolls. The Museum at New Hampton is known locally as "a dandy little museum," and indeed it is. Supported by the Township of Lebanon, it is a classic example of the enterprise and commitment of countless individuals and groups working to keep our heritage alive in every town, village, and crossroads of America.

FOR THE DRIVER: Take GSP south to Exit 140A (75¢) or NJT south to Exit 14 (70¢). From either, pick up US 22 west and proceed past Somerville until 22 merges with I-78. Shortly take 2nd Clinton exit for Clinton-Pittstown (Exit 15), turn right from ramp onto W Main St (Rte 173), go about ¼ mi, and turn left to Old Red Mill and Clinton Historical Museum Village, just before bridge. From here cross Raritan to Hunterdon County Art Center, opposite museum on Center St.

Leaving art center, continue on Center St, bearing right and proceeding to jct with NJ 31. Turn left on 31 and go north toward Hampton. If you're in the mood for something more active than sightseeing, there are two fine park facilities on your way. Shortly on 31 you will pass SPRUCE RUN RESERVATION (201-638-8572), which offers boating, swimming, camping, fishing, picnic areas and grills, and a range of winter sports. Special consideration was given to wheelchair accessibility in the design of Spruce Run; it is partially barrier-free and has ramps to the bathing beach and fishing pier. To reach the entrance, go north on 31 past jct with Rte 513 to Van Syckles Rd and turn left. If you turn right on Rte 513 it will take you to VOORHEES STATE PARK (201-638-6969), with hiking trails, picnic areas, children's playground, scenic overlook, observatory, and cardiovascular fitness course. Voorhees is not wheelchair-accessible at present, but modifications are in the works.

Continue north on 31 past Spruce Run and Voorhees towards Hampton, but don't take Hampton turnoff. Wait for road on right with sign for New Hampton (this is Musconetcong River Rd, but it's not marked). Go just under 1 mi on this to Museum at New Hampton, passing the New Hampton General Store and other fine antique shops on the way.

Canoeing, Loop-de-Looing, Choo-Chooing

TRIP B-13

CRANFORD BOAT AND CANOE COMPANY, Cranford
BOWCRAFT AMUSEMENT PARK, Scotch Plains
MODEL RAILROAD CLUB, Union

DISTANCE: From GWB to farthest point, Bowcraft, about 40 mi. Fast and average speeds.

Cranford Boat and Canoe Company, Springfield & Orange Aves., Cranford, NJ 07016 (201-272-6991). *Open spring thru fall daily 11-7. Rentals by the hour, week, month, or season.*

Known locally as the "Canoe Club," Cranford's offers safe flatwater mini-expeditions into a quiet preserve. We'll paddle up the Rahway River, winding through varied scenery. There are other rivers nearby to explore, as well as dams to conquer. We'll learn the correct way to handle a canoe, if we didn't know before. Be sure to obey all safety regulations.

Bowcraft Amusement Park, Rte. 22, Scotch Plains, NJ 07076 (201-233-0675). *Open daily all year; arcade 9am-11pm, miniature golf 9am-10pm, batting cages 10am-10pm; rides open at noon. Free admission and parking, fee per activity. Refreshment stand, picnic areas. Most facilities not wheelchair-accessible.*

This lively, well-groomed playland offers activities to suit most ages and interests. The sports lineup includes miniature golf and batting practice, and there's a video arcade with all the latest electronic games. Junior daredevils can try the kiddie motorcycle jump, helicopter ride, bumper cars, flying turtles, tilt-a-whirl, and kiddie scrambler, among other rides. The more sedate will enjoy the antique train ride and merry-go-round.

Model Railroad Club, Box 1146, Union, NJ 07083 (201-964-9724). *Open to the public Sat 1-4. Adults $1, children 50¢. Difficult for wheelchairs.*

If you ever dreamed of waking up one Christmas morning to find a little train chugging around the tree, you'll love the Model Railroad Club. There are currently 3,500 feet of track, and the club eventually intends to complete a scale-model point-to-point railroad running from Hoboken to Pittsburgh. From a special visitor's balcony you can watch the trains in operation on the Hudson, Delaware & Ohio Line, the Trenton Northern Power & Electric Traction Line, and the Rahway Valley Short Line. There are displays and exhibits, including one that explains how to start the hobby and where to purchase supplies (no sales here, though). Once a year, from the week before Thanksgiving to the week before Christmas, on weekends, visitors are invited to a full public show and allowed to walk through the operating aisles.

FOR THE DRIVER: Take GSP south to Exit 137 (75¢) and bear right from ramp onto NJ 28 west, or take NJT south to Exit 13 (95¢) to NJ 439 to NJ 28 west, passing jct with GSP. Go to 3rd light on 28 (Springfield Ave), turn right, and go 2 blocks to Orange Ave and Cranford Boat and Canoe, on right.

Continue on Springfield Ave past Nomahegan Park to end of street. Turn left, still on Springfield, to jct with US 22. Take second entrance, 22 west, and go about 1½ mi to Bowcraft's, on right.

From here, go back on 22 east to Jefferson Ave in Union. Turn right to Model Railroad Club.

Ancient Flowers, Modern Bulbs

TRIP B-14

BIBLE GARDENS OF ISRAEL, Woodbridge

EDISON STATE PARK AND MEMORIAL TOWER,
   Menlo Park

1746 DRAKE HOUSE MUSEUM, Plainfield

DISTANCE: From GWB to Plainfield, about 40 mi. Fast and average speeds.

Bible Gardens of Israel, Beth Israel Memorial Park, Rte. 1, Wood-bridge, NJ 07095 (201-634-2100). *Open all year 9-4:30 Mon-Fri, Sun. Free. No picnicking, no pets. Smooth, level walks; manageable for wheelchairs.*

Here are miniature gardens made up of plants mentioned in the Bible. There are four main displays: the Garden of the Promised Land, the Garden of Moses, the Garden of Jerusalem, and the Garden of the Kings. The architecture features marble from Mount Carmel and stones from the Holy Land. People of all faiths come to enjoy the plantings in this unique park.

Edison State Park and Memorial Tower, Christie St., Menlo Park, Edison, NJ 08820 (201-549-3299 or 287-0900). *Museum and tower open all year Wed-Fri 12:30-4, Sat-Sun 12:30-4:30; also open Tues 12:30-4 Memorial Day to Labor Day. Free. Park is under development; no picnicking or other facilities at present. Museum wheelchair-accessible.*

This Art Deco tower was erected in 1937 on the exact site of the laboratory where Thomas Edison perfected the incandescent lamp and developed more than 400 other patented inventions. Edison's original workshop was moved lock, stock, and barrel to the Ford Museum in Dearborn, Michigan, but there's a scale model of it on display at the museum here, along with models of Edison's first tinfoil phonograph (1877) and the first practical light-bulb (1879). We cannot climb the tower, but inside at its base we'll see the ever-burning light that Edison himself switched on in 1929. Atop the tower, 131 feet above us, is a 14-foot, 8-ton amber glass replica of the lamp that lit the way into the 20th century.

1746 Drake House Museum, 602 W. Front St., Plainfield, NJ 07060 (201-755-5831). *Open all year Sat 2-4 and by appointment; call for arrangements and fees. Difficult for wheelchairs.*

During the Battle of Short Hills in 1777 this striking house served as Washington's headquarters and now serves a more pacific function as headquarters of the Plainfield Historical Society. Built in 1746, it has been restored and filled with period furnishings. An interesting diorama depicts the fighting in the nearby Watchungs, where the Continental Army maintained defensive outposts to keep watch on British troop movements.

FOR THE DRIVER: Take GSP south to Exit 130 (75¢). Here take US 1 south, but at 1st jughandle cross over and come back on US 1 north. Just beyond pkwy overpass follow sign, on right, to Beth Israel Memorial Park and Bible Gardens.

From gardens, continue north on US 1 to Greene Ave and turn left, following sign to Iselin. Just beyond Mount Lebanon Cemetery and railroad overpass, turn left at light onto NJ 27 towards Metuchen. Proceed past pkwy briefly to Christie St and turn right to Edison Park.

Go back to 27 and turn right towards Metuchen. At stoplight at Main St (Rte 531) turn right, following sign to Plainfield. At Oak Tree Ave light turn briefly, then right onto Park Ave (still Rte 531), and go about 3 mi to 5th St, passing on left the newly renovated CEDAR BROOK PARK (201-527-4900), a particular attraction from early May to mid-June, when the irises and then the dogwoods are in full bloom.

At 5th St (NJ 28) turn left and follow 28 through town, turning twice with it. Drake House is at 2nd turn, W Front St, where 28 goes left.

From Drake House, you can continue down W Front St (still NJ 28) about 2 mi to Washington Ave (Rte 529), turn right, and go north on 529 briefly to WASHINGTON ROCK STATE PARK (201-754-7940), where you can picnic and take in the fine view. A monument here marks the site of one of General Washington's observation posts.

Woodbridge, Edison, and Plainfield are interesting old towns that have seen a lot of changes since they were settled in the late 17th century; students of history and architecture will find much to see in all three. For FURTHER INFORMATION about Woodbridge and Edison, contact the Middlesex County Cultural and Heritage Commission, 841 Georges Rd, North Brunswick, NJ 08902 (201-745-4489), which publishes excellent brochures for historic walking tours through both towns; the. Woodbridge Metropolitan Chamber of Commerce, 52 Main St, Woodbridge, NJ 07095 (201-636-4040); the Historical Association of Woodbridge Township, c/o Barron Arts Center, 582 Rahway Ave, Woodbridge, NJ 07095 (201-634-0413); the Edison Township Historical Society, 328 Plainfield Ave, Edison, NJ 08820; and the Edison Chamber of Commerce, PO Box 281, Edison, NJ 08817 (201-287-1951). For more on Plainfield, contact the Central Jersey Chamber of Commerce, 120 W 7th St, Plainfield, NJ 07060 (201-754-7250).

Giants, Devils, and Other Spectacles

TRIP B-15

MEADOWLANDS SPORTS COMPLEX, East Rutherford

DISTANCE: From GWB, about 5 mi. Fast speeds.

Meadowlands Sports Complex, East Rutherford, NJ 07073 (201-935-8500). *Sports, racing, concerts, special events throughout the year. Fully wheelchair-accessible.*

Okay, so you've never forgiven the Giants and the Jets for moving to the stadium here. So you don't have to go to the football games. You can choose basketball with the Nets, hockey with the Devils, soccer with the Cosmos, thoroughbred and harness racing with some of the best horses around, tennis with the world's top seeds, and (maybe) baseball (maybe soon), if the Meadowlands is successful in its aggressive quest for a major league team. Or how about Ringling Brothers, the Ice Capades, the Grand Prix, a Springsteen concert, or any other of the impressive array of events that attracted some 8½ million people last year. A stone's throw from mid-Manhattan, and more than likely on your way home from most parts of New Jersey, the Meadowlands may offer just what you're looking for to top off your day's trip.

FOR THE DRIVER: Take NJT to Exit 16W (30¢) or Lincoln Tunnel to NJ 3 west towards Rutherford and follow signs for sports complex.

A Fascinating Sub Trip

TRIP B-16

USS LING, North Hackensack

VON STEUBEN HOUSE STATE HISTORIC SITE,
   River Edge

VAN SAUN COUNTY PARK, Paramus

DISTANCE: From GWB, about 8 mi. Fast and average speeds.

USS Ling, 150 River St., Hackensack, NJ 07601 (201-487-9493 or 342-3268). *Open 10-5 daily Feb-Nov, 10-5 Thurs-Sun Dec-Jan. Adults $2.50, children and senior citizens $1.50. Guided ½-hr tours, free parking, small gift shop. Not wheelchair-accessible.*

The *Ling* is a real submarine, used in World War II, later part of the reserve fleet, then a training vessel. Since 1973 she has been berthed on the Hackensack River, donated as a memorial to those who lost their lives in submarine service. The 312-foot-long vessel is kept in perfect working condition, and we can tour the crew quarters, the engine rooms, the torpedo rooms and conning tower, and more. We learn about some of the problems of submarine technology and some of the improvements instituted since the *Ling* was built. Ashore there's a museum with related displays. The ship is heated, but in winter it's wise to dress warmly. As for agility, it helps to have some, but many senior citizens have made the tour and enjoyed every minute.

Von Steuben House State Historic Site, Main St., River Edge, NJ 07661 (201-487-1739). *Open all year Wed-Sat 10-12 and 1-5, Sun 2-5; closed Thanksgiving, Christmas. Low porch and lintel; no ramps, but will accommodate wheelchairs.*

This attractive dwelling, built in 1695, was enlarged by the Zabriskie family in 1752 and is sometimes known as the Zabriskie House. Because the Zabriskies were Tories, the house was confiscated during the Revolution and given to Baron von Steuben in gratitude for his help in training the Continental Army. The Baron eventually chose not to live in the house and sold it back to the Zabriskies. Today it is the headquarters of the Bergen County Historical Society. Visitors will find a good sampling of period furniture, glassware, antiques, and Indian artifacts.

Van Saun County Park, 216 Forest Ave., Paramus, NJ 07652 (201-262-3771). *Grounds open all year daily dawn-dusk; free. Zoo open 9-5 Memorial Day to Labor Day, 9-4:30 other times; free (admission fee may go into effect in 1987); train rides Apr-Sept Tues-Sun 10-5, 25¢ per person, children under 2 free. Picnic facilities, fishing, playgrounds, playing fields, horseshoe pitch, shuffleboard, bike trail, ice skating, sledding, tennis (fee), concession stand. Zoo fully wheelchair-accessible, park largely barrier-free.*

This popular park is likely to be crowded at the height of the summer season, but the kids will enjoy the zoo, with a nice collection of North and South American animals, a farmyard display, train rides, and a large walk-through aviary. Van Saun is also worth a visit in spring, when the early gardens bloom. Particularly attractive is the garden at Washington Spring, from whose waters the general is said to have drunk.

FOR THE DRIVER: Take I-80 west off GWB to Exit 66, Hudson St, just across the Hackensack River. Coming off ramp, turn left on Vreeland at stop sign and go 1 block to Hudson St. Turn left and go to 5th light on Hudson, turn right here onto E Kansas, then turn left at light onto River St. Go about ¼ mi to *Ling,* on right, just before Bergen County Record Building.

From *Ling,* turn right on River St (NJ 503) and follow it north. About ¼ mi past jct with NJ 4, turn right on Main St in River Edge. Continue to dead end and Steuben House.

Go back to NJ 4 and go west to Forest Ave exit. At traffic light remain on Forest and continue north briefly to Van Saun County Park, watching for signs on right.

To return to city, go east on 4 back to GWB.

Discovering Silk City

TRIP B-17

LAMBERT CASTLE, Paterson
PATERSON MUSEUM, Paterson
GREAT FALLS HISTORIC DISTRICT, Paterson
AMERICAN LABOR MUSEUM, Haledon

DISTANCE: From GWB, about 15 mi. Fast speeds.

Lambert Castle, Valley Rd., Paterson, NJ 07503 (201-881-2761). *Open all year Wed-Sun 1-4; closed major holidays. Adults $1, over 65 50¢, children under 15 free. Difficult for wheelchairs.*

This imposing stone structure was built in 1892 by Catholina Lambert, an immigrant who made a fortune as a silk manufacturer during Paterson's heyday as "Silk City of the World." The Passaic County Historical Society maintains it as a museum with changing local exhibits and displays of decorative arts, paintings, and antiques, including a 5,400-piece spoon collection. The building itself features a wealth of architectural detail and reflects the opulent lifestyle of its rags-to-riches owner.

Paterson Museum, Thomas Rogers Building, 2 Market St., Paterson, NJ 07501 (201-881-3874). *Open daily all year, Mon-Fri 10-4:30, Sat-Sun 12:30-4:30; closed major holidays. Suggested donations: $1 adults, children free. Fully wheelchair-accessible.*

Organized in 1925, the Paterson Museum began rather humbly as a collection of rocks and artifacts dug up by local residents and donated to the public library. It grew steadily in size and scope, and in 1982 was relocated to the restored Thomas Rogers Locomotive Erecting Shop (1873) in the Great Falls Historic District. In addition to an exceptional collection of rocks, minerals, and gems, there are archeology and natural history displays and exhibits that show Paterson's evolution as a textile and manufacturing center. We can also see the shell of the 14-foot prototype submarine built in 1878 by John P. Holland, a pioneer of modern submarine technology, and a slightly later model, Holland's *Fenian Ram,* intended by its designer to sink the British navy, thereby winning freedom for Ireland.

Great Falls Historic District, McBride Ave. & Spruce St., Paterson, NJ 07501 (201-279-9587 or -1270). *Grounds open daily all year. Museum open daily all year, Mon-Fri 10-4:30, Sat-Sun 12:30-4:30, closed major holidays; adults $1, children under 12 free. Guided tours $1 adults, children under 12 free; brochures for free self-guided tours available at museum. Annual Great Falls Festival on Labor Day weekend, special events all year. Museum is wheelchair-accessible, with displays all on 1 level; wheelchairs can navigate streets.*

A hundred feet wide and 77 feet tall (about half the height of Niagara Falls), the Great Falls of the Passaic River can be counted on for a spectacular display in any season. Attracted by the tremendous power of the falls, Alexander Hamilton and other members of the Society for Establishing Useful Manufactures (S.U.M.) founded Paterson in 1791 as the first planned industrial city in the newly independent United States. Pierre L'Enfant, planner of Washington, D.C., designed raceways (now renovated) for the various mills, and Paterson grew rapidly. In 1835 Samuel Colt began manufacturing his revolvers here, and soon the silk boom made Paterson "Silk City of the World." The iron industry was turning out Rogers locomotives at a great rate by the late 19th century, and the aeronautics industry came to town after World War I.

Changing technology gradually made the mills and factories of Great Falls obsolete, and today it is a national historic site preserving an important chapter in American industrial history. We can walk along the old cobbled streets, see the houses of workmen and mill owners, and visit the factories and museum. A footbridge over the falls affords a magnificent view. The old hydroelectric station, currently under renovation, is scheduled to be operational in fall 1986, once again generating power for Paterson and environs. Because of the work, the 1986 Great Falls Festival will not take place, but try to catch it next year—it's a marvelous event.

American Labor Museum, Botto House National Landmark, 83 Norwood St., Haledon, NJ 07508 (201-595-7953). *Open all year Wed-Sun 12-4. Adults $1, children under 12 free. Free parking, picnic area, gift shop. Not wheelchair-accessible at present, but future modifications are planned.*

We all know, especially in this Statue of Liberty centennial year, that America is a nation of immigrants, built by the sweat and toil of men, women, and children from all over the world. Interestingly, the American Labor Museum in Haledon is the only museum in the United States dedicated to the history of working people—their lives on and off the job, their culture, their organizing struggles, their aspirations. The museum building itself is a peculiarly apt symbol: in 1908, after emigrating from Italy and laboring 12 hours a day 6 days a week for 15 years in New Jersey's textile mills, Pietro and Maria Botto built this house, 12 rooms of their own with garden, the American Dream come true. They installed a grape arbor and bocce court in the garden and ran the house as an ethnic social center for fellow Italian immigrants. In 1913, when more than 24,000 workers struck the Paterson silk mills, the Bottos offered their house as a gathering place, and for 6 historic months it was the scene of meetings, rallies, strategy sessions, and stirring oratory from some of the greats of the labor movement, including Elizabeth Gurley Flynn, John Reed, and Big Bill Haywood. The Paterson strike was a turning point in the battle for the 8-hour day and other labor reforms.

Through its varied collections, exhibits, ethnic festivals, concerts, film series, lectures, workshops, and seminars, the American Labor Museum recreates these events and the texture of working people's lives around the turn of the century. For those interested in delving further, there are extensive pictorial and archival materials in the library and research collection, open to the public by appointment.

For a rare slice of ordinary life during the decades of this country's industrial transformation, or for a rare visit to a historic site in New Jersey where George Washington did not sleep, go to the American Labor Museum.

FOR THE DRIVER: From GWB take I-80 west to Squirrelwood Rd, get off and make a U-turn onto I-80 east. Exit at Clifton/NJ 20 and go south on 20 to first exit, Valley Rd. Get off 20 here, turn right, and look for entrance to Lambert Castle, shortly on right.

From Lincoln Tunnel take Rte 3 west to jct with US 46, 1 mi or so past Clifton. Here take Montclair/Paterson exit to Valley Rd. Turn right on Valley and go about 2½ mi to Lambert Castle, on left.

The castle is located in GARRET MOUNTAIN RESERVATION (201-742-6373), a woodland park on top of a 502-foot plateau, offering good views, picnic areas (by permit), hiking trails, fishing, boating, and stables.

From Lambert Castle, return to Valley Rd and turn left. At jct with NJ 20 go north, following "Downtown Paterson" signs to end of 20. Here, at Grand St light, go straight ahead on Jersey St to end at Market St. Turn left. You are now in the heart of Great Falls Historic District. Paterson Museum is last building on left on Market St (watch for locomotives). Park across street in public lot.

From the falls, cross the Passaic River on Wayne Ave and turn left on Front St briefly to Preakness Ave. Turn right, proceed a few blocks to Union Ave, and turn right again. Shortly, at W Broadway, turn left. At 3rd light make sharp right onto Barbour St, then 2nd left onto Mason Ave. American Labor Museum is at end of block, on left.

A Shopping Spree at the Jersey Malls

TRIP B-18

RIVERSIDE SQUARE, Hackensack

BERGEN MALL, Paramus

GARDEN STATE PLAZA, Paramus

PARAMUS PARK, Paramus

FASHION CENTER, Paramus

WILLOWBROOK MALL, Wayne

DISTANCE: From GWB, about 10 mi to Paramus, about 20 mi to Wayne. Mainly fast speeds.

No guide to northern Jersey would be complete without a word about the shopping malls. There are acres of them, offering something for just about every budget and taste. For a change of pace and a different kind of one-day adventure, consider taking in a mall or two.

Each mall resembles a small city, and each has its own personality; some are geared towards that elegant feeling, others towards kids and strollers and a carnival atmosphere. All have seasonal attractions and almost constant diversions of various kinds: petting zoos, rides for the kids, car and boat exhibits, crafts, fashion and art shows, performances and concerts, perhaps a display of hang-gliding equipment or a farmers' mart. In general, foliage (living) abounds, plenty of benches provide rest zones for shoppers, natural light shines through cleverly constructed skylights. The malls listed here are all enclosed and temperature-controlled, and have wheelchair-accessible parking and facilities.

Riverside Square, Rte. 4 & Hackensack Ave., Hackensack, NJ 07601 (201-489-0151). *Open Mon-Fri 10-9:30, Sat 10-6; closed Sun. Parking for 3,000 cars.*

Opened in March 1977, this is the newest and probably the most elegantly luxurious of the malls on our trip. The selection of anchor stores sets the theme: here are Bloomingdale's, Saks Fifth Avenue, and Conran's, with about 90 smaller shops and boutiques lining walkways of 2 floors. Softly shaded nature tints are used in the decor. Food is both plain and gourmet; a special section is set apart to permit diners to eat on benches amid the sun- or moonlit landscaping.

Bergen Mall, Rte. 4 at Forest Ave., Paramus, NJ 07652 (201-845-4050). *Open Mon-Sat 10-9:30; closed Sun. Village Mall open Mon, Tues, Wed, Sat 11-5:30, Thurs-Fri 11-9:30; closed Sun. Parking for over 4,800 cars.*

There's almost a World's Fair atmosphere here, with rows of flags and a large shimmering ball that is a gushing fountain. Anchor stores are Sterns, Ohrbach's, and Newberry's, with about 80 other shops handling a big variety of merchandise. Sterns' floral department fronts on the center promenade, and within it is a restaurant, one of several in the mall where both snacks and larger meals are available. Here, too, is the well-known Playhouse on the Mall (201-368-1943), featuring Broadway shows and musicals.

Downstairs is a quaint little slice of the past called Village Mall, with a number of narrow streets and cubbyhole "shoppes" selling craft materials, leatherwork, objets d'art, and antiques, including dollhouses and toys. Also downstairs are the auditorium, post office, headquarters for several youth organizations, and a bank.

Garden State Plaza, Rtes. 4 & 17, Paramus, NJ 07653 (201-843-2404). *Open Mon-Sat 10-9:30; closed Sun. Parking for about 7,500 cars.*

This large mall is a newly renovated "state-of-the-art enclosed regional shopping center." Attractive shopping lanes are named for flowering trees embellishing each one in spring—magnolias, cherries, dogwood. Anchor stores are Bamberger's, Gimbel's, and J. C. Penney, with a supporting cast of about 120 other stores and services. Snacks or meals are available in the Food Court.

Paramus Park Mall, Rte. 17 near Midland Ave., Paramus, NJ 07652 (201-261-8000). *Open Mon-Sat 10-9:30; closed Sun. Parking for over 4,000 cars.*

Between Abraham & Straus and Sears, nearly 100 stores line an enormous S-shaped walkway with a variety of merchandise appealing to many ages and tastes. Youngsters are beguiled by special shows and a carousel. In the 2-story center section escalators and a "bubble" elevator rise amidst banks of plantings and waterfalls to a second level with a picnic area. Here are 20 more shops, including a restaurant featuring all kinds of crêpes and a Farrell's Ice Cream Parlour. The others sell an unbelievable assortment of good food at good prices, to be eaten at one of the many tables on the surrounding gallery. Menus range from Greek, Pennsylvania Dutch, Chinese, Italian, and Mexican to fish 'n' chips, McDonald's, Nathan's hot dogs, and deli concoctions. A health food center caters to those who prefer something different.

Fashion Center, Rte. 17 near Ridgewood Ave., Paramus, NJ 07652 (201-444-9050). *Open Mon-Fri 10-9:30, Sat 10-6; closed Sun. Parking for over 1,800 cars.*

The tone of this mall is set by its anchor stores, B. Altman and Lord & Taylor. There is a less hurried atmosphere here, a feeling of relaxed shopping in a very pleasant setting of fountains and soft lights. Among the more than 20 additional stores are F. A. O. Schwarz, Brooks Brothers, and 3 restaurants.

Willowbrook Mall, Rtes. I-80, 23 & 46, Wayne, NJ 07470 (201-785-1616). *Open Mon-Sat 10-9:30, Sun 11-6. Parking for 9,000 cars.*

This is one of the biggest, and a single visit won't cover nearly all of it. Four anchor stores here—Bamberger's, Ohrbach's, Sterns, and Sears—are just part of a lineup of more than 175 shops on two levels. One section is a fashion gallery with hanging gardens and fountains and places to relax away from the throngs. All kinds of eating places on hand.

FOR THE DRIVER: From GWB take NJ 4 west and proceed to exit to Hackensack Ave, at Bloomingdale's. Turn in here for Riverside Square. The Von Steuben House (Trip B-16) can be reached from this same exit.

Return to 4 west, take briefly to exit to Forest Ave, and follow signs to Bergen Mall, on left.

To continue to Garden State Plaza, follow signs back to 4 west and continue to NJ 17 south. Take this across the road and exit at mall.

Take 17 north about 3 mi to entrance on right to Paramus Park. From here, take Abraham & Straus Drive north of mall to light and follow signs to Fashion Center, or take 17 north briefly.

For Willowbrook Mall, from GWB take I-80 west about 20 mi to jct with NJ 23. Follow signs to 23 south. Just beyond cloverleaf is entrance to Willowbrook. If driving to Wayne from Paramus, take NJ 17 south to I-80 west and proceed as just described.

After the Mall

TRIP B-19

DEY MANSION, Wayne

VAN RIPER-HOPPER HOUSE/WAYNE MUSEUM, Wayne

DISTANCE: From GWB, about 20 mi. Mainly fast speeds.

Dey Mansion, 199 Totowa Rd., Wayne, NJ 07470 (201-696-1776). *Open all year Tues, Wed, and Fri 1-4, Sat-Sun 10-4; closed New Year's, Thanksgiving, Christmas. Adults $1, under 16 free; additional fees for special events. Guided tours lasting about 40 min, picnic area. Not wheelchair-accessible.*

Located in Preakness Valley Park, this attractive Georgian mansion was built in 1740 by Dirck Dey (pronounced "Die"), a prosperous Dutch gentleman. A knowledgeable builder, Dey used the finest fieldstone, Flemish brick, and hand-hewn timbers in the construction of the house. His son, Colonel Theunis Dey, became a friend of George Washington's during the Revolution, and when the Continental Army was camped in the Preakness Valley, he offered the general use of the house as headquarters. Washington was here in July 1780, when he received news of the French allies' landing on Rhode Island with badly needed supplies and reinforcements, and he returned that fall after the failure of Benedict Arnold's treason at West Point. The mansion, maintained by the Passaic County Park Commission, holds great appeal for anyone interested in furnishings; all the articles are period originals in perfect condition. The outbuildings, including a barn, wagon shed, smokehouse, forge, and springhouse, have also been restored.

Van Riper-Hopper House/Wayne Museum, 533 Berdan Ave., Wayne, NJ 07470 (201-694-7192). *Open all year Fri-Tues 1-5; closed New Year's, Thanksgiving, Christmas. Free. No ramps, difficult for wheelchairs.*

This Dutch colonial house stands on land once belonging to the

Lenni Lenape Indians. The original portion was built in 1786 and is celebrating its bicentennial this year. An excellent example of careful planning, the house faces south in order to take advantage of the sun's light and heat. There are furnishings dating from the 1780s to the 1880s, an exhibit room with changing displays, an archeological research laboratory (Saturdays only), and special programs throughout the year.

FOR THE DRIVER: Take I-80 west off GWB through Paterson to 2nd exit for NJ 62, marked "62 South, Little Falls." Almost at once follow small sign and fork right on US 46 west to Dover. Shortly exit, right, to Riverview Drive and stay on it for about 1 mi, following signs to Wayne. At intersection just before golf course is Totowa Rd. Turn right here to Dey Mansion, on left.

Go back to Riverview Drive, turn right, and proceed briefly to Valley Rd. Turn right and continue on Valley Rd several mi to end, with Point View Restaurant directly in front of you. Here turn right at Berdan Ave and watch for Wayne Museum, on left.

On this trip you are very close to the two Wayne malls on Trip B-18 and the Paterson sites on Trip B-17.

Westward Ho!

TRIP B-20

LAKE HOPATCONG
HOPATCONG STATE PARK, Landing
WILD WEST CITY, Netcong

DISTANCE: From GWB, about 50 mi. Mainly fast speeds.

Lake Hopatcong is New Jersey's largest lake and one of its most popular resort areas. It is 900 feet above sea level and 9 miles long, with 40 miles of shoreline. Recreational opportunities abound: swimming (there are 10 public beaches), fishing, boating, water skiing, horseback riding, tennis, golf, ice fishing, ice boating, etc. For FURTHER INFORMATION, contact the Hopatcong Chamber of Commerce, PO Box 135, Hopatcong, NJ 07843 (201-398-0288), or the Skylands Tourism Regional Council, PO Box 467C, Convent Station, NJ 07961 (201-231-7000 X7416, or, in NJ 800-624-0485, outside NJ 800-424-0485).

Hopatcong State Park, Landing, NJ 07850 (201-398-7010). *Grounds open all year daily, 8-8 Memorial Day to Labor Day, 8-4:30 other times; beach open 10-6 daily Memorial Day to Labor Day. Parking fee Memorial Day to Labor Day $4 per car weekends and holidays, $2 weekdays, free Tues; no fee at other times. Swimming, fishing, boat launching ramp (rentals available at nearby marinas outside park), picnic facilities and grills, playgrounds. No alcohol, no hunting. Leashed pets only, no pets at beach. Partially barrier-free, well-graded lawn to swimming area, wheelchair-accessible picnic facilities and restrooms.*

This scenic 107-acre park is a good place to get your feet wet in Lake Hopatcong. It contains a section of the old Morris Canal, which was the chief means of moving coal and ore across the state from the 1830s to the 1880s.

Wild West City, Rte. 206, Netcong, NJ 07857 (201-347-8900). *Open weekends 10:30-6 May to mid-June and Labor Day thru Oct (weekdays school groups only), daily 10:30-6 mid-June to Labor Day, including holidays. Adults $4.50, children under 12 $4. Picnic area, petting zoo. Most facilities wheelchair-accessible.*

Here's a place that looks just like the set of your favorite TV westerns. Try the horseback, pony, or hay rides, take a foray into Indian territory on an old Iron Horse, watch the famous gunfight at the OK Corral, and beware of gunslingers on the stagecoach. Top off the day by swinging into the Golden Nugget Saloon for a meal and a show.

FOR THE DRIVER: Take I-80 west off GWB to Exit 28, proceed to stoplight, turn left, and go about ½ mi to Hopatcong State Park and lake. From here you can take a scenic drive around the lake.

Go back towards I-80 and pick up US 46 west to jct with US 206. Take 206 north towards Newton, passing turnoff to Waterloo Village (Trip B-21). A little beyond, on right, is road to Wild West City.

New Jersey, Too, Has a Waterloo

TRIP B-21

WATERLOO VILLAGE RESTORATION, Stanhope

ALLAMUCHY MOUNTAIN STATE PARK, Hackettstown

DISTANCE: From GWB, about 55 mi. Mainly fast speeds.

Waterloo Village Restoration, Stanhope, NJ 07874 (201-347-0900). *Open Tues-Sun 10-6 mid-Apr thru Oct, Tues-Sun 10-5 Nov-Dec; closed Jan to mid-Apr. Admission: Tues-Fri adults $6, senior citizens $4.50, children 6-12 $3; Sat-Sun adults $7.50, senior citizens $5, children 6-12 $3; under 6 free. Guided tours, picnic area, snack bar. Special events throughout summer, annual bluegrass festival. Pets discouraged. Dirt roads, many steps, difficult for wheelchairs.*

Costumed guides escort us through what was once a bustling town on the Morris Canal, known as Andover Forge in Revolutionary times. Today's restored village, located in Allamuchy Mountain State Park, was named for an iron foundry that in turn was named for Napoleon's epic defeat in 1815. The buildings are original and still stand exactly where they stood in the 18th and 19th centuries. We can visit 20 different sites, including homes, a gristmill, a stagecoach inn, a general store, a smithy, and an apothecary shop, and watch working craftspeople making candles, spinning and weaving, throwing pottery, and more.

Allamuchy Mountain State Park, Hackettstown, NJ 07840 (201-852-3790). *Open all year daily, daylight hours. Free. Picnic areas, fishing, hiking, camping (fee), playground, cross-country skiing, sledding. Leashed pets only, no pets in campgrounds. Stephens Section partially barrier-free and wheelchair-accessible.*

This attractive 10,000-acre park is mainly a wilderness area. The large northern section, where Waterloo Village is located, has hiking trails and good fishing at Saxton Falls, a waterfall on the Musconetcong River. Most of the park's facilities are located in the Stephens Section, about a mile below.

FOR THE DRIVER: Take I-80 west off GWB to Exit 25, US 206. Take 206 north to 2nd traffic light and turn left at sign for Waterloo Village, in Allamuchy Mountain State Park.

From village, turn left on park road and go south to Saxton Falls and Stephens Section of park.

Fish, Fowl, and the Legend of Jenny

TRIP B-22

ROCKPORT GAME FARM, Hackettstown

PEQUEST TROUT HATCHERY AND NATURAL
RESOURCE EDUCATION CENTER, Oxford

LAND OF MAKE BELIEVE, Hope

JENNY JUMP STATE FOREST, Hope

DISTANCE: From GWB, about 60 mi. Fast and average speeds.

Rockport Game Farm, Box 27A, Rockport Rd., Hackettstown,
NJ 07840 (201-852-3461). *Open daily all year. Free.*

Acres of pheasants await you here after a beautiful drive through
the Jersey hills. This sea of feathers makes an imposing sight, and
the farm also keeps some exotic birds, deer, and other game.
There's not much to see when the birds are young and kept indoors, but the drive alone is well worth the trip.

Pequest Trout Hatchery and Natural Resource Education Center,
Pequest Rd., Oxford, NJ 07863 (201-637-4125). *Open all year Fri-
Sun 10-4. Free. Tours; slide shows twice a day at 11 and 2.
Wheelchair-accessible.*

This could just be the hit of today's trip. It's a must for the
fishermen in the family, but even the amateur will be impressed.
Anglers (and cooks) will stand drooling at the sight of thousands
of trout that will soon stock the New Jersey waters. Indoors, the
first steps in the hatching process (September-October) may be
observed through glass partitions, and there will be special programs and videotapes at the Natural Resource Education Center
when it is completed. Your visit to Pequest may inspire you to
head up the road to Allamuchy Mountain State Park (Trip B-21)
and try your luck in the Musconetcong.

Land of Make Believe, Great Meadows Rd., Hope, NJ 07844 (201-
459-5100). *Open 10-5 Memorial Day weekend and weekends
in June, daily 10-5 late June to Labor Day, Sun only 10-5 Labor*

Day to Christmas; closed other times. Adults $5.50, children $6.50 (fee covers all rides and activities). Free parking, picnic area, refreshment stand, gift shop. Many facilities wheelchair-accessible.

Nestled at the foot of Jenny Jump Mountain, this family amusement park is just the place for kids who want to visit Santa at the North Pole, pilot the Red Baron or a restored Word War II DC-3, take a Civil War train ride or the Alfalfa Express hayride, converse with a talking scarecrow and a talking horse, or frighten themselves silly in the Haunted House. There's also a restored house where Jenny may have lived at the time of her legendary jump (see below).

Jenny Jump State Forest, PO Box 150, Hope, NJ 07844 (201-459-4366). *Open all year daily, daylight hours. Free. Picnics, camping (fee), hiking and nature trails, playground, cross-country skiing, sledding. Leashed pets only, no pets in campgrounds. Park office and restrooms wheelchair-accessible.*

The settler looked up in horror to where his daughter was picking berries above the clearing, saw the raised tomahawks of the Indians coming up behind her, and cried out, "Jump, Jenny, jump!" Legend has it that Jenny did. A small but exceedingly scenic park commemorates this tale, and we're invited to explore either by car or on foot. Here lived the Minsi (Wolf) tribe of the Lenape Indians. Campsites now rest on ground where Indian artifacts have been found. The main attraction is the superb view from the well-marked drives and trails.

FOR THE DRIVER: Take I-80 west off GWB to Exit 26, Hackettstown/US 46. Follow 46 southwest to Hackettstown and jct with Grand Ave, at light. Turn left on Grand and go about 3 mi south to Rockport Game Farm, well marked by signs.

Return to Hackettstown and US 46. Continue west on 46 about 10 mi to Pequest Hatchery, again well marked by signs.

Go back on 46 east a few mi to Great Meadows. Here turn left on Rte 611 (Saint Peter and Paul Church on corner) and go north 2-3 mi to Land of Make Believe, entrance on right.

Continue north on 611 about 2 mi to State Park Rd and Jenny Jump. From here, for return trip, continue north to Hope and I-80, and back to GWB.

Rumpelstiltskin, Rocks, Recreation

TRIP B-23

FAIRY-TALE FOREST, Oak Ridge

FRANKLIN MINERAL MUSEUM, Franklin

ACTION PARK/VERNON VALLEY GREAT GORGE, McAfee

DISTANCE: From GWB, about 50 mi. Fast and average speeds.

Fairy-Tale Forest, Oak Ridge Rd., Oak Ridge, NJ 07438 (201-697-5656). *Open Easter thru Oct: mid-June to Labor Day daily, Mon-Sat 10-5, Sun and holidays 10-6; weekends 10-5 Easter to mid-June, Labor Day thru Oct; gate closes 1 hr before closing time. Adults $3.75, children 2-12 $2.75. Snack bar, picnic area, souvenir shop. Paved walks manageable for wheelchairs.*

Children can hardly wait to enter this enchanted woodland filled with scenes and characters from their favorite stories. Hand-crafted life-size characters inhabit the castles, cottages, and gingerbread houses that dot this 20-acre storybook land. The kids can visit Rapunzel's tower, the Old Woman's shoe, Goldilocks' cabin, Jack's beanstalk, and a 3-ring circus, renewing their acquaintance with Red Riding Hood, Snow White, Humpty Dumpty, Little Miss Muffet, contrary Mary, and other fairy-tale notables along the way. There's also a merry-go-round, a fire engine, and the Candy Rock Train. Grab your glass slippers and follow the breadcrumbs to Oak Ridge!

Franklin Mineral Museum, Evans St., Franklin, NJ 07416 (201-827-3481). *Open mid-Apr to mid-Nov: mid-Apr thru June and Sept to mid-Nov Fri-Sat 10-4, Sun 12:30-4:30; July-Aug Wed-Sat 10-4, Sun 12:30-4:30; closed Easter. Museum admission $2 adults, $1 elementary and high school students; same fees charged again for admission to Buckwheat Dump. Guided tours, gift shop. Museum is wheelchair-accessible, but not dump.*

There are some 300 different minerals on display here, almost all of them from the Franklin-Ogdensburg area, the beneficiary of a unique sequence of geological events that began about a billion years ago. In the course of these unimaginable eons, several major periods of mountain building produced the world's richest zinc ore body, along with 26 minerals not found anywhere else on earth. Recently (in the last million years or so, that is), glaciation, erosion, and weathering have continued the process of mineral formation, and new specimens are still being discovered.

The Franklin Mineral Museum contains permanent and traveling collections, as well as what may be the most spectacular display of fluorescent minerals anywhere to be found. The mine replica simulates the operations of the New Jersey Zinc Company, which donated all the equipment and materials used in the reconstruction. The museum also administers the Buckwheat Dump, where we can prospect on our own and take home up to 20 pounds of minerals (10 pounds for kids). We're welcome to bring our own gear, or rent or purchase ultraviolet lamps and other equipment at the gift shop.

Action Park/Vernon Valley Great Gorge, PO Box 848, McAfee, NJ 07428 (general information 201-827-2000; ski conditions and year-round activities hotline 201-827-3900).

Action Park. *Open Memorial Day to mid-Oct: daily Memorial Day to Labor Day, Sun-Thurs 10-9, Fri-Sat 10-10; weekends Labor Day to mid-Oct, Sat 10-10, Sun 10-9. Adults (anyone over 48" tall—some activities are geared to size) $17, children $13; weekends during peak season (mid-June to late Aug) adults $18, children $13. Admission fee covers all activities except Grand Prix racecars, operated as a separate concession. No pets, no food or beverages allowed in park; picnic area and refreshments available nearby. Restrooms, walks, and some water park activities wheelchair-accessible.*

The *New York Times* calls Action Park "the most distinctive expression of the amusement park in our age"—and they're not talking ferris wheels and Kewpie dolls. With more than 50 different activities and the world's largest water park at your disposal, you can easily spend an entire day in this beautiful mountain setting. For a break from the Avalanche Flume Ride, Incredible Roaring Springs, Tidal Wave Pool, Awesome Surf Hill, Human Cannonball, speedboats, go-carts, etc., try the Broadway Revue or the rock-and-roll show, or quench your thirst at the German

Brewery. In summer Action Park puts on an annual 10-day German Festival and other special events.

Vernon Valley Great Gorge. *Open daily Thanksgiving to Apr, weekdays 9am-10:45pm, weekends and holidays 8:30am-10:45pm. Fees (lower to upper ranges, depending on days and hrs): season pass (worthwhile if planning 10 or more trips) $175-$330 adults, $160-$260 under 13, inquire about special family rates; lift ticket $13-$24 adults, $13-$19 under 13; equipment rentals $4.50-$15; private lessons $30-$35; 1-day packages (lift ticket, lessons, rentals) $28-$44 adults, $25-$39 under 13. Patrolled slopes, lodges, spa (free to overnight guests), Cobblestone Shopping Village. Inquire about Handicapped Skiers' Program, available at lesson rates.*

Here, spread over 3 mountains, are over 25 miles of interconnected skiing terrain, with 17 lifts and 52 trails graded for difficulty. The world's largest snowmaking system can lay 8 miles of 3-foot-deep fresh snow overnight. An army of maintenance workers keeps the slopes well groomed for maximum performance, and patrols make sure that safety regulations are observed.

FOR THE DRIVER: From GWB take I-80 west to Exit 53 and pick up NJ 23 north through Butler about 18 mi to Oak Ridge Rd. Here follow signs to Fairy-Tale Forest, on left.

From here, continue on 23 north towards Franklin and Sussex. Coming into Franklin, just past jct with Rte 517 is a small shopping center. Continue briefly on 23 to Buckwheat Rd and turn left, following signs for Franklin Mineral Museum.

Return to NJ 23 and continue northwest to jct with NJ 94. Here go right (north) about 4 mi to Action Park and Great Gorge, well marked by signs.

Creatures and Crafts in Scenic Northwest Jersey

TRIP B-24

SPACE FARMS ZOO AND MUSEUM, Sussex
HIGH POINT STATE PARK, Sussex
STOKES STATE FOREST, Branchville
PETERS VALLEY CRAFTS CENTER, Layton

DISTANCE: From GWB, about 70 mi. Fast and average speeds.

Space Farms Zoo and Museum, Beemerville Rd., Sussex, NJ 07461 (201-875-5800). *Open 9-6 daily May thru Oct. Adults $5, children 3-12 $2.50. Picnic area, playground, restaurant, gift shop. Grounds somewhat hilly but manageable for wheelchairs, buildings wheelchair-accessible.*

The denizens of Space Farms are not extraterrestrials but over 500 native North American mammals, birds, and reptiles, along with a few exotic species from foreign parts, all collected by the Space family. The Spaces have been operating the 400-acre farm since 1927 and pride themselves on their tradition of "tender, loving care in tune with nature." In addition to viewing the animals in their natural habitat, you can visit the museum buildings and see Grandpa Ralph Space's remarkable collection of Americana—antique cars, toys, dolls, clocks, muskets, inventions, gadgets, Indian artifacts, and everything but the kitchen sink (that's in Grandma Space's restaurant, serving short-order specialties with an old-fashioned touch).

High Point State Park, RR 4, Box 287, Sussex, NJ 07461 (201-875-4800). *Open all year daily, daylight hours. Admission Memorial Day to Labor Day and weekends in May and Oct, $2 per car weekdays (Tues free), $3 weekends and holidays; other times 50¢ per person, under 12 and over 62 free. Picnicking, refreshments, swimming and bathhouse, hiking and nature trails, boating, fishing, camping (fee), cross-county skiing, ice skating, ice fishing, snowmobiling, sledding, dog sledding. Leashed pets only. Wheelchair-accessible beach and restrooms.*

The highest point in New Jersey (1,803 feet) lies in this beautiful 14,000-acre park. From the top of the 220-foot war memorial that marks the spot, we can see the Delaware River, the Poconos, the Catskills, and the juncture of three states, New York, New Jersey, and Pennsylvania. The view is especially magnificent in laurel time and in the fall. Part of the Appalachian Trail winds through High Point, and spring-fed Lake Marcia provides a refreshing dip. There's also a lodge in the park, currently under restoration.

Stokes State Forest, RR 2, Box 260, Branchville, NJ 07826 (201-948-3820). *Open all year daily. Free admission to park; Memorial Day to Labor Day admission to Stony Lake day use area $1 per car weekdays, $3 weekends and holidays.* Picnicking, playground, refreshments, swimming and bathhouse, boating, camping (fee), fishing, hiking and nature trails, bridle paths, cross-county skiing, snowmobiling, ice skating, ice fishing, sledding. Stony Lake, picnic areas, and newer buildings wheelchair-accessible.

This park of over 15,000 acres on the Kittatinny Ridge offers some of the finest scenery in New Jersey. Don't miss Tillman Ravine, a natural gorge in the southern corner of the park, or 1,600-foot-high Sunrise Mountain, with superb views of the surrounding landscape.

Peters Valley Crafts Center, Layton, NJ 07851 (201-948-5200). *Store and gallery open all year daily 10-5; studios open to the public for interpretive programs in July-Aug or by appointment. Spring, summer, and fall workshops in blacksmithing, ceramics, jewelry, textiles, photography, woodworking; $10 registration fee, tuition from $40 for day workshops to $150 for 9-day workshops. Annual summer craft fair. Ramp into store; otherwise not wheelchair-accessible.*

Located in the Delaware Water Gap National Recreation Area (Trip B-25), Peters Valley is a year-round residential community where skilled craftspeople are invited to live and work in exchange for teaching workshops in their various specialties. Recent workshops have covered such topics as hand-forged tools, the "lost wax" process of ceramic shell casting, contemporary teapots, kiln building, goldsmithing, enameling, electroforming and electroplating, landscape and portrait photography, photography on/in/and fabrics, quilting, collage art, handbound books, knotting and coiling, embroidery, silk painting, rustic furniture, and joinery. In addition to the workshops, there are associate, internship, and assistantship programs for qualified students. The gallery and store feature work by the resident craftspeople and other nationally known artists. If you have more than a casual interest in crafts, you may want to consider a membership ($15-$100) entitling you to waiver of $10 registration fee and other privileges.

FOR THE DRIVER: Take I-80 west off GWB to Exit 53 and pick up NJ 23 north to Sussex. At jct with Rte 565, turn left, following signs to Space Farms. Shortly make a right-angle turn and continue straight ahead to Rte 519, turning left and proceeding to farms as indicated by signs.

From here, go north on 519 about 5 mi to NJ 23, then north on 23 another few mi to High Point State Park, or go south on 519 about 6 mi to US 206, then north on 206 about 3 mi into Stokes State Forest. High Point borders Stokes on the south, and you can drive from one to the other on interconnected park roads, taking a scenic route along the crest of the mountain. Ask for maps at park offices.

As you leave Stokes going north on 206, you will come to jct with Rte 521. Turn left here and go about 1 mi to jct with Rte 615, then left again about 2 mi on 615 to Peters Valley.

To go directly to Peters Valley from New York, take I-80 west to Exit 34, NJ 15, then 15 north to US 206 north to Stokes. Just before Stokes, Rte 521 meets 206 on left. Do not turn here. Continue through Stokes until 521 branches off again on left, then proceed as above.

A Majestic Gateway to the Poconos

TRIP B-25

DELAWARE WATER GAP NATIONAL RECREATION AREA, New Jersey/Pennsylvania

DISTANCE: From GWB, about 75 mi. Fast speeds.

Delaware Water Gap National Recreation Area, Bushkill, PA 18324 (717-588-6637). *Grounds open daily all year; Kittatinny Point Information Station open Apr-Oct daily 9-5; Dingmans Falls Visitor Center open May to Labor Day daily 9-5; Millbrook open Apr-Oct daily 9-5; Slateford Farm open Memorial Day to Labor Day Wed-Sun 12-5. No fees. Picnicking; swimming at Hidden Lake, Smithfield Beach, and Milford Beach (lifeguards); fishing, canoeing (rentals available outside park), hiking trails, self-guided nature trails; ice fishing, ice skating, cross-country skiing, snowmobiling, all in designated areas only. Detailed park maps, trail and river guides available at Kittatinny Point Information Center. Leashed pets only. Braille Trail at Pocono Environmental Education Center, some facilities manageable for wheelchairs.*

Stretching for 35 miles along the banks of the Delaware River, these 70,000 largely unspoiled acres hold a wealth of scenic and recreational opportunities. The most spectacular sight is the gap itself, where, over countless millennia, the Delaware River carved a path between the Kittatinny Ridge in New Jersey and the Pocono Mountain Plateau in Pennsylvania. The gap, about 900 feet across at river level, widens to span a mile at the crest, making a dramatic cleft in these ancient mountains, which were once as high as the Rockies. There are three marked gap overlooks, one on the site of the old Kittatinny House, a popular resort hotel destroyed by fire in 1931, one at Point of Gap, with exhibits illustrating the gap's formation, and one at Arrow Island, with access to a self-guided trail.

Wildlife abounds here, and you can hike along 13 marked trails graded for difficulty, including a 25-mile section of the Appalachian Trail. The Dingmans Falls Trail, an easy hike through a picturesque gorge dotted with stands of hemlock and rhododendron, leads to the Poconos' highest waterfalls, Dingmans and the aptly named Silver Thread Falls. There's a visitor center here with exhibits and audiovisual programs. Two educational centers in the middle of the park, operated by local schools in cooperation with the National Park Service, offer year-round environmental programs: POCONO ENVIRONMENTAL EDUCATION CENTER, RD 1, Box 268, Dingmans Ferry, PA (717-828-2319), and WALPACK VALLEY ENVIRONMENTAL EDUCATION CENTER, Box 134, Walpack Center, NJ 07881 (201-948-5749). There's no camping in the national recreation area, but WORTHINGTON STATE FOREST (201-841-9575), located within its boundaries at the southern end, allows camping, as do High Point State Park and Stokes State Forest (Trip B-24), outside the boundaries to the north.

In addition to the natural attractions, there are two developed park sites of historic interest. Slateford Farm is a partially restored 19th-century house with outbuildings near the site of an old slate quarry. Millbrook, a small rural town left behind by the march of progress, has been restored to life as a 19th-century village, with homes, general store, church, school, blacksmith and shoemaker's shops, gristmill, and other buildings.

A word of caution: if you're hiking, swimming, rock climbing, or canoeing, be sure to read and obey all safety regulations.

FOR THE DRIVER: Take I-80 west off GWB all the way to Millbrook exit, last exit in New Jersey, just before toll bridge (25¢) into Pennsylvania. Kittatinny Point Information Center is just off this exit, in southern end of park, not far from Point of Gap. Inquire here for detailed map. You can also enter the park from various points north on the Jersey side, including the sites on Trip B-24. Once inside the park you can drive its length on internal roads, crossing to the Pennsylvania side at several points on toll bridges (all 25¢). Within the park boundaries are a number of privately operated sites, including those on Trip B-26.

Over the River and to the Falls

TRIP B-26

POCONO INDIAN MUSEUM, Bushkill

MAGIC VALLEY VILLAGE AND WINONA FIVE FALLS, Bushkill

BUSHKILL FALLS, Bushkill

DISTANCE: From GWB, about 90 mi. Mostly fast speeds.

We're on the other side of the gap now, in the land of the heart-shaped bathtub, but there's much more to the Poconos than honeymoon hotels. We'll find plenty of dramatic scenery, unspoiled wilderness, forests, parks, and just about any form of recreation we fancy. The mountains are breathtaking during laurel season (usually the last three weeks in June, depending on the weather), when they are blanketed by delicate pinkish blossoms as far as the eye can see. A laurel tour by car is an excellent way to see the Poconos, and you can get a list of recommended scenic laurel routes, as well as FURTHER INFORMATION about the area, from the Pocono Mountains Vacation Bureau, 1004 Main St., Stroudsburg, PA 18360 (717-421-5791 or 800-POCONOS).

Pocono Indian Museum, Rte. 209, Bushkill, PA 18324 (717-588-9338). *Open all year daily except Christmas, 9-8 in July-Aug, closing times vary during rest of year. Adults $2.50, children 6-12 $1, under 6 free. Guided tours, gift shop (ski shop in winter). Will accommodate wheelchairs; entrance has flight of low steps, but displays are all on 1 level.*

Here a series of nicely mounted displays, including pottery, artifacts, and a real bark house, tells the story of the Delaware Indians who inhabited this area centuries ago. Today there are only a few Delaware Indians left, and the museum preserves a vanished way of life. There's also an exhibit of Plains Indian peacepipes, tomahawks, war bonnets, and one other unique item of headgear—a 130-year-old scalp. The museum remains open in winter, but the gift shop operates as a ski shop.

Magic Valley Village and Winona Five Falls, Rte. 209, Bushkill, PA 18324 (717-588-9411). *Open early Apr to mid-Oct daily 10-dusk. Adults $4.75, senior citizens and children 6-12 $3.75, under 6 free. Self-guided tours of falls, petting zoo, shows, snack bar. Will accommodate wheelchairs.*

Hundreds of years ago, according to legend, the Indian princess Winona leapt into these rushing waters to stop her father's tribe from warring with her lover's tribe. Starting from a height of 175 feet, 5 cascades tumble down mossy rocks amid hemlocks, pines, and mountain laurel. We can hike to the falls from the turn-of-the-century theme park, where artisans work at traditional Pennsylvania crafts while gunslingers shoot it out in the streets. There are puppet and magic shows, animals to pet, and music at the Opry House.

Bushkill Falls, Rte. 209, Bushkill, PA 18324 (717-588-6682). *Open Apr-Nov daily 9-dusk. Adults $3.50, senior citizens $2.75, children 6-12 $1, under 6 free. Picnic area and grills, nature trails, wildlife exhibit, fishing, 2-seater paddleboat rentals ($1.25 per boat), miniature golf ($1 per person), shops, refreshment stand. Shops and restrooms wheelchair-accessible, but not falls.*

From its headwaters high in the northeastern Poconos, Bushkill Creek rushes down to a 100-foot cliff near the Delaware as if eager to take the plunge into a beautiful green pool and then down another 70 feet through a dramatic boulder-strewn gorge. This is Bushkill Falls, "the Niagara of the Poconos," one of several waterfalls to which we can hike on well-marked trails of varying difficulty. It's a gorgeous spot, carefully but unobtrusively maintained. At the entrance to the falls are the picnic and recreational areas, a taxidermy exhibit of native wildlife, an art gallery, and a number of shops, including a silversmith, an ice cream parlor, and a fudge kitchen.

FOR THE DRIVER: Take I-80 west off GWB through New Jersey and across the Delaware (25¢) into Pennsylvania. At Exit 52, take US 209 north through Marshalls Creek, passing ADVENTURE TOURS (717-223-0505), one of several places in the area where you can rent canoes. Continue north on 209 about 5 mi to Pocono Indian Museum. A few mi beyond, on left, is turnoff for Magic Valley Village. Bushkill Falls is another few mi north on 209.

Bushkill lies within the boundaries of the Delaware Water Gap National Recreation Area (Trip B-25).

From Stroudsburg to the Lehigh Valley

TRIP B-27

QUIET VALLEY LIVING HISTORICAL FARM,
  Stroudsburg

HOUSE OF BASKETS, Gilbert

JIM THORPE, Carbon County

HICKORY RUN STATE PARK, White Haven

DISTANCE: From GWB to Stroudsburg, about 80 mi, fast speeds; from Stroudsburg to Jim Thorpe, about 55 mi, average speeds.

On this trip we'll take a long drive from Stroudsburg, gateway to the Poconos, west to the town of Jim Thorpe in Carbon County. For FURTHER INFORMATION, contact the Pocono Mountains Vacation Bureau, 1004 Main St., Stroudsburg, PA 18360 (717-421-5791 or 800-POCONOS), and the Carbon County Tourist Promotion Agency, PO Box 90, Railroad Station, Jim Thorpe, PA 18229 (717-325-3673).

Quiet Valley Living Historical Farm, Box 2495, RD 2, Stroudsburg, PA 18360 (717-992-6161). *Open daily late June to Labor Day Mon-Sat 9:30-5:30, Sun 1-5:30; annual Harvest Festival on Columbus Day Weekend. Adults $5, children 3-12 $2.50, under 3 free. Continuous guided tours; last tour leaves at 4. Picnic area.*

No pets. Will accommodate wheelchairs and other handicaps; call in advance.

Quiet Valley is a journey back in time to a self-sufficient colonial farm run much as it was in 1765 when a hardworking Pennsylvania Dutch family first settled here. The costumed staff members are more than tour guides; they are actors playing the roles of family members going about their daily chores of spinning, weaving, meat smoking, gardening, and tending the animals. As they take us through the farm's 14 buildings, some original, they describe their lives as colonists and demonstrate such skills as forging (not money), wool dyeing, candle dipping, and broom making. In the age of mass production, these activities may come as a revelation to the kids, who will also enjoy petting the animals and trying the hay jump in the barn.

House of Baskets, Gilbert, PA 18331 (717-992-6336). *Open all year daily 9-6, including Sun and holidays. No admission fee. Not wheelchair-accessible.*

If you're in the market for more baskets to put your eggs in, this is the place for you! It's a lovely old house filled to the rafters with baskets of every size and description, wicker furniture, toys, and crafts. You're welcome to browse.

Jim Thorpe is well outside our normal day-trip range, but it's a unique place, and worth the extra mileage. It takes its name from the great native American athlete who astonished the world with an unprecedented record-breaking performance at the 1912 Olympics. Jim Thorpe was not born here, nor did he ever pass through here while he was alive. The story of how the town came to be named for him is a story of hard times: hard times for the man, who was unfairly stripped of his Olympic medals (recently restored) on a technicality, and hard times for Mauch Chunk (the Indian name for "Bear Mountain") and East Mauch Chunk, booming coal and railroad towns in the 19th century, declining and economically strapped in the 20th. In 1953 Jim Thorpe died in poverty after a long, painful illness, and his wife sought to have him buried with a public memorial in his home state, Oklahoma. Oklahoma said no. Hearing of the plight of Mauch Chunk and East Mauch Chunk, Mrs. Thorpe proposed to lend the towns her husband's name in return for their assistance in memorializing him. Though the two Chunks had been squabbling for years, the citizens were inspired by this idea, transcended their differences, and merged to become Jim Thorpe, Pennsylvania.

Jim Thorpe lies at the bottom of a gorge on the Lehigh River, flanked by sheer mountainsides, in a region sometimes known as "the Switzerland of America." The town's appearance is as fascinating as the story of its name. In its heyday it spawned a slew of self-made millionaires who built the palatial residences and impressive public buildings we see today. Perhaps the most striking of these is the ASA PACKER MANSION (717-325-3229), an Italianate extravagance built by the founder of Lehigh University, who came to Mauch Chunk penniless in 1828 and became a wealthy railroad tycoon. ST. MARK'S EPISCOPAL CHURCH, commissioned as a memorial by Asa Packer's widow, is a striking Gothic Revival structure built into a hillside. The fine townhouses on MILLIONAIRES ROW contrast with the humbler residences on STONE ROW, where Asa Packer's foremen and engineers lived. There's railroad history in the bricks of the JERSEY CENTRAL RAILROAD STATION (1888) and the bed of the SWITCHBACK GRAVITY RAILROAD (1827-1870), and labor history too, at the CARBON COUNTY JAIL (1869), where five Molly Maguires were hanged in 1877.

The Lehigh River offers some terrific whitewater rafting. If you want to shoot the rapids, try JIM THORPE RIVER ADVENTURES (717-325-2570) or POCONO WHITEWATER RAFTING CENTER (717-325-3657). There's also recreation at man-made MAUCH CHUNK LAKE (717-325-3669) 3 miles west of town, and a great view of the Lehigh Valley from FLAGSTAFF MOUNTAIN PARK (717-325-4554) about 3 miles north of town.

Hickory Run State Park, RD 1, Box 81, White Haven, PA 18661 (717-443-9991). *Open daily all year. No entry fee. Picnicking, playgrounds and fields, nature center, hiking trails, swimming beach (Memorial Day to Labor Day), fishing, camping (fee), snack bar, ice fishing, ice skating, sledding, snowmobiling, cross-country skiing. Leashed pets in day-use area, no pets on beach or campsites. Picnic area, restrooms, and beach wheelchair-accessible.*

Here are 15,500 acres of wooded hills threaded with clear streams and waterfalls. The park's special feature is a lake 2,000 feet long and 500 feet wide, with scenically contoured shores and trees stretching down to the water—but there's no water. Instead, boulders: pinkish, rounded, and piled up like heaps of jellybeans. This is the glacial Boulder Field, a National Natural Landmark. One of the more startling views is of energetic "swimmers" clambering across the lake to the opposite shore.

FOR THE DRIVER: Take I-80 west off GWB through New Jersey and across the Delaware (25¢) into Pennsylvania. In Stroudsburg take Exit 46S onto US 209 south. Take Shafer School House Rd exit off 209 briefly to Business 209. Turn left here, following well-marked route to Quiet Valley.

Go back to 209 south and continue to sign for Brodheadsville. Exit here and continue on this road (it becomes PA 115, then US 209 again) about 1 mi south of Brodheadsville to House of Baskets.

Continue south on 209 across the Pennsylvania Tpk Extension. Just before is BELTZVILLE STATE PARK (215-377-3170), with fishing, hiking, swimming, winter sports, and other activities. About 2 mi after tpk extension 209 turns sharply right and goes north into Jim Thorpe.

Take PA 903 north out of Jim Thorpe and go about 15 mi, crossing tpk extension, to PA 534. Turn left and go through Albrightsville back across tpk extension to Hickory Run State Park.

For return trip, go back on 534 to jct with 903. Turn left on 903 and go north to jct with PA 115. Turn left on 115 and go 1 mi or so to jct with I-80 east to New York.

Further Adventures in the Poconos

TRIP B-28

CAMELBACK SKI AREA, ALPINE SLIDE AND
    WATERSLIDE, Tannersville

POCONO KNOB, Mount Pocono

MEMORYTOWN U.S.A., Mount Pocono

PENNSYLVANIA DUTCH FARM, Mount Pocono

HOLLEY ROSS POTTERY, LaAnna

DISTANCE: From GWB to Mount Pocono, about 95 mi. Fast and average speeds.

Now we're moving into the heart of the Poconos resort area. For FURTHER INFORMATION contact the Pocono Mountains Vacation Bureau, 1004 Main St., Stroudsburg, PA 18360 (717-421-5791 or 800-POCONOS).

Camelback Ski Area, Alpine Slide, and Waterslide, Tannersville, PA 18372 (717-629-1661); ski phone 800-532-8201 in PA, 800-233-8100 outside PA). *Open for skiing (fee) daily Dec-Mar. Slides open, weather permitting, weekends mid-May to Memorial Day and early Sept to Columbus Day, daily late June to Sept (Waterslide may open later and close earlier), 10-5 daily until Labor Day, 10-4 thereafter. Alpine Slide $3.50 adults, $3 children under 12; waterslide $1 per ride; bargain days Mon in July-Aug, multiple-ride tickets available. Golf driving range and baseball batting range (fees), restaurant, cafeteria. Not wheelchair-accessible.*

There's year-round fun at this recreational facility, which is a fully equipped ski area in winter. In summer kids love to splash down the 300-foot-long chutes of the Waterslide or ride the chairlift to the top of the ski area and career down the 3,263-foot Alpine Slide. Camelback is located in but not part of BIG POCONO STATE PARK (717-629-0320), which offers picnicking, hiking trails, and bridle paths.

Pocono Knob is a scenic overlook on Mount Pocono that affords an excellent view of the Delaware Water Gap and beyond, on a clear day extending as far as the Blue Ridge Mountains to the south and High Point, New Jersey, to the northeast.

Memorytown U.S.A., HCR 1, Box 10, Mount Pocono, PA 18344 (717-839-7176). *Open daily all year for dining, lodging, shopping. Free entry and parking. Manageable for wheelchairs.*

A series of restored buildings from the early 1800s—originally barns, a corn crib, a carriage shed, etc.—today houses a small, pleasant shopping complex with Indian Trading Post, Country Store and General Emporium, Hex Shop, Centennial Print Shop and Museum, and more. We can dine at the Heritage Inn, serving a Pennsylvania Dutch supper buffet on Friday and Saturday evenings, or quench our thirst at Tavern by the Lake while the kids go off to the paddleboats and go-carts.

Pennsylvania Dutch Farm, Mount Pocono, PA 18344 (717-839-7680). *Open Apr-Nov daily 10-5. Farm tour $2.50 adults, $1.25 children under 12; hayrides $1.50 adults, $1 children under 12. Pets discouraged. Manageable for wheelchairs.*

"Drive the lane down and tour the farm over" is the slogan here as we visit an authentically furnished Amish home and see exhibits on Amish life. We can also explore the barn and pet the farm animals. The gift shop sells Pennsylvania Dutch foods, jellies, hex jewelry, and such.

Holley Ross Pottery, LaAnna/Cresco, PA 18326 (717-676-3248). *Showroom open early May to mid-Dec daily, Mon-Sat 9:30-5:30, Sun 1-5:30; demonstrations Mon-Fri 11 and 3:30. Free. Mostly wheelchair-accessible.*

Here we can not only browse through a large collection of dinnerware, glassware, cookware, lamps, planters, and gift items, but see the process by which they are made. It's fascinating to watch the pottery thrown and fired, and a small woodland park provides an attractive setting for picnics.

FOR THE DRIVER: Take I-80 west off GWB through New Jersey and across the Delaware (25¢) into Pennsylvania. Continue on 80 to Exit 45 and proceed northwest on PA 715 briefly towards Tannersville. Watch for turnoff shortly on left to Camelback, about 3 mi west.

Go back the way you came and continue briefly on 715 to jct with US 611. Here turn left and go north through Scotrun to Mount Pocono, passing signs for Memorytown and Pennsylvania Dutch Farm. Just beyond railroad overpass is Knob Rd, a small road with a sign for Mount Pocono Motel. Turn right here and take this up to Pocono Knob, encircling the Knob and returning to US 611. Turn left, go back down 611, and turn left at signs for Memorytown and adjoining Pennsylvania Dutch Farm, 1 mi or so east on Grange Rd.

Continue on Grange Rd to jct with PA 940. Turn right here and go several mi to jct with PA 390. Turn left and go north briefly on 390 to jct with PA 191. Turn left on 191 and continue north through Cresco to Mountainhome. Here 390 meets 191 again and goes off to right. If you follow 390 briefly, you come to CALLIE'S CANDY KITCHEN (717-595-2280), where the kids will be mesmerized by the vast array of confections for sale. Callie's specializes in chocolate-covered fresh strawberries and will give candy-making demonstrations on request. Beyond Callie's, on left, is Playhouse Lane and the well-regarded POCONO PLAYHOUSE (717-595-

7456), with Broadway shows at decidedly non-Broadway prices ($10-$12 a ticket). North of playhouse, a left turn on Cresco Rd will lead you to BUCK HILL FALLS, lovely 200-foot waterfalls surrounded by birch groves and hemlock stands. You can follow this road around and back to PA 191 and turn right for Holley Ross Pottery, or, from Mountainhome at jct of 191 and 390, go left on 191 and take it north about 9 mi to Holley Ross in LaAnna.

Here we are about 10 mi from the southern tip of Lake Wallenpaupack (Trip B-29) via 191 north to PA 507 northeast to the lake; PA 390 north from Mountainhome also goes to the lake. A few mi west of LaAnna is a host of recreational activities in TOBYHANNA AND GOULDSBORO STATE PARKS (717-894-8336), which can be reached by going north of LaAnna briefly on 191 and turning left on PA 423.

In and Around the Poconos' "Big Lake"

TRIP B-29

LAKE WALLENPAUPACK AND ENVIRONS

DISTANCE: From GWB to first stop at lake, about 110 mi. Fast and average speeds.

Lake Wallenpaupack is the centerpiece of this trip to the northeast Poconos. From here we'll make a loop back into New York to see some of the sights just across the Delaware in the southernmost Catskills region (see Trips C-15 to C-20 for the Catskills). Since our trip is planned mainly for the enjoyment of the drive, the directions are incorporated with brief descriptions of the principal attractions along our route. For FURTHER INFORMATION about the lake area, contact the Lake Wallenpaupack Association, PO Box 398, Hawley, PA 18428 (717-226-2141), the Hawley-Lake Wallenpaupack Chamber of Commerce, PO Box 150, Hawley, PA 18428 (717-226-3191), the Pike County Chamber of Commerce, Milford, PA 18337 (717-296-8700), the Wayne County Chamber of Commerce, 865 Main St., Honesdale, PA 18431 (717-253-1960), or the Pocono Mountains Vacation Bureau, Lake Region Division, Box 3, Stroudsburg, PA 18360 (717-421-5791 or 800-POCONOS); for the New York area, contact the Sullivan County Office of Public Information, County Government Center, Monticello, NY 12701 (914-794-3000 X160 or 800-882-CATS in NYS, 800-343-INFO outside NYS).

Lake Wallenpaupack is 5,600 acres of tempting blue water with 52 miles of shoreline and the Pocono Mountains as a backdrop. The lake region was home to the Minisink, Lenape, and Paupack Indians; "Wallenpaupack" is a Lenape word meaning "stream of swift and slow waters." And it *was* a stream, until the Pennsylvania Power and Light Company dammed it in 1926. Today the lake is a major year-round recreation area, and the hydroelectric plant is used mainly during periods of peak demand.

To reach Lake Wallenpaupack, we take I-80 west off GWB to Exit 53 west of Paterson. Here we pick up NJ 23 northwest to Port Jervis and junction with I-84. We take I-84 west to Exit 6 and from here follow PA 507 northeast along the southern shore of the lake. Shortly after exit are signs and a turnoff, left, for CLAWS 'N' PAWS (717-698-6154), about 6 miles northwest, and always a hit with the kids. In addition to a tiger, wolf, bear, puma, et al., the Lipko Chimps perform here; there's the usual collection of tame deer and llamas to pet, along with a chance to caress a python or alligator.

There are a number of resorts and recreation areas around the lake. Going northeast on 507, we shortly come to one of the more popular, WHITE BEAUTY VIEW RESORT AND MARINA (717-857-0234 or 800-233-4130), where we can choose our favored method of entering the water: swimming, skin and scuba diving, water skiing, sailing, parasailing, motorboating, or a sedate ride on their scenic cruiser.

From White Beauty we'll continue on 507 about 12 miles, to the northeast end of the lake, where the dam is located. At junction with US 6, we'll turn left on 6 and go about ¼ mile to the LAKE WALLENPAUPACK ASSOCIATION INFORMATION CENTER (717-226-2141). About ¼ mile further on 6 the PENNSYLVANIA POWER AND LIGHT COMPANY (717-226-3702) maintains a visitor center where we can see exhibits and get the story of the lake straight from the people who created it 40 years ago.

Continuing on US 6 west to Hawley, we'll pass junction with PA 590 on left. This goes around the lake on the north side and is an alternate route to Claws 'n' Paws, about 12 miles west on 590. Just west of Hawley on US 6 is a red railroad car, the GRAVITY COACH, which ran between Pittston and Hawley from 1850 to 1880. It was part of the Pennsylvania Gravity Railroad, operating on 22 inclined planes from Hawley to Scranton. The cars, loaded with coal and passengers, were hauled uphill by stationary engines and went downhill on their own with Galilean gusto.

From Hawley we continue west on US 6 about 12 miles to Honesdale, founded in 1826 by the Delaware & Hudson Canal Company and named for the company's president, Philip Hone. In town, at 810 Main St., is the WAYNE COUNTY HISTORICAL SOCIETY MUSEUM (717-253-3240), housed in the old canal company office. A little further on US 6, across a bridge, is a replica of the STOURBRIDGE LION, the first operating steam locomotive in the United States, shortly supplanted by mules when the railbed proved too weak to hold it. If we're tired of driving, STOURBRIDGE RAIL EXCURSIONS (717-253-1960) will take us on a scenic ride to Lackawaxen.

Now we go back on US 6 east several miles to junction with PA 652. Here we turn left and go about 10 miles northeast across the Delaware to Narrowsburg, New York. We bear left on 652 after the bridge and turn left at second stoplight onto NY 97. Here we find the FORT DELAWARE MUSEUM OF COLONIAL HISTORY (914-252-6660), a replica of a 1755 stockade, maintained by Sullivan County in honor of the Connecticut Yankees who settled the Delaware Valley. Costumed staff members demonstrate how the original occupants of this frontier fortification actually lived, and there are special events throughout the summer. There's fine canoeing and kayaking around Narrowsburg; we have our choice of white water or gentle river currents, and of numerous rental and tour facilities in the area, including BOB AND RICK LANDER'S DELAWARE RIVER CANOE TRIPS (914-252-3925), a couple of miles south of the fort.

Continuing south about 10 miles on 97, we come to Minisink Ford. Here, opposite Minisink Battleground Park, is ROEBLING BRIDGE, the first suspension bridge designed by John Roebling, a smaller version of his most famous creation, the Brooklyn Bridge. Built between 1846 and 1849, it is currently undergoing repairs and may be closed to auto traffic. But we need to stretch our legs anyway, so we'll walk across the bridge to Lackawaxen, Pennsylvania, and turn right on PA 590, just over the bridge, for a visit to the ZANE GREY MUSEUM (717-685-7522), former home of the New York dentist who penned *Riders of the Purple Sage* and 102 other books at the rate of 100,000 words a month. It was here in

Lackawaxen, said America's most prolific author of westerns, that he first experienced *really* wild country.

Back across the bridge, we'll head for our last stop, continuing south on 97 a few miles to junction with NY 55 in Barryville. Here we'll turn left and go north 7 miles to the ELDRED PRESERVE (914-557-8316), where the main attraction is year-round trout fishing at 3 stocked ponds in 2,000 acres of rustic woodlands. Eldred also offers lodging and dining, tennis, swimming, hiking, and other recreational facilities.

To return to New York City from Eldred, we'll go back to 97, take it south to Port Jervis, and go back on NJ 23 to I-80 east.

Up the Hudson on the West Bank

• *To many New Yorkers the Hudson is the Enchanted Valley, a wizard's mixture of history and legend, evoking memories of Dutch mariners, British grenadiers, Continental veterans, conjuring vistas of Bear Mountain, the wooded Highlands, the Catskills rising in the west. Houses of stone that have lasted 300 years, miles of apple orchards and vineyards, parks and waters for outdoor fun, embellished by the imagination of Washington Irving and Fenimore Cooper—from Manhattan to Rip Van Winkle's hideout, every mile is an exhilarating experience.*

Exit Points
George Washington Bridge (GWB), Major Deegan Expwy

Main Roads
New York Thruway (NYT), Palisades Interstate Pkwy (PIP), US 9W

Connections
NYT is a continuation of I-87, Major Deegan Expwy in the Bronx. To reach Major Deegan, take
—Henry Hudson Pkwy (NY 9A) to Cross Bronx Expwy (I-95 north) to Major Deegan;
—FDR Drive to Willis Avenue Bridge to Major Deegan;
—Triborough Bridge to Major Deegan;
—Bronx-Whitestone Bridge or Throgs Neck Bridge to Cross Bronx Expwy (I-95 south) to Major Deegan.
To connect with Major Deegan farther north, take
—Henry Hudson Pkwy (NY 9A) to Saw Mill River Pkwy (SMRP) to Cross County Pkwy east;
—Bronx River Pkwy or Hutchinson River Pkwy (HRP) to Cross County Pkwy west.
To connect with NYT near Tappan Zee Bridge (on east bank), take
—US 9 (Broadway) north to jct with NYT near Tarrytown;
—Henry Hudson Pkwy (NY 9A) to SMRP to jct with NYT near Tarrytown;
—Sprain Brook Pkwy, Bronx River Pkwy, HRP, or I-95 (becoming New England Thruway) north to Cross Westchester Expwy (I-287) west to jct with NYT near Tarrytown.
To connect with NYT from GWB (on west bank, north of Tappan Zee Bridge), take
—PIP north to Exit 9;
—US 9W north to South Nyack and jct with NYT.
To reach PIP
—from GWB, follow signs (PIP begins on Jersey side of bridge);
—from NYT, cross Tappan Zee Bridge and take Exit 13;
—from US 9W, take 9W north, paralleling PIP, almost to New York State line, where 9W and PIP intersect.
To reach US 9W
—from GWB, follow signs (9W begins on Jersey side of bridge);
—from NYT, cross Tappan Zee Bridge and take Exits 10 or 11;
—from PIP, take Exit 4 near New York State line.

Tolls

One-way highway tolls (collected in both directions) are given in "For the Driver" at the end of each trip and are calculated from the New York City line unless otherwise indicated. NYT tolls are collected on a barrier system (40¢ at Yonkers, 25¢ at Spring Valley, 50¢ at Harriman) from the city line to Harriman and on a ticket system north of Harriman. It is assumed in "For the Driver" that you cross all barriers from the city line to your destination; if not, you don't pay. *NYT tolls in "For the Driver" do not include the $1.50 toll on the Tappan Zee Bridge* (collected southbound to New York City, no toll collected northbound).

There is one barrier toll on SMRP (25¢ at Yonkers), one on HRP (25¢ at Pelham), and one on the New England Thruway (40¢ at New Rochelle); if you use these roads to get to Area C, you pay when you cross these barriers.

For New York City bridge and tunnel tolls, see p. xvi; remember to add these to the highway tolls as appropriate, depending on your route.

Hudson River Crossings

In addition to the Tappan Zee Bridge (NYT from Nyack to the Tarrytown area), the following Hudson River bridges link Area C (west bank) with Area D (east bank). Depending on your point of departure, you may want to travel up the east bank and use one of these bridges to cross to your destination in Area C; or you can use them to combine trips in Areas C and D.

Bear Mountain Bridge (US 6/US 202 from Bear Mountain State Park to Peekskill area)	
Newburgh-Beacon Bridge (I-84 from Newburgh to Beacon)	50¢ collected
Mid-Hudson Bridge (US 44/NY 55 from Highland to Poughkeepsie)	eastbound, no toll
Kingston-Rhinecliff Bridge (NY 199 from Kingston to Rhinecliff)	collected westbound
Rip Van Winkle Bridge (NY 23 from Catskill to Hudson)	

On a Clear Day, a Remarkable Panorama

TRIP C-1

PALISADES INTERSTATE PARK, New Jersey Section
ROCKEFELLER LOOKOUT
ALPINE LOOKOUT
STATE LINE LOOKOUT

DISTANCE: From GWB to the farthest point, State Line, about 11 mi. Mainly fast speeds.

Palisades Interstate Park, New Jersey Section, PO Box 155, Alpine, NJ 07620 (201-768-1360). *Grounds open daily all year, weather permitting, daylight hours. Park headquarters open all year Mon-Fri 8:30-4:30. Free except for areas in Trips C-2 and C-3. No climbing; no alcohol, picnicking, or barbecuing except in 4 designated areas (see Trip C-2); no ground fires; no pets in picnic areas or developed areas, leashed pets only on trails. Some facilities wheelchair-accessible, as noted.*

Discovered in 1524 by Giovanni da Verrazano, the Palisades ("fence of stakes") are volcanically formed basalt cliffs overlooking the Hudson River. In 1900 Congress established the Palisades Interstate Park Commission to protect the cliffs from destruction by quarrying. The park consists of over 80,000 acres of land in New York (Trips C-4, C-5, C-7, and C-8) and New Jersey; the 2,500-acre New Jersey Section, extending about 11 miles from Fort Lee (Trip C-3) to the New York State Line, is a National Historic Landmark and a National Natural Landmark. Here, minutes from Manhattan, we'll stand on cliffs 300 to over 500 feet high as we survey a panorama that includes the mighty Hudson, the New York skyscrapers, Long Island, Westchester, and far beyond. Looking straight down we'll have awesome views of tops of trees that literally grow up the sides of the precipice. Below, along the shore, are picnic grounds and boat basins (Trip C-2).

The New Jersey Section contains two designated National Recreation Trails, the Long Path and the Shore Trail, both beginning at the George Washington Bridge. The famous Long Path, marked by blue squares, winds along the clifftops past Rockefeller, Alpine, and State Line Lookouts, crosses into New York, and con-

tinues through Harriman State Park into the Catskills; when complete, it will link New York City with the Adirondacks and Lake
Placid, some 400 miles away. The Shore Trail follows the low
route to the New York State Line and is marked by white squares.
Six sets of stairs marked by overlapping blue and white squares
connect the two trails. Average hiking time is 30 minutes per mile;
camping, cooking, and cliff climbing are strictly prohibited, and
hikers must be off the trails by dark. For FURTHER HIKING INFOR-
MATION and detailed maps, contact the New York-New Jersey
Trail Conference, 232 Madison Ave., New York, NY 10016 (212-
696-6800).

Many cultural, educational, and recreational programs take place
in the park throughout the year. Call or write park headquarters
for a bimonthly calendar of events.

Rockefeller Lookout. *20-min parking limit, no fee. One curb,
but fair wheelchair access to vista points.*

We're across the Hudson from the Riverdale section of the
Bronx, just above Manhattan Island. To our right is the George
Washington Bridge, and behind it, the New York skyscrapers.
Beyond them is the Long Island Sound and Long Island. The hills
north of the bridge rise to become Washington Heights, highest
point on Manhattan. During the Revolution this was the site of
Fort Washington, one of the city's ill-fated defenses. Fort Tryon
Park stretches along the clifftops, and at the upper end stands the
Cloisters, a medieval museum maintained by the Metropolitan
Museum of Art.

Underneath the New York end of the bridge at Jeffreys Hook
we can just make out the Little Red Lighthouse, slated for demolition when the bridge went up, but spared through protests and
publicity. Look straight down the side of the cliffs for stagger-
ingly effective views of treetops mingling with gigantic columns
of rock.

Alpine Lookout. *20-min parking limit, no fee. Steps and gravelly walk to promontory.*

On our way here from Rockefeller Lookout we pass the GREEN-
BROOK SANCTUARY of the Palisades Nature Association (call or
stop by park headquarters for hours and further information). At
the lookout, part of the Long Path takes us to the very edge of
the cliffs, among the great craggy pillars that poured out of the

earth and solidified so many eons ago. We're safely fenced in, but naturally we'll stay on the marked trails and keep the kids in tow. That's Yonkers across the river (Trip D-1).

State Line Lookout. *1-hr parking limit, no fee. Hiking, cross-country ski trails marked and graded for difficulty (rentals available), year-round refreshment stand, art and craft shows, antique shows, special events. Parking and restrooms wheelchair-accessible.*

We're now across from Hastings-on-Hudson, and we're 532 feet tall. Our best view is to the north where the Tappan Zee Bridge carries the New York Thruway across 3 miles of river between Tarrytown and Nyack. The Long Path still clings to the top of the cliffs, and we can join it for a hike.

FOR THE DRIVER: From both levels of GWB, follow signs for PIP, which runs the length of the park. Rockefeller Lookout is about 3 mi north, just off pkwy on right. Alpine Lookout is another 3 mi north on right; park headquarters is just above, off Exit 2 on right; and State Line Lookout is off Exit 3 on right, about 3 mi north of Alpine.

Exploring the Palisades from Below

TRIP C-2

PALISADES INTERSTATE PARK, New Jersey Section
ROSS DOCK
ENGLEWOOD AREA
UNDERCLIFF
ALPINE AREA

DISTANCE: From GWB to farthest point, Alpine, about 6 mi. Average speeds.

Palisades Interstate Park, New Jersey Section (See Trip C-1 for general information). *Shore areas open during daylight hours, weather permitting; season and facilities vary as noted; hours may also vary with staff availability. Alcohol, picnicking and barbecuing (no ground fires, bring your own grill and charcoal) permitted in these 4 areas only. Fishing and crabbing from seawalls,* *docks, and shoreline permitted in season, no license necessary. No swimming, no climbing, no pets.*

Ross Dock. *Open (when collector is on duty) weekends and holidays mid-Apr to early May and in Oct, daily early May thru Sept. Parking fee: cars $2, motorcycles $1. Picnicking, hiking, fishing, playgrounds, basketball court. Picnic area wheelchair-accessible.*

This is the first picnic area we reach as we come over the George Washington Bridge. The view is especially interesting because we're almost beneath the bridge.

Englewood Area. *Open daily all year. Parking fee: weekends and holidays most of Apr and most of Oct, daily late Apr to early Oct, cars $2, motorcycles $1; other times free. Picnicking, hiking, fishing, playground, boat basin (launching ramp $5), refreshment stand in season. Picnic area and restrooms wheelchair-accessible.*

Here is the park's largest picnic area, with fine views and a trail to the clifftops. The Dyckman Street Ferry used to dock at Englewood.

Undercliff. *Open (when collector is on duty) weekends and holidays Memorial Day to Labor Day. Parking fee: cars $2, motorcycles $1. Picnicking, hiking, fishing. Picnic area wheelchair-accessible.*

This small area on the cliff side of Henry Hudson Drive has fine views and trails leading down to the river.

Alpine Area. *Open daily all year. Parking fee: weekends and holidays early Apr to early May and early Sept to late Oct, daily early May to early Sept, cars $2, motorcycles $1. Picnicking, hiking, fishing, playground, boat basin (launching ramp $5), special events, outdoor concerts (free after payment of parking fee) Wed 8pm in July-Aug. Picnic area and restrooms wheelchair-accessible.*

Above us hang the great cliffs, with trees growing at all angles from the rock crevices. Man-made embellishments include picturesque pavilions and the historic Blackledge-Kearny House (c. 1750), once Cornwallis's headquarters (it's closed to the public, but we can peek through the windows). Trails lead along the riverbank and right up the side of the Palisades. If these seem pretty steep to us, we might note that during the Revolution the British soldiers climbed them, carrying all their equipment, on their way to capture Fort Lee.

FOR THE DRIVER: From GWB follow signs for PIP. Go north to Exit 1 and follow signs for Henry Hudson Drive and Englewood Area, at bottom of cliff. Ross Dock is about 1½ mi south, Undercliff is just above Englewood, and Alpine is about 5 mi north of Undercliff, all via Henry Hudson Drive.

Note that Henry Hudson Drive is closed completely from early Nov to mid-Apr. From mid-Apr to early Nov it is open during daylight hours to cars only, except on weekends and holidays until noon, when Englewood-Alpine section is reserved for bicyclists, joggers, and pedestrians (otherwise prohibited on drive and approach roads). When this section is closed to cars, you can still reach Englewood and Ross Dock as described above, but you can't drive from Englewood to Undercliff to Alpine via Henry Hudson Drive; you can hike from Englewood to Undercliff (less than 1 mi), and you can drive to Alpine via PIP Exit 2. When drive is closed completely, Ross Dock and Undercliff are also closed; use PIP for Englewood and Alpine.

Vistas of Past and Present Just Across the Bridge

TRIP C-3

FORT LEE HISTORIC PARK

DISTANCE: Just over GWB on the Jersey side. Mainly fast speeds.

Fort Lee Historic Park, Hudson Terrace, Fort Lee, NJ 07024 (201-461-1776). *Grounds open daily all year, daylight hours. Visitor center open weekends in Feb noon-5, Mar to Memorial Day Wed-Sun 10-5, Memorial Day to Labor Day daily 10-5, Labor Day thru Dec Wed-Sun 10-5; closed Jan. Parking fee Apr-Oct $2 cars, $1 motorcycles; other times free. Picnicking (no grills or fires), souvenir stand, self-guiding trails. No climbing, no bikes, no pets. Visitor center main floor and restrooms wheelchair-accessible, wide paved paths thru grounds.*

Fort Lee played a disheartening role in the early phases of the American Revolution, when the British were fighting for control of the Hudson. In July 1776, to block them, George Washington ordered the fortification of a number of sites on both sides of the river, including this fort named for General Charles Lee, a mercurial man who envied Washington and whose treason almost handed the British a victory at the Battle of Monmouth later that year (see Trip A-9). In August a large British force landed on Long Island and drove the American defenders across Brooklyn into Manhattan. Throughout the fall skirmishes raged where skyscrapers now stand, and Washington fell back to Harlem Heights and White Plains (Trip D-3). In November the Americans suffered a major defeat at Fort Washington, in what is today upper Manhattan. With its sister fort in British hands, Fort Lee lost its strategic importance and was already being evacuated when a surprise attack forced a hasty flight, resulting in further losses of men and badly needed supplies. That December, as Washington retreated deeper into New Jersey, Tom Paine penned the famous line "These are the times that try men's souls."

Fort Lee Historic Park, administered by the Palisades Interstate Park Commission, commemorates those trying times. The visitor center, just east of the original fort, features historic exhibits, audiovisual displays, and a short film (shown only on weekends). Outside, two overlooks give spectacular views of the George Washington Bridge, the New York skyline, and the Hudson River (minus attacking British armada). Winding trails take us through the southern part of the 33-acre park to reconstructed gun batteries and an 18th-century soldier's hut where demonstrations of colonial life are staged by the park staff. Of course, momentous battles still rage in this area daily during rush hour, but it's hard for us to imagine it as a wilderness outpost of America's war for independence. A visit to Fort Lee Historic Park helps change our perspective, taking us out of New York City into America's past.

FOR THE DRIVER: Take upper level of GWB to 1st Fort Lee exit, after exit for PIP. Bear right and proceed down ramp to Hudson Terrace, at traffic light. Turn right and go about 50 ft past next light to park entrance, on left.

The End of the Road for Major André

TRIP C-4

GEORGE WASHINGTON MASONIC SHRINE/DE WINT
  HOUSE, Tappan

ANDRÉ HILL, Tappan

TALLMAN MOUNTAIN STATE PARK, Sparkill

DISTANCE: From GWB, about 13 mi. Average speeds.

George Washington Masonic Shrine/De Wint House, 20 Livingston
Ave., Tappan, NY 10983 (914-359-1359). *Open all year daily
10-4; closed Christmas. Donations. Pets discouraged. Well-graded
paths, a step or two into house; will accommodate wheelchairs.*

General Washington made the De Wint House (c. 1700) his
headquarters five times, and he was here the last week of September 1780, when Major John André, accused as a spy in the Benedict Arnold conspiracy to betray West Point, was captured and
brought to Tappan. A military court appointed by Washington
held an inquiry on September 29 and determined that André should
be hung as a spy. Washington is said to have signed the order for
his execution at a table now in this house. The house was subse-
quently bought by the Masons and is preserved as a memorial to
Washington, a member. On the grounds is a carriage house (1800)
containing historic artifacts.

André Hill, Tappan, NY. British headquarters in New York tried
but failed to secure André's release through a prisoner exchange.
André wrote General Washington asking for a soldier's death by
shooting, but his request was denied on the grounds that he had
been condemned as a spy and must suffer a spy's punishment. On
October 2, 1780, resplendent in the full dress uniform of a British
officer, he was taken from his place of detention in a local tavern
(this building, remodeled as a restaurant called The '76 House but
now closed indefinitely, can still be seen off Main St. in Tappan),
escorted up the hill to the drumbeat of "The Dead March," and
hanged. A charming and cultivated man, he was mourned by many
on both sides and became something of a romantic figure after his

execution. André was buried where he died; in 1821 his remains were moved to Westminster Abbey in London.

Tallman Mountain State Park, Sparkill, NY (914-359-0544). *Part of Palisades Interstate Parks; see Trip C-5 for general information and fees. Park vehicle use fee in effect mid-June to early Sept. Picnicking, hiking trails, cinder track, playground, handball courts, tennis courts (free), swimming pool, refreshment stands in summer.*

This scenic park, administered by the Palisades Interstate Park Commission, is a stone's throw from the northern tip of the New Jersey Section of the Palisades (Trips C-1 and C-2), and right across the river from Sunnyside, home of Washington Irving (Trip D-2).

FOR THE DRIVER: From GWB take PIP north to Exit 4, US 9W, then take 9W north towards Nyack. Shortly, at traffic light, turn left on Oak Tree Rd and follow it a block past jct with NY 303 to De Wint House, entrance on left.

Return to Oak Tree Rd, turn left, and continue until it merges with Main St in Tappan. The '76 House is to the right on Main, just across the street. For André Hill, turn left on Main and continue uphill bearing right. There's a marker at the execution site.

Go back on Oak Tree Rd past De Wint House and return to jct with US 9W. Continue north briefly to Tallman Mountain State Park, on right.

Up the Hudson to High Tor

TRIP C-5

PALISADES INTERSTATE PARKS, New York

NYACK BEACH STATE PARK, Upper Nyack

ROCKLAND LAKE STATE PARK, Congers

HIGH TOR STATE PARK, Haverstraw

DISTANCE: From GWB to farthest point, High Tor, about 30 mi. Average and slow speeds.

Palisades Interstate Parks, Bear Mountain State Park, Bear Mountain, NY 10911 (914-786-2701). *Open daily all year, daylight hours. Vehicle use fees, when in effect (see individual entries): park areas $2.50 per car, $1.50 weekdays after 4pm; beach areas*

$3.50 per car, $1.50 weekdays after 4pm. Payment of 1 vehicle use fee per day good for admission to any other park or recreation area in Palisades system (pay $1 difference if going from park area to beach area); if dining at Bear Mountain Inn, vehicle use fee is subtracted from bill. Pool and skating fees: adults 50¢, children 6-12 25¢, under 6 free; bathhouse lockers 25¢ plus $1 key deposit, valuables storage 50¢; skate rentals $1 plus $2 deposit. Boat rentals: $2.50 per person per hr weekends and holidays, $2 weekdays, plus $15 deposit. No ground fires; cooking permitted in park grills and fireplaces. No camping except in Harriman State Park (see Trip C-8). Leashed pets only. All parks within system have wheelchair-accessible restrooms and ramps at parking lots, beach areas, pools, and picnic areas. Note: Some of the Palisades pools and beaches were closed intermittently during the 1986 season due to a shortage of lifeguards; check in advance.

The three parks on this trip, as well as Tallman Mountain State Park on the last trip and many of the parks and historic sites on the next several trips, are administered by the Palisades Interstate Park Commission. Unlike the New Jersey Section of the Palisades (Trips C-1 and C-2), the New York parks are scattered throughout several counties. The above information applies to all the Palisades parks in New York unless otherwise indicated in the individual entries. Exact opening and closing dates and operating hours tend to vary slightly from year to year; park activities are free except for charges specified above, and entry to the parks is free when vehicle use fees are not in effect; fees listed are those in effect for the 1986 season. For further information call the specific park that interests you or contact the Palisades Interstate Park Commission at the Bear Mountain headquarters.

Nyack Beach State Park, Upper Nyack, NY (914-268-3020). *Park vehicle use fee in effect weekends Memorial Day to mid-June and Labor Day to early Oct, daily mid-June to Labor Day. Picnicking, hiking trails, ballfields, fishing, boat launching ramp, cross-country skiing.*

This small 61-acre park is hard to beat for scenery. The main attraction is the river itself (no swimming allowed); kids love to play on its banks, adults think first of the fishing. Trails start here for a hike to Rockland Lake, just above, or a 2-mile trek to High Tor.

Rockland Lake State Park, Congers, NY (914-268-3020). *Park vehicle use fee in effect weekends Memorial Day to mid-June, daily mid-June to Labor Day. Picnicking, hiking and exercise trails, swimming pools (south pool opens Memorial Day, north pool opens mid-June), playing fields, basketball courts, boat launching ramp, fishing, ice skating, sledding, cross-country skiing, nature center, rowboat rentals ($4 per hr or $16 per day plus $16 deposit), tennis courts ($1.50 per hr singles, $2 per hr doubles), golf courses ($2.75-$9 for 18 holes depending on course and hour; equipment rentals and lessons available), refreshment stands in season. Golf, tennis, fishing, and boating season Apr-Nov. No pets.*

Built around an attractive small lake, this park provides a wide range of activities. A network of trails spreads out in several directions for hiking, and the nature center has a boardwalk into a swamp area where plants of the region are marked for identification. Wildfowl gather here and during winter are a constant attraction.

High Tor State Park, Haverstraw, NY (914-634-8074). *Park vehicle use fee in effect daily mid-June to Labor Day. Picnicking, hiking, swimming pool, refreshment stand in season.*

Located up the side of the famous High Tor Mountain, this rugged park is popular mainly for hiking and swimming. Hiking here is for the more experienced. You can climb High Tor or Low Tor, or take any of the connecting trails south to Hook Mountain, Rockland Lake, or Nyack Beach State Parks. The Long Path goes through High Tor on its way west to Harriman State Park (Trip C-8).

FOR THE DRIVER: From GWB, take PIP north to Exit 4 and pick up US 9W north to Nyack. In town turn right on High St., just after jct with NY 59, and proceed to Broadway. Turn left and follow Broadway into Nyack Beach State Park.

Go back down Broadway about 1 mi and turn right on Old Mountain Rd, proceeding uphill to top. Follow signs to US 9W and continue north on 9W about 1 mi to Rockland Lake State Park.

Continue north on 9W to jct with NY 304 to New City. Turn left on 304 to Ridge Rd (1st small road), then turn right on Ridge and go to end at South Mountain Rd. Turn left on South Mountain for 1-2 mi to High Tor State Park, on the mountainside on right.

From here you can go back to South Mountain Rd and turn left back to US 9W the way you came, or turn right on South Mountain to Central Hwy, turn right and take Central Hwy over Little Tor Mountain to jct with US 202, and turn right on 202 back to US 9W south or left on 202 to Palisades Interstate Pkwy south for return trip.

Religious Tranquility, Revolutionary Turmoil

TRIP C-6

MARIAN SHRINE, West Haverstraw
STONY POINT BATTLEFIELD STATE HISTORIC SITE, Stony Point

DISTANCE: From GWB, about 35 mi. Fast and average speeds.

Marian Shrine, Filors Lane, West Haverstraw, NY 10993 (914-947-2200). *Open May-Oct daily 9-6; closed other times. Weekday services at noon (mass) and 3:30; weekend masses (11am, noon); blessing of pilgrims in morning; tours, procession, benediction in afternoon. Picnicking allowed, pets discouraged. Well-paved walks, ramp to main building, annual handicapped day.*

Here a beautiful woodland path winds past 15 white Carrara marble statues that comprise the Rosary. While not as spectacular as Graymoor, the Franciscan monastery across the river to the north (Trip D-9), the Marian Shrine has an intimacy all its own; the guardians are the Salesians of St. John Bosco. Visitors may attend mass at an outdoor altar under a marble dome. There's a good deal of walking, for the statues are spaced some distance apart. The expressions on the finely sculpted faces make a good subject for photographers, and there are lovely views of the Hudson and the distant mountains.

Stony Point Battlefield State Historic Site, PO Box 182, Stony Point, NY 10980 (914-786-2521). *Open late Apr to late Oct: grounds Wed-Sun 8:30-5, museum Wed-Sun 9-4:30. Free. Picnicking (no cooking), self-guided tours, special events. Leashed pets only. Parking, building entrances, and most public areas and restrooms wheelchair-accessible.*

This site, administered by the Palisades Interstate Park Commission, commemorates the night of July 15-16, 1779, when General "Mad" Anthony Wayne and his Light Infantry stormed the

British garrison at Stony Point and recaptured the fort. It was a classic surprise attack, mounted by way of a sandbar traversible only at very low tides, with the soldiers using bayonets for silence. The victory gave a tremendous boost to American morale. Today markers enable us to walk out the battle: we learn where the Americans made their assault on the seemingly impregnable fort, where the outer and inner lines of the British abatis were located, where the final hand-to-hand combat took place. At the tip of the point we come upon a picturesque lighthouse, built in 1826 and currently being restored.

In the museum we'll find documents on the history of Stony Point, maps of the battleground, audiovisual displays, and costumed interpreters. There's also material on the Arnold-André treachery (look for a self-portrait by André) and artifacts from the war. Outside we have fine vistas of Haverstraw Bay and the lower Hudson Valley.

FOR THE DRIVER: From GWB take PIP north to Exit 13, Willow Grove Rd. Turn right (east) on Willow Grove and go about 1 mi to Filors Lane. Turn right and proceed to Marian Shrine, shortly on right.

From shrine turn right on Filors Lane and continue east to US 9W. Go north on 9W to turnoff for Stony Point Battlefield, on right shortly after jct with NY 210.

You can return to the city on 9W south or take it back to jct with NY 210, turn right, and go west about 2½ mi to PIP south.

A Trip to Bear Mountain

TRIP C-7
BEAR MOUNTAIN STATE PARK
BEAR MOUNTAIN INN

DISTANCE: From GWB, about 40 mi. Mainly fast speeds.

Bear Mountain State Park, Bear Mountain, NY 10911 (914-786-2701). *Part of Palisades Interstate Parks; see Trip C-5 for general information. Park vehicle use fee in effect all year, daily early May to Labor Day, weekends and holidays only at other times. Perkins Memorial Drive open daily late Mar to early Oct. Trail-*

side Museum and Zoo open all year daily 9-5. Picnicking (cooking permitted, but bring your own grill; no cooking facilities in park), hiking trails, playing fields, fishing, swimming pool (Memorial Day to Labor Day), roller and ice skating, sledding, cross-country skiing, boat rentals (Apr-Oct), miniature golf (fee), year-round refreshment stand. Annual Christmas festival and winter ski jumping tournaments.

Bear Mountain State Park, New York City's year-round playground, covers more than 5,000 acres of the Highlands that gave the Hudson its reputation as the Rhine of America. The popular Trailside Museum and Zoo has exhibits on the history and natural history of the area. The beautiful scenery and wide variety of activities attract great throngs, so try to plan your trip for a weekday.

One of the best mountain drives available near the city is the ride to the top of Bear Mountain on Perkins Memorial Drive. Along the way there are continual vistas from scenic overlooks, and historic markers telling of battles that took place directly below. From the observation tower atop the mountain we can see the High Point tower in New Jersey (Trip B-24), the New York skyscrapers, and, much closer, Anthony's Nose just across the river and Sugar Loaf Hill to the north. There are picnic areas below the tower, and a road to the scenic drive leading to the well-photographed overlook above Bear Mountain Inn.

Bear Mountain Inn, Bear Mountain, NY 10911 (914-786-2731). *Open all year for lodging and dining. Dining hours 8-11am, 12-3pm, 5-9pm (10pm on weekends). Inquire about overnight rates, weekend packages, seasonal specials. Wheelchair-accessible parking and restrooms, sidewalk ramps, elevator to dining room, level grounds.*

Operated as a concession within Bear Mountain State Park, the inn has a 50-year tradition of hospitality and fine dining. Overlooking Hessian Lake, surrounded by majestic mountains, it's a perfect place for a meal or cocktail. A major attraction is the sumptuous Saturday night smorgasbord, with live music and dancing throughout the evening. If you dine at the inn when the park vehicle use fee is in effect, the fee will be deducted from your bill.

FOR THE DRIVER: From GWB take PIP north to the end at Bear Mountain traffic circle. Turn right to inn and parking lot. At south end of parking lot turn right onto Seven Lakes Pkwy and proceed to Perkins Memorial Dr, shortly on right.

Note that at Bear Mountain circle you can drive over the Bear Mountain Bridge (50¢ toll eastbound) to the east bank of the Hudson and some of the sites in Area D. Just south of the bridge is IONA ISLAND, once a navy base where bombs and ammunition were assembled during both World Wars. In the mid-1960s the navy gave Iona to the Palisades Interstate Park Commission for development as a recreation area, but nothing came of these plans. It is now a winter sanctuary for the endangered bald eagle. The island itself is closed to the public but can be viewed from the causeway.

More of the Great Outdoors

TRIP C-8

HARRIMAN STATE PARK
ANTHONY WAYNE AREA
SILVER MINE AREA
LAKE TIORATI
LAKE SEBAGO
LAKE WELCH

DISTANCE: From GWB to Anthony Wayne Area, about 38 mi; from here, 2-10 mi to other sites. Fast and average speeds.

Harriman State Park, Harriman, NY (914-786-2701). *Part of Palisades Interstate Parks; see Trip C-5 for general information.*

Adjacent to Bear Mountain State Park on the southwest, Harriman is a much larger area (over 46,000 acres) and includes more rugged terrain and many undeveloped areas. Like Bear Mountain, it offers a wide range of activities and facilities for year-round use.

Anthony Wayne Area (914-942-2650). *Park vehicle use fee in effect daily mid-June to Labor Day. Picnicking, hiking trails, playground, swimming pool (may be closed due to staff shortages; check in advance), cross-country skiing, refreshment stand in summer. No pets.*

With attractive picnic and play areas fanning out around a large pool, this is a good spot for those who don't like things too rustic.

Silver Mine Area (914-429-2608). *Park vehicle use fee in effect daily mid-June to Labor Day. Picnicking, hiking, fishing. Downhill skiing facilities closed but may reopen as a concession; check in advance.*

This is a lovely woodland park by a picturesque mountain lake. Paths and picnic areas all around the lake make it a fine place to spend an afternoon. Fall foliage is outstanding here.

Lake Tiorati (914-351-2568). *Beach vehicle use fee in effect weekends and holidays Memorial Day to mid-June, daily mid-June to Labor Day. Picnicking, hiking trails, swimming beach, boat launching ramp, fishing, ice skating on lake, tent camping sites (small fee), refreshment stand in summer.*

A large, clear lake, Tiorati offers a refreshing swim, and little tufts of islands provide intriguing destinations for fishermen.

Lake Sebago (914-351-2583). *Beach vehicle use fee in effect daily mid-June to Labor Day. Picnicking, hiking trails, playing fields, swimming beach, fishing, boat rentals, boat launching ramp, ice skating on lake, cross-country skiing, refreshment stand in season, cabin rentals (call Sebago Cabins, 914-351-2360, for season and fees). No pets.*

One of the larger beaches in the area, this is another superb setting, with fine walks and good views all around.

Lake Welch (914-947-2444). *Beach vehicle use fee in effect weekends and holidays Memorial Day to mid-June, daily mid-June to Labor Day. Picnicking, hiking trails, playing fields, swimming beach, fishing, boat launching ramp, boat rentals, snowmobile trail, refreshment stand in summer, tent and trailer camping at Beaver Pond (small fee; reserve in advance thru Ticketron).*

This is another large beach area, able to handle the biggest summer crowds. The swimming and boating are excellent, and there's a lovely hedged lawn for sunbathing.

FOR THE DRIVER: From GWB, take PIP north to Exit 15 and Anthony Wayne Area. From here follow signs to Seven Lakes Pkwy and turn left. Silver Mine Area is about 2 mi south on Seven Lakes, and Lake Tiorati is another 1½ mi south on Seven Lakes.

Continue south on Seven Lakes past LAKES ASKOTI AND SKANNATATI (fishing only), LAKE KANAWAUKE (picnicking and hiking; park vehicle use fee in effect mid-June to Labor Day), and jct with NY 210. Shortly is Lake Sebago. From here, go back up Seven Lakes Pkwy to Lake Welch Pkwy and turn right to Lake Welch, about 2½ mi.

If you are not going to Anthony Wayne or Silver Mine, there are more direct routes to the other areas. From PIP Exit 13, go west on Gate Hill Rd and NY 210 to Lake Welch. At Lake Welch, turn left off 210 onto Johnstown Rd to Lake Sebago. For Lake Tiorati, take PIP Exit 14A and go west on Tiorati Rd to lake. Just after exit you can also turn left on Lake Welch Pkwy to Lake Welch.

Good Manors in Northern Jersey

TRIP C-9

RINGWOOD STATE PARK, Ringwood
RINGWOOD MANOR SECTION
SHEPHERD LAKE SECTION
SKYLANDS MANOR SECTION

DISTANCE: From GWB, about 35 mi. Mainly fast speeds.

Ringwood State Park, Box 1304, Ringwood, NJ 07456 (201-962-7031). *Grounds open all year daily dawn-dusk. Fees charged separately for each section from Memorial Day to Labor Day (see below). Leashed pets only. Special events throughout year. Partially barrier-free.*

Ringwood Manor Section. *Manor open May to early Oct Tues-Sun 10-4; closed Mon. Entry fee $2 per car weekends and holidays, $1 weekday (Tues free). Picnic area, hiking and nature trails, fishing in Ringwood River, ice fishing, sledding, cross-country skiing, refreshment stand. Manor entrance wheelchair-accessible.*

A picturesque park with a millpond and formal gardens surrounds a 78-room manor house built in the 18th century and Victorianized in the 19th. Some of the rooms are furnished with valuable pieces collected by two well-known families over the years: Peter Cooper, founder of Cooper Union, lived at Ringwood, and later Abraham Hewitt, the ironmaster, resided here. General Washington made it his headquarters occasionally. Outside a waterwheel stands on the site of an old iron forge.

Shepherd Lake Section. *Entry fee Memorial Day to Labor Day $4 per car weekends and holidays, $2 weekdays (Tues free). Picnic facilities (fireplaces), hiking, playground, swimming, fishing, boating (ramp and rentals), ice skating, ice fishing, sledding, cross-country skiing, year-round skeet shooting (201-962-6377), refreshment stand. Swimming area and restrooms wheelchair-accessible.*

Here 541 acres of the Ramapo Mountains are ours to enjoy. The lake is spring-fed, and the fishing is excellent if you like trout, pickerel, and northern pike. Hiking trails into the mountains afford good views at elevations of 500 to 1,040 feet above sea level.

Skylands Manor Section. *Manor open by appointment only. Entry fee $2 per car weekends and holidays, $1 weekdays (Tues free). Hiking trails, ice fishing, cross-country skiing, snowmobile trails, sledding. House all on 1 floor, manageable for wheelchairs.*

Skylands Manor House is a beautiful rustic estate built in 1924 and patterned after an English baronial mansion. The 44 rooms are unfurnished, but the walls, ceilings, fireplaces, stained glass windows, and paneling, imported from European castles, are noteworthy. The elegantly landscaped botanical gardens can be toured on request. Here are more good hiking trails with splendid views of the surrounding country.

FOR THE DRIVER: Take NYT north towards Albany to Exit 15 at Suffern (65¢). Here pick up NY 17 north to Ringwood-West Milford exit (Sloatsburg Rd) and turn left for 2-3 mi into Ringwood State Park. Entrance to Shepherd Lake is off this road on left, entrance to Ringwood Manor is a little further on right, and entrance to Skylands Manor is beyond Ringwood at Morris Rd.

Certain Reservations in the Ramapos

TRIP C-10

CAMPGAW MOUNTAIN COUNTY RESERVATION,
Mahwah
DARLINGTON COUNTY PARK, Mahwah
RAMAPO VALLEY RESERVATION, Mahwah
BERGEN COUNTY WILDLIFE CENTER, Wyckoff

DISTANCE: From GWB, about 5 mi. Fast and average speeds.

Campgaw Mountain County Reservation, Campgaw Rd., Mahwah, NJ 07443 (201-327-7804). *Open daily all year, daylight hours. No entry fee. Picnicking, hiking trails, playgrounds, bridle paths, camping (fees), snowmobiling, downhill skiing mid-Mar to mid-Dec (call 201-327-7800 or -7801 for snow conditions and fees). Leashed pets only. Wheelchair-accessible restrooms, easy paved roads.*

Here's a good place for a not too strenuous hike along old Indian trails that wind through hemlock groves or skirt the swamplands. The park contains a wildlife refuge and plenty of play areas for the kids. Campgaw Mountain Ski Area, with a 1,650-foot main slope and snowmaking facilities, is a popular and reasonably priced attraction in winter.

Darlington County Park, Darlington Ave., Mahwah, NJ 07443 (201-327-3500). *Open Apr to late Nov daily 10am to ½ hr after sunset, weather permitting. Admission: weekends and holidays $5 adults, $2 children 5-17; weekdays $4 adults, $2 children 5-17; under 5 and over 62 free. Picnicking (cooking permitted, bring your own grill), swimming, fishing, playing fields, handball courts, basketball courts, tennis courts, golf course (fees), snack bar. No pets. Wheelchair-accessible restrooms, ramps to beach area.*

There are three lakes here, two for swimming and one for fishing. Adjacent to Campgaw Mountain, the park provides a beautiful setting for family outings.

Ramapo Valley Reservation, Ramapo Valley Rd., Mahwah, NJ (201-825-1388). *Open all year daily 8-4:30. Free. No cars beyond entrance, no swimming; picnic areas, hiking trails, fishing, canoing, camping. Leashed pets only. Difficult for wheelchairs.*

Here are some trails for the more adventuresome, under really tall timber. There's more climbing than walking, and the boulders are piled high. Among several hikes is one up the mountainside to a clear lake a mile or so away, not far from the Skylands section of Ringwood State Park.

Bergen County Wildlife Center, Crescent Ave., Wyckoff, NJ 07481 (201-891-5571). *Grounds open all year daily, 8-8 in summer, 8-sunset other times. Building open all year daily 8-4:45. Free. No pets. Building fully wheelchair-accessible and barrier-free.*

Here's a good place to take the kids for an all-around introduction to Mother Nature. The 81-acre grounds feature a nature trail, a wildlife pond, and seasonal displays of rhododendron, azaleas, and wildflowers. There's some captive wildlife on view, and the museum has an observatory, informative natural history exhibits, and two large aquariums, one for saltwater species and the other for their freshwater cousins.

FOR THE DRIVER: Take NYT north towards Albany to Exit 15 at Suffern (65¢). Here pick up Rte 17 south to New Jersey and jct with US 202, shortly below NYT. Take 202 southwest about 2 mi to Darlington Ave. Turn left here and go a short distance to fork in road. Bear right up hill on Campgaw Rd for Campgaw Mountain Reservation; bear left, continuing on Darlington, for Darlington County Park.

Go back to US 202 (Ramapo Valley Rd), turn left, and continue briefly to entrance to Ramapo Valley Reservation, on right.

Continue south on 202 to Oakland and jct with NJ 208. A right turn here will take you to scenic Skyline Drive through RAMAPO MOUNTAIN STATE FOREST (201-337-0960), a beautiful and largely undeveloped wilderness area. For Bergen County Wildlife Center, turn left on 208, towards New York City, and go abut 2 mi to Summit Ave exit, on right. Get off 208 here and bear left, crossing back over 208 to Franklin Ave. Turn right on Franklin and follow it through center of Wyckoff, across a small railroad track, and across Godwin Ave 3 or 4 blocks to Crescent Ave. Turn right here and watch for sign to center, almost immediately on left.

To Standardbred Country via Merrie Olde England

TRIP C-11

NEW YORK RENAISSANCE FESTIVAL, Tuxedo
HALL OF FAME OF THE TROTTER, Goshen
HISTORIC TRACK, Goshen
MUSEUM VILLAGE OF ORANGE COUNTY, Monroe

DISTANCE: From GWB to Museum Village via Sterling Forest and Goshen, about 70 mi. Fast and average speeds.

New York Renaissance Festival, Rte 17A, Sterling Forest, Tuxedo, NY 11978 (914-351-5171, in NYC 212-645-1630). *Festival runs for 7 or 8 weekends beginning in early Aug, 11am-6pm; schedule varies each year (check in advance). Admission (includes all entertainment): adults $9.50 Sat, $10 Sun; senior citizens $8.50 Sat, $9 Sun; children 6-12 $3.75 Sat-Sun, under 6 free; season pass (good for admission every day of festival) $27.50. Free parking; special Short Line Festival Bus from Port Authority in Manhattan (212-736-4700). Grounds and restrooms wheelchair-accessible.*

If you think all the romance has gone out of the world, try shedding your cares and a couple of centuries at the New York Renaissance Festival, where you can thrill to the spectacle of knights in shining armor jousting on horseback as in days of yore, lend an ear to the strolling minstrels, laugh along with the jesters and mimes, sate yourself on hearty fare and noble drink, fritter away your farthings at the gaming tables, and watch the Equity players strut and fret their hour upon the stage at the Globe Theater. Struth, all this and more, as you like it, in the lovely setting of Sterling Forest. The festival is now in its ninth year, and going strong.

Hall of Fame of the Trotter, 240 Main St., Goshen, NY 10924 (914-294-6330). *Open all year Mon-Sat 10-5, Sun 12-5; closed week-*

ends Jan-Feb. Adults $1, children 50¢; movie and tour $2 per person. No steps into building, wide aisles on 1st floor; no wheelchair access to 2nd floor.

The former Good Time Stable has been converted into a museum dedicated to the Standardbred trotters who made this area famous. More than 100 exhibits in the large box stalls and hay chutes capture the flavor of harness racing and tell the story of this quintessentially American sport, the great national pastime of the 19th century, still entertaining millions of enthusiastic fans today. There's an original painting of Hambletonian, the Standardbred "daddy of 'em all," as well as Currier and Ives lithographs, wood carvings, bronzes, and statuary. Dioramas and films depict the immortal horses and drivers, and there are lifelike statuettes of the sport's great personalities in the United States Harness Writers Association Living Hall of Fame. We can browse in the Peter D. Haughton Memorial Library or in the Weathervane Shop, which sells horseshoes, jewelry, and all manner of items related to harness horses.

Historic Track, Box 192, Goshen, New York 10924 (914-294-5333). *Open for walking tours all year daily, all hours. Free. Racing in spring and summer; schedule and fees vary (check in advance). Picnicking, refreshment stand, special events all season. Grounds easy for wheelchairs; grandstand not wheelchair-accessible, but races can be watched from other locations.*

This National Historic Landmark, harness racing's oldest track (1838), still offers an exciting program of Grand Circuit races, Sire Stakes events, trotting bred exhibition races, and matinee races where amateur drivers vie for the coveted trophy—a horse blanket. Even if there are no races scheduled on the famous half-mile during our visit, we can see the horses in their stables and watch them go through their paces during their daily workout.

Museum Village in Orange County, Museum Village Rd., Monroe, NY 10950 (914-782-8247). *Open May to early Dec: May-June and Sept-Dec Wed-Fri 10-2, Sat-Sun 12-5; July-Aug Wed-Fri 10-5, Sat-Sun 12-5; open Mon holiday weekends, otherwise closed Mon-*

Tues. Adults $4.75, senior citizens $3.50, children 6-16 $2.75, under 6 free. Picnic area, snack bar, shops, special events all year. No pets. Will accommodate wheelchairs; call in advance.

Here's an outdoor museum that gives us a vivid taste of life in preindustrial America. At 33 buildings clustered around the Village Green, we can see demonstrations of such indispensable 19th-century skills as weaving, blacksmithing, cobbling, wood carving, sheep shearing, sausage stuffing, and the making of candles, brooms, soap, cider, and other basics. A collection of steam and gas engines heralds the arrival of 20th-century technology, while a natural history exhibit takes us back to prehistoric times and for once invites us to "please touch" the bones of a well-preserved mastodon.

The Museum Village specializes in such contrasts, with exhibits that remind us how laborious life was before the invention of modern appliances like the vacuum and the Cuisinart but may also make us long for the simpler days of Dr. Daniel's Housecleaning Fluid and Gargle. Throughout the year there are special events, including antique shows, Christmas shopping and caroling, festive dinners, Halloween tricks and treats, and an annual kite-flying day where you can buy or build your own aerodynamic contribution to the Hudson Valley skies.

FOR THE DRIVER: Take NYT north towards Albany to Exit 15 at Suffern (65¢) and pick up NY 17 north about 10 mi to jct with NY 17A/210. Turn left and go about 3 mi west to Sterling Forest and New York Renaissance Festival, on left (parking on right). In winter there's downhill skiing here at STERLING FOREST SKI CENTER (914-351-2163).

Continue on 17A/210 to jct with Rte 5 at Greenwood Lake, where the cannon Molly Pitcher used during the Battle of Monmouth was cast. Here 210 branches off to the left, and you may want to follow it south for a scenic drive into New Jersey, where it becomes NJ 511 and takes you to a nice family recreation area at the southern end of GREENWOOD LAKE (201-728-3721). From here, you can follow 511 to Awosting Rd, turn left, and return to NY 17A/210 via Awosting, E Shore, and Sterling Forest Rds; or you can follow 511 to turnoff for Ringwood (Trip C-9); or you can remain on 511 to WANAQUE RESERVOIR, impressive not only for its 28-billion-gallon capacity but also for its beauty in fall and its apparent attractiveness to aliens (numerous flying saucers have been sighted in the area). As you proceed around the reservoir on 511, you will meet Skyline Drive, which goes through Ramapo Mountain State Forest (Trip C-10).

From jct of 17A/210 and Rte 5, continue on 17A about 6 mi to Warwick, passing MOUNT PETER SKI AREA (914-986-4992), another nice spot to hit the slopes in winter. In Warwick there are a number of interesting buildings maintained by the Warwick Historical Society (914-986-2720): SHINGLE HOUSE on Forester Ave, the oldest house in the village, said to have been roofed and sided with singles all made from a single tree; the 1810 HOUSE on Main St, with some fine Duncan Phyfe pieces and displays of Americana; and the OLD SCHOOL BAPTIST MEETING HOUSE on Church St.

In Warwick 17A meets NY 94, and the two become Main St. Go north on this about 6 mi to Florida, where 94 branches off to right. Go straight and continue on 17A about 4½ mi to Goshen. In Goshen at jct with NY 17/US 6, 17A becomes NJ 207 and passes Good Time Park, once the proud home of the Hambletonian (1930-42, 1944-56), now a deserted, weed-choked lot. Proceed on 207 through stoplight (Goshen's one and only) to Minisink Memorial and Orange Blossoms Monument near entrance to Historic Track; just beyond is Hall of Fame of the Trotter, on right as road bends left. Track is behind Hall of Fame, and you can walk to either from the other.

Go back to jct with NY 17/US 6 (Quickway) and take it east about 10 mi, passing GOOSEPOND MOUNTAIN STATE PARK (914-786-2701), an unspoiled wilderness tract with hiking trails and bridle paths. Get off Quickway at Exit 129, Museum Village Rd, and follow signs to Museum Village of Orange County.

For return trip, continue east on Quickway to NYT.

Duty, Honor, Country

TRIP C-12

 UNITED STATES MILITARY ACADEMY, West Point
  WEST POINT MUSEUM
  WEST POINT CHAPELS
  FORT PUTNAM
 WARNER HOUSE, CONSTITUTION ISLAND, West Point

DISTANCE: From GWB, about 45 mi. Mainly fast speeds.

United States Military Academy, West Point, NY 10996 (914-938-2638). *Grounds open all year daily dawn-dusk. Visitor center open all year daily 8:30-4:15; closed Thanksgiving, Christmas, New Year's. All facilities and parking free. Self-guided tour, picnic areas, gift shops, restaurant and cafe at Hotel Thayer on grounds (open daily all year). Leashed pets only. Some areas wheelchair-accessible; inquire at visitor center. Commercial tours available through West Point Tours, Inc., Box 268, Highland Falls, NY 10928 (914-446-4724), not affiliated with academy; tours operate weekends late March to June and Sept-Oct, daily June-Aug; adults $2, children under 12 $1.50.*

West Point, site of the military academy established by Act of Congress in 1802, figured prominently in the Revolutionary War, though it was never a battleground. It was one of four strategically situated fortifications along the mid-Hudson, and it was here, in 1778, that the great 150-ton chain was laid across the river to Constitution Island to block British ships. It was as commander of West Point in 1780 that General Benedict Arnold made his name a synonym for "traitor" by plotting to betray the Point into British hands.

The Hudson bends sharply here before continuing towards Poughkeepsie, providing fine scenic vistas at Trophy Point, where we can see some of the 300-pound links of the river chain and a battle monument to the Civil War dead. There are many other monuments and memorials scattered throughout the grounds, including a 9-foot bronze American Soldier by Felix Deweldon, designer of the Iwo Jima Flag Raising Memorial. If our timing is right, we can watch the current crop of cadets drilling on the Plain, the same parade ground where Baron von Steuben drilled the ragtag soldiers of the Continental Army. The visitor information center is the best place to start our visit to West Point. Here we can see displays and a film on cadet training, and pick up maps and brochures for a self-guided tour.

West Point Museum. *Open all year daily 10:30-4:15; closed Christmas, New Year's. Will accommodate wheelchairs. New museum, currently under construction, is projected to open in fall 1987 (hours may change) and will be fully wheelchair-accessible.*
"Weapons change," said General George S. Patton, "but man

who uses them changes not at all." This quotation is called to mind as we view an imposing array of military arms, flags, uniforms, and memorabilia. There are dioramas of past wars, some of the Selden Chapin military miniatures, including his Grand Armée of Napoleon, and weapons from the war with Spain, the Boxer Rebellion, the Civil War, Vietnam. Other displays include a 6-ton World War I tank, George Washington's personal "gentleman's pistols," and Napoleon's sword and pistols. The Alexander Craighead Collection of Military Battle Art, on permanent exhibition, is the largest public collection of military art in the United States.

West Point Chapels. *Open all year daily 8:30-4:15. No photographing during chapel services.*

Cadet Chapel, built in 1910, is an impressive cross-shaped structure in "military Gothic," with an exceptionally large pipe organ and magnificent stained glass windows. It holds services on Sundays at 10:30 a.m. (also summer services at Trophy Point). Catholic Chapel, another fine building, holds Sunday services at 8, 9, 10:30, noon, and 5. Jewish Chapel, completed in fall 1984, has a gallery museum that chronicles Jewish participation in America's military history. Services are at 7:30 Friday evenings. Old Cadet Chapel, dating from 1836, holds a Lutheran service Sunday mornings at 10:30. In the chapel is a file with the names of those buried in the adjoining cemetery, including Revolutionary War heroine Margaret Corbin, General Custer, General Winfield Scott, and astronaut Edward White, killed in a space test in 1967.

Fort Putnam. *Open mid-May to mid-Nov daily 10:30-4.*

This restored Revolutionary War fort offers period exhibits and a commanding view of West Point and the Hudson River. The fort was built in 1778-79 to provide protection for Fort Clinton, downriver near what is now the Trailside Museum in Bear Mountain State Park (Trip C-7).

Warner House, Constitution Island, Box 41, West Point, NY 10996 (914-446-8676). *Boat operates late June thru Sept Wed-Thurs at 1pm and 2pm, leaving from South Dock at West Point for 2-hr tour. Adults $5, students and senior citizens $4, children under 5 $2. Prepaid reservations required; call Mon-Fri 10-11:30am. No* *picnics, no pets, no photographing in house. Difficult for wheel-chairs.*

This lovely old house, with a stone foundation wall dating from Revolutionary times, was the home of the Warner family from 1836 to 1915 and is furnished with their original possessions. The Warner sisters, Susan and Anna, taught Bible classes at West Point and were well-known writers: Susan penned a 19th-century best-seller, *The Wide, Wide World,* and Anna is best remembered for her words to "Jesus Loves Me." Our tour includes 15 rooms of the house, a short walk to the ruins of Revolutionary War fortifications, and a visit to a beautiful memorial garden planted with flowers described by Anna Warner in *Gardening by Myself* (1872).

FOR THE DRIVER: From GWB, take PIP north to Bear Mountain traffic circle. Follow signs for 9W north to West Point. Go a few mi on 9W to jct with NY 218 and turn right to Highland Falls and West Point. When road forks, follow sign on right to West Point main gate (Thayer Gate South). Visitor center is just outside gate on right; new museum will be right near visitor center.

After entering grounds, turn left on Mills Rd, just beyond Cavalry Flats. Follow sign for thru traffic, bearing right. Just before Lusk Reservoir and Michie Stadium (where Army home games are played), on left, are signs for Fort Putnam. Beyond stadium, on right, is sign for Cadet Chapel. Continue downhill for Jewish Chapel and Catholic Chapel, both on left.

At bottom of hill a right turn on Washington Rd takes you past Trophy Point and parade grounds to Thayer Hall on Cullum Rd, where museum is currently located. A left takes you to Old Cadet Chapel and through grounds to Washington Gate, where you can pick up US 9W south for return trip. To add a beautiful drive, turn right at Washington Gate and go over Storm King Mountain on NJ 218 past sign for Museum of the Hudson Highlands (Trip C-13) to jct with US 9W.

For boat trip to Constitution Island and Warner House, after entering Thayer Gate South, pass Hotel Thayer and turn right on Williams Rd. Go to bottom of hill and cross railroad tracks to South Dock, parking on left.

At West Point you can pick up a free copy of a spunky little publication called *The West Point DayHops Newsguide,* Box 70, Highland Falls, NY 10928 (914-446-3613), also available at Bear Mountain and other sites and sponsoring advertisers in the region. It's crammed with information and directions for suggested day trips to points of interest within a half-hour or so from West Point.

The Army's Winter of Discontent

TRIP C-13

WASHINGTON'S HEADQUARTERS STATE HISTORIC
SITE, Newburgh

KNOX'S HEADQUARTERS STATE HISTORIC SITE,
Vails Gate

NEW WINDSOR CANTONMENT, Vails Gate

MUSEUM OF THE HUDSON HIGHLANDS,
Cornwall-on-Hudson

DISTANCE: From GWB to farthest point, Newburgh, about 60 mi. Fast
and average speeds.

Washington's Headquarters State Historic Site, 84 Liberty St.,
Newburgh, NY 12550 (914-562-1195). *Open all year: Apr-Dec Wed-
Sat 10-5, Sun 1-5; Jan-Mar Sat 10-5, Sun 1-5, and by appointment; closed Thanksgiving, Christmas, New Year's. Free. Parking and house wheelchair-accessible; museum accessible on 1st
floor, otherwise difficult for wheelchairs.*

In the fall of 1782, after 7 years of war, more than 8,000 soldiers
and officers of the Continental Army camped in the Newburgh
area to await news of the peace negotiations in Paris. The three
historic sites on this trip, all administered by the Palisades Interstate Park Commission, tell the story of this last long encampment of Washington's army.

The Jonathan Hasbrouck House in Newburgh served as Washington's headquarters from April 1782 to August 1783. Here he
issued orders, declined a suggestion that he become America's
first king, and in general spent the days none too happily, if we
can judge from a letter he wrote on January 10, 1783: "Time will
pass heavily on in this dreary mansion in which we are fast locked
by frost and Snow." The house, begun in 1725 and completed by
1770, is furnished as it might have been when Washington was
here. It stands on 7 acres overlooking the Hudson. On the grounds
is the 53-foot Tower of Victory, erected to commemorate the 100th
anniversary of the disbanding of the Continental Army. Nearby
is a museum with exhibits and audiovisual displays.

Knox's Headquarters, PO Box 207, Vails Gate, NY 12584 (914-561-5498). *Open Apr-Oct Wed-Sat 10-5, Sun 1-5; closed otherwise except by appointment. Free. Picnicking, craft demonstrations, concerts, special events. Parking and house entrance wheelchair-accessible, interior difficult for wheelchairs.*

This attractive Georgian house of stone and frame construction was the home of John Ellison, an 18th-century merchant. General Horatio Gates used it as his headquarters in the winter of 1782-83, while he was in command of the New Windsor Cantonment. Earlier in the war it sheltered Generals Henry Knox and Nathanael Greene. A short walk from the house is the Jane Colden Native Plant Sanctuary, a beautiful sight in spring when the wildflowers bloom, and just beyond are the ruins of the Ellison gristmill and an old stone bridge to the main road.

New Windsor Cantonment, PO Box 207, Vails Gate, NY 12584 (914-561-1765). *Open late Apr thru Oct Wed-Sat 10-5, Sun 1-5. Free. Picnicking, military demonstrations, special events. Leashed pets only. Fully wheelchair-accessible.*

Some 8,000 soldiers of the Continental Army spent the last months of the Revolutionary War on this site, living in 800 log huts and waiting for news of peace. The winter was a hard one; the men were in rags, and their meager pay was long overdue. Some of the officers began circulating mutinous documents known as the Newburgh Addresses, calling on the army to take matters into its own hands. Washington showed a fine political instinct in his handling of the situation, sympathizing with their grievances while appealing to their patriotism. In the end the officers unanimously reaffirmed their support for their general and the cause for which they had fought so long. On April 19, 1783, exactly 8 years after "the shot heard round the world" was fired at Concord, the Cessation of Hostilities was announced to the army, and the soldiers dispersed to their homes in the newly independent United States of America.

Today at New Windsor Cantonment the daily routine of the Continental Army's last encampment is recreated in a "living history area." Every afternoon uniformed interpreters hold a military drill and demonstrate the firing of Revolutionary War muskets and cannon. At the visitor center there are audiovisual displays and two floors of exhibits, including the original medal created by Washington for enlisted men, the Badge of Military Merit, predecessor of the Purple Heart.

Museum of the Hudson Highlands, The Boulevard, Cornwall-on-Hudson, NY 12520 (914-534-7781). *Open all year Mon-Thurs 2-5, Sat 12-5, Sun 1:30-5; closed Fri; closed July 4th, Thanksgiving, Christmas, New Year's. No pets. Ramps at parking lot and into building.*

In a granite gorge on the side of a mountain, surrounded by self-guiding nature trails, stands a prize-winning piece of architecture housing a unique museum with natural history displays, cultural exhibits, and an assortment of live animals native to the region. The walls are adorned with attractive murals, and a newly renovated exhibit area depicts habitats of the Hudson Valley.

FOR THE DRIVER: From GWB, take PIP north to Bear Mountain traffic circle and pick up 9W north 16 mi to Newburgh. At Broadway (NY 17K) turn right and go 5 lights to Liberty St. Turn right on Liberty and go 2 blocks to Washington's Headquarters.

Go back to US 9W and take it south to NY 94. Turn right on 94 and go 2-3 mi to Forge Hill and Knox Headquarters.

Continue briefly on 94 to jct with NY 32 and NY 300 (Temple Hill Rd). Turn right on 300 and go about 1 mi to New Windsor Cantonment, on right.

Go back down NY 300 to jct with NY 94 and NY 32. Take 32 south past turnoff for Storm King Art Center (Trip C-14) to T-jct just beyond (NY 107, not marked). Turn left here and proceed into Cornwall-on-Hudson. Your road merges shortly with NY 218; proceed on this, bearing right, to Payson Rd, and turn right here, following signs for Museum of the Hudson Highlands.

For your return trip, continue on 218 over Storm King Mountain to jct with US 9W south.

Vintage Art and Wine

TRIP C-14

STORM KING ART CENTER, Mountainville

BETHLEHEM ART GALLERY, Newburgh

BROTHERHOOD WINERY, Washingtonville

DISTANCE: From GWB, about 55 mi. Fast and average speeds.

Storm King Art Center, Old Pleasant Hill Rd., Mountainville, NY 10953 (914-534-3115). *Grounds open early Apr to late Nov Wed-Mon 12-5:30; building open late May to late Oct Wed-Mon 12-5:30; both closed Tues. Suggested donation $2 per person. Picnic area. No pets on grounds. Wheelchair-accessible parking and restroom facility, ramp into museum and 1st-floor exhibits, parts of gardens manageable for wheelchairs.*

More than 100 large-scale contemporary sculptures are on display here in 350 acres of landscaped gardens overlooking Schunemunk Mountain. The museum, an elegant cut-stone mansion in the Normandy style, houses a superb collection of sculptures by well-known American and European artists. The center's impressive permanent holdings are supplemented by loans from other museums and changing sculpture exhibits throughout the year. From the gardens we look out through 5 enormous granite Ionic columns to magnificent vistas of rolling foothills. If our thirst for scenic beauty still isn't quenched, we can take a hike through the Mountainville Nature Conservancy of the Storm King Art Center, about 4 miles west of here (the museum staff will be happy to supply directions).

Bethlehem Art Gallery, Jackson Ave., RD 2, Newburgh, NY 12550 (914-496-4785). *Open all year Mon-Sat 10-5, evenings Tues-Wed 7-9; closed Sun. No admission fee. Artwork for sale, restorations, appraisals, custom framing, art supplies, art instruction. Parking and entrance wheelchair-accessible, gallery all on 1 level.*

The atmosphere here is quite different from that at Storm King. It's a bustling place that exhibits locally produced art and is known for its historic tiles, limited-edition prints of the Hudson Valley, and original paintings at affordable prices. If the Muse suddenly strikes you, you can buy everything you need to set up your easel on the riverbank and try your hand at the landscape that has captured the imagination of so many artists.

Brotherhood Winery, 35 North St., Washingtonville, NY 10992 (914-496-3661). *Open Feb to mid-Apr Sat-Sun 11-4, mid-Apr to* *mid-Nov daily 11-4; closed major holidays. Free parking; $2 per person for 1¼-hr tours leaving about every hr. No pets. Wheelchair-accessible parking, tour difficult for wheelchairs.*

This is the oldest winery in America, but if you're expecting hilly vineyards with rows of brown-robed monks picturesquely plucking grapes, forget it. Only the name Brotherhood remains in this modern commercial enterprise to remind us that the original cellars were built by French monks in the early 1700s. The tour takes us on a long subterranean ramble through dank caverns among the great white-oak aging casks. We'll visit the processing/bottling plant and see a slide presentation on wine and champagne making over the years, with tips on the proper way to serve and enjoy the fruits of the vine. Eventually we're invited to step up to an almost endless bar and sample some of the merchandise. The winery is busiest during the fall harvest, when the grapes are brought in by truck, but any season is good for the tour, and there are special events throughout the year (theater/lunch programs, Maine clambakes, grape stomps, feasts in the Bacchus Room, etc.). No matter when you go, bring a jacket or sweater; even in summer the cellars are cool.

FOR THE DRIVER: Take NYT north towards Albany to Exit 16 ($1.15). Immediately after toll turn right off Quickway (US 6/NY 17) and go north 10 mi on NY 32, watching for blue-and-white signs to Storm King Art Center. Just past T-jct (NY 107, not marked), cross a green steel bridge over a small creek and turn left on Orrs Mills Rd. Go 1 mi to 1st left, Old Pleasant Hill Rd, turn here, and go ½ mi to art center, on left.

Go back to NY 32 and continue north to jct with NY 94 in Vails Gate (Trip C-13). Make a left on 94 and go 2 mi southwest to Jackson Ave (Bethlehem Church at corner). Turn right here and go about ½ mi to Bethlehem Art Gallery.

Return to NY 94 and turn right, continuing west to Washingtonville. Just before center of town is North St. Turn right and drive up the block to Brotherhood Winery, entrance on right.

Note that Brotherhood is only one of many WINERIES IN THE HUDSON VALLEY on both banks of the river. For a detailed brochure on the other wineries of the region, write the Hudson River Wine Council, PO Box 608, Marlboro, NY 12542, or contact the Hudson River Valley Association, 72 Main St., Cold Spring-on-Hudson, NY 10516 (914-265-3066).

For return trip, continue into Washingtonville on 94 to jct with NY

208, take 208 south about 6 mi to Quickway, and take this east a few mi to NYT.

Two Breathtaking Introductions to the Catskills

TRIP C-15

WURTSBORO AIRPORT, Wurtsboro
ICE CAVES MOUNTAIN, Cragsmoor

DISTANCE: From GWB, about 95 mi. Fast and average speeds.

We're approaching the Catskill Mountains, a region beyond an average day's round trip from New York City. There's a wealth of beautiful scenery, cultural attractions, and historic sites here; we'll explore some of the highlights and take some lovely drives. Bear in mind that as we go up, the temperature goes down; the mountains are generally 10 to 15 degrees cooler than the valley.

In this and the next few trips, we're nearing the southern Catskills, home of those famed resort hotels that have nurtured so many comedians. Each resort is a self-contained world of its own, and there are many such worlds to choose from if you've got time for more than a day trip. For FURTHER INFORMATION about accommodations and about the southern Catskills generally, contact the Chamber of Commerce of Ulster County, 7 Albany Ave., Kingston, NY 12401 (914-338-5100), the Ulster County Public Information Office, County Office Building, Box 1800, Kingston, NY 12401 (914-331-9300), and the Sullivan County Office of Public Information, County Government Center, Monticello, NY 12701 (914-794-3000, X160). There are also two toll-free Catskill information numbers: in New York State 800-882-CATS, outside New York State 800-343-INFO.

Wurtsboro Airport, Rte. 209, Wurtsboro, NY 12790 (914-888-2791). *Open daily all year, weather permitting, 8:30-6 (or dusk, whichever comes first). Sailplane demonstration rides (15-20 min) $25, introductory lesson (15-20 min) $30, varying fees for more advanced instruction. Will accommodate handicapped persons if able to sit in plane.*

Whether you want to experience the peaceful, thrilling, unbelievable sensation of soaring like a bird, or simply watch this fascinating sport from the sidelines, you'll find your visit here unique. Graceful, slim-lined Schweizer sailplanes are towed into the air by high-performance Cessnas, then released to glide, silhouetted against magnificent mountain scenery. Wurtsboro has been a soaring site since 1927 and offers instructional programs for experienced pilots as well as beginners.

Ice Caves Mountain, Box 111, Cragsmoor, NY 12420 (914-647-7989). *Open Apr-Nov daily 9-dusk. Adults $5, children 6-12 $2.50, under 6 free. Self-guided tour, picnic area. Leashed pets only. Scenic drive to Sam's Point and top of mountain, but no wheelchair access to caves.*

This National Natural Landmark in the Shawangunk (pronounced "Shongum") Mountains offers marvels formed by millions of years of geological activity. A beautiful drive up the mountain takes us to Sam's Point, a massive stone plateau jutting a half-mile (2,255 feet) into the sky and affording a spectacular panoramic view of five states. According to legend a trapper named Sam jumped from here to escape an Indian war party and lived to tell about it, but you won't want to try this for yourselves unless you brought a sailplane with you from Wurtsboro.

Beyond Sam's Point a trail leads us past attractions like Crystal Chasm, the Balanced Rock, and Rainbow Tunnel to the glacial caves where the ice never melts. We can listen through a crack to the voice of Lost River, discover caverns, underground lakes, and cool grottos, and find stone shapes for every fantasy among the rugged rock formations. The trail has handrails and is well maintained, but be sure to stay on it and exercise normal caution. We can walk it in a half-hour or so, but why hurry? At the top of the mountain is Lake Maratanza, a haven for migratory birds. This is Ellenville's water supply, and there's no fishing or swimming allowed.

FOR THE DRIVER: Take NYT north towards Albany to Exit 16 ($1.15), then Quickway (US 6/NY 17) west to Exit 113. Here take US 209 north 2½ mi to Wurtsboro Airport.

Continue north on 209 to Ellenville. In town turn right on NY 52 and go about 5 mi to turnoff for Cragsmoor and Ice Caves Mountain, on left, then another few mi to entrance and scenic drive.

As you drive along on NY 52, don't be surprised if you see winged figures swooping over the highway. Ellenville is known as "The Hang-Gliding Capital of the East"; its topography and thermals make it ideal for this increasingly popular sport. If you want to give it a whirl, visit AERIAL TECHNIQUES SKY SCHOOL, Rte. 209, Ellenville, NY 12428 (914-647-3344).

A Huguenot Haven on the Hudson

TRIP C-16

HUGUENOT STREET, New Paltz

LOCUST LAWN, Gardiner

SNYDER ESTATE, Rosendale

DISTANCE: From GWB to farthest point, Rosendale, about 90 mi. Mainly fast speeds.

The three sites on this trip are owned and operated by the Huguenot Historical Society, PO Box 339, New Paltz, NY 12561 (914-255-1660), one of those dedicated local organizations to which we owe the preservation of so much of our nation's history. The Huguenots, French followers of John Calvin, suffered heavy persecution at the hands of France's Catholic monarchy throughout the 17th century. Many thousands of them fled, including the 12 families who settled along the Hudson in 1677 and named their community after *die Pfalz,* an area near the Rhine where they had found temporary refuge before sailing for the New World.

Huguenot Street, New Paltz, NY *Open Memorial Day thru Sept Wed-Sun 10-4; closed Mon-Tues. Complete tours (2¼ hrs) $5 adults, $4 senior citizens, $1 children 7-12, under 7 free; short tours (1¼ hrs) $2.50 per person; tour of 1 house $1.50 per person. No pets. Deyo Hall, gift shop, and restroom wheelchair-accessible; some houses on 1 level but most with steps.*

Here is the oldest street in America where the original houses still stand. The land was purchased by the Duzine (the heads of the 12 founding Huguenot families) from the Esopus Indians in

1677, for once on generous terms. At first the families lived in log huts, gradually replaced by the sturdy stone structures we see here today, among them the Jean Hasbrouck House (1692-1712), in the medieval Flemish style; the Bevier-Elting House (1698) with its large windows and roomy porch; DuBois Fort (1705), built to satisfy the English governor's demand for "a place of Retreat and Safe-guard"; and the French church (1717), reconstructed in 1972 after 10 years of painstaking research. Most of the houses were continually occupied by the descendants of the builders for 250 years, and the furnishings include heirlooms considered too precious to be left behind during the long flight from France.

Locust Lawn, Gardiner, NY. *Open Memorial Day thru Sept Wed-Sun 10-4; closed Mon-Tues. Guided tours $2 adults, $1 children under 14. Wildlife sanctuary, nature trails. No ramps into buildings; difficult for wheelchairs.*

This handsome Federal mansion was built in 1814 by Colonel Josiah Hasbrouck, a descendant of one of the original Huguenot families that settled around New Paltz. Hasbrouck fought in the Revolutionary War, served in Congress, and was one of the wealthiest men of his day, as is apparent from the beautiful furnishings, fine china, and paintings (including portraits by Ammi Phillips and works of the Hudson River School) that adorn his home. The marbelized plaster walls in the central hall were the trademark of the well-known architect Cromwell of Newburgh. The outbuildings include a slaughterhouse, smokehouse, and carriage house.

Also on the grounds, near Plattekill Brook, is a much older building, the Terwilliger homestead, reflecting Hudson River Valley, French Huguenot, and Dutch architectural styles. Evert Terwilliger, who began the house in 1738, is buried here with his wife and slaves. Just west of Locust Lawn is the Little Wings Wildlife Sanctuary, where woodland trails offer pleasant strolls and a chance to observe some of the 28 species of resident birds.

Snyder Estate, Rosendale, NY (914-658-9900). *Open by appointment only. Guided tour $2 adults, $1 children 6-14, under 6 free. No ramps, steps into house; difficult for wheelchairs.*

The old stone portion of this 19th-century homestead was the residence of Jacob L. Snyder and his wife, Catherine Hasbrouck.

Jacob discovered natural cement rock on his property and did a thriving business supplying cement for the Delaware & Hudson Canal, begun in 1825. Thus began a Snyder cement dynasty that lasted until Jacob's great-great-great grandson, Andrew J. Snyder II, was forced to close his Century Cement Corporation in 1970. Today the estate provides a fascinating glimpse of industrial history as we learn about the manufacture of the distinctive, durable Rosendale cement and the vicissitudes of the Snyder business over the years.

FOR THE DRIVER: Take NYT north towards Albany to Exit 18 at New Paltz ($1.80). Go west into town on NY 299 (Main St) to jct with NY 32. Turn right and go north on 32 to Huguenot St, shortly on left.

Go back to NY 32. Locust Lawn is 4 mi south on 32. For Snyder Estate go 8 mi north on 32 to jct with NY 213 and turn left. Go 2 mi west on 213 to estate, entrance on right.

On your way south on 32 to Locust Lawn, at jct with Minnewaska Trail (US 44/NY 55), you can turn right and go west a few mi to WIDMARK FARMS (914-255-6400), a family beekeeping operation complete with black bears to steal the honey. There are bee demonstrations, bear performances, honey for sale, and animals to pet.

In New Paltz, you may want to visit the STATE UNIVERSITY OF NEW YORK COLLEGE AT NEW PALTZ (914-257-2229) for concerts, plays, music festivals, and regular shows at the planetarium (914-257-2066).

Sparkling Blue Waters, Clear Mountain Air

TRIP C-17

MOHONK MOUNTAIN HOUSE, New Paltz

LAKE MINNEWASKA DAY PARK, Lake Minnewaska

DISTANCE: From GWB, about 90 mi. Mainly fast speeds.

Mohonk Mountain House, Mohonk Lake, New Paltz, NY 12561 (914-255-1000, in NYC 212-233-2244). *Open daily all year for lodging, dining, activities. Day visits: $15 per person for lunch and access to grounds; $5 per person weekends, $4 weekdays, for hiking pass and use of picnic lodge; $4 gate fee for evening activ-*

ities. No swimming for day visitors; overnight guests have prior-
ity in use of other facilities. Picnicking, hiking trails, game room,
lawn sports, fishing by Mohonk day permit ($3), boat and paddle-
boat rentals ($4 per hr), carriage rides ($8 per person per hr), 9-
hole golf course (Apr-Oct; $4 per round weekdays, $5 per round
weekends, carts $8 per round), clay tennis courts (May-Nov; $9
per court per hr), platform tennis ($5 per court per hr), horseback
riding (Apr-Oct; $10 per hr), cross-country skiing (equipment
rentals $14-$23 per day), ice skating (skate rentals $2 per hr),
fitness center with masseuse (fees). Special events and programs
all year. Inquire about daily and weekly rates, special packages.
No pets. Building and some paths wheelchair-accessible.

One of the last great turn-of-the-century mountain resorts, Mohonk is an enormous, rambling Victorian castle overlooking a small,
clear, deep freshwater lake. This improbable and quite fantastic
structure was built as a retreat by Alfred Smiley and his twin
brother, Albert, Quakers dedicated to the cause of world peace,
and is still run by the Smiley family. More than 135 miles of trails
and carriage roads wind through some 5,000 acres of stunning
Shawangunk mountain scenery in the Mohonk Preserve, a haven
for hikers, naturalists, bird watchers, and rock climbers eager to
test their mettle on the sheer Trapps cliffs. The marvelous view
from Skytop Tower encompasses several states and is especially
gorgeous in spring when the laurel blooms and in fall when the
foliage turns.

Mohonk runs a plethora of programs offering something for
everyone virtually year-round: nature outings, Hudson Valley
heritage tours, Tower of Babble intensive foreign language study,
chamber music, cooking classes, stargazing, sports tournaments,
computer courses, children's activities, a new science fiction
weekend with Isaac Asimov, and the annual Mystery Weekend,
where guests divide into teams to solve a dastardly crime con-
cocted by mystery writer Donald E. Westlake. Day visitors can
participate in some of these programs, but many last several days
and most require advance reservations.

Mohonk is proud of its traditions and dedicated to the preservation of its beautiful surroundings. In 1986 world peace may be
further away than it was in 1869 when Alfred Smiley first looked
out over the Shawangunks from Skytop, but a day's peace is no
further away than the mountain house he built.

Lake Minnewaska Day Park, PO Box 162, Lake Minnewaska, New York 12446 (914-255-6000)). *Open daily all year, Mon-Fri 9-6, Sat-Sun 9-6:30. Season pass $75 adults, $25 children 6-16; unlimited adult day pass $6 weekends, $5 weekdays (senior citizens $4 weekends and weekdays); limited adult day pass (Peterskill Park only) $3 weekends and weekdays; flat rate for children 6-12 $1, under 6 free. Picnicking (grills provided), hiking, playing fields, swimming, canoeing (rentals), scuba diving (no equipment rentals), camping (fees), cross-country skiing (rentals), snack bar. No pets. No ramps, but wheelchairs can manage some areas; portable johns only.*

This private estate, 1,300 mountaintop acres in the Shawangunks, is run by the Phillips family. The clear blue waters of the lake are great for cave diving, canoeing, and swimming; there's a wading beach for the kids and a dock diving area for more advanced swimmers, both with lifeguards. We can enjoy scenic hiking to the mountain crest or through Peterskill Park with its three cascading waterfalls, or we can take a vigorous 5-mile hike to Awosting Lake in MINNEWASKA STATE PARK (914-786-2701), part of the Palisades Interstate Parks system, with more good hiking trails, bridle paths, beach area, and cross-country skiing in winter.

FOR THE DRIVER: Take NYT north towards Albany to Exit 18 at New Paltz ($1.80). Turn left on NY 299 (Main St) and follow it west thru New Paltz. Cross bridge over Wallkill River, take first right after bridge, and go about ¼ mi to fork in road. Bear left at fork and proceed up Mountain Rest Rd to Mohonk Mountain House gate.

Go back to NY 299 and continue west to Minnewaska Trail (US 44/NY 55). Turn right and go west carefully (this scenic road has many hairpin turns) 5 mi to Lake Minnewaska Day Park, entrance on left. Just beyond on Minnewaska Trail is entrance to Minnewaska State Park.

Historic Kingston, New York's First Capital

TRIP C-18

SENATE HOUSE STATE HISTORIC SITE
VOLUNTEER FIREMEN'S HALL AND MUSEUM ·
OLD DUTCH CHURCH
HISTORIC STOCKADE WALKING TOUR

DISTANCE: From GWB, about 95 mi. Mainly fast speeds.

Senate House State Historic Site, 312 Fair St., Kingston, NY 12401 (914-338-2786). *Open late Apr to Dec Wed-Sat 10-5, Sun 1-5; off-season by appointment. Free. Tours, concerts, special events. Will accommodate wheelchairs; call in advance.*

The Senate House, administered by the Palisades Interstate Park Commission, holds an important place in the history of New York State. Built by Wessell Ten Broeck in 1676 of rock-cut limestone, with one wall of Holland brick, it was already a century old when the first state legislature convened there on September 9, 1777. On October 7 the legislature adjourned upon learning that British troops were moving up the Hudson towards Kingston, and on October 16 the British landed and set the town afire. The house was damaged in the fire and repaired by its owner, Abraham Van Gaasbeek. Only the porch is "new"—it dates from 1888. There's a lovely rose garden behind the house, and the museum has historical exhibits and a collection of paintings by John Vanderlyn, a Kingston native and a student of Gilbert Stuart's.

Volunteer Firemen's Hall and Museum, 265 Fair St., Kingston, NY 12401 (914-331-0866 or -4065). *Open Apr thru Oct Fri 11-3, Sat 10-4. Free. First floor manageable for wheelchairs.*

In 1981 Kingston's seven volunteer fire companies and the Exempt Firemen's Association leased this 1857 fire station of the Wiltwyck Hose Company from the city as a meeting hall. As a labor of love, the members turned the first floor into a museum and opened it to the public in April 1982. In the parlor we find hand-carved black walnut furniture and the inevitable firehouse player piano (it works). Also on display is an extensive collection of antique firefighting equipment, memorabilia, and prints. Books and documents testify to the valor of the early firemen and trace the history of firefighting in Kingston, which began when the city ordered a fire engine from England in 1754. Three years and many fires later, this primitive but functional apparatus arrived and served admirably for two decades, until it went up in smoke when the British burned Kingston in 1777.

Old Dutch Church, Main & Wall Sts., Kingston, NY 12401 (914-338-6759). *Open by appointment only. Free. Entrance, interior, and restrooms wheelchair-accessible.*

This attractive 19th-century church is home to one of the oldest congregations in America, established in 1659. The church museum holds artifacts and documents of historical interest, including a letter from George Washington. George Clinton, first governor of New York (1777-1795), vice-president under Jefferson and Madison, and one of the earliest New York politicians to manipulate election results (in the 1792 gubernatorial race against John Jay), is buried in the cemetery.

Historic Stockade Walking Tour, 28 Green St., Kingston, NY 12401 (914-338-1004). *Tours by appointment only. Adults $1.50, children $1. Not manageable for wheelchairs.*

Here's a good way to see all the important sites in Kingston's historic district. This hour-long tour generally starts at the Old Dutch Church, goes along the perimeter of the stockade erected in 1658 by order of Dutch governor Peter Stuyvesant, and ends at the Senate House, taking in several other buildings along the way.

If you want to take the tour on your own, stop in at the newly opened Urban Cultural Park Center on Clinton Ave., across from the Senate House. Here you can see a movie on Kingston and pick up a detailed brochure with background information and walking instructions.

FOR THE DRIVER: Take NYT north towards Albany to Exit 19 ($2.15). Follow signs for Kingston; halfway around rotary, exit at Washington Ave. Go 2 blocks to Front St, turn left, and go 4 blocks to Fair St. Here turn right and proceed to Senate House, immediately on left. Volunteer Firemen's Hall is just down the block, across John St. From here go to next corner, turn right at Main St, and go 1 block to Old Dutch Church, at Main and Wall.

Note that you are only minutes from Rondout Landing and the sites on Trip C-19. If you want to combine the two trips, see "For the Driver" under C-19.

Solitude and Scenery Along the Historic Hudson

TRIP C-19

SLABSIDES, West Park
RONDOUT WATERFRONT DISTRICT, Kingston
HUDSON RIVER MARITIME CENTER
TROLLEY MUSEUM OF NEW YORK
HUDSON RIVER CRUISES

DISTANCE: From GWB, about 95 mi. Mainly fast speeds.

Slabsides, West Park, NY 12493 (914-384-6556). *Grounds and trails open daily all year, tours by appointment only; open houses twice a year, on 3rd Sat in May and 1st Sat in Oct. Free. No picnicking, no smoking, no fires, no pets. Not wheelchair-accessible, but drive is nice.*

John Burroughs (1837-1921) was a great American naturalist who lived on a farm near Esopus and wrote expressively in a Thoreauvian vein. He decided to convert a marshy woodland area near his home into a garden, and the results were so attractive that he knew he must build a retreat here. With the help of a local carpenter, he fashioned a rustic cabin and even made some of his own furniture. Burroughs came to this sanctuary often, sometimes bringing his friends—among them, Teddy Roosevelt, Thomas Edison, Henry Ford, fellow naturalist John Muir, and Walt Whitman, whose poetic gift Burroughs was the first to recognize.

Today the "Sage of Slabsides" is no more, but the feeling of quiet and solitude remains. By far the best means of appreciating Slabsides is the tour led by his granddaughter. Postcards, slides, booklets, and copies of her biography of Burroughs are also available. The John Burroughs Natural History Society and the John Burroughs Association, composed of friends who made possible the preservation of the cabin, meet at Slabsides twice a year, and the public is welcome to attend.

Rondout Waterfront District, Kingston, NY. Kingston's historic port on Rondout Creek has been revitalized as an urban cultural park, and today it once again bustles with activity, as it did in the days when the Rondout linked the city with the Delaware & Hudson Canal. There are many fine shops, restaurants, and galleries in this beautiful section of the city.

Hudson River Maritime Center, Rondout Landing, Kingston, NY 12401 (914-338-0071). *Open all year Wed-Sun 12-5. Adults $1, children 50¢. Ramp into building, parts of interior manageable for wheelchairs; staff will accommodate.*

Here is a living museum of Hudson River maritime history, started out of a storefront in 1980, now the hub of the waterfront renaissance. In the museum we can see a variety of marine artifacts and exhibits, with special attention to the steamboat era and the days of the elegant paddlewheeler *Mary Powell,* queen of the Hudson from the Civil War until after World War I. Outside we can watch shipwrights at work building and rigging all sorts of craft, from shad boats to vessels of the kind that sailed the Hudson a century ago. There are also outdoor floating displays, and more exhibits in the restored Kingston Lighthouse, accessible via a short, pleasant ride on the museum boat, the *Rondout Belle.*

Many yachts, sailboats, tugs, launches, cruisers, and coastal liners make Rondout Landing a port of call, and the Maritime Center has recently acquired a fast, graceful racing catamaran, the *Hudson Valley Spirit,* America's first regionally sponsored racing boat. A number of Hudson River cruise ships leave from here, including the *Rip Van Winkle* (see below). Every year the center sponsors two delightful events: the Shad Festival, during the running of the shad in spring, with the day's catch donated by the local fishermen, pan-fried before our eyes, and served up to the accompaniment of sea chanteys; and the Pumpkin Festival, when the sloop *Clearwater* (see Croton Point Park, Trip D-5) sails up the Hudson and unloads its cargo of soon-to-be jack-o'-lanterns in a great gold-orange heap for the inspection of the valley's children.

Trolley Museum of New York, 89 E. Strand, Kingston, NY 12401 (914-331-3399). *Open Memorial Day to Columbus Day, 12-5* *weekends and holidays, 12-5 daily July-Aug. Adults $1, children 50¢. Visitor center and gift car wheelchair-accessible.*

Landlubbers will appreciate this museum on wheels, an old-time trolley offering a 1½-mile scenic ride along the Hudson. There's a selection of antique cars on display, as well as more trolley lore in the new visitor center.

Hudson River Cruises, 524 N. Ohioville Rd., New Paltz, NY 12561 (914-255-6515). *Operates May thru Oct, Sun in May-June and Sept-Oct, daily late June to Sept; leaves Kingston 9:30am, arrives West Point 1pm, departs West Point 2:30pm, arrives Kingston 6pm. Round trip $15 adults, $8 children under 12; 1-way $10 adults, $5 children under 12. Smorgasbord buffet and full bar service (not included in ticket price). Inquire about schedule and fees for Fri-Sat evening music and dance cruises. No pets. Not wheelchair-accessible.*

Here's a relaxing, delightful way to take in the sights and sounds of the Hudson River Valley. We'll have to get up with the sun to make it to Kingston by departure time, but this day-long cruise to West Point aboard the 500-passenger *Rip Van Winkle* is well worth the effort. Our guide will regale us with a capsule history as we glide past wild stretches of shoreline, dramatic mountains (including the aptly named Storm King), vineyards and orchards, lavish estates, quaint lighthouses, island castles, and soaring bridges. We can loll on deck while the boat docks at West Point (Trip C-12) or purchase tickets aboard for a 1¼-hour tour of the US Military Academy ($2) before heading back up the lovely, legendary river.

FOR THE DRIVER: Take NYT north towards Albany to Exit 18 ($1.80) at New Paltz. Here go east on NY 299 to jct with US 9W. Turn left and go north about 4 mi to West Park. Beyond the main part of town, at Park Lane, turn left and continue, bearing left, as Park Lane becomes Floyd Ackert Rd. At sign for Burroughs sanctuary, park on road and walk ½ mi on Burroughs Drive to cabin.

Return to 9W and continue north about 8 mi. After passing through Port Ewen, cross bridge over Rondout Creek, proceed to light at bottom of hill, and turn left at Garraghan Drive. Go about 2 blocks to end of street and turn left at light, onto Broadway. Follow Broadway to waterfront, turn left, and park anywhere. Hudson River Maritime Center is right here, and trolley museum is just beyond, across street.

If coming from Senate House or other sites on Trip C-18, follow Broadway to end at waterfront, being careful to remain on Broadway when it makes a lefthand jag at Burger King; watch for sign here to waterfront. On your way, at 601 Broadway, you will pass the ULSTER PERFORMING ARTS CENTER (914-339-6088), a 1927 vaudeville house in the Neoclassical Revival style, offering a varied year-round program of theater, music, dance, and concerts by the resident Hudson Valley Philharmonic.

Deeper into the Catskills

TRIP C-20

ONTEORA TRAIL, NY 28 from Kingston

RIP VAN WINKLE TRAIL, NY 23A from Catskill

MOHICAN TRAIL, NY 23 from Catskill

DISTANCE: From GWB to Kingston, about 95 mi; to Catskill, about 120 mi. Fast and average speeds.

On this trip we're moving into the heart of the Catskill Mountains. We'll take in some truly magnificent scenery and pass many points of interest along the way. Since we're mainly out for the drive, brief descriptions of some of these attractions are incorporated with the directions. Remember that this area is in a different weather pattern from New York City. Spring comes late here; by the same token, two or three weeks before the leaves turn in the city they'll be at their peak in the mountains. For FUR-THER INFORMATION about the northern and western Catskills, contact the Greene County Promotion Department, Box 467, Catskill, NY 12414 (518-943-3223 or -6559), and the Delaware County Chamber of Commerce, 56 Main St., Delhi, NY 13753 (607-746-2281). The toll-free information number for the southern Catskills can also give you information on the entire Catskills area: in NYS 800-882-CATS, outside NYS 800-343-INFO.

Onteora Trail, NY 28 from Kingston. Kingston, which we've been exploring on our last two trips, is one of the gateways to the Catskills. From NYT Exit 19 at Kingston ($2.15), we'll drive west on

NY 28, but first we'll go 3 miles south on Old Rte. 209 to Hurley, capital of New York for one month in 1777 after Kingston was burned by the British, birthplace of Sojourner Truth, and a station on the Underground Railroad. Here we can visit the HURLEY PATENTEE MANOR (914-331-5414), a Dutch cottage built in 1696 and enlarged in 1745 as an English country mansion. Once a year, on the second Saturday in July, the town dresses up in 17th-century garb for STONE HOUSE DAY (914-331-4121), when the public is invited to tour 10 privately owned Dutch stone houses (be sure to look for the witch-catcher in the chimney of the Polly Crispell House). Brochures for a self-guided walking or driving tour are available in town or from the Hurley Heritage Society, Box 661, Hurley, NY 12443.

Returning on Old 209 to NY 28, we'll turn left and go west. Almost immediately we'll enter CATSKILL FOREST PRESERVE (518-457-2500), an enormous tract of almost 700,000 acres where we can hike through some of the wildest, most unspoiled country in the East. Part of the State Forest Preserves, the park stretches across Ulster and Greene Counties into Sullivan and Delaware Counties; most of the sites we'll be visiting on this drive and the next lie within its boundaries.

Proceeding west on NY 28 several miles, we come to the tip of the 12-mile-long ASHOKAN RESERVOIR (914-657-2304), whence comes a large proportion of New York City's daily water supply. The underground hydroelectric plant is not open to the public, and there's no picnicking here, but fishing and boating are allowed by permit. Or we can just look: mountains unfold in all directions, cloud formations and reflections in the clear waters are superb. Often when the fall foliage has petered out along the Thruway and across the river, this area is still ablaze with color. We can continue along the north side of the reservoir on NY 28 or take the southern route around it on 28A, which brings us back to 28 on the other side of Boiceville.

Continuing west on NY 28 from the eastern end of the reservoir, we come to the attractive small town of West Hurley. Just beyond is junction with NY 375. We'll take this north about 3 miles for a side trip to Woodstock.

Woodstock has been a mecca for artists since 1902, when Ralph Radcliffe Whitehead, a student of John Ruskin's, established the Byrdcliffe Crafts Colony here. The WOODSTOCK ARTISTS ASSOCI-

ATION (914-679-2940), founded in 1910, still thrives, offering a summer lecture series and changing exhibits. We can also visit the WOODSTOCK GUILD OF CRAFTSMEN (914-679-2079), which stages multimedia events in its Kleinert Gallery (914-679-2815) and operates a co-op shop (914-679-2688) selling locally made crafts. The WOODSTOCK ART TOUR (914-679-7969) gives us a chance to meet some of the town's artists and visit their studios. For entertainment there's the WOODSTOCK PLAYHOUSE (914-679-2436), the oldest summer stock theater in New York, and the MAVERICK SUMMER MUSIC CONCERTS (914-679-8746), the oldest chamber music series in the country, begun in 1916. For FURTHER INFORMATION, contact the Woodstock Chamber of Commerce, PO Box 36, Woodstock, NY 12498 (914-679-6234). By the way, that famous hippie happening of 1969 actually happened on a farm about 60 miles west of here.

Back on NY 28, we continue west to Boiceville, at the western tip of Ashokan Reservoir. Here we'll make a stop at the TOTEM INDIAN TRADING POST AND MUSEUM (914-657-2531) to see a display of totem poles, an Indian statue garden, and a collection of Indian artifacts, crafts, clothing, and jewelry.

Another 8 or 9 miles on 28 bring us to Phoenicia and an INFORMATION CABOOSE with brochures on local recreational and cultural attractions. We can hike, swim, camp, and find a variety of winter activities at ROMER MOUNTAIN PARK (914-688-7440), or we can board the CATSKILL MOUNTAIN RAILROAD (914-688-7400) for a scenic 2.8-mile ride along Esopus Creek. This is trout country, but fly fishermen aren't the only ones who flock to the creek; the untamed waters make it a favorite haunt of innertubers. If we don't have our own tube with us, we can rent one at Romer Mountain Park (which also has snowtubing in winter) or at several shops in the area. Note that NY 214 goes north from Phoenicia to Hunter Mountain and NY 23A (see next drive).

About 13 miles west of Phoenicia, still on NY 28, we come to Highmount, where we can hit the slopes at two fine ski facilities: BELLEAYRE MOUNTAIN SKI CENTER (914-254-5601; ski phone 800-942-6904 in NYS, 800-431-6012 outside NYS) and HIGHMOUNT SKI CENTER (914-254-5265). Belleayre has cross-country skiing too, and in summer we can picnic here and take a scenic chairlift ride to the summit.

We're now at the edge of Catskill Park. We'll stop here, but NY 28 goes on through Delaware County to Oneonta.

Rip Van Winkle Trail, NY 23A from Catskill. From NYT Exit 21 ($2.70) we'll drive west along this stunning wilderness route through Greene County, legendary home of Rip Van Winkle. When we leave NYT we'll be in the town of Catskill, where art enthusiasts will want to visit the THOMAS COLE HOUSE (518-943-6533) on Spring St. Cole, the founder of the Hudson River School, lived here from 1836 to 1848 and did some of his most important work in the studio. Catskill also hosts an annual summer OLD CATSKILL DAYS FESTIVAL (518-943-4591).

As we go west from Catskill to Palenville, NY 23A crosses NY 32, which goes north to Cairo and NY 23 (see next drive). Along the way are many lovely waterfalls and some interesting attractions. Left off 32 is a turnoff for the CATSKILL GAME FARM (518-678-9595), which more than 30 years ago began a conservation project to preserve species endangered in the wild and today has large breeding herds of rare and vanishing animals. There are more than 2,000 furred and feathered creatures here, including rhinos, giraffes, zebras, cheetahs, and tame deer for the children to pet. Just up the road a piece on 32 is CARSON CITY (518-678-5518), an old Wild West town with gunslingers, can-can girls, museum, and Indian show; and just beyond that is the CATSKILL REPTILE INSTITUTE (518-678-5590), with a complete line of ophidians, from snakes in the grass to the deadly king cobra.

Back on 23A, a little west of junction with 32, we come to Palenville, whose annual CIRCUS ARTS FESTIVAL (518-678-9021, 212-254-4614 in NYC) is a real treat for big-top aficionados. Also here is PALENVILLE INTERARTS COLONY (518-678-9021), with music, dance, drama, mime, and experimental theater performances by the Bond Street Theater Coalition.

Leaving Palenville, 23A takes us into Catskill Park (see previous drive) and on to HAINES FALLS. The falls, high and beautiful, are off our route a little in Twilight Park. Tucked away in the forest, accessible by trail from North Lake State Park off 23A in Haines Falls, is New York's highest waterfall, KAATERSKILL, which James Fenimore Cooper described so vividly in *Leatherstocking Tales*.

From Haines Falls we'll continue west on 23A to Hunter, where a tempting array of activities awaits us at the Catskills' second-highest mountain (4,025 feet). HUNTER MOUNTAIN SKI BOWL (518-263-4223, ski phone 800-548-6648 in NYS, 800-FOR-SNOW outside NYS), a vast 3-mountain complex with 44 slopes and snowmaking facilities that insure over 140 ski days per season, can easily accommodate thousands of skiers an hour; in summer and fall we can take the Hunter Mountain Sky Ride for wonderful views of the Catskills. The well-known HUNTER MOUNTAIN FESTIVALS (518-263-3800) run virtually nonstop from July 4th to Labor Day and include an Italian Festival, German Alps Festival, Country Music Festival, National Polka Festival, International Celtic Festival, and Indian Festival.

NY 23A continues another 13 miles or so through Lexington to Prattsville, where it merges with our next route, NY 23.

Mohican Trail, NY 23 from Catskill. From NYT Exit 21 ($2.70) we again go west from Catskill, through more gorgeous mountain scenery, but now we're north of where we were on our last drive. Shortly we pass Leeds, with the oldest STONE BRIDGE in New York (1780), and South Cairo, with its slightly incongruous MAHAYAN BUDDHIST TEMPLE, an ornate specimen of Chinese architecture.

Approaching Cairo, we'll pass junction with NY 32, where we can go south to the Catskill Game Farm, Carson City, and the Catskill Reptile Institute (see previous drive). If we're passing through on Labor Day, we'll catch the CAIRO COUNTRY FAIR AND CIRCUS (518-622-2073).

From Cairo we can take side trips south a few miles on NY 24 to Purling and the old gristmill at SHINGLEKILL FALLS, or north about 7 miles on NY 145 to East Durham, "The Emerald Isle of the Catskills," which hosts a major IRISH FESTIVAL AND IRISH FEIS (518-634-7100). Also here, on Wright St., is the BUTTERFLY MUSEUM AND FARM (518-634-7759), where they'll give you a home where the viceroys roam while the monarchs and swallowtails play. No, really, it *is* a butterfly farm, a tribute to the life's work of butterfly collector and cultivator Max Richter, and a boardinghouse into the bargain.

Continuing west on 23, we wind our way up to Windham, where we'll find a fine downhill skiing facility, SKI WINDHAM (518-734-

4300; ski phone 800-342-5116 in NYS, 800-833-5056 outside NYS). There's a classy atmosphere at this once private ski club, which has a 3,050-foot mountain and excellent snowmaking facilities.

NY 23 continues west to Prattsville, where it meets NY 23A, our previous drive. We can turn left here and make a circle around the heart of Greene County by going east on 23A back to Catskill, or we can continue west to Prattsville, Oneonta, and beyond.

Along the East Bank of the Hudson

• *Here are lands of great natural beauty, hills and valleys endowed with folklore, colonial settlements, Revolutionary memorials, parks and reservations. We'll follow the Hudson River northward through historic Westchester County into Putnam and Dutchess Counties. Proceeding inland across the southeastern strip of New York State above Long Island, we reach attractions near the border of Connecticut.*

Exit Points
Saw Mill River Pkwy (SMRP), New York Thruway (NYT)

Main Roads
NYT, SMRP, I-684, Taconic State Pkwy (TSP)

Connections

To reach NYT, see connections given in "Traveling to Area C," p. 119

To reach SMRP, take Henry Hudson Pkwy (NY 9A) or Major Deegan Expwy (I-87) north through the Bronx and follow signs.

Several other highways run north out of the city roughly parallel to SMRP: Bronx River Pkwy (becoming TSP), Sprain Brook Pkwy, Hutchinson River Pkwy (HRP). SMRP can be reached from any of these by taking them to Cross County Pkwy or Cross Westchester Expwy (I-287) and taking these west to jct with SMRP. Depending on destination, they can also be used as alternate routes for SMRP.

SMRP, Sprain Brook Pkwy, and Bronx River Pkwy (becoming TSP) all intersect at Hawthorne Interchange north of Tarrytown.

To reach I-684, take SMRP, NYT, Sprain Brook Pkwy, or Bronx River Pkwy north to jct with Cross Westchester Expwy (I-287), then take this east to jct with I-684; or take HRP north across I-287 to jct with I-684; or take I-95 (becoming New England Thruway) north to Cross Westchester Expwy west to jct with I-684.

Tolls
Toll information for Area D is the same as for Area C (p. 120) except that you will not be using the Tappan Zee Bridge. For New York City bridge and tunnel tolls, see p. xvi; remember to add these to highway tolls as appropriate, depending on your route.

Hudson River Crossings
The bridges linking the east and west banks of the Hudson are listed on p. 120. You may want to use these to combine trips in Areas C and D.

A Trip to De Jonkheer's Town

TRIP D-1

PHILIPSE MANOR HALL STATE HISTORIC SITE,
  Yonkers
HUDSON RIVER MUSEUM, Yonkers
UNTERMYER PARK AND GARDENS, Yonkers
SHERWOOD HOUSE, Yonkers

DISTANCE: From GWB, about 5 mi. Fast and average speeds.

Our next several trips take us to Westchester County, land of the
Manhattan and Mohican Indians before the Dutch West India
Company bought and battled them out, site of George Washing-
ton's desperate struggle to keep the British at bay in the early
years of the Revolution, home of America's first internationally
acknowledged writer, Washington Irving. For FURTHER INFOR-
MATION contact the Westchester Tourism Council, 148 Martine
Ave., White Plains, NY 10601 (914-285-2941), and the Hudson
River Valley Association, 72 Main St., Cold Spring-on-Hudson,
NY 10516 (914-265-3066).

Philipse Manor Hall State Historic Site, Warburton Ave. & Dock
St., Yonkers, NY 10701 (914-965-4027). *Grounds open all year
daily; manor open late May to late Oct Wed-Sat 12-5, Sun 1-5.
Free. Guided tours, last tour leaves 4:30. Special events all season. Will accommodate wheelchairs; call in advance.*
  This handsome Georgian manor house was begun in 1682 by
Frederick Philipse, a Dutch immigrant who became Peter Stuyvesant's carpenter-contractor and, under the British, first lord of
the manor of Philipsburg. By trading and shipping he made himself owner of houses, mills, and 90,000 acres on both sides of the
Hudson up to Croton. During the Revolution the Philipse family
remained loyal to the Crown, and the manor was confiscated.
George Washington is said to have been interested in Mary Philipse, sister of the lord of the manor. At one time the house served
as the Town Hall of Yonkers, and the northern wing was stripped
to create a courtroom and a council chamber. In addition to its

intrinsic architectural interest, the house contains exhibits on the painstaking restoration process, historical exhibits, and the Cochran portrait collection, including works by Copley, Gilbert Stuart, Charles Willson Peale, Rembrandt Peale, and Benjamin West.

Hudson River Museum, Trevor Park-on-Hudson, 511 Warburton Ave., Yonkers, NY 10701 (914-963-4550). *Open all year Wed 10-5:30, Thurs 10-9, Fri-Sat 10-5:30, Sun 12-5:30. Adults $4, children under 12 $1. Planetarium admission/shows: adults $2/$3, children $1/$1.50. Concerts, lectures, cafe, gift shop, summer jazz and chamber music concerts, special events throughout year. Fully wheelchair-accessible.*

With its triple focus on art, local history, and science, the Hudson River Museum is a fascinating place to spend a day. Here we can go from Indian relics to contemporary art, from the *Half Moon* to the Space Age. In the modern building we'll find galleries with changing exhibits in a wide variety of media, from ceramics to video, and the Andrus Planetarium, with excellent programs on astronomy and the latest developments in space science. Andrus has just acquired a $475,000 star projector that will make it one of the most sophisticated planetariums in the Northeast; it is scheduled to be installed and operational by March 1987. We can also tour the adjoining John Bond Trevor Mansion (1876), a beautifully preserved Hudson River Eastlake chateau. Across the river, we get a marvelous view of the Palisades (Trips C-1 and C-2).

Untermyer Park and Gardens, N. Broadway and Greystone Pl., Yonkers, NY 10701. *Open all year daily. Flat but gravelly; difficult for wheelchairs, but manageable with help.*

This elaborate formal garden is perched on one of the highest natural elevations in the Hudson River Valley, on the grounds of the former Greystone estate, owned by New York governor Samuel Tilden and then by Samuel Untermyer, a self-made millionaire. It was Untermyer who developed the Grecian Gardens and willed the property to the city of Yonkers as a public park. In 1973 the city undertook a 6-year, $2.5 million restoration project to repair the fountain network, Greek Temple and statues, Assyrian Portal, ornate marble mosaics, and other striking features of the Grand Beaux Arts landscape design, one of the few in America.

Sherwood House, 340 Tuckahoe Rd., Yonkers, NY 10707 (914-965-1243). *Open mid-May thru Oct, Thurs and Sun 2-5. Adults $1, children 50¢; additional fees for some special programs. Craft demonstrations; annual strawberry, folksinging, and square-dance festivals. Not wheelchair-accessible; special tour for blind visitors.*

One of the few pre-Revolutionary structures in the area, this colonial farmhouse has been restored by the Yonkers Historical Society. Escorted by costumed guides, visitors will see the large fireplace and beehive bake oven, historical exhibits, and many fine antiques. The main part of the house was built in 1740 by Thomas Sherwood, a tenant farmer on the Philipse Manor, and was purchased by his son Stephen when the Philipse lands were sold at auction after the Revolution. In the early 1800s Dr. John Ingersoll bought the house and built an addition for use as an office, charging his patients 50¢ a visit ($1 for house calls). Sherwood House has recently been added to the National Register of Historic Places.

FOR THE DRIVER: Take SMRP north to Yonkers Ave exit (25¢), immediately after jct with Cross County Pkwy, or take NYT north to Exit 4 (no toll) and take Cross County Pkwy briefly to SMRP north to Yonkers Ave exit, passing exit off NYT for YONKERS RACEWAY (914-968-4200), famed home of night harness racing. Coming off ramp, turn right on Yonkers Ave, then right at stoplight onto Ashburton Ave, following it as it goes right at top of hill, then left down hill. Continue on Ashburton about 1 mi to Warburton Ave. Turn left on Warburton and go 3 blocks south to Dock St and Philipse Manor, at Larkin Plaza.

From manor go back on Warburton past Ashburton, then north about 6 blocks to Trevor Park and Hudson River Museum, shortly after Warburton crosses Glenwood Ave.

Continue north on Warburton just over 1 mi to Odell Ave. Turn right and follow Odell uphill to N Broadway (US 9). Turn right on N Broadway and go about ½ mi south to Untermyer Park and Gardens, just past hospital.

Go back to Odell and turn right, crossing SMRP to Saw Mill River Rd (NY 9A). Turn right, go about ½ mi south to Tuckahoe Rd, and turn left, following signs for NYT. Beyond NYT entrance watch for sign to Sprain Brook Pkwy south. Just before ramp is a small road, on right, to Sherwood House.

A Day in Sleepy Hollow

TRIP D-2

SLEEPY HOLLOW RESTORATIONS
SUNNYSIDE, Tarrytown
PHILIPSBURG MANOR, North Tarrytown
VAN CORTLANDT MANOR, Croton-on-Hudson
LYNDHURST, Tarrytown
HISTORICAL SOCIETY OF THE TARRYTOWNS,
Tarrytown
UNION CHURCH OF POCANTICO HILLS, North
Tarrytown
OLD DUTCH CHURCH, North Tarrytown

DISTANCE: From GWB to Tarrytown, about 20 mi. Fast and slow speeds.

All the sites on this trip are in the Tarrytown area except for Van Cortlandt Manor, about 11 miles north in Croton-on-Hudson. Van Cortlandt is included with the other two Sleepy Hollow Restorations because they are all under the same management and because they make an enlightening day's tour in and of themselves, reflecting distinct periods of American history from colonial days through the Revolution up to the Civil War. But there's plenty to see in historic Tarrytown, whose name may derive from the Dutch word *tarwe*, meaning "wheat," or, as Washington Irving conjectured, from the tendency of the early menfolk to tarry too long in the local tavern. In any case, if you wish to tarry too, save Van Cortlandt Manor for Trip D-5, where we visit some other sites in and around Croton.

Sleepy Hollow Restorations, 150 White Plains Rd., Tarrytown, NY 10591 (914-631-8200). *Open 10-5 daily Apr thru Nov, 10-5 Wed-Mon Dec thru Mar; closed Thanksgiving, Christmas, New Year's. Admission per site $4 adults, $3.50 over 60, $2.50 children 6-14; 2-site combination (good for 4 months) $7 adults, $6.25 over 60, $4.50 children 6-14; 3-site combination (good for 6 months) $10 adults, $9 over 60, $6.50 children 6-14; under 6 free. Guided tours,* *free parking, picnic facilities, gift shop; exhibits, films, demonstrations, and special events throughout the year. No pets. Will accommodate wheelchairs; call in advance.*

Sunnyside, Tarrytown, NY. Washington Irving, the first American to achieve a literary reputation abroad, made his home here in what he described as "a little old-fashioned stone mansion, all made up of gable ends, and as full of angles and corners as an old cocked hat." An apt description of this most picturesque of houses, and an apt dwelling for the author of "The Legend of Sleepy Hollow" and "Rip Van Winkle." Sunnyside is just as it was in Irving's day, and we can look out over the same views he loved so much, of the Tappan Zee and the beautiful clear pond he called his "little Mediterranean."

Philipsburg Manor, North Tarrytown, NY. This Dutch colonial farm and trade center was one of the headquarters of the Philipse family's 90,000-acre empire on the Hudson (see Philipse Manor, Trip D-1). The stone manor house has been restored to its appearance in 1720, and the farm still operates much as it did then: costumed farmers till the soil, milkmaids tend the cows, and the great millstones of the water-driven gristmill turn wheat into flour. Philipsburg is rich in history and lore. It was here that Major André was captured after conspiring with Benedict Arnold to betray West Point (see Trip C-4); it was here, with the Headless Horseman hot on his heels, that Ichabod Crane tried but failed to get over the millpond bridge. Today we see much the same landscape that Ichabod saw in his headlong flight, and we can walk over the Headless Horseman Bridge to the Old Dutch Church and cemetary (see below).

Van Cortlandt Manor, Croton-on-Hudson, NY. Situated on a rise at the confluence of the Croton and Hudson Rivers, this handsome manor was the home of Philip Van Cortlandt, scion of a powerful New York family, hero of the Revolutionary War, and member of Congress. The house has been carefully restored and beautifully furnished, and there's a flavor here that puts the visitor right back among the industrious Dutch occupants. We'll watch demonstrations of crafts and cooking, and examine priceless antique furnishings, many from the original estate. Then we'll stroll down the Long Walk through gardens and orchards to the atmospheric Ferry House, a popular stop for weary travelers on the old Albany Post Road, with a Tap Room for the noisier, bawdier crowd, and a Common Room reserved for meals and games for the quieter patrons.

Lyndhurst, 635 S. Broadway, Tarrytown, NY 10591 (914-631-0046). *Open late Mar to early Nov Tues-Sun 10-4:15, early Nov thru Dec Sat-Sun 10-3:30; closed Thanksgiving, Christmas, New Year's. Adults $4, senior citizens $3, students 6-18 $2, under 6 free. Guided tours, gift shop. Annual Summer of Music (July-Aug), Children's Day (June), craft and antique shows, other special events. No pets. Entrance and 1st floor wheelchair-accessible.*

This masterpiece of Gothic Revival architecture, maintained by the National Trust for Historic Preservation, was designed by Alexander Jackson Davis for New York City mayor William Paulding and was later owned by merchant George Merritt and railroad speculator Jay Gould. The interior is not so much a restoration as a reconciliation among the styles of the three families who lived here. Apparently nothing was ever thrown away, so the place is a treasure house of Victorian elegance. There are Tiffany glass windows, rugs of silk and silver thread, paintings by well-known artists, examples of *trompe l'oeil* decor (wood painted to look like marble, ceilings painted to look like wood), and many other striking details.

Historical Society of the Tarrytowns, 1 Grove St., Tarrytown, NY 10591 (914-631-8374). *Open all Year Tues-Sat 2-4; closed Thanksgiving, Christmas, New Year's, July 4th. Donations accepted. Gift shop. Steps into building; not wheelchair-accessible.*

This museum in the elegant 1848 home of the first president of the Village of Tarrytown contains eight rooms of exhibits, including a Victorian parlor, the Room of the Old Tarrytowns, a weapons room, two American Indian rooms, a children's room filled with dolls and toys, and the Captor's Room, where paintings, lithographs, and documents record the capture of Major John André by three local militiamen in September 1780 (see Trip C-4). The building itself is in the Italianate Victorian style with a dormered mansard roof reflecting the influence of the French Second Empire. Down the street at 19 Grove the Historical Society maintains a research center with an extensive library, map collections, and the Requa Archeological Laboratory and Library, housing 35,000 artifacts recovered during a 7-year dig at the Requa tenant farmstead on the Philipsburg Manor grounds.

The Historical Society buildings are only two of the many interesting architectural specimens that abound in Tarrytown. The society will happily supply you with a detailed, informative brochure outlining walking or driving tours of the town's landmarks and historic districts.

Union Church of Pocantico Hills, North Tarrytown, NY. *Open Apr-Dec, Wed, Fri, and Sun 2-5. Donation $2 per person. Will accommodate wheelchairs. Tours and further information available through Sleepy Hollow Restorations, 150 White Plains Rd., Tarrytown, NY 10591 (914-631-8200).*

In the sanctuary of this lovely stone church we'll go back for a moment far beyond colonial days to the time of the Old Testament prophets depicted on seven extraordinary stained-glass windows created by Marc Chagall. The stained glass gives a special translucence to the unmistakable forms and palette of this modern master. There are also two other windows by Chagall on biblical themes, and a hauntingly beautiful rose window by Matisse, commissioned as a memorial to Abby Aldrich Rockefeller.

Old Dutch Church, Broadway & Pierson, North Tarrytown, NY 10591. *Maintained under auspices of First Reformed Church of North Tarrytown (914-631-1123). Grounds open all year daily; Sun services 10am June-Aug.*

This ancient landmark in Sleepy Hollow stands on a hill that was partly cut away to accommodate US 9, which crosses the Headless Horseman Bridge over the Pocantico River just below. The church was built by Frederick Philipse around 1685 for his family and the tenants of the manor. The belfry atop the gambrel roof contains the original bell cast in Holland with the legend, in Latin, "If God be for us, who can be against us?" Philipse and his wife, Catherine Van Cortlandt, are buried under the chancel. Just north of the church is Sleepy Hollow Cemetery, the "sequestered glen" that Washington Irving called "one of the quietest places in the whole world." Today the author rests here, and so do William Rockefeller, Andrew Carnegie, Samuel Gompers, and many others, famous and little known.

FOR THE DRIVER: Take NYT north to Exit 9 at Tarrytown (40¢) and pick up US 9 (Broadway) south 1 mile to Sunnyside, on right.
Go back to US 9, turn left, and go north ¾ mi to Lyndhurst, on left.
Continue north on 9 about 1 mi past jct with NYT to Neperan Rd. Turn right up hill and go 2 blocks to Grove St and Historical Society of the Tarrytowns.
Go back to US 9, turn right, and go north briefly to jct with NY 448. Turn right here and go 1½ mi east to Union Church of Pocantico Hills. Return to 9.
Near jct with 448 is PATRIOT'S PARK, on left just off US 9, with a statue marking the capture of Major André. A little further north is Philipsburg Manor, at foot of hill. Just beyond, across Headless Horseman Bridge, is entrance to Old Dutch Church and Sleepy Hollow Cemetery.
Just west of Philipsburg Manor is KINGSLAND POINT PARK (914-631-1068), with picnicking, hiking, and fishing, and off its shores is TARRYTOWN LIGHTHOUSE (914-285-2652), a center for nature and historic heritage programs, with exhibits portraying lighthouse life over the past century.
For Van Cortlandt Manor, continue north on US 9 about 9 mi to Croton Ave exit and turn right to manor.

In Washington's Footsteps at White Plains

TRIP D-3

WASHINGTON'S HEADQUARTERS MUSEUM,
North White Plains
MILLER HILL RESTORATION, North White Plains

DISTANCE: From GWB, about 25 mi. Average speeds.

Washington's Headquarters Museum, Virginia Rd., North White Plains, NY (914-949-1236). *Operated by Westchester County Department of Parks, Recreation and Conservation, Michaelian Office Building, White Plains, NY 10601 (914-285-2652). Open all year Wed-Sun 10-4. Free. Self-guided tour, curator on duty. Annual Washington's Birthday Celebration, special weekend pro-*

grams. Wheelchair-accessible parking, walks, and restrooms; ramp to 1st floor of house.

George Washington slept here in this white clapboard house, the center of a busy 100-acre colonial farm owned by Elijah and Ann Miller. The original portion was built in 1738, with the west wing added in 1770. During the Battle of White Plains in October-November 1776, the Miller home served as headquarters for Washington, whose ragtag army had just been driven out of New York City by British forces under General Howe. The American troops retreated up the Bronx River Valley and established a line of defense on Chatterton Hill in what is now northern White Plains. It took the British only 15 minutes to dislodge them from this position, but then a timely rainstorm forced a lull in the battle. Washington used the opportunity to regroup his men on Miller Hill, which was much steeper and easier to defend. From here they were able to repulse the combined British and Hessian forces, and Howe finally retreated at daybreak on November 5.

The Miller homestead was right in the thick of the action, and today we can see it much as it looked when Washington stayed here. Everything on view is authentic or an exact duplicate: Washington used the table and chair in the parlor; the clothes press in the bedroom belonged to Ann Miller's father and bears a musket pellet authenticating its patriot pedigree; Mrs. Miller baked in the brick beehive oven in the kitchen, still in occasional use for samplings of baked beans, cookies, and breads; and the Miller family laundry was done in the large wooden box in the kitchen, with a bell tied to the stick "agitator" to make sure the child-powered "washing machine" completed its cycle. In the 1970s the house was renovated by the Historic Workshop of the National Trust for Historic Preservation in Tarrytown, and it now shows the original look of the floorboards, walls, doors, and trim. The White Plains chapter of the DAR donated the furniture and keeps it in perfect condition. Be sure to pay your respects to the huge sycamore whose boughs shade the western corner of the house, and whose roots have lifted the bedroom floor 4 inches. It's said to be 300 years old, and it's been inducted into the Hall of Fame for Trees in Washington, D.C.

Miller Hill Restoration, North White Plains, NY. *Open daily all year for viewing. Free.*

Here the final shots of the Battle of White Plains were fired. Restored earthworks show where Washington's troops dug in and held off the Redcoats, while a battle diagram enables us to follow the course of the combat.

FOR THE DRIVER: Take Bronx River Pkwy north to Exit 26, Virginia Rd. Turn right on Virginia Rd, proceed across railroad tracks, and watch for Washington's Headquarters Museum, shortly on left.

Continue a short distance on Virginia Rd, watching for signs on left to Miller Hill.

Across Westchester by Pond, Marsh, and Lake

TRIP D-4

WAMPUS POND, Armonk

MARSH SANCTUARY, Mt. Kisco

TEATOWN LAKE RESERVATION, Ossining

DISTANCE: From GWB to Wampus Pond, about 30 mi; from Wampus to Teatown via Marsh, 10-15 mi. Fast and slow speeds.

Wampus Pond, Rte. 128, Armonk, NY 10504 (914-273-3230). *Open all year daily dawn-dusk. Parking fee $2.25 per car May-Sept. Picnicking, fishing, boat rentals and ramp, ice skating. Leashed pets only. Not wheelchair-accessible.*

Here's a small, scenic park a little off the beaten track. It's a nice place to picnic or plunk your line in the pond and wait for the one that got away.

Marsh Sanctuary, Rte. 172, Mt. Kisco, NY 10549 (914-241-2808). *Grounds open all year daily dawn-dusk; museum open all year Mon-Fri 9-4. Free. No pets. Not wheelchair-accessible.*

On a rustic hillside surrounded by blossoming shrubs and wildflowers stands, of all unlikely things, a small Greek amphitheater. Built in 1913, it is the setting for a variety of activities, both cultural and botanical. The sanctuary has two parts. Brookside, the more developed one, has 15 acres of gardens and trails. The other consists of some 75 acres of woods and marshland accessible by trail and boardwalk, providing opportunities for serious study of plant and bird life.

Teatown Lake Reservation, Spring Valley Rd., Ossining, NY 10562 (914-762-2912). *Grounds open all year daily dawn-dusk; museum open all year Tues-Sat 9-5, Sun 1-5. Free. No pets. Museum has 1 step, lake area flat and partially wheelchair-accessible; wheelchair access planned in future.*

This Nature Education and Environmental Field Station is devoted to environmental preservation and sponsors an ambitious range of school and community programs, in addition to seminars and slide programs for the general public. It's an ideal setting for such an endeavor: the 400 acres of serene woodlands crisscrossed by 12 miles of trails are calculated to induce an appreciation for nature in even the most hardened urbanite. Teatown is a perfect place for nature walks and relaxed contemplation. There's also a fine museum with changing natural history exhibits and a small animal rehabilitation program for injured wildlife.

By the way, there's a wonderful story behind the name Teatown. Some time before the American Revolution, a Bronx merchant moved to the area, bringing with him a stash of tea. The local women, catching wind of the sudden appearance of this rare commodity, stormed the merchant's farm and were held at bay by the women of the household. The stalemate was finally broken when the merchant capitulated to the irate ladies and agreed to ship in a steady supply of black-market tea.

FOR THE DRIVER: Take NYT north to Exit 8 (40¢). Here take I-287 east to White Plains and pick up I-684 north towards Brewster. Go about 6 mi to exit for Armonk and NY 22. Take 22 west briefly into Armonk and turn right at jct with NY 128, Armonk Rd. About 1½ mi up 128 is Wampus Pond. Note that Armonk is very close to the Connecticut border and some of the sites on the early trips in Area E.

Continue north on 128 a few mi to NY 117, Bedford Rd, and turn right here briefly to NY 172, still Bedford Rd. Turn right on 172 and watch for Brookside section of Marsh Sanctuary at McLain St, shortly on left. To reach woodlands and marsh area, continue on 172 to Sarles St, turn right, and go about 2 mi to entrance, marked by orange posts.

Go back on 172 to jct with 117, turn right, and continue north briefly into Mt Kisco. Turn left on NY 133 and proceed west past SMRP about 1 mi to Seven Bridges Rd. Turn right and go to end at Croton Reservoir, then turn left on NY 100 briefly to NY 134. Turn right on 134 and proceed across TSP, passing KITCHAWAN FIELD STATION (914-941-8886), a lovely wooded area operated by the Brooklyn Botanic Garden. Shortly after 134 crosses TSP, watch for Spring Valley Rd, one of several small roads on right. Turn here for Teatown Lake Reservation.

Various Points of View

TRIP D-5

CROTON POINT PARK, Croton-on-Hudson

CROTON GORGE, Cortlandt

GEORGE'S ISLAND PARK, Montrose

INDIAN POINT ENERGY EDUCATION CENTER,
   Buchanan

BLUE MOUNTAIN RESERVATION, Peekskill

DISTANCE: From GWB to farthest point, Blue Mountain, about 40 mi. Fast and average speeds.

Croton Point Park, PO Box 64, Croton-on-Hudson, NY 10520 (914-271-3293). *Grounds open all year daily dawn-dusk; parking fee $2.25 per car May-Sept. Beach open late June to Labor Day Sat-Sun 10-7; adults $2, senior citizens $1 weekdays, children $1, under 5 free. Picnicking, playing fields, hiking, canoe launching ramp (fee), camping (fee), fishing, refreshment stand. No pets. Wheelchair-accessible parking and restrooms.*

This popular recreation center of more than 500 acres is the site of the annual Great Hudson River Festival sponsored by the sloop CLEARWATER (914-454-7673), which has spearheaded the drive to clean up the Hudson and also participates in many other river festivals and special programs. The park offers fine views up and down the river, and in winter we can often see ice boating. Almost every guidebook neglects to mention the gnarled old tree with the huge knothole where you have to put your leaf-ticket before you can go down the steep winding path to the river. It was off this point, in September 1780, that the British man-of-war *Vulture* lay at anchor waiting to pick up Major John André after his secret interview with Benedict Arnold near Haverstraw. But when Americans at King's Ferry opened fire with a small howitzer, the ship had to drop downriver; André was compelled to take the land route and was captured at Tarrytown (Trip D-2).

Croton Gorge, PO Box 64, Croton-on-Hudson, NY 10520 (914-271-3293) *Grounds open all year daily dawn-dusk. Parking fee $2.25 per car May-Sept. Picnicking, play areas, hiking, fishing, cross-country skiing, sledding. Leashed pets only. Wheelchair-accessible parking.*

This rugged park hugging the side of Croton Dam is a little patch of wild in the heart of suburbia. When the reservoir is high, water cascades over the dam in a sparkling display of freedom on its way to the Old Croton Aqueduct and thence to the taps of New York City. The view from the top of the dam is worth the climb, but you can drive there too.

George's Island Park, Dutch St., Montrose, NY 10548 (914-737-7530). *Grounds open all year daily dawn-dusk. Parking fee $2.25 per car May-Sept. Picnicking, playing fields, hiking, fishing, launching ramp (fee). Leashed pets only. Wheelchair-accessible parking and restrooms.*

Here is a particularly scenic park on Montrose Point, across from Stony Point (Trip C-6). Trails extend along the crest of rocky shores dotted with intriguing little coves and patches of beach. Many species of small wildlife and birds make their homes here.

Indian Point Energy Education Center, Buchanan, NY 10511 (914-737-8174). *Open all year Tues-Sat 10-5. Free. Self-guided tours. Partial wheelchair access; ramps into building, and all 3 levels of exhibits can be reached.*

Picturesquely situated on a fault line, the Indian Point Energy Education Center at Con Ed's nuclear power plant offers a variety of exhibits on nuclear energy and shows us what our friend the atom is up to these days. We can also see the control room simulator used to train plant operators, a working solar energy system, a wind generator, and displays on energy conservation, the environment, and the history and ecology of the Hudson River Valley. Whatever our position on nuclear power, Indian Point provides a unique opportunity to learn more about how the awesome energy of the atom is harnessed. For those more inclined to stand outside with a picket sign, the view certainly beats Three Mile Island.

Blue Mountain Reservation, Welcher Ave., Peekskill, NY 10566 (914-737-2194). *Grounds open all year daily dawn-dusk; parking fee $2.25 per car May-Sept. Beach open Memorial Day to Labor Day Tues-Sun 10-7; adults $2, senior citizens $1 on weekdays, children $1, under 5 free. Sportsman Center (914-737-7450) open all year Sat and holidays 9-5, Sun 11-5, also Thurs-Fri 10-5 Apr-Dec; $2-$6 per hour. Picnicking, hiking, playgrounds, bridle paths, fishing, ice skating, cross-country skiing, sledding, refreshment stand. No pets. Parking, restrooms, and beach wheelchair-accessible.*

Two of Westchester's highest peaks are within this forest preserve. We can hike to Blue Mountain (680 feet) and Mount Spitzenberg (560 feet), or we can ride up on the bridle paths instead. Swimming is in Loundsbury Pond. The Sportsman Center has safe and diversified target ranges for trap and skeet shooting, rifles, pistols, and archery.

FOR THE DRIVER: Take SMRP to Hawthorne Interchange (25¢) and pick up NY 9A north about 7 mi until it merges with US 9. Continue north briefly to Croton Point Ave, turn left, and proceed across railroad tracks into Croton Point Park. A right turn on Croton Point Ave, then another right at 1st light, will take you to Van Cortlandt Manor (Trip D-2).

Go back to US 9, turn left, and go north briefly to next exit, NY 129. Turn right and go northeast on 129 about 2 mi to Croton Gorge entrance, just below dam. A little past park entrance, on right, is Croton Dam Rd, which takes you across the top of the dam for good views.

Return to 9, turn right, and go north about 3 mi to exit for Montrose and Buchanan. Turn left here onto 9A and go past veterans' hospital to Dutch St. Turn left on Dutch to George's Island.

Go back to 9A, turn left, and continue a short way to a group of traffic lights; at 3rd light, on Bleakley Ave, turn left and follow signs for about 1 mi to Con Ed plant at Indian Point.

Return to 9A, turn left, and drive to Welcher Ave. Turn right and proceed up hill, crossing Washington St. Signs here direct you to Blue Mountain Reservation.

History, Art, and Music in Upper Westchester

TRIP D-6

JOHN JAY HOMESTEAD STATE HISTORIC SITE,
  Katonah

WARD POUND RIDGE RESERVATION, Cross River

CARAMOOR CENTER FOR MUSIC AND THE ARTS,
  Katonah

BEDFORD COURTHOUSE MUSEUM, Bedford Village

KATONAH GALLERY, Katonah

MUSCOOT FARM PARK, Somers

DISTANCE: From GWB to Katonah, about 40 mi. Fast and average speeds.

John Jay Homestead State Historic Site, PO Box AH, Katonah, NY 10536 (914-232-5651). *Grounds open all year daily 8-dusk. Building open Memorial Day to Labor Day Wed-Sat 10-5, Sun 1-5; guided tours every ½ hr, last tour begins at 4:30; call for hours before Memorial Day and after Labor Day. Free. Concerts, nature walks, holiday programs, annual chess tournament, special events all year. Steps into house, but wheelchairs can get around 1st floor once inside.*

John Jay, our first Chief Justice, was a towering figure in the early history of the United States. He was a principal negotiator of the peace treaty that ended the Revolution, coauthor with Madison and Hamilton of the *Federalist Papers* arguing for ratification of the Constitution, and author of the 1794 treaty with England that bears his name. He also served the state of New York in many different capacities. After 27 years of public life he retired to this homestead, built on land purchased by his maternal grandfather, Jacobus Van Cortlandt, from the Indian sachem Katonah in 1703. Jay's descendants lived here continuously until 1953, and the house is furnished primarily with their belongings. The rear of the original farmhouse has just been extensively restored, and the Iselin room has been turned into a family portrait gallery that includes paintings by John Trumbull and Gilbert Stuart.

Ward Pound Ridge Reservation, Rtes. 35 & 121, Cross River, NY 10518 (914-763-3493). *Grounds open all year daily dawn-dusk; parking fee $2.25 per car May-Sept. Trailside Nature Museum (914-763-3993) open all year Wed-Sun 9-5; free. Picnicking, hiking, bridle paths, fishing, camping (fee), snowmobiling, sledding, cross-country skiing, refreshment stand. Leashed pets only. Wheelchair-accessible parking.*

Over 4,000 acres of park spread over a scenic mountain provide a great place to spend the day. There are miles of trails with lovely scenic vistas, two rivers for fishing, and the small but interesting Trailside Nature Museum, with natural history exhibits and various interpretive programs. An annual Fiddling Celebration takes place at Ward Pound Ridge in summer.

Caramoor Center for Music and the Arts, PO Box R, Katonah, NY 10536 (914-232-5035). *Museum open Apr-Nov Thurs and Sat 11-4, Sun 1-4, by appointment Wed and Fri; adults $4, children under 12 $2; guided tours, picnicking. Annual music festival late June thru Aug; tickets $10-$25. Museum and festival wheelchair-accessible; call in advance.*

The former home of New York lawyer Walter T. Rosen, a lavish Mediterranean-style estate built between 1930 and 1939, today operates as a museum housing his extensive collection of paintings, sculpture, Italian Renaissance furniture, medieval tapestries, and Chinese art. Here we can wander through entire rooms from European villas and palaces, stroll through the impressive formal gardens, and picnic in the apple orchard. In summer the highly respected Caramoor Music Festival brings some of the world's best classical artists to this lovely setting in the rolling hills of northern Westchester.

Bedford Courthouse Museum, Bedford Village, NY 10506 (914-234-9328). *Open mid-Mar to mid-Dec Wed-Sun 2-5; closed major holidays. Adults 75¢, senior citizens and children under 12 25¢. A few steps into 1st-floor courtroom, 2nd floor not wheelchair-accessible.*

Our tour of this 1787 courthouse begins in the courtroom where, 150 years ago, John Jay's son William was one of the presiding judges. Typical accoutrements of a court of the stagecoach period surround the bench. Upstairs there are two original jail cells and a museum with memorabilia covering 300 years of town history. The museum, maintained by the Bedford Historical Society, was formerly located in the little stone school across the green, now restored as a typical one-room schoolhouse of the last century (open same hours as museum, no additional charge). A map outlining a walking tour of Bedford Village is available at the courthouse, which will celebrate its bicentennial in 1987; check for special events.

Katonah Gallery, 28 Bedford Rd., Katonah, NY 10536 (914-232-9555). *Open all year Tues-Fri 2-5, Sat 10-5, Sun 1-5; docent tours 2:30 Tues, Thurs, Sun; closed Mon and during installation of new exhibits (check in advance). Free. Festivals and special events during exhibits. Will accommodate wheelchairs.*

Established in 1953, the Katonah Gallery has mounted six or more major exhibits annually for the last three decades. There is no permanent collection here; instead the staff researches and creates exhibits assembled from the holdings of museums and private collectors around the country. Among the many noteworthy past exhibits have been "Luminism in American Art," "The Face of Egypt," "Shadow Puppets of Southeast Asia," and "Indians of the Lower Hudson Valley" for the Westchester tricentennial celebration. The exhibits change every six to eight weeks.

Muscoot Farm Park, Rte. 100, Somers, NY 10589 (914-232-7118). *Open May-Oct Wed-Sun 10-4. Free. Picnicking, fishing. Leashed pets only. Wheelchair-accessible parking and restrooms.*

This 777-acre spread recreates farm life at the turn of the century. We can see the 28-room main house and original outbuildings, farm animals, antique cultivating equipment, and, on weekends, demonstrations of beekeeping, sheep shearing, blacksmithing, and other vanishing skills of America's rural past.

FOR THE DRIVER: Take Hutchinson River Pkwy north to I-684 north (25¢), or SMRP north past Hawthorne Interchange to I-684 north (25¢). Follow 684 to Exit 6 for Katonah-Cross River. Here go east on NY 35 to 1st stoplight at jct with NY 22 (Jay St). For John Jay Homestead, turn right on 22 and go about 1½ mi south to entrance, on left. For Ward Pound Ridge Reservation, continue east on 35 about 3 mi to Cross River and park entrance.

From Jay Homestead, continue south on 22 about 1 mi to jct with Girdle Ridge Rd, turn left, and go ½ mi to Caramoor gates, on right.

Return to 22 and go south about 3 mi to Bedford Courthouse, in center of Bedford Village.

Go north on 22 back to jct with 35. Turn left and go west across I-684 briefly to Bedford Rd (NY 117). Turn left and proceed to Katonah Gallery, shortly on left.

Go back to 35, turn left, and continue west about ¾ mi to jct with NY 100. Turn left on 100 and follow it into Muscoot Farm Park.

American Enterprise, Oriental Gardens

TRIP D-7

READER'S DIGEST, Pleasantville

HISTORIC ELEPHANT HOTEL AND CIRCUS MUSEUM,
  Somers

HAMMOND MUSEUM AND ORIENTAL STROLL
  GARDENS, North Salem

DISTANCE: From GWB to farthest point, Hammond Museum, about 55 mi. Fast and average speeds.

Reader's Digest, Pleasantville, NY 10570 (914-769-7000). *Open all year Mon-Fri during business hours; tours by appointment only. Free. Not wheelchair-accessible.*

Motorists driving along the Saw Mill River Parkway in Westchester have long been familiar with the outlines of some red-brick buildings grouped around a main building with a handsome white cupola. This is the headquarters of one of the world's most widely read magazines, the *Reader's Digest*. On our tour we can visit the editorial and executive offices, scan the corridors for our Most Unforgettable Character, and soak up Life in These United States. Besides the luxurious furnishings, many of them antiques, we'll find a notable collection of French impressionist and modernist paintings. We won't get to see how they condense those books, though—the printing is not done on the premises.

Historic Elephant Hotel and Circus Museum, Somers, NY 10589 (914-277-4977). *Open all year Fri 2-4 and by appointment. Free. Not wheelchair-accessible.*

Show-biz history was made in this small town. Once the center of a thriving cattle industry, it won national attention around 1810 when a farmer named Hachaliah Bailey (no relation to James Bailey of Barnum & Bailey fame) came into possession of an elephant, Old Bet, the second ever seen in the United States. His brother, a sea captain, had bought her in London and shipped her up the Hudson to Ossining. The elephant caused such a sensation that Bailey took her on tour and exhibited her for a fee. In Maine poor Bet went foraging for a snack in a tasty-looking potato field, and the farmer shot her. Despite Bet's unhappy end, Bailey's neighbors were inspired by his example, rounded up the most exotic four-footed critters they could find, and started road shows, making Somers a hotbed of circus entrepreneurship. From his profits Bailey built the Elephant Hotel, today the Somers Town Hall, housing offices and a museum with old posters, circus paraphernalia, and a display of miniatures collected by circus people on their travels. In 1829 Bailey raised a monument to Old Bet in front of the building, a large effigy made of wooden blocks standing high on a granite plinth.

Hammond Museum and Oriental Stroll Gardens, Deveau Rd., North Salem, NY 10560 (914-669-5135). *Museum open May thru Dec Wed-Sun 11-5; gardens open May thru Oct Wed-Sun 11-5; both closed Mon-Tues except on legal holidays. Separate admission to museum and gardens: $2 adults, $1 children under 12. No pets. Museum fully wheelchair-accessible, gardens have one major wheelchair-accessible path.*

Here, apart from the rush of life, we can stroll through 3½ acres of artfully landscaped Oriental gardens that transport us to another world, another culture, another time. We'll come upon rippling waterfalls, a river of blue lava stones gliding past banks of miniature plants, an island garden of rock ruled by Jizo, patron saint of children. Adjacent to the gardens is a museum of the humanities founded in 1957 by Natalie Hays Hammond in memory of her parents. A showcase for art treasures from around the world, it mounts a major exhibit every year on themes ranging from heraldry to ecology, from needlepoint to world religions. The museum also sponsors a program of dramatic readings, concerts, lectures, ballets, period plays, and masques. At Hammond, all these disparate forms of expression receive their due as different ways of telling the human story.

FOR THE DRIVER: Take SMRP north to Hawthorne Interchange (25¢) and continue north on SMRP about 4 mi. At stoplight at Roaring Brook Rd and Reader's Digest Rd turn right to Reader's Digest headquarters.

Go back to SMRP, turn right, and continue north towards Brewster and jct with I-684. Go about 5 mi north on I-684 to jct with NY 116. Turn left and go west on 116 into Somers and jct with NY 100/US 202. Turn left on these briefly to where they branch; here is Historic Elephant Hotel and Circus Museum.

Go back to NY 116, turn right, and proceed past I-684 and Titicus Reservoir to NY 124, at top of hill. Turn left, go ¼ mi to Deveau Rd, and turn right on Deveau to Hammond Museum.

From Mary's Lovely Knoll to Beautiful Boscobel

TRIP D-8

MARYKNOLL SEMINARY, Maryknoll

GRAYMOOR, Garrison

DICK'S CASTLE, Garrison

BOSCOBEL, Garrison

FOUNDRY SCHOOL MUSEUM, Cold Spring

DISTANCE: From GWB to Cold Spring, about 55 mi. Fast and average speeds.

On this trip we cross the Westchester County line into Putnam County, named for General Israel Putnam, one of the leaders of the gallant stand at Bunker Hill in 1775. For FURTHER INFORMATION contact Putnam County Tourism, 72 Main St., Cold Spring, NY 10516 (914-265-3066).

Maryknoll Seminary, Maryknoll, NY 10545 (914-941-7590). *Open all year daily 9-5; gift shop open Mon-Sat 2-5, Sun 1-4:30. No* *admission fee. Pets discouraged. Some facilities wheelchair-accessible; call in advance.*

Maryknoll is the headquarters of the Catholic Foreign Mission Society of America. At the seminary on the west property and across the road at the Maryknoll Sisters Center, priests and nuns are trained for service in foreign missions. From here they go out to all corners of the world to work among the poor and oppressed in churches, schools, health clinics, farms, and community projects. On our visit we can see photo exhibits on the Maryknoll missions around the globe, stop at the various chapels and shrines, or climb to the upper cloister for splendid views of the countryside. The international gift shop at the Sisters Center has an unusual and intriguing selection of items.

Graymoor Christian Unity Center, Garrison, NY 10524 (914-424-3671). *Grounds open all year; inquire about services, tours, pilgrimages, weekend retreats, weekly meetings, special programs. Picnic facilities. Pets discouraged. Grounds and some buildings manageable for wheelchairs.*

Here, situated on top of a high hill, commanding a magnificent view, is the monastery of the Franciscan Friars of the Atonement. Pilgrims from around the world come here to attend services, visit the shrines and chapels, and make the Stations of the Cross at the Crucifixion Group. The Unity Center is an interfaith conference and retreat facility where people of all beliefs can heed the injunction of Isaiah 2:3, "Come, let us go up the mountain of the Lord."

Dick's Castle, Rte. 9D, Garrison, NY 10524. *Not open to public.*

Perched high on a hill overlooking the Hudson, this striking Moorish structure of Spanish medieval design was begun early in the century by Mr. and Mrs. Evans R. Dick to house themselves and their large collection of artwork. After spending nearly $3,000,000, they were forced to give up the project due to financial reverses. The castle remained on its hilltop while vandals destroyed great chunks of its ornamentation, tramps spent nights on its floors, and general decay reduced it to a crumbling, photogenic ruin. In 1944 an engineer named Anton Chmela bought "Dick's

Folly" with the idea of turning it into a museum of American industry. He and his family opened the castle to the public for some years, but the burden of restoration was too much for them. It passed into the hands of an art foundation with ambitious plans for turning it into a Hudson River Valley museum, but they too found the job too daunting, and now the property is on the market again. At present you can't see much of Dick's Castle—it's closed, the drive is roped off, and you can only glimpse it from the road if you're driving south on 9D—but if you're a dreamer with a little cash to spare, perhaps that's just as well.

Boscobel, Rte. 9D, Garrison, NY 10524 (914-265-3638). *Open Wed-Mon Mar thru Dec, 9:30-4 in Mar and Nov-Dec, 9:30-5 Apr thru Oct; closed Thanksgiving, Christmas. Guided tours only; last tour begins ½ hr before closing. Adults $4, children 6-14 $2, under 6 free. Gift shop, concerts, annual Christmas candlelight tours, special events all season. No pets, no spike heels. Grounds wheelchair-accessible, mansion difficult for wheelchairs.*

A flawless example of New York Federal architecture, Boscobel (1804) overlooks a rocky gorge in the Hudson Highlands where the river cuts through the Appalachian Mountain range. This is indeed a *bosco bello*, "beautiful wood." Boscobel's builder, States Morris Dyckman, wanted the finest of everything for his dream house, and despite his wife's pleas for economy, he spared no expense. This, he told her, would be their "last sacrifice to Folly." Today we can be glad he had his way.

Both the building and its interior decor were patterned after the style of Robert Adam—delicate, flowery, pleasing to the eye. The mantels and moldings are exquisitely designed; the furnishings include Duncan Phyfe pieces and much of Dyckman's original china, silver, and library. Outside across the portico are carvings resembling graceful draperies of wood. We can also tour the stunning formal rose gardens, the orangerie and herb garden, and several original outbuildings, including the "necessary house."

After visiting Boscobel, you will wince to learn that it nearly fell victim to the wrecker's ball in the 1950s. It now stands 15 miles north of its original site, whence it was transported piece by piece and restored with generous support from Lila Acheson Wallace, founder of the *Reader's Digest* (Trip D-7).

Foundry School Museum, 63 Chestnut St., Cold Spring, NY 10516 (914-265-4010). *Open Mar-Dec Wed 9:30-4, Sun 2-5, and by appointment. Free; donations accepted. No ramps into building, but all exhibits are on 1 floor; will accommodate wheelchairs.*

This small museum, operated by the Putnam County Historical Society, is a treasure house filled with Americana and fascinating exhibits on local history and industry. It's located in a refurbished 150-year-old schoolhouse originally used by the children of the factory workers at neighboring West Point Foundry. Permanent exhibits include paintings, scale models of a Hudson River sloop and the grand old paddlewheeler *Mary Powell,* and artifacts connected with foundry operations, both military and household. There's good material for research in the library and archives.

FOR THE DRIVER: Take SMRP to Hawthorne Interchange (25¢) and pick up NY 9A north about 4½ mi to traffic light at NY 133. Turn right, towards Millwood, drive a few blocks to Brookside Lane, and turn left to Maryknoll, across Ryder Ave.

From Maryknoll turn right on Ryder back to 9A and follow it north, merging with US 9 and continuing through Peekskill across a small bridge to rotary. Here continue north on US 9 about 4 mi to Graymoor, on right.

Just beyond Graymoor, NY 403 branches left off 9 to Garrison. Take 403 to jct with NY 9D and turn right, going north on 9D past Garrison (which played turn-of-the-century Yonkers in the movie *Hello Dolly!*) a few mi to a steep unpaved road, on right, just before a small bridge. This is the entrance (closed) to Dick's Castle, which you can only see from 9D going south. Look for it on your way home. Continue north on 9D briefly to Boscobel entrance, on left.

When you leave Boscobel, continue north on 9D, which bears left, then right, into Cold Spring. Just after sign for Cold Spring, make a sharp left onto side road, Chestnut St, to Foundry School Museum.

A little north of Foundry School Museum on 9D, at traffic light, is jct with NY 301. A right turn here will take you 4 or 5 mi east to CLARENCE FAHNESTOCK MEMORIAL STATE PARK (914-225-7207), a popular 4,000-acre recreation area with picnicking, hiking, bridle paths, swimming beach, boat rentals and ramp, and camping. Or you can turn left at light onto Main St for a brief side trip to an unusual scenic vista. Go as far as you can after turn, then turn left on Lunn Terrace, crossing railroad tracks to Market St. Turn right on Market back to Main St, then left to waterfront. Here, on the banks of the Hudson, you'll find a 1920s bandstand and a lovely view across the river to Crow's Nest and Breakneck Mountains, Storm King Mountain to your right, West Point and Constitution Island below (Trip C-12). A left on Market St will take you to the restored CHAPEL OF OUR LADY, the oldest Catholic church in New York outside Manhattan.

From jct of 9D and 301, you can easily continue north on 9D to Madam Brett and Van Wyck Homesteads, first stops on next trip.

Bound for Poughkeepsie

TRIP D-9

MADAM BRETT HOMESTEAD, Beacon

VAN WYCK HOMESTEAD MUSEUM, Fishkill

LOCUST GROVE/YOUNG-MORSE HISTORIC SITE, Poughkeepsie

CLINTON HOUSE STATE HISTORIC SITE, Poughkeepsie

GLEBE HOUSE, Poughkeepsie

VASSAR COLLEGE, Poughkeepsie

DISTANCE: From GWB to Poughkeepsie, about 75 mi. Fast and average speeds.

Now we're in Dutchess County, an area rich in history, scenic beauty, culture, and old money. For FURTHER INFORMATION contact the Dutchess County Tourism Promotion Agency, PO Box 2025, 46 Albany Post Rd., Hyde Park, NY 12538 (914-229-0033).

Madam Brett Homestead, 50 Van Nydeck Ave., Beacon, NY 12508 (914-831-6533 or 897-4046). *Open May thru Oct Fri-Sun 1-4. Adults $2, students 13-18 $1, under 13 50¢. Two steps into building; wheelchairs can navigate 1st floor once up steps.*

Here is one of the oldest buildings in Dutchess County. Catheryna and Roger Brett moved into this house on Christmas Day, 1709, and it was occupied by their direct descendants for seven generations thereafter, until 1954. During the Revolutionary War, Beacon was a link in the long chain of alarm pyres stretching from the Hudson Highlands south to Morristown, New Jersey (Trip B-8), erected at General Washington's command to warn of the approach of British troops. The Brett Homestead served as a supply depot for the Continental Army, and the lady of the house, Catheryna's granddaughter, entertained Washington, Lafayette, and von Steuben here. Today the house and formal gardens are maintained by the local chapter of the DAR.

Van Wyck Homestead Museum, Fishkill Historical Society, Box 133, Fishkill, NY 12524 (914-896-9560). *Open Memorial Day to Labor Day Sat-Sun 1-5 and by appointment; call for arrangements and fees. Steps into building; difficult for wheelchairs.*

This Dutch colonial house stands on ground purchased from the Wappinger Indians in the 1680s by Francis Rombout, who struck a deal for "all the land he could see" and then climbed to the top of Mount Beacon to enlarge his prospects. Rombout's daughter, Catheryna Brett, inherited his property and in 1732 sold 959 acres of it to Cornelius Van Wyck, who built a three-room house that is the east wing of the present structure. During the Revolution, Fishkill served as Washington's Northern Army headquarters, and the Van Wyck house was requisitioned for military use. After the war it reverted to the Van Wyck family, who lived here for the next 150 years, until the Fishkill Historical Society acquired the house and turned it into a Revolutionary War museum.

Locust Grove/Young-Morse Historic Site, 370 South Rd., Poughkeepsie, NY 12602 (914-454-4500). *Open Memorial Day thru Sept Wed-Sun and holidays 10-4. Adults $3, senior citizens $2.50, children 7-16 $1, under 7 free. Guided tours, last tour starts at 3. Picnic facilities, hiking trails. No ramps, but 1st floor manageable for wheelchairs once up porch steps.*

Since the Locust Grove property was granted to Colonel Peter Schuyler in 1688, it has passed through many hands, including those of Samuel F. B. Morse, inventor of the telegraph, who bought it in 1847 and remodeled the house as a Tuscan villa. The dining room addition and the large collection of fine furnishings were the work of the Young family, who owned Locust Grove from 1901 to 1975 and set aside a trust to maintain it as a historic site and wildlife sanctuary. Today we can see early telegraph equipment, Morse memorabilia, fine furnishings, and changing exhibits from the Young collection of dolls, fans, costumes, books, and assorted Americana.

Clinton House State Historic Site, 549 Main St., Poughkeepsie, NY 12601 (914-471-1630). *Open all year by appointment Mon-Fri 9-3; closed major holidays. Free. Ramp into building; will accommodate wheelchairs (call in advance). Address written inquiries to Dutchess County Historical Society, PO Box 88, Poughkeepsie, NY 12602.*

This museum is named for New York's first governor, George Clinton, who used it as his office when Poughkeepsie was the temporary state capital in 1777. It is operated by the Dutchess County Historical Society primarily as a research facility and has an excellent collection of manuscripts, books, maps, and other documents on local history.

Glebe House, 635 Main St., Poughkeepsie, NY 12601 (914-454-0605). *Open July-Aug Sun 1-4 and by appointment; call Clinton House (above) for arrangements. Free. No ramp, but wheelchairs can enter thru back door.*

Glebe House has a colorful history dating back to pre-Revolutionary times, when it was built as the rectory of the Episcopal Church. In its first decade it was home to the Reverend John Beardsley, exiled in 1777 for his vigorous support of the Crown. Thereafter, though "glebe" means "parsonage," the house was put to more profane uses, serving as a rectory again for only four years. During the Revolution it was occupied by quartermasters of the Continental Army; in 1796 it was purchased by Peter DeReimer, whose daughter Elsie eloped from an upstairs window three years later; in the late 19th century the property went into decline and had a checkered career as a beer garden and picnic grove, among other things. Today it has been restored to reflect the life of a middle-class family in the early 1800s.

Vassar College, Press and Information Office, Poughkeepsie, NY 12601 (914-452-7000). *Buildings open during academic year Mon-Sat 9-5, Sun 1-5, and by appointment in summer. Free. Fully wheelchair-accessible.*

Founded by Poughkeepsie brewer Matthew Vassar in 1861, Vassar College was a pioneering experiment in higher education for women. Today it is a coeducational college known for its academic quality and the beauty of its 1,000-acre campus. More than 200 species of trees, some exotic, offer their shade to 100 distinctive buildings designed by such noted architects as James Renwick, Jr. (the 1865 Main Building, after the Tuileries, reportedly planned so that it could be converted to a brewery if females proved uneducable), Marcel Breuer (Ferry House), and Eero Saarinen (Noyes House). The Norman-style chapel has five Tiffany windows, and the great stained-glass window in Thompson Library depicts Elena Lucrezia Cornaro Piscopia receiving the first doctorate awarded to a woman (by the University of Padua in 1678). The $7.2 million Seeley G. Mudd Chemistry Building, opened in 1984, boasts the latest in energy-saving technology and laboratory equipment. Of particular interest is the Vassar College Art Gallery (X2645), with a fine permanent collection of 8,500 works, including 19th-century English drawings, 20th-century art, Hudson River landscapes, Rembrandt etchings, and Dürer engravings.

FOR THE DRIVER: Take SMRP to Hawthorne Interchange (25¢) and pick up TSP north to jct with NY 301. Drive west on 301 through Fahnestock Park across US 9 to jct with NY 9D in Cold Spring. Here you are very close to the last few stops on Trip D-8. Turn right and go into Beacon on 9D (Wolcott Ave). A few blocks ahead, across a small bridge, is Teller Ave. Turn right here and proceed to Madam Brett Homestead, at Van Nydeck Ave, 1 block before stoplight.

Continue to stoplight and go straight on what is now Business Rte 52 until it merges with NY 52 into Fishkill. At jct with US 9, turn right on 9 and go about 1 mi south, just past jct with I-84, to Van Wyck Homestead entrance on Snook Rd.

Go back to US 9 and go north about 9 mi to Locust Grove, at Beachwood Ave stoplight.

Continue north on 9 into downtown Poughkeepsie. Take exit for US 44/NY 55 and go east to White St. Turn left and go 1 block to Main St and Clinton House. Turn right on Main and go 2 blocks to Glebe House, on left.

Continue down Main St. to Raymond Ave, turn right, and go about 1 mi to Vassar, main entrance on left.

"I Will Arise and Go Now, and Go to Innisfree . . ."

TRIP D-10

INNISFREE GARDEN, Millbrook

DISTANCE: From GWB, about 80 mi. Mainly fast speeds.

Innisfree Garden, Millbrook, NY 12545 (914-677-8000). *Open all year Wed-Fri 10-4, Sat-Sun 11-5; over 16 $1.50 Sat-Sun, otherwise free. No pets. Not wheelchair-accessible.*

The late Walter Beck was a landscape artist in the most literal sense. He spent the better part of a lifetime studying Oriental techniques of painting, calligraphy, and gardening, and in 1930 he began applying them to the creation of what is sometimes known in the East as a cup garden. With nature as his canvas, he used rocks, terraces, and retaining walls to create areas of tension and motion around streams, waterfalls, and the lake that forms the first "floor" of his garden. The result of his 22 years of work at Innisfree was an exquisitely wrought garden "painting" that still delights the eye and mind.

FOR THE DRIVER: Take SMRP to Hawthorne Interchange (25¢) and pick up TSP north to Poughkeepsie and exit for US 44. Take 44 east to Millbrook and watch for Tyrrel Rd on right, just beyond jct with NY 82. Turn here and follow signs to Innisfree.

Innisfree is about 15 mi northeast of Poughkeepsie and about 12 mi east of Hyde Park. It can easily be combined with one or more of the stops on Trips D-9 and D-11.

FDR and the CIA

TRIP D-11

ROOSEVELT-VANDERBILT NATIONAL HISTORIC SITE,
    Hyde Park
HOME OF FRANKLIN D. ROOSEVELT NATIONAL
    HISTORIC SITE

FRANKLIN D. ROOSEVELT LIBRARY AND MUSEUM
ELEANOR ROOSEVELT NATIONAL HISTORIC SITE
VANDERBILT MANSION NATIONAL HISTORIC SITE
CULINARY INSTITUTE OF AMERICA, Hyde Park

DISTANCE: From GWB, about 80 mi. Mainly fast speeds.

Roosevelt-Vanderbilt National Historic Site, Hyde Park, NY 12538 (914-229-9115). *FDR Home and Vanderbilt Mansion open daily 9-5 Apr thru Oct, Thurs-Mon 9-5 Nov thru Mar; closed Thanksgiving, Christmas, New Year's. Adults $1.50, under 16 and over 62 free; fee includes admission to home, mansion, and library. See separate listing for Eleanor Roosevelt site. Leashed pets only on grounds. All 4 sites fully wheelchair-accessible.*

The Franklin D. and Eleanor Roosevelt National Historic Sites, together with the Roosevelt Library and Museum, constitute a moving memorial to the First Family that saw the nation through the Depression and the Second World War. The nearby Vanderbilt Mansion is, among other things, an apt expression of the class interests President Roosevelt was often accused of betraying by his social and economic policies. The library is maintained by the National Archives in a cooperative visiting arrangement with the National Park Service, which administers the other three sites.

Home of Franklin D. Roosevelt National Historic Site. Franklin Delano Roosevelt was born in this house on January 30, 1882, and kept it as his family home all his life. With the recorded voice of Eleanor Roosevelt guiding us, telling us anecdotes about this room or that, we sometimes have the uncanny feeling we're really visiting the living family, not just a house. We'll see some magnificent furnishings: the beautifully wrought Dresden chandelier and mantel set bought by Roosevelt's father in 1866, fine pieces from Italy and the Netherlands, a Gilbert Stuart painting of one of FDR's illustrious ancestors.

Echoes of more recent history are heard in Roosevelt's office, his "Summer White House," where in June 1942 he and Winston Churchill signed the agreement that led to the development of the atomic bomb. Upstairs we find the boyhood room used by Roosevelt and his sons after him. Perhaps most moving is FDR's own bedroom, with his favorite photos, Fala's leash and blanket on the chair where the little Scottie always slept, and the books and magazines the president left scattered about on his last visit here in March 1945, shortly before his death.

The name Roosevelt, from the Dutch, means "field of roses." How fitting, then, that in a beautiful garden of roses, surrounded by century-old hemlocks and perennial flower beds, both Franklin and Eleanor now rest. The tombstone is of Imperial Danby, the same white marble used in the Thomas Jefferson Memorial in Washington. A sundial stands just beyond the graves; at its base is a small plaque flush with the ground and hard to see from the walk. Here, still close to his master, lies Fala.

Franklin D. Roosevelt Library and Museum (914-229-8114). *Open all year daily 9-5; closed Thanksgiving, Christmas, New Year's.*

Those who experienced the Roosevelt years will be reminded of many things here as they peruse newsworthy gifts from foreign rulers, oddities (remember him as the Sphinx?), family heirlooms, photos, naval paintings, ship models, and more. Be sure to go downstairs to see the Ford specially fitted for Roosevelt to drive after he contracted polio. The FDR Library was the first presidential library and houses Roosevelt's papers.

Eleanor Roosevelt National Historic Site. *Access via shuttlebus from FDR home Apr thru Oct, leaving every 30 min daily 10-5; adults $1.95, children 4-15 $1.10, under 4 free. Access by private car on weekends in Mar and Nov; get map at FDR home. Site closed Dec thru Feb and weekdays in Mar and Nov.*

Eleanor Roosevelt was a tireless worker for social justice and political reform. During Franklin Roosevelt's 12 years as president, she performed with dignity and grace the difficult role of First Lady to "that man in the White House." It was here at her country retreat, Val-Kill, that she relaxed from the cares of public life and entertained friends, relatives, and a fair contingent of foreign dignitaries. Val-Kill was dedicated as a memorial to Eleanor Roosevelt and opened to the public on October 11, 1984, the centennial of her birth. It reflects both her personal tastes and her work for the wide range of causes she adopted.

Vanderbilt Mansion National Historic Site. A turn-of-the-century palatial mansion, this relic of the Gilded Age is considered one of the best examples of the Beaux Arts style in the country. Designed by the architectural firm of McKim, Mead and White, with interiors by the leading contemporary decorators, it was the country home of a grandson of railroad baron Cornelius Vanderbilt, and it expresses the influence of European art on American wealth in those days. It is filled with fine marble, mahogany woodwork, throne chairs, tapestries, beaded crystal chandeliers, heavily napped rugs (one weighs 2,300 pounds), hand-embroidered silk. The glittering opulence impresses, in different ways, everyone who visits the mansion—which, with 59 rooms, 22 fireplaces, and quarters for 60 servants, is considered the most modest of the various Vanderbilt estates.

Culinary Institute of America, Hyde Park, NY 12538 (offices 914-452-9600, admissions 452-9430 X327, reservations 471-6608). *Open all year: Escoffier Restaurant open Tues-Sat for prix fixe lunch (noon-1, $18) and dinner (6:30-8:30, $36); American Bounty Restaurant open Tues-Sat for à la carte lunch (11:30-1, $9.50-$12.75) and dinner (6:30-8:30, $11-$17); St. Andrew's Cafe open Mon-Fri for lunch (11-1) and dinner (6-8). Reservations and jackets required at Escoffier and American Bounty. All 3 restaurants wheelchair-accessible via elevator at back of building.*

Do you worry about the state of the world? Suffer from indigestion every time you watch the news? Relax. Since 1946 a total of more than 17,000 CIA graduates have filled key positions in the world's fine restaurants, hotels, private clubs, resorts, industrial and research centers, institutional and corporate dining rooms. Strategically placed on the proverbial way to a man's heart, these products of CIA training labor ceaselessly to make the world safe for gastronomy.

The Culinary Institute of America was founded after World War II as a storefront school for 16 returning veterans. Today it has almost as many students as Vassar, all learning the myriad arts of fine cooking and dining, and all eager to practice on you. It's a fair enough exchange: without hocking the family jewels, you can dine sumptuously at the Escoffier, a 3-star restaurant offering *haute cuisine;* savor an array of regional specialties at the American Bounty Restaurant; or partake guiltlessly of gourmet health food at St. Andrew's Café. The meals—about 4,000 of them a day—are prepared by the students under the watchful eyes of 90 chefs and instructors from 18 different countries. Tours of the facilities are reserved for prospective students or groups by advance arrangement, but visitors are welcome to browse in the well-stocked bookstore, which also sells a line of kitchen accessories not readily available elsewhere.

The CIA's weekly shopping list includes 1,500 pounds of sugar, 1,500 pounds of flour, 2,200 dozen eggs, 400 pounds of bananas, 100 pounds of garlic, 2,000 pounds of butter, and no guns.

FOR THE DRIVER: Take SMRP north to Hawthorne Interchange (25¢) and pick up TSP north to Salt Point Tpk exit above Poughkeepsie. Go west on this across NY 9G to US 9, turn left, and go south about 2 mi to FDR home. Library is here also; take shuttlebus to Val-Kill or ask for map when bus is not running.

From FDR home turn left on 9 and go north briefly to Vanderbilt Mansion, entrance on left.

From mansion, turn right on 9 and go about 2 mi south of FDR home to Culinary Institute of America.

Rhinebeck from Below—and Above

TRIP D-12

MILLS-NORRIE STATE PARK, Staatsburg

MILLS MANSION STATE HISTORIC SITE

OLD RHINEBECK AERODROME, Rhinebeck

DISTANCE: From GWB to Rhinebeck, about 95 mi. Mainly fast speeds.

Mills-Norrie State Park, Staatsburg, NY 12580 (914-889-4646). *Open all year daily, daylight hours. No entry fee. Picnicking and grills, playground, hiking trails, fishing, marina (914-889-4200), camping and cabins (late May to late Oct; fees), snowmobiling, sledding, cross-country trails and rentals, refreshment stand. Leashed pets only, no pets in picnic areas or campsites. Picnic area and restrooms wheelchair-accessible.*

This attractive park on the Hudson offers fine facilities for a day's outing. There are really two parks here, one the Mills historic site (see below), and the other the Norrie recreation area. On the grounds of the Norrie section is Norrie Point Inn, formerly a popular spot for waterfront dining and dancing, now an environmental education center run by Dutchess County Community College.

Mills Mansion State Historic Site (914-889-4100). *Grounds open all year daily 6am-10pm. Mansion open Memorial Day to Labor Day Wed-Sat 10-5, Sun 1-5; guided tours, last tour begins 4:30. Free. Picnicking, golf course (fees). No pets. Will accommodate wheelchairs; call in advance.*

The Mills Mansion was originally a Greek Revival structure built in 1832 by Morgan Lewis, Revolutionary War officer and governor of New York from 1804 to 1807. It was later the home of Ogden and Ruth Livingston Mills, who hired the noted architectural firm McKim, Mead and White to enlarge and remodel it in the Neoclassical style. Mills was a prominent financier, his wife was a member of an established New York political family, and their son served as secretary of the treasury under Herbert Hoover. The mansion reflects the lifestyle of America's wealthy and powerful over several generations. The gorgeous marble fireplaces, rich wood paneling, and gilded plasterwork make an appropriate setting for Flemish tapestries, fine artwork, and ornate furnishings in the Louis XV and Louis XVI styles. The grounds are beautifully landscaped and afford a sweeping panorama of the Hudson.

Old Rhinebeck Aerodrome, Rhinebeck, NY 12572 (914-758-8610). *Open mid-May thru Oct daily 10-5. Air show Sat-Sun 2:30; preshow activities begin at 2. Mon-Fri $1.50 adults, $1 children 6-10; Sat-Sun show $6 adults, $3 children 6-10; under 6 free. Free parking, picnic facilities. Show and displays wheelchair accessible.*

This one-of-a-kind "museum in the sky" is a showcase for Cole Palen's collection of vintage aircraft dating from 1900 to 1937. Palen sank everything he had into acquiring and maintaining these rare specimens, which take to the air every weekend for a thrilling 1½-hour show. The daring young men in their flying machines, sporting aviator garb out of World War I, are aided in takeoffs and landings by a ground crew that apparently knows exactly how to handle planes without brakes or automatic starters, on runways of dirt that slope just enough to give the necessary boost. Before and after the show, we can take a barnstorming ride in a 1929 open cockpit biplane piloted by a dead ringer for Eddie Rickenbacker. The planes, some of which have starred in movie and TV productions, are on display for our inspection every day during the season.

FOR THE DRIVER: Take SMRP north to Hawthorne Interchange (25¢) and pick up TSP north to Salt Point Tpk exit above Poughkeepsie. Go west on this across NY 9G to US 9, turn right, and go north past Vanderbilt Mansion (Trip D-11) about 4 mi to Mills-Norrie State Park, entrance on left. This puts you in Norrie section of park; Mills Mansion is about 1 mi north off US 9.

Continue north on 9 a few mi to Rhinebeck. At jct of 9 and NY 308 is the BEEKMAN ARMS INN (914-876-7077), built in 1700 and said to be the oldest continuously operating hotel in the country. Its Tap Room is an attractive and popular spot for drinks and dining. Rhinebeck is a picturesque old town, and you may want to spend some time here shopping, sightseeing, or attending one of the events at the DUTCHESS COUNTY FAIRGROUNDS, which hosts an antiques show and a well-known juried crafts show in addition to the annual fair. For FURTHER INFORMATION, contact the Rhinebeck Chamber of Commerce, PO Box 42, Rhinebeck, NY 12572 (914-876-4778).

From Beekman Arms, continue north on US 9 past jct with 9G a short way to Stone Church Rd, opposite church. Turn right here and follow signs to Old Rhinebeck Aerodrome.

For a different route home, continue north briefly on US 9 to jct with NY 199 in Red Hook, another quaint town full of antique shops, surrounded by farms where you can pick your own fresh produce in season. As perhaps you've noticed, in the Hudson River Valley there are many mansions, and another of these, MONTGOMERY PLACE, is a few mi west of Red Hook via 199. This lavish 19th-century estate will be offering tours sometime in 1987; watch for the opening. Meanwhile, to return to New York City, turn right on 199 and go east 5 or 6 mi to jct with TSP south.

Up the Hudson to Hudson

TRIP D-13

CLERMONT STATE HISTORIC PARK, Germantown

OLANA STATE HISTORIC SITE, Hudson

AMERICAN MUSEUM OF FIRE FIGHTING, Hudson

DISTANCE: From GWB to Hudson, about 120 mi. Mainly fast speeds.

Clermont State Historic Park, RR 1, Box 215, Germantown, NY 12526 (518-537-4240). *Grounds open all year daily 8am to ½ hr after dusk. Mansion open Memorial Day to last Sun in Oct Wed-Sat 10-5, Sun 1-5, including holidays; guided tours, last tour begins 4:20. Picnicking, hiking, cross-country skiing. Annual July 4th festivities, pumpkin festival, and Christmas program; concerts, craft demonstrations, antiques seminars, and other special events. Leashed pets only, no pets in picnic area. Grounds and mansion fully wheelchair-accessible.*

Here is the ancestral estate of Robert R. Livingston, a member of the Continental Congress, one of the five framers of the Declaration of Independence, and a man with a finger in many another historic pie. As first chancellor of New York State, he administered the presidential oath of office to the Father of Our Country, George Washington, and as minister to France under Thomas Jefferson, he negotiated the Louisiana Purchase. In 1802 he agreed to finance Robert Fulton in the experiments that led to the first commercially practical steamboat. Fulton named the boat *Clermont* in Livingston's honor, and it stopped at the estate on its maiden voyage up the Hudson in 1807.

Originally built in 1730, the house was burned by the British in 1777 in reprisal for Livingston's staunch advocacy of American independence, and rebuilt largely through the determined efforts of Livingston's wife, Margaret Beekman Livingston. Clermont remained in the hands of the Livingston family until 1962, when the state of New York acquired it, restored it to its appearance in 1930, and opened it as a public park and memorial to one of its first families. Today we can tour the house, stroll through the lovely restored gardens, and picnic on the grounds, enjoying a glorious view across the Hudson to the Catskills rising in the west.

Olana State Historic Site, Hudson, NY 12534 (518-828-0135). *Grounds open all year daily 8:30-sunset; free. House open Memorial Day thru Oct: Memorial Day to Labor Day Wed-Sat 10-4, Sun 1-4; fall hours vary (call in advance). Admission to house by guided tour only, adults $1, children 50¢; tours begin every 20 min, maximum 12 persons per tour; advance reservations strongly recommended. Picnicking, carriage trails, ice skating, cross-*

country skiing. Annual Victorian Christmas; concerts and special
events throughout season. Leashed pets only on grounds, no
photographing in house. Shale drives make grounds difficult for
wheelchairs, but house tour is wheelchair-accessible.

"As the good woman said of her mock-turtle soup, 'I made it
out of my own head.' " Thus, with what can only be called magnificent understatement, did Frederick Edwin Church describe his
31 years of work on Olana, the striking castle he designed and
built on an Italian layout with strong Persian decorative elements.
Church was a noted painter of the Hudson River School and stud-
ied with its founder, Thomas Cole, who first introduced him to
the site where Olana now stands. Like the other members of the
school, Church painted native American landscapes and Hudson
River scenes, but he had a preference for foreign and exotic subjects—a preference aptly reflected in Olana, in contrast to the
homey, plain, and very American-looking residence of Thomas
Cole across the river in Catskill (Rip Van Winkle Trail, Trip C-
20).

The main portion of Olana was built between 1870 and 1876,
with some additions in the 1880s. As Church constantly reworked
his paintings, so he constantly fashioned and refashioned Olana,
proclaiming it "finished" only in 1891, when he turned it over to
his son. The interior, meticulously restored just as Church planned
it, is a marvel of intricately patterned tiles, gilded arches, vibrant
colors, exquisite furnishings from Persia, Kashmir, and other Near
Eastern lands. Church's work—some of which adorns Olana's
walls, along with two paintings by Thomas Cole—is noted for its
delicate rendering of light, and this same sensitivity is displayed
in the design and placement of the windows, each framing a scenic view, each capturing a different quality of light.

Church lavished equal attention on his 250 acres of property,
which was farmland when he purchased it in the 1860s. Today it
is a beautiful woodland, each of the thousands of trees selected
by Church and planted with a painterly eye for composition. He
even created the beautifully contoured lake at the foot of the hill
to "balance" the view of the Hudson against the Catskills. Indeed, driving through Olana's grounds is like driving through one
of Church's paintings—a romantic landscape conceived in the
artist's mind's eye and executed with utmost care on the canvas
of the Hudson River Valley.

American Museum of Fire Fighting, Harry Howard Ave., Hudson, NY 12534 (518-828-7695). *Open Apr thru Oct Tues-Sun 9-4:30. Free. Ramps into building.*

This museum, operated by the Firemen's Association of the State of New York, contains one of the oldest and largest collections of firefighting equipment and memorabilia in the country. There are thousands of items here, from firehats, badges, banners, and speaking trumpets to paintings, prints, and lithographs. And, of course, the engines, scores of them, stalwart antiques spanning two centuries of firefighting, from the horse-drawn days through the steam era to the early motorized trucks of the 1920s. The oldest specimen is the Newsham engine, built in England in 1725, imported to New York in 1731, and in continuous service for the next 154 years. Fittingly, the museum is located in the Firemen's Home, close to some of the men who used the equipment to battle the flames of yesteryear.

FOR THE DRIVER: Take SMRP north to Hawthorne Interchange (25¢) and pick up TSP north towards Albany. At jct with NY 199 turn left and proceed west past jct with US 9 in Red Hook to jct with NY 9G. Turn right and go north on 9G. Just over Columbia County line (see Trip D-14), turn left on Rte 6 and follow signs to Clermont, entrance on right.

Continue north on 9G about 15 mi. As Rip Van Winkle Bridge comes into view, watch for road to Olana, on right about 1 mi before bridge.

Return to 9G, turn right, and go north briefly to jct with NY 23. Bear left and continue north to Hudson on what is now 9G/23B (Columbia St). Soon you pick up signs to Firemen's Home. Follow these, continuing 1 block beyond the point where 9G/23B turns right. The next corner is State St. Turn right past library, then bear left on Carroll to next corner, Short St. Turn left (this is now Harry Howard Ave) and proceed to top of hill and Firemen's Home, on left. Drive to parking lot at right of buildings. American Museum of Fire Fighting is in last building on left.

For return trip, go back to 9G/23B and follow 23B east towards Claverack. This joins NY 23, which continues east to TSP south.

Bound for the Berkshires

TRIP D-14

UPPER COLUMBIA COUNTY

DISTANCE: From GWB to farthest point, about 145 mi. Fast and average speeds.

Upper Columbia County. On our last trip we crossed from Dutchess County into Columbia County, a lovely area between the Catskills and the Berkshires. It's a bit far for a day trip from New York City, but we'll have time to take a spin through the countryside north of Hudson and then east to the Massachusetts line, noting some of the points of interest along the way. For FURTHER INFORMATION, contact the Columbia County Chamber of Commerce, 729 Columbia St., Hudson, NY 12534 (518-828-4417); for more on the many scenic, cultural, and recreational attractions of the popular Berkshires region, which is mainly in Massachusetts but includes parts of eastern Columbia County, contact the Berkshire Hills Conference/Visitors Bureau, Berkshire Common, Pittsfield, MA 01201 (413-443-9186 or 800-BERKSHR).

Our first stop will be Kinderhook, birthplace of Martin Van Buren, the eighth president of the United States, and the first president to be born an American citizen. We can easily reach Kinderhook by continuing north on US 9 from Hudson, last stop on Trip D-13 (note also that the Rip Van Winkle Bridge runs from Hudson across the river to Catskill and some of the sites on Trip C-20). If we're coming directly from the city, we'll take SMRP north to Hawthorne Interchange (25¢) and pick up TSP north to NY 23, about 6 miles past the exit for LAKE TAGHKANIC STATE PARK (518-851-3631), with year-round fishing and facilities for a wide range of winter and summer sports. We'll turn left on 23 and go west to Hudson, where we'll pick up US 9 north about 11 miles to Kinderhook. On our left as we come into town is the JAMES VANDERPOEL HOUSE OF HISTORY (518-758-9265), an 1819 building in the Federal style, maintained by the Columbia County Historical Society as a museum. In addition to a fine collection of Duncan Phyfe and Chippendale furniture, the museum has materials on local history and documents relating to Martin Van Buren. It's a good place to get directions for a walking tour of Kinderhook, a town frequented by Washington Irving, his fictional creation Ichabod Crane, and the pre-treasonous Benedict Arnold, among others. The Columbia County Historical Society also operates the LUYKAS VAN ALEN HOUSE (518-758-9265), a little south of town on NY 9H. Built in 1737, it has been restored as a museum of 18th-century Dutch culture and Hudson Valley art.

By the way, anyone with a particular interest in the Dutch influence on the development of the Hudson Valley will also enjoy the BRONCK HOUSE MUSEUM (518-731-8386), almost directly across the river from Kinderhook, about 10 miles north of Catskill (Trip C-20) off US 9W, accessible via the Rip Van Winkle Bridge. This complex of stone houses and farm buildings was begun in 1663 by Pieter Bronck, whose father, a Dane in the employ of the Dutch West India Company, settled in and gave the family name to the Bronx. The buildings, all carefully researched and restored by the Green County Historical Society, include two vintage Hudson Valley Dutch stone houses; several Dutch barns, among them the unique 13-sided Freedom Barn, with one wall for each of the 13 original states; and a "stepmother's house," built in the 1820s in deference to the sensibilities of the Bronck daughters, who refused to live under the same roof with their father's second wife. There are many interesting artifacts and period tools on display here, as well as a fine collection of paintings by such noted American artists as Thomas Cole, Ammi Phillips, Ezra Ames, and John Frederick Rensett.

Back on the east side of the Hudson, a little south of the Van Alen House on NY 9H, is the MARTIN VAN BUREN NATIONAL HISTORIC SITE (518-758-9689). Van Buren bought this 1797 estate, known as Lindenwald, in 1839 during his term as president. The house is currently under restoration, but a portion of it is open for tours, and the gardens are lovely.

From Lindenwald, we'll go back on 9H past junction with 9 to Route 28B. Here we turn right and go east through Valatie and Chatham Center, continuing on what is now Route 13. A mile or so past Chatham Center, on our left just below the Berkshire spur of the New York Thruway, is the SHAKER MUSEUM (518-794-9100) at Old Chatham. Here, spread throughout eight buildings, is an extensive collection of artifacts, crafts, tools, documents, and books relating to the American settlements of the United Society of Believers in Christ's Second Appearing, popularly known as Shakers because of the trembling ecstatic displays that accompanied their religious worship. An offshoot of the English Quakers, the Shakers believed that the Deity was both male and female, and that their leader, Mother Ann Lee (1736-1784), was the incarnation of the female divine principle, as Jesus had been the incarnation of the male. Persecuted in England, Mother Ann and eight followers emigrated to America in 1774 and settled at Watervliet, New York, near Albany. By 1850, when the movement reached its height, there were some 6,000 Shakers living in 18 communities, mostly in the Northeast. They practiced equality of the sexes, open confession of sins, communal ownership of property, pacifism, and celibacy, perpetuating themselves by conversion and the adoption of orphans. They were also an ingenious people, noted for their many practical inventions and the beautiful simplicity of their furniture designs. Today, though the Shaker movement has all but died out, the culture, craftsmanship, and ideals of these gentle people continue to fascinate.

The Shaker Museum provides an excellent introduction to Shaker history. Now we'll deepen our acquaintance by driving northeast from Old Chatham on Route 13 past the New York Thruway a few miles to junction with US 20 at Brainard. Here we'll turn right and go east through New Lebanon, site of the first permanent Shaker community (1787), continuing across the Massachusetts line to the HANCOCK SHAKER VILLAGE (413-443-0188), at junction of US 20 and MA 41. This settlement, established in 1790, remained an active Shaker community until 1960 and was known to its inhabitants as the City of Peace. Today we can tour 20 original buildings and watch craftspeople preserving the Shaker traditions of fine workmanship. The village also sponsors a busy program of special events, and some of the crafts and furniture are for sale in the restored 1910 horse barn.

Our drive to the Hancock Shaker Village takes us along the southern edge of PITTSFIELD STATE FOREST (413-442-8992), a 10,000-acre tract that has camping and recreational facilities and is especially beautiful during azalea time, usually late May to mid-June. At the village, we are only 5 miles west of Pittsfield, with its many museums, ski areas, and historic buildings, including ARROWHEAD (413-442-1793), the house where Herman Melville lived while writing *Moby Dick*. About 7 miles south of Pittsfield is TANGLEWOOD (413-637-1940), former home of Nathaniel Hawthorne, present home of the famed Berkshire Music Festival, held annually in summer.

These are only a few of the countless attractions of the Berkshire region of Massachusetts. We can't begin to explore them all in the space of a day, but now we'll have our bearings when we come back with more time at our disposal.

From Pittsfield, our quickest route home is to go south on US 7 and then US 20 to Lee and pick up I-90, Massachusetts Turnpike west (35¢) following signs for Albany. This becomes NYT (25¢), which takes us to TSP south and back to New York City.

Into Middle and Upper Connecticut

• *Our next trips take us across the New York line into Connecticut, mainly the middle and upper regions of the western part of the state. Most of these trips are full-day extensions covering territory beyond an average short drive from New York City. However, fast roads allow us to reach a wide variety of attractions easily.*

We begin on the New York side of the line and move into Connecticut. For hundreds of unspoiled colonial towns filled with pre-Revolutionary homes, for entire areas that have been designated historic districts, for the quietly beautiful New England countryside, these drives are unexcelled.

Exit Point
I-684

Main Roads
I-684, I-84

Connections
To reach I-684, take
—Saw Mill River Pkwy (SMRP), New York Thruway (NYT), Sprain Brook Pkwy, or Bronx River Pkwy to jct with Cross Westchester Expwy (I-287), then take this east to jct with I-684;
—Hutchinson River Pkwy (HRP) north across I-287 to jct with I-684;
—I-95 (becoming New England Thruway) to Cross Westchester Expwy west to jct with I-684.
To reach I-84, take
—I-684 north to Brewster.
For alternate routes to destinations in Area E, use
—HRP (becoming Merritt Pkwy/Wilbur Cross Pkwy in Connecticut) or I-95 (becoming New England Thruway becoming Connecticut Tpk) and then take connecting roads north from these to I-84 or to destination.

Tolls
There are no tolls on I-684 and I-84. If you use NYT, SMRP, HRP, or New England Thruway to get to Area E, see toll information for Area C, p. 120. If you use Merritt/Wilbur Cross in Connecticut, see toll information for Area F, p. 159. For New York City bridge and tunnel tolls, see p. xvi; remember to add these to highway tolls as appropriate, depending on your route.

219

Local Heroes

TRIP E-1

SOUTHEAST MUSEUM, Brewster, New York

SQUANTZ POND STATE PARK, New Fairfield, Connecticut

DISTANCE: From GWB to Squantz Pond, about 75 mi. Fast and average speeds.

Southeast Museum, Main St., Brewster, NY 10509 (914-279-7500). *Open late Mar to late Dec Tues-Wed 12-4, Sat-Sun 2-4. Free. Annual Craft Emporium in Oct, special events throughout season.*

This fine regional history museum was founded in 1963 when the tiny town of Southeast was observing its tricentennial. Preparing for the celebration, the townsfolk began rifling through their cellars and basements in quest of historic artifacts and were so impressed with the results that they decided to open a museum in the Old Town Hall of Southeast (1896).

There are four permanent exhibits on display here: the David McLane railroad exhibit, on the history of the Harlem line, which ran between New York City and Brewster; an exhibit on condensed milk, invented in 1863 by Gail Borden, who opened a factory that operated here for 50 years; a collection of circus memorabilia from the days when the Brewster area was home base for various local traveling menageries (see Historic Elephant Hotel and Circus Museum, Trip D-7); and the Trainer collection of rare minerals from the Tilly Foster iron mine, active through most of the 19th century, until it collapsed in 1897. In addition, the museum mounts three major exhibits a year on changing themes, drawing on its extensive collection of antique farm implements, old quilts, period clothing, and assorted Americana reflecting 19th-century material culture.

Squantz Pond State Park, New Fairfield, CT 06810 (203-795-4165). *Open all year daily 8-sunset. Use fee Memorial Day to Labor Day $2 per car weekdays, $4 weekends and holidays; otherwise free. Picnicking, hiking trails, swimming, scuba diving, fishing, canoe* *rentals, ice skating, food concession. No pets. Wheelchair-accessible phones and toilets.*

Here's a scenic 172-acre park in a picturesque region of rural Connecticut. It's a fine place for picnicking or nature photography after an afternoon of absorbing the multifarious facts of local history. The drive to Squantz Pond, partially along the shores of CANDLEWOOD LAKE (203-775-6256), is especially pretty. Connecticut's largest lake, Candlewood is 14 miles long with more than 60 miles of shoreline and offers further opportunities for swimming, fishing, boating, and picnicking.

FOR THE DRIVER: Take I-684 north to Brewster. Just after exit for I-84 to Danbury, take Brewster exit for US 6 west and US 202/NY 22 south. After they branch, remain on 6 (Main St) briefly into block-and-a-half-long downtown Brewster, where it's hard to miss the Southeast Museum.

Go back as you came to jct of 6, 202, and 22. Bear left and go north on 22 briefly to Rte 54, Milltown Rd. Turn right and follow this across the New York State line to jct with CT 39, Bull Pond Rd. Turn left and proceed north and east on 39 about 8 mi to Squantz Pond State Park.

To the Connecticut Berkshires

TRIP E-2

MUSEUM OF NATURAL HISTORY, Pawling, New York
WEBATUCK CRAFT VILLAGE, Wingdale
MACEDONIA BROOK STATE PARK, Kent, Connecticut
SLOANE-STANLEY MUSEUM, Kent
KENT FALLS STATE PARK, Kent
NORTHEAST AUDUBON SOCIETY CENTER, Sharon
HOUSATONIC MEADOWS STATE PARK, Sharon
LAKE WARAMAUG STATE PARK, Kent

DISTANCE: From GWB to farthest point, Sharon, about 110 mi. Fast and average speeds.

On this trip we take a long ride all the way to the northwest corner of Connecticut, singling out some of the highlights along our route. If we're just out for a scenic drive, we can cover the distance in a day, but if we're interested in spending some time at the various stops, we'll want to divide this into two or more trips, and perhaps include some of the attractions and side trips mentioned in "For the Driver." For FURTHER INFORMATION about western Connecticut, contact the Litchfield Hills Travel Council, PO Box 1776, Marbledale, CT 06777 (203-868-2214). They'll be happy to send you a variety of thorough, informative, lively brochures and a complete calendar of events for this very eventful region.

Museum of Natural History, Akin Free Library, Quaker Hill, Pawling, NY 12564 (914-855-5099). *Museum open mid-May to mid-Oct Thurs-Sun 2-4; adults 50¢, children 15¢. Library open all year, mid-May to mid-Oct Thurs-Sun 2-4, other times Sat-Sun 2-4. Museum exhibits wheelchair-accessible.*

Mrs. Olive Gunnison, longtime resident of Quaker Hill, spent the better part of a lifetime acquiring specimens of rocks, minerals, insects, and birds from all over the world. This museum houses her personal collection, informatively displayed in four large rooms. There is also a room devoted to the history of Quaker Hill, which takes its name from the band of Quakers who settled here in the early 1700s. Today their meetinghouse still stands, surrounded by picturesque countryside and beautiful estates that have attracted many famous residents over the years, including Lowell Thomas, Edward R. Murrow, and Thomas E. Dewey. The Akin Free Library has extensive materials on local history and genealogy and is currently preparing a Dewey Memorial Room.

Webatuck Craft Village, Hunt Country Furniture, PO Box 500, Wingdale, NY 12594 (914-832-6464). *Open Mar-Dec Wed-Sat 10-4:30, Sun 12-4:30. No admission fee. Picnicking, fishing, special exhibits. Many steps, uneven paths; difficult for wheelchairs.*

Here's a good place for an afternoon of shopping in a relaxed, scenic setting. Spread over the grounds of Hunt Country Furniture, the Webatuck Craft Village has a silversmith, a potter, a stained-glass artisan, and several other shops, including the Flower Loft, the Webatuck Trading Company, featuring crafts and gift items from all over the country, and Folkcraft Instruments, selling beautiful handmade harps, dulcimers, and psalteries. The Hunt Country Furniture showroom, a converted 1747 inn with the original flooring and chestnut beams, displays a variety of handcrafted pine, oak, and cherry furniture in handsome original designs. The Webatuck craftspeople do not do demonstrations as such, but we're welcome to watch them at work, and there are occasional guest craftspeople and shows throughout the year. We're also invited to picnic along the banks of Ten Mile River or try our luck with rod and reel in its trout-stocked waters.

Macedonia Brook State Park, Kent, CT 06757 (203-927-3238). *Open all year daily 8-sunset. Free. Picnicking, hiking trails, playing field, fishing, camping (fees), cross-country skiing. Leashed pets only, in picnic areas only. Wheelchair-accessible picnic shelter, campsites, playing field, and phones.*

A gift to the state from the White Memorial Foundation in Litchfield (Trip E-5), these 2,300 acres contain excellent trout streams, bubbling natural springs, and two peaks affording superb views of the Catskills and the Taconic Mountains from an elevation of about 1,400 feet.

Sloane-Stanley Museum, Kent, CT 06757 (203-927-3849 or 566-3005). *Open May thru Oct Wed-Sun 10-4:30. Adults $1.75, senior citizens 75¢, children 50¢. Partially manageable for wheelchairs.*

This extensive collection of early American farm implements, tools, and paintings, housed in a New England barn, was brought together by Eric Sloane, author and artist, on land donated by the Stanley tool manufacturing company of New Britain. Captions accompany the tools, which are displayed in such a way as to demonstrate how they were used. In the early 18th century, Kent was a center of the iron ore industry, and the ruins of the old Kent blast furnace (1826-1892) are here on the museum grounds, along with an early New England log cabin replica built by Eric Sloane.

Kent Falls State Park, Kent, CT 06757 (203-927-3238). *Open all year daily 8-sunset. Free. Picnicking, hiking trails, playing field, fishing. Leashed pets only, in picnic areas only. Picnic area, playing field, and phones wheelchair-accessible.*

Here Connecticut's loveliest waterfall cascades down several levels to a brook. A wide, winding path leads to the head of the falls, which are particularly beautiful in spring when the water is high and in fall when the leaves turn. All around are pine forests with inviting trails for hiking.

Northeast Audubon Center, Rte. 4, Sharon, CT 06069 (203-364-0520). *Trails open all year daily dawn-dusk. Building open all year daily, Mon-Sat 9-5, Sun 1-5; closed major holidays. Museum admission $1 adults, 50¢ children, free to Audubon Society members. Self-guided tour, picnic tables, gift shop, bookstore. No pets. Building not wheelchair-accessible; easy trail for young and elderly may be manageable for some wheelchairs.*

This 684-acre sanctuary of the National Audubon Society is a good place for birdwatching, observation of the spring and fall migrations, or quiet walks through meadows and forests dotted with lakes, ponds, and brooks. The museum and interpretive center has both live and static natural history exhibits, a Children's Discovery Room, and the Hal Borland Seasonal Room.

Housatonic Meadows State Park, Sharon, CT 06069 (203-672-6139). *Open all year daily 8-sunset. Picnicking, hiking trails, fishing, boating, camping (fees), cross-country skiing. Free. Leashed pets only, in picnic areas only. Wheelchair-accessible picnic area, campsites, phones, and toilets.*

This 452-acre park along the rushing Housatonic River is noted for a 2-mile stretch of water reserved for fly fishing. Non-anglers will enjoy the beautiful woodlands and fine hiking trails.

Lake Waramaug State Park, Kent, CT 06757 (203-868-0223). *Open all year daily 8-sunset. Use fee Memorial Day to Labor Day $1 per car weekdays, $2 weekends and holidays; otherwise free. Picnicking, hiking trails, playing field, swimming, scuba diving, fishing, camping (fees), ice skating, cross-country skiing, food concession. Leashed pets only, in picnic areas only. Wheelchair-accessible picnic shelter, playing field, campsites, and toilets.*

Waramaug, an Indian word meaning "good fishing place," is an apt name for Connecticut's third-largest natural lake, and one of its most beautiful. The 95-acre park located on its northwest shore hosts the annual Women's National Rowing Regatta in May.

FOR THE DRIVER: Take I-684 north to Brewster. Here pick up NY 22 and continue north about 11 mi towards Pawling. At jct with NY 55, continue north on 22/55 merged, shortly coming to Quaker Hill Rd. Turn right here at stoplight and sign for Museum of Natural History, Akin Free Library.

Return to 22/55, turn right, and continue north 5-6 mi. At Wingdale, just beyond Harlem Valley State Hospital, 55 goes on ahead and 22 forks left. Here you have several choices. If it's blueberry season (usually mid-July into August, depending on the weather), you can follow 22 to the blinking light, turn left at sign to Wingdale, and drive about 4 mi up a winding road to BLUEBERRY PARK (914-782-8664), where you can pluck to your heart's content. You pay by the amount you pick—a lot less than at city markets, and freshness is guaranteed. Best to bring your own containers and wear comfortable shoes. If you continue north on 22 through the blinking light about 15 mi, you can have a different kind of experience with the fruits of the vine at CASCADE MOUNTAIN VINEYARDS (914-373-9021) on Flint Hill Rd in Amenia, New York. The drive up to this 100-acre winery is lovely, and when you get there you can take a free tour, taste some of the prize-winning wines, and savor other local delicacies, including a fine Columbia County camembert. Note that Amenia is only a few mi from Sharon, Connecticut; if you go to the vineyards, you can drive over to Sharon and continue this trip from there (see directions below).

From jct of 22 and 55 at Wingdale, proceed east on 55 towards Connecticut, following signs to Webatuck Craft Village and Hunt Country Furniture.

Continue east on 55 across Connecticut line to jct with US 7 in the quaint village of Gaylordsville. For the next stops on this trip, you turn left here and go north on 7, but you may also want to drive south about 7 mi to New Milford, passing VOLTAIRE'S (203-354-4200), with an exceptional selection of craft items for sale and changing fine arts exhibits in the gallery; at jct with US 202, turn left and go east briefly to New Milford Green, surrounded by antique shops, restaurants, boutiques, and historic buildings, including the NEW MILFORD HISTORICAL SOCIETY MUSEUM (203-354-3069), with fine collections of portraits, miniatures, furniture, china, antique clothing, dolls, and toys.

From jct of 55 and 7 in Gaylordsville, go north on 7 towards Kent, passing Bull's Bridge Rd, where a left turn will take you across the Housatonic on BULL'S BRIDGE, one of two covered bridges in Connecticut still open to automobile traffic (you'll come to the other one soon). Over 200 years old, it's a favorite subject for photographers. Near here on US 7 is the BULL'S BRIDGE GLASS WORKS AND GALLERY (203-927-3448), featuring vases, lamps, paperweights, bottles, and glass-blowing demonstrations.

Continue north on 7 about 4 mi to jct with CT 341 in Kent. Here turn left and proceed briefly to Macedonia Brook State Park, entrance on right. Return to 7 and Kent Center, where there are a number of fine shops and galleries, including the PARIS-NEW YORK-KENT GALLERY (203-927-3357), praised by the *New York Times* as a "top-quality private art gallery," and the HOUSE OF BOOKS (203-927-4104), specializing in books by local authors and limited-edition prints by Eric Sloane and David Armstrong. The Sloane-Stanley Museum is about 2 mi north of Kent Center on US 7, and another 3-4 mi north of that, on right, is Kent Falls State Park.

From Kent Falls, continue north on 7 several mi to Cornwall Bridge and jct with CT 4, passing CORNWALL BRIDGE POTTERY (203-672-6545), where you can watch pots fired in a 35-foot-long wood-burning kiln and inspect the many beautiful items in the showroom. At jct with 4, you again have several choices. A left turn onto 4 west takes you to the Northeast Audubon Center in Sharon, another quintessential New England village with many lovely 19th-century homes and the inevitable green and Congregational church. A little further on 4, past the distinctive HOTCHKISS CLOCK TOWER, is jct with CT 343, where you can turn left and go west briefly to the SHARON PLAYHOUSE (203-364-5909), a professional summer theater and art gallery. Note that in Sharon you are about 10 mi south of Salisbury via CT 41/US 44. Here is yet another lovely old town, in a particularly scenic area, and if you're taking this drive in the fall, you may catch the famed SALISBURY ANTIQUES FAIR (203-824-0306), one of the oldest such fairs in Connecticut, now in its 30th year.

If you've gone to Sharon, return on CT 4 to Cornwall Bridge and jct with US 7. Turn left and go north on 7 into Housatonic Meadows State Park. A little beyond the north end of the park is the postcard-pretty village of West Cornwall, where you'll find the second COVERED BRIDGE over the Housatonic. This one, designed by covered-bridge maven Ithiel Town (see Bucks County Covered Bridges Tour, Trip A-14), has been in continuous use since 1837. Also here, in the center of West Cornwall, is the CORNWALL BRIDGE POTTERY STORE (203-672-6545), an outlet for the work done at Cornwall Bridge Pottery (see above) as well as for fine ceramics, glassware, fabrics, and paintings by other craftspeople and artists. For art of a more specialized sort, check out the AUTO ART GALLERY (203-672-6055) on Dibble Hill Rd, which claims the largest collection of contemporary automotive artwork in the world—paintings, prints, posters, sculptures (perhaps auto mobiles?), and other unique aesthetic expressions of America's love affair with the car. About 1 mi south of the covered bridge is CLARKE OUTDOORS (203-248-8924), where you can rent everything you need for kayaking or canoeing on the Housatonic.

From West Cornwall, go back down 7 through Cornwall Bridge and continue south briefly to jct with CT 45. Turn left and go south on 45 through Warren to Lake Waramaug Rd, just before New Preston. Turn right here to Lake Waramaug State Park.

For the quickest route back to New York City, continue south briefly on 45 to jct with US 202, then south on US 202 through New Milford, where 202 merges with US 7, to Danbury. Here take I-84 west into New York and pick up I-684 south.

On General Putnam's Trail

TRIP E-3

PUTNAM MEMORIAL STATE PARK, Redding
DANBURY SCOTT-FANTON MUSEUM AND
HISTORICAL SOCIETY, Danbury

DISTANCE: From GWB to Danbury, about 65 mi. Mainly fast speeds.

Putnam Memorial State Park, Redding, CT 06875 (203-938-2285). *Grounds open all year daily 8-sunset; museum open mid-May to mid-Sept daily 8-4, mid-Sept to mid-Oct Sat-Sun 8-4. Free. Picnicking, playing field, hiking and nature trails, fishing, ice skating. Leashed pets only, in picnic area only. Museum and picnic area wheelchair-accessible.*

In the winter of 1778-79, several thousand Continental troops under the command of General Israel Putnam wintered near Danbury on this site, which is now preserved as a Revolutionary War memorial. Some of the foundations and chimneys of the original soldier cabins are still visible, and the museum houses other relics of the encampment. An oak tree that sprouted from an acorn of the famous Charter Oak of Hartford (see Trip E-9) flourishes in the park, and there's a scenic picnic and play area around a small lake.

Danbury Scott-Fanton Museum and Historical Society, 43 Main St., Danbury, CT 06810 (203-743-5200). *Open all year Wed-Sun 2-5; closed major holidays. Donations accepted. Historic buildings not wheelchair-accessible; Huntington Hall has a few steps, but exhibits are all on l level.*

An important supply depot for the Continental Army during the American Revolution, Danbury was looted and burned by British and Hessian forces in 1777. In the early 1970s, history sleuths were surprised to find evidence that the Scott-Fanton House, presumed to have been spared the torch because of Tory ownership, was actually built around 1785 by John Rider, a carpenter and ardent patriot. Restored to its appearance around the time of Rider's death in 1833, the house contains authentic furnishings, a large collection of carpenter's and joiner's tools, and a costume display.

Behind the Scott-Fanton House is the Dodd Shop, with exhibits showing the development of the hat industry in Danbury from the humble three-a-day output of Zadoc Benedict's 1790 factory to the booming mechanized production that made it "Hat Capital of the World" from the early 20th century into the 1950s. Also behind the house is Huntington Hall, a modern building with changing exhibits and a research library.

The Danbury Historical Society also owns the house in Rogers Park where Charles Ives was born in 1874. Ives, considered the father of modern American music, won a Pulitzer Prize for his Third Symphony in 1947. Built around 1780 by a New York silversmith, the house was purchased in 1829 by Ives's great-grandfather and remained in the family until 1960, six years after the composer's death. At present the Ives House is closed to the public, but there are plans in the works to move it to the Scott-Fanton site and open it as a museum. In the meantime we can visit the Ives Parlor in the Scott-Fanton House, which contains one of the composer's pianos and other memorabilia.

FOR THE DRIVER: Take I-684 north to Brewster. Here pick up I-84 east to Danbury. Get off at Exit 5, turn right at stoplight onto Main St, and proceed down Main about 2 mi to Danbury Scott-Fanton Museum, on left just past St. Peter's Church. Note that Danbury is at the southern tip of Candlewood Lake, about 8 mi south of Squantz Pond State Park (Trip E-1), and about the same distance north of Ridgefield (Trip F-5).

Continue on Main St to the end, passing Rogers Park, where the Ives House is located. Turn left here at stoplight onto South St. Proceed a few mi on South St (which becomes CT 53) to jct with CT 302. Bear left and go through Bethel to jct with CT 58. Turn right and go south about 2 mi to Putnam Memorial State Park.

There are a number of other historical and cultural sites in the Danbury-Bethel area, as well as an array of municipal parks, lakes, and golf courses. For FURTHER INFORMATION, contact the Housatonic Valley Tourism Commission, Box 406, Danbury, CT 06810 (203-743-0546).

From Glebe to Crèche to Wigwam

TRIP E-4

GLEBE HOUSE, Woodbury
FLANDERS NATURE CENTER, Woodbury
ABBEY OF REGINA LAUDIS, Bethlehem
GUNN HISTORICAL MUSEUM, Washington
AMERICAN INDIAN ARCHAEOLOGICAL
INSTITUTE, Washington

DISTANCE: From GWB to farthest point, Washington, about 90 mi. Fast and average speeds.

Glebe House, Hollow Rd., Woodbury, CT 06798 (203-263-2855). *Open Apr-Oct Sat-Wed 1-5, Nov Sat-Wed 1-4, Dec thru Mar by appointment. Suggested donation $2 adults, 50¢ children. Will accommodate wheelchairs.*

This picturesque building, some of it dating back to 1690, was part of the glebe (minister's farm) of Woodbury's first Episcopal priest, John Rutgers Marshall, who took up residence here in 1771. Marshall, like many other Anglicans, was a Tory sympathizer who vigorously opposed American independence and wrote pamphlets attacking the ideas of Thomas Paine. It is sometimes said that Marshall built a secret tunnel in Glebe House to escape in case of trouble, but researchers now believe that this "tunnel," really little more than a basement crawl space, predates Marshall's occupancy. In 1783, when the cause of American independence was won, a group of Anglican clergymen met at Glebe House and elected Samuel Seabury first American bishop of the Protestant Episcopal church.

Like many of the homes in Woodbury's historical district, Glebe House was built by a local housemaker called Herd (who lived in the nearby red house on Hollow Rd., now maintained by the Old Woodbury Historical Society). The gambrel roof and other additions to the central room date from the 1730s or 1740s. Today the house has period furnishings, documents relating to the development of the Episcopal church in America, and charming colonial gardens. Costumed guides occasionally give tours and recreate the life of the household during colonial times.

Flanders Nature Center, Flanders Rd., Woodbury, CT 06798 (203-263-3711). *Trails open all year daily dawn-dusk; trailside center open Sun aft; office open Mon-Fri 9-5. Free. No horses on trails, no pets on Church Hill Rd. trail. Difficult for wheelchairs.*

This 1,000-acre wildlife sanctuary and outdoor education laboratory offers a choice of two hiking trails through varied terrain and habitats. The wildflower trail is delightful in spring, and the marsh walk is particularly popular with birdwatchers. There are some good exhibits at the trailside environmental center and small natural history museum.

Abbey of Regina Laudis, Bethlehem, CT 06751 (203-266-7727). *Grounds open all year daily; art shop (203-266-7637) open all year Tues-Sun 11-noon and 1:30-4; crèche on display late Apr to mid-Jan daily 11-4. Donations accepted. Annual Abbey Fair in early Aug. Difficult for wheelchairs.*

The main attraction at this Benedictine abbey in Bethlehem is, appropriately enough, a nativity scene crafted by artists of 18th-century Naples. The Neapolitan crèche is displayed in an antique barn perhaps not so unlike that faraway stable where the Christ child was born. Also here is the Little Art Shop of the Abbey of Regina Laudis, selling religious articles, wool from the abbey sheep, and many items handcrafted by the Benedictine nuns. Visitors are welcome to attend mass or vespers at the chapel.

Gunn Historical Museum, Wykeham Rd., Washington, CT 06793 (203-868-7756). *Open Apr-Dec Tues-Thurs 1-4, Sat 12-3. Free. Difficult for wheelchairs.*

Here's an interesting place, a 1781 house crammed with artifacts reflecting life in Washington in the 18th and 19th centuries— furniture, paintings, toys, dolls and dollhouses, gowns, thimbles, needlework, spinning wheels, homespun, tools, kitchenware, china. In addition to these collections, there are exhibits on the history of Washington since colonial times.

American Indian Archaeological Institute, Curtis Rd., Washington, CT 06793 (203-868-0518). *Open all year daily, Mon-Sat, 10-*

4:30, Sun 1-4:30; closed New Year's, Easter, Thanksgiving, Christmas. Adults $2, children 6-18 $1, under 6 free. Tours by appointment, gift shop, craft workshops, weekend film series. Wheelchair access into building, all exhibits on 1 level.

The American Indian Archaelogical Institute is a serious research and educational facility devoted to the history of America's original inhabitants and the study of early cultures. The exhibits include a mastodon skeleton 12,000 years old, 10,000-year-old Paleo-Indian artifacts from the oldest known Indian campsite in Connecticut, a simulated dig site, and a reconstructed Indian village with wigwams and a longhouse, the distinctive bark-covered structure that symbolized the mutual responsibilities of the Five Nations of the Iroquois Confederacy. There are nature trails on the grounds, and the institute borders STEEP ROCK RESERVATION, a 600-acre preserve with hiking trails and picnic facilities.

FOR THE DRIVER: Take I-684 north to Brewster. Here pick up I-84 east to Danbury. Continue past Danbury to Exit 15 at Southbury and take US 6 east (actually going north at this point) about 4 mi to Woodbury, passing 3 sets of traffic lights. Shortly watch for sign for Woodbury Historic District and Pilgrim's Mall, on left. Just after Pilgrim's Mall parking lot, take an immediate left on Hollow Rd to Glebe House. This section of US 6 (Main St in Woodbury), often referred to as Antique Avenue, is lined with what is possibly the densest concentration of antique shops in Connecticut.

Your route to Glebe House, US 6 between Southbury and Woodbury, is a lovely stretch of road passing many fine old houses. During the Revolutionary War it was a major thoroughfare for the Continental Army, and General Rochambeau marched his troops along it in 1781 to join General Washington for the Yorktown campaign, the closing battle of the war. But there's more here than historic reverberations. Shortly after leaving I-84, just beyond Southbury Plaza, a left turn off US 6 takes you to the HERITAGE VILLAGE BAZAAR, a pleasant shopping area with 25 specialty stores and several restaurants and art galleries. Further along on 6, at jct with CT 64, a right turn takes you to LAKE QUASSAPAUG ("clear water") in Middlebury, open to the public for swimming and boating. On its shores is QUASSY AMUSEMENT PARK (203-758-2913, in CT 800-FOR-PARK), with rides, games, arcade, swimming, and special events.

From Glebe House, continue east on US 6 about 1 mi to Flanders Rd, just outside Woodbury Center. Turn left here and go about 3 mi to Church Hill Rd, a dirt road leading to office of Flanders Nature Center.

Continue on Flanders Rd 1-1½ mi to Abbey of Regina Laudis.

From abbey, continue on Flanders Rd about 1½ mi to CT 61, turn left on 61, and continue north through Bethlehem to jct with CT 109 in Morris. Turn left on 109 towards Washington Depot. At jct with CT 47, turn left and continue south on 47 after 109 branches right, proceeding to Washington Green and Gunn Historical Museum.

Continue south on 47 briefly to jct with CT 199. Turn right and go 1¼ mi to sign for American Indian Archaeological Institute.

For return trip, go back on 199 to jct with 47 and take 47 north a few mi to jct with US 202. A right turn here takes you to MOUNT TOM STATE PARK (203-868-0223), with swimming, boating, picnicking, and other recreational facilities. A left turn takes you south via US 202 and US 7 to I-84 west to I-684 south and back to New York City.

A Day in Litchfield

TRIP E-5

LOURDES IN LITCHFIELD SHRINE
LITCHFIELD HISTORICAL SOCIETY MUSEUM
TAPPING REEVE HOUSE AND LAW SCHOOL
WHITE MEMORIAL FOUNDATION

DISTANCE: From GWB, about 100 mi. Fast and average speeds.

With its tree-lined streets, gracious homes, and traditional village green, Litchfield appears to have bypassed the 20th century as well as a good part of the 19th. It's a classic New England town of the late 18th century, rich in history, pleasing to the eye, soothing to the harried urban soul. For FURTHER INFORMATION about Litchfield and environs, contact the Litchfield Hills Travel Council, PO Box 1776, Marbledale, CT 06777 (203-868-2214), or the Town Clerk, West St., Box 488, Litchfield, CT 06759 (203-567-9461).

Lourdes in Litchfield Shrine, Rte. 118, Litchfield, CT 06759 (203-567-8434). *Grounds open daily all year. Pilgrimage season May to mid-Oct; call for schedule of services. Donation. Picnic area, gift shop. Pets discouraged. Grotto, near parking lot, is manageable for wheelchairs.*

At this 35-acre shrine of the Montfort Missionaries, an outdoor chapel faces a replica of the grotto at Lourdes, France, where the Virgin Mary is said to have appeared to Saint Bernadette in 1858. To one side, the Way of the Cross starts up a wooded trail that winds to the top of the hill, ending with a flight of steps up to Calvary. Visitors are welcome to attend mass, vespers, and the outdoor Sunday services held during the pilgrimage season.

Litchfield Historical Society Museum, East & South Sts., Litchfield, CT 06759 (203-567-5862). *Open mid-Apr to mid-Nov Tues-Sat 11-5; closed holidays, including Tues after Mon holiday. Donations accepted. Steps into building, parts of interior manageable for wheelchairs.*

Unlike many local museums whose rooms are crammed full of Americana, this one has four spacious galleries where every article on display stands out. The exhibits include early American furniture, locally produced silverware and clocks, a section on Litchfield County history, and a fine collection of paintings by Ralph Earl, among them a portrait of Mariann Wolcott, wife of one of Litchfield's most prominent citizens, Oliver Wolcott, who signed the Declaration of Independence, served in the Continental Congress, and was governor of Connecticut in 1796-97. You'll want time to browse here.

Tapping Reeve House and Law School, South St., Litchfield, CT 06759 (203-567-5862). *Open mid-May to mid-Oct Thurs-Mon 12-4; closed July 4th, Labor Day, Mon holidays. Adults $1, children free. Steps into buildings, difficult for wheelchairs.*

America's first law school was established in this house in 1773 by Tapping Reeve, lawyer and jurist. He began by holding classes in the parlor, later moving to the school building next door. Reeve was married to Aaron Burr's sister, and Burr was one of his earliest pupils, the first in a long line of distinguished graduates, among them Vice-President John C. Calhoun, Horace Mann, three Supreme Court justices, six Cabinet secretaries, and 130 members of Congress. In addition to fine antiques and period furnishings, we can inspect documents relating to the Reeve family, the school's curriculum, and the early history of the legal profession in the United States. The house, the law building, and the attractive gardens are maintained by the Litchfield Historical Society.

White Memorial Foundation, Rte. 202, Litchfield, CT 06759 (203-567-0857). *Grounds open all year daily; free. Conservation Center (203-567-0015) open all year, spring thru fall Tues-Sat 9-5 and Sun 11-5, winter Tues-Sat 8:30-4:30 and Sun 11-5; adults $1, children 50¢. Picnicking, hiking and nature trails, fishing, bridle paths, camping (fees), cross-country skiing. Leashed pets only. Conservation Center fully wheelchair-accessible; paved paths and picnic areas manageable for wheelchairs; Braille Trail.*

Connecticut's largest nature sanctuary, on the shores of Connecticut's largest natural lake, offers 4,000 acres of forest, marshlands, ponds, and streams sheltering a diversity of trees, flowers, ferns, mosses, birds, fish, and wildlife. Some 35 miles of trails provide ample opportunity for hiking, horseback riding, bird-watching, nature study, or relaxed contemplation. Beautiful Bantam Lake offers its shores for picnicking and its waters for fishing. The Conservation Center is an excellent natural history museum with an extensive library, a children's room, and displays explaining the varied habitats and ecological systems within the sanctuary.

FOR THE DRIVER: Take I-684 north to Brewster. Here pick up I-84 east to Waterbury and take Exit 19 to CT 8 north. Before continuing north towards Litchfield, you may want to take a side trip off CT 8 at Exit 33 to Waterbury's MATTATUCK MUSEUM (203-753-0381) in its new location at 144 W Main. Here, in addition to notable collections of decorative and fine arts and a junior museum with Indian and colonial displays, is the fascinating Waterbury Industrial History Exhibit, which portrays the development of Connecticut's fourth-largest city as a center for the production of brass and brass objects, from buttons to shell housings. For FURTHER INFORMATION on Waterbury, contact the Greater Waterbury Chamber of Commerce, 32 N Main St, PO Box 1469, Waterbury, CT 06721 (203-757-0701).

Continue north on CT 8 about 16 mi to Exit 42. Here take CT 118 west towards Litchfield. About 1 mi before Litchfield Center, just past jct with CT 254, is Chestnut Hill Rd, where a left turn takes you to HAIGHT VINE-YARD AND WINERY (203-567-4045) for free tours and tasting. A little beyond turnoff for Haight is Lourdes in Litchfield Shrine, just off 118 on right.

From Lourdes, continue west briefly on 118 to jct with US 202. Here, on the village green, is Litchfield's stately CONGREGATIONAL CHURCH (1829), one of the most photographed churches in New England. Continue on 202 to the other side of the green and jct with CT 63 (North St above 202, South St below). Here, on the corner, is the Litchfield Historical Society Museum. If you park near the green, you can walk to various historic sites in Litchfield. Many of these are still privately owned homes, but once a year, usually the second Saturday in July, they are open to the public for tours; inquire at the Historical Society Museum.

From the museum, go down South St past the SAMUEL SEYMOUR HOUSE (now the rectory of the Episcopal church), where John Calhoun stayed as a student at Tapping Reeve's law school next door. Across the street is the OLIVER WOLCOTT HOUSE, to which, during the Revolutionary War, came Washington, Lafayette, Alexander Hamilton, and the equestrian statue of George III, the latter toppled from its pedestal in Bowling Green, New York City, by the Sons of Liberty, dragged all the way to Litchfield, and melted down into bullets by the women of the town. Further down South St is Old South Rd, a righthand fork that takes you to the ETHAN ALLEN HOUSE, where the famed Revolutionary War hero and leader of the Green Mountain boys once lived.

Go back to the green. Here look for a narrow road leading behind the shops on West St to COBBLE COURT, a 19th-century cobblestone courtyard ringed by quaint shops. Continue across US 202 on 63, now North St, to a number of other historic spots: the HOME OF BENJAMIN TALLMADGE, a Revolutionary War officer, confidential agent, and aide to George Washington; SHELDON'S TAVERN, another of Washington's many resting places; the site of the BIRTHPLACE OF HENRY WARD BEECHER AND HARRIET BEECHER STOWE, whose father, the influential clergyman Lyman Beecher, preached at the Congregational church from 1810 to 1826 (the house now here is not the house in which they were born); and the site of MISS PIERCE'S ACADEMY, the first girls' school in the United States, founded by Sarah Pierce in 1792.

At this point you may wish to continue north on 63 about 6 mi to Goshen, an interesting town not far from some of the sites on the drive in Trip E-2. On your way into town, you pass the GOSHEN FAIRGROUNDS, home of one of Connecticut's largest agricultural fairs. In the center of town is the GOSHEN HISTORICAL SOCIETY MUSEUM (203-491-2665), emphasizing local history and Indian artifacts. About 6 mi west of Goshen, in Mohawk Mountain State Park, is MOHAWK MOUNTAIN SKI AREA (203-672-6100 or 672-6464), with excellent facilities for downhill and cross-country skiing.

In Litchfield, at jct of 63 and 202, go southwest on 202 about 2 mi to White Memorial Foundation and Bantam Lake. From here, the quickest route home is to continue south on US 202 and US 7 back to I-84 west to I-684 south.

Laurel Time in Northwest Connecticut

TRIP E-6

TORRINGTON TO RIVERTON

DISTANCE: From GWB to farthest point, about 120 mi. Fast, average, and slow speeds.

Torrington to Riverton. This trip is primarily a scenic drive, and its special appeal depends upon the time of year. For several weeks in June, lavish displays of mountain laurel burst forth, fully justifying Connecticut's reputation as the Laurel State. Here we make a loop through one of the prime laurel areas, noting the attractions along our route. The best time for viewing varies with the weather, but the blossoms are usually out by mid-June. For FURTHER INFORMATION, contact the Litchfield Hills Travel Council, PO Box 1776, Marbledale, CT 06777 (203-868-2214).

From New York City, we'll take I-684 north to Brewster. Here we'll pick up I-84 east to Waterbury and take Exit 19 to CT 8 north, as we did on Trip E-5. We'll go north on 8, passing junction with CT 118 west to Litchfield. About 3 miles beyond, we come to Torrington, birthplace of abolitionist John Brown and center of brass manufacture. Before getting down to brass tacks, Torrington was known as "Mast Swamp" because the local pines supplied so many masts for sailing vessels.

At junction of CT 8 and CT 4, we'll take 4 west, but first we may want to make a brief detour to the HOTCHKISS-FYLER HOUSE (203-482-8260) on Main St. in the center of Torrington. A grand Victorian mansion built in 1900, the house features parquet floors, mahogany paneling, hand stenciling, and fine furnishings; local history exhibits are on view in the adjacent museum. Also on Main St. is the WARNER THEATER (203-489-7180), a former art deco movie palace, now a National Historic Landmark offering a year-round schedule of concerts.

Proceeding through Torrington's business district on 4 west, we shortly come to Mountain Rd. and turn right to INDIAN LOOKOUT WILDLIFE PRESERVE (203-482-4372). Here, in 1947, Paul

Freedman began to clear his 6 acres of mountainside to allow the laurel on it to survive and spread. He and his wife landscaped the area, mingling other plants and trees to provide a natural, balanced setting. The 6 acres grew to 100, and in 1958 the public was first invited to this fairyland of pink that hangs over the whole mountain like a bank of clouds. Every year since, the preserve has been open for scenic walks during laurel season. Those unable to walk may drive through at specified hours; call in advance.

Returning to CT 8, we continue north about 9 miles to Winsted, hub of the laurel season festivities. The town, which hosts an annual LAUREL FESTIVAL AND BALL (203-379-1805 or -7280) to celebrate the state flower, is also noted for its beautiful ecclesiastical architecture. In Winsted at junction with CT 44, we'll take 44 west briefly to CT 263 west to the corner of Prospect St., where we can visit the SOLOMON ROCKWELL HOUSE (203-379-8433), built in 1813 by a well-to-do iron manufacturer. Sometimes called "Solomon's Temple," the house is of interest today for its Greek Revival architecture and its collections of rare portraits, clocks, chairs, glass-plate negatives, and memorabilia from the Revolutionary and Civil Wars. About 4 mi further west on 263 in Winchester Center is the quaint KEROSENE LAMP MUSEUM (203-379-2612), displaying a private collection of 500 hanging and standing lamps used in homes, schools, factories, and railroad cars from 1856 to 1880.

Returning to Winsted on CT 44, we'll continue east to New Hartford, passing the NEW HARTFORD HISTORICAL SOCIETY MUSEUM (203-379-7235), located in the library in the center of town. Continuing east on 44, we'll turn left at junction with CT 219 and go north to LAKE MCDONOUGH (203-379-3036 or 278-7850) for boating, fishing, picnicking, hiking, and swimming. At junction of 219 and CT 318, we'll turn left on 318, crossing the Saville Dam and Spillway of the Barkhamsted Reservoir. Here we may want to stop and take some pictures of the superb panorama, a mosaic of hills, lakes, and woodlands forming a backdrop for the cascading white waters of the spillway, particularly beautiful during laurel season.

Continuing west briefly on 318, we'll come to junction with CT 181. Here we'll turn left and go west and south on 318/181 about 1 mi. Just before a small metal bridge, we'll turn right on a narrow road that winds along the Farmington River through PEOPLES STATE FOREST, a lovely area for picnicking and hiking. Across the river is AMERICAN LEGION STATE FOREST, with ruggedly beautiful terrain for hiking and camping.

The serpentine road through Peoples State Forest takes us north to junction with CT 20 in Riverton, where we'll take a left over the bridge to the HITCHCOCK CHAIR COMPANY FACTORY STORE (203-379-4826). Riverton was formerly named Hitchcocks-ville. Here in 1826 Lambert Hitchcock, founder of the village, built a factory for the production of a special kind of chair decorated with fine stenciling that included his name and that of the town. The chairs became famous for quality and style, and today are considered valuable antiques. After the founder's death the factory gradually became inactive. In 1946 a new company was formed to reopen it for the reproduction of chairs and cabinet furniture. Today we can visit the gift shop and look through picture windows into the adjoining factory where the maple, oak, and cherry furniture is handcrafted. Near the factory, off CT 20 on River Rd., is the HITCHCOCK MUSEUM (203-379-1003) in the former Old Union Church (1829), housing a superb collection of antique painted and stenciled furniture.

From Riverton, we'll continue west on CT 20 about 1½ miles to junction with CT 8, turn left, and retrace our steps back to New York City.

Clocks and Locks of Old Connecticut

TRIP E-7

HERSHEY LAKE COMPOUNCE, Bristol

AMERICAN CLOCK AND WATCH MUSEUM, Bristol

LOCK MUSEUM OF AMERICA, Terryville

STANLEY-WHITMAN HOUSE, Farmington

HILL-STEAD MUSEUM, Farmington

DISTANCE: From GWB to Farmington via Bristol, about 110 mi. Fast and average speeds.

On this trip we go from the eastern Litchfield Hills region of Connecticut into the Farmington Valley. For FURTHER INFORMATION about Litchfield Hills, contact the Litchfield Hills Travel Council, PO Box 1776, Marbledale, CT 06777 (203-868-2214); for Farmington and points north, contact the Farmington Valley/West Hartford Visitors Bureau, 41 E. Main St., Avon, CT 06001 (203-674-1035).

Hershey Lake Compounce, 822 Lake Ave., Bristol, CT 06010 (203-582-6333 or 800-826-7889 in CT, 800-243-7275 in NYS except from 716 area code). *Open daily in summer 10-10; weekends in Sept, Sat 10-10, Sun 10-8; call for opening date and spring schedule. Theme park admission $9.95 ages 10-61, $6.95 over 61, $8.95 ages 4-9, 3 and under free; waterslide (10-8:30) $3.25 per ½ hr; beach (10-dusk) $2.50 per person per day; parking $2 per car. No radios or tape recorders, no picnics or food except from park restaurants and concessions, no pets. Restrooms and many park facilities wheelchair-accessible.*

"America's oldest amusement park. *And* its newest." So goes the slogan for the turn-of-the-century theme park at Lake Compounce, in operation for 140 years, recently acquired by the Hershey Entertainment and Resort Company. The operator of Pennsylvania's famed Hersheypark gave Lake Compounce a multimillion-dollar facelift and reopened it in the summer of 1986 with many new rides and shows to add to the traditional fun. Kids will love the Berkshire Rapids flume ride down the mountain, the heart-stopping ups and downs of the Wildcat rollercoaster, the stomach-churning gyrations of the Tunxis Twirl, and a host of other diversions including a historic train and carousel, antique autos, bumper cars, miniature golf, a "penny arcade," and games of skill. There are special rides for younger children, a wide selection of restaurants and eateries, two theaters and a troupe of roving players performing scenes from Mark Twain, a shopping area, and a beach at sparkling Lake Compounce. A skillful blending of time-tested attractions and modern innovations, Hershey Lake Compounce extends the joys of the classic American amusement park to new generations of the young and young-at-heart.

American Clock and Watch Museum, 100 Maple St., Bristol, CT 06010 (203-583-6070). *Open Apr thru Oct daily 11-5. Adults $2.50,* *senior citizens $2, children 8-15 $1.25, under 8 free. Steps into building, some exhibit areas manageable for wheelchairs.*

Bristol has been renowned for its clocks since 1790, when Gideon Roberts began making and selling them locally. It is a fitting home for the American Clock and Watch Museum, where more than 1,800 timepieces, from majestic grandfather clocks to Mickey Mouse watches, are on display in clearly labeled exhibits that unfold the history of American horology. The museum consists of two buildings, the Miles Lewis House (1801), a fine specimen of the post-Revolutionary mansion house, and the Ebenezer Barnes Wing, erected in 1955 using paneling and other materials salvaged from the first permanent residence (1728) in Bristol. In a fireproof vault in the Barnes Wing is the Edward Ingraham Library, a comprehensive collection of reference materials on the American clock and watch industries, open to serious researchers by appointment.

Lock Museum of America, 130 Main St., Terryville, CT 06786 (203-589-6359). *Open May thru Oct. Tues-Sun 1:30-4:30. Adults $1, children under 12 free. Largely wheelchair-accessible.*

If you're ever going to find the key to whatever it is you're looking for, this may be the place. It's a one-of-a-kind collection of more than 22,000 items tracing the American lock industry back to its local beginnings in the early 19th century. There are all kinds of locks and keys for every purpose, from the grim (handcuffs, leg irons) to the utilitarian (trunks, cabinets, safes) to the merely decorative.

Stanley-Whitman House, 37 High St., Farmington, CT 06032 (203-677-9222). *Open May thru Oct Tues-Sun 1-4, Mar-Apr and Nov-Dec Sun 1-4; closed major holidays. Adults $2, children 6-14 $1, under 6 free. A few steps into building; will accommodate wheelchairs.*

This National Historic Landmark is one of the most beautifully restored colonial houses in the country. The original portion was built around 1663 and is a good example of the "framed overhang" style popular in England and transplanted by the settlers. Many of the furnishings were made by local craftsmen, and the herb and flower gardens have been planted to reflect 17th- and 18th-century horticultural tastes.

Hill-Stead Museum, 35 Mountain Rd., Farmington, CT 06032 (203-677-4787). *Open Wed-Sun 2-5 all year except mid-Jan to mid-Feb; also closed major holidays. Adults $3, students over 11 $2, children under 11 $1. Guided tours. No steps into building, elevator to 2nd floor.*

A gracious turn-of-the-century mansion, Hill-Stead was designed by Stanford White for industrialist Alfred A. Pope, an early and prescient connoisseur of impressionist art. In addition to the fine furnishings, Chinese porcelains, bronzes, and assorted *objets,* Pope's outstanding collection of paintings by Monet, Degas, Manet, Whistler, and other impressionist artists is on display here, preserved as he left it by his daughter, Theodate. An interesting figure in her own right, Theodate was one of the first women architects in the United States and counted many artists and writers among her acquaintances. During her years at Hill-Stead, her guests included Mary Cassatt, Henry James, Isadora Duncan, and John Masefield.

FOR THE DRIVER: Take I-684 north to Brewster. Here pick up I-84 east past Waterbury to Exit 31, turn left off ramp, and take CT 229 north about 3 mi, following signs for Hershey Lake Compounce.

Continue north on 229 about 2 mi to end, at jct with US 6. Turn left and proceed toward Bristol on 6. At jct with CT 69, turn left onto Maple St, crossing railroad tracks, and proceed to next stoplight. American Clock and Watch Museum is on corner, on left. Note that Bristol is the site of BALLOONS OVER BRISTOL (203-589-4111), a 3-day event held annually on Memorial Day weekend, with hot-air balloonists from all over the country guiding their colorful craft aloft in the skies of Farmington Valley.

Return to US 6, turn left, and continue west 3½-4 mi to Terryville and Lock Museum, at 130 Main St (US 6).

From Terryville, go back through Bristol on US 6 and continue east to jct with CT 10. Turn left and go north briefly to Farmington, a picture-perfect New England town of great charm. Watch for stoplight at Mountain Rd, turn right, and proceed to High St and Stanley-Whitman House. A little further on Mountain Rd, on left, is a small lane to Hill-Stead.

For return trip, go back to CT 10 and continue to center of Farmington and jct with CT 4. Turn right and go a short way to I-84 west, following signs.

Footprints in the Sands of Time

TRIP E-8

WEBB-DEANE-STEVENS MUSEUM, Wethersfield
OLD ACADEMY MUSEUM, Wethersfield
BUTTOLPH-WILLIAMS HOUSE, Wethersfield
DINOSAUR STATE PARK, Rocky Hill

DISTANCE: From GWB to Wethersfield, about 110 mi. Mainly fast speeds.

We're now in one of Connecticut's oldest settled regions, an early commercial center because of its strategic location on the Connecticut River. For FURTHER INFORMATION about Wethersfield and the nearby towns of Rocky Hill, Glastonbury, and Newington, contact the Olde Towne Tourism District, 2400 Main St., Glastonbury, CT 06033 (203-659-1219).

Webb-Deane-Stevens Museum, 211 Main St., Wethersfield, CT 06109 (203-529-0612). *Open all year Tues-Sat 10-4, also Sun 1-4 mid-May to mid-Oct. Adults $1.50 per house or $4 combination ticket, children 50¢ per house. Difficult for wheelchairs.*

Here are three handsome 18th-century houses restored to reflect the lifestyles of their owners—a merchant, a diplomat, and a tradesman. The oldest of them, the Joseph Webb House (1752), was the site of a historic meeting between Washington and Rochambeau in 1781, during which the two generals formulated the strategy that led to the British defeat at Yorktown, the concluding battle of the Revolutionary War. Not only did Washington sleep here, but the bedroom boasts the *very same* wallpaper that was hung in his honor on that occasion!

The Silas Deane House (1766) was the residence of a diplomat who was instrumental in securing French aid for the Revolutionary cause, and who recruited a number of distinguished foreign military officers (Lafayette, Pulaski, von Steuben, De Kalb) to serve with the Continental Army. During the Revolution, Silas Deane was unjustly accused of profiteering, but his reputation was posthumously cleared. His home, built for entertaining on a grand scale, has many unique structural details and a spaciousness unusual in houses of the period.

The last of the buildings, the Isaac Stevens House (1788), is the least formal, reflecting the simpler tastes of its owner. In addition to the authentic period furnishings (1640-1840) that adorn all three houses, there is an interesting collection of children's toys and ladies' bonnets here.

Old Academy Museum, 150 Main St., Wethersfield, CT 06109 (203-529-7656). *Open mid-May to mid-Oct Mon-Fri 1-4, Sat 12-5, and by appointment. Adults $1, children 6-12 50¢, under 6 free. Ramps into building, 1st-floor facilities wheelchair-accessible, but not gallery; museum is currently under renovation and will be fully wheelchair-accessible when work is completed, probably spring 1987.*

Built in 1804 by the First School Society, this Federal-style redbrick building had later incarnations as a female seminary, public library, and town hall. Now it is the home of the Wethersfield Historical Society, with changing exhibits on local history, a genealogical library, the Connecticut Horticultural Society Library, and the library of the Rushlight Club, established to research and preserve the history of lighting methods and fixtures. From the museum we have access to the Captain James Francis House (1793), where the furnishings and displays reflect the life of the Francis family over 170 years.

Buttolph-Williams House, Marsh & Broad Sts., Wethersfield, CT 06109 (203-529-0460 or 247-8996). *Open mid-May to mid-Oct daily 1-5. Adults $1, senior citizens 75¢, children 25¢. Will accommodate wheelchairs.*

From 1692, when this house was built, to 1752, the date of the Webb House (see above), some radical changes in living occurred. The Buttolph-Williams House is a typical "mansion house" of an earlier and more rugged era, and we have a chance to observe the contrast if we visit both. The house has been carefully restored, and the collections of 17th-century pewter, delft, fabric, and furnishings are outstanding. Of special interest is the kitchen, said to be the best preserved, most fully equipped kitchen of its period in New England.

Dinosaur State Park, West St., Rocky Hill, CT 06067 (203-529-8423). *Grounds open all year daily 9-4:30; free. Museum open all year Tues-Sun 9-4:30; adults $1, children 50¢. Picnicking, hiking and nature trails, playing field. Leashed pets only, in picnic area only. Picnic area, playing field, museum, and museum restrooms wheelchair-accessible.*

While excavating a construction site some years ago, a bulldozer operator turned up a stone slab imprinted with curious markings that were soon identified as the three-toed tracks of dinosaurs of the Jurassic Period. Excited paleontologists from the Connecticut Geological Survey and Yale's Peabody Museum (Trip F-10) went to work with their spades, eventually unearthing over 2,000 prints estimated to be 200 million years old. About 500 of the tracks are enclosed under a geodesic dome, and the rest have been electrically sanded and sealed to protect them from weathering. One area of the 60-acre park has been set aside for visitors who wish to make plaster casts of the tracks to take home. In the museum we can inspect a skeletal cast and a life-size model of the creature that left its footprints here, while a greenhouse and a living reptile exhibit suggest something of the lifestyle and period furnishings of this long-extinct race of behemoths. A National Natural Landmark, Dinosaur State Park is a surefire hit with kids, whose fascination with *Tyrannosaurus rex, Brontosaurus,* et al., generally exceeds even their attachment to *Dungeons and Dragons* and MTV.

FOR THE DRIVER: Take I-684 north to Brewster. Here pick up I-84 east past Waterbury to Exit 27 and jct with CT 66 east. Take 66 east about 8 mi to jct with I-91.

Alternate route to I-91: Take HRP/Merritt Pkwy/Wilbur Cross Pkwy north to Exit 67 and jct with I-91 ($1.30), or take I-95 north (40¢) to Exit 47 and jct with I-91 in New Haven.

Take I-91 north to Exit 26 in Wethersfield. After ramp turn left on Marsh St (not marked) and follow it around to Main St, passing Buttolph-Williams House at Marsh and Broad Sts. At corner of Marsh and Main St is First Church of Christ, and diagonally across from it (left on Main) is Webb-Deane-Stevens Museum. A little further down Main, across street, is Old Academy Museum.

Go back on Main to Marsh. Turn right to Broad St and Buttolph-

Williams House, on right. Before leaving Old Wethersfield, you may want to take a walk and see the many other HISTORIC BUILDINGS—116 pre-1840 houses within a dozen blocks, as well as a variety of later 19th-century structures—that make this town so attractive. Note also that Wethersfield is only a few mi south of Hartford (Trip E-9).

Turn right on Broad St, passing village green, and proceed to Maple St, CT 3. Turn right on Maple briefly to jct with CT 99, at light. Turn left and go south on 99 past jct with I-91 to West St and sign for State Veterans' Hospital. Turn right and watch for Dinosaur State Park, across road from hospital.

For return trip, continue on West St briefly to jct with I-91. Take 91 south to CT 66 and go back the way you came, or continue south on 91 to Wilbur Cross/Merritt Pkwy/HRP south ($1.30) or I-95 south (40¢).

A Memorable Day in Hartford

TRIP E-9

   SCIENCE MUSEUM OF CONNECTICUT
   ELIZABETH PARK
   CONNECTICUT HISTORICAL SOCIETY
   MARK TWAIN AND HARRIET BEECHER
      STOWE HOUSES
   STATE CAPITOL
   RAYMOND E. BALDWIN MUSEUM OF
      CONNECTICUT HISTORY
   WADSWORTH ATHENEUM
   CONSTITUTION PLAZA
   TRAVELERS TOWER
   OLD STATE HOUSE
   BUTLER-McCOOK HOMESTEAD

DISTANCE: From GWB, about 120 mi. Fast speeds.

Hartford, capital of Connecticut and "Insurance Capital of the World," was established in 1635-36 by Thomas Hooker and a band of discontented Puritan families from Massachusetts. It has a rich historical, cultural, and architectural heritage, and its downtown area is considered one of the country's more successful examples of urban renewal. We can't explore all the attractions of Hartford in a day, but we can single out one or two that especially appeal to us, or we can get a good general introduction to the city by going on The Walk, a self-guided journey to the main points of interest downtown. For a brochure describing The Walk, and for FURTHER INFORMATION about Hartford and environs, contact the Greater Hartford Convention and Visitors Bureau, 1 Civic Center Plaza, Hartford, CT 06103 (203-728-6789).

Science Museum of Connecticut, 950 Trout Brook Drive, West Hartford, CT 06119 (203-236-2961). *Open all year daily, Mon-Sat 10-5, Sun 1-5; closed Labor Day, Thanksgiving, Christmas, New Year's. Nature center closed Mon during school year; call for schedule of planetarium shows. Adults $3.50, senior citizens and children 3-12 $2, children 2 and under 50¢. Will accommodate wheelchairs; call in advance.*

Formerly the Children's Museum of Hartford, the Science Museum has retained its appeal for young people while greatly expanding its range of exhibits. Outside, a 60-foot cement sperm whale welcomes us, beckoning us to the wonders within: a marine aquarium with an 11,000-gallon Caribbean reef tank; a small zoo where we can meet a variety of birds, mammals, and reptiles, both native and exotic; a panoply of stars twinkling in the skies of the Gengras Planetarium; a physical science discovery room where we can experiment with the invisible forces that govern our universe; an interactive heart exhibit that shows us how the old ticker works while allowing us to check our pulse and blood pressure; and a hands-on room where we can, among other things, pet the fish. All in all, there's something here to engage and enlighten everyone, from the youngest child to the most scientifically retrograde adult.

Elizabeth Park, Prospect & Asylum Aves., Hartford, CT (203-722-6490). *Grounds open all year daily dawn-dusk; greenhouses open all year daily (except holidays) 10-4. Free. Snack bar, lounge, and auditorium in Pond House. Outdoor displays manageable for wheelchairs.*

This city-owned park is famous for its rose gardens, with more than 900 varieties blossoming in gorgeous profusion every spring, usually peaking in late June. In addition, there are 14,000 other plants on display during the summer months, and varied vegetation year-round in the greenhouses. The park sponsors a program of outdoor concerts in summer and offers ice skating on the pond in winter.

Connecticut Historical Society, 1 Elizabeth St., Hartford, CT 06105 (203-236-5621). *Museum open all year Mon-Sat 1-5; library open all year Mon-Sat 9-5; both closed Sun and holidays, also Sat from Memorial Day to Labor Day. Free. Partially manageable for wheelchairs.*

The leading repository of museum materials on state history, the Connecticut Historical Society has eight galleries of changing exhibits and permanent displays, including two particularly fine furniture collections, the Barbour collection of Connecticut pieces from the colonial and Federal periods, and the George Dudley Seymour collection of 17th- and 18th-century pieces. We can also see Connecticut-made silver, pewter, toys, glassware, pottery, and stoneware. The art of the tavern sign is well represented by more than 70 specimens, suggesting that a fair number of past Connecticut residents were not customers of the Phoenix Mutual Life Insurance Company, which accepted only teetotalers when it was established in Hartford in 1851. The society also maintains a vast library of almost 2 million historical manuscripts, 70,000 books, 3,500 bound volumes of newspapers and periodicals, extensive genealogical holdings, and assorted maps, prints, and photographs.

Mark Twain and Harriet Beecher Stowe Houses, Nook Farm, 77 Forest St., Hartford, CT 06105 (203-525-9317). *Open all year, June thru Aug daily 10-4:30, Sept thru May Tues-Sat 9:30-4 and Sun 1-4; closed New Year's, Easter, Labor Day, Thanksgiving, Christmas. Twain House $3.75 adults, $1.50 children under 17; Stowe House $3 adults, $1.25 children under 17; combination ticket $6 adults, $2.75 children under 17; preschoolers free; rates may change in fall or winter 1986. Steps into houses, ground floors manageable for wheelchairs, but no access to upper floors. Nook Farm Visitor Center wheelchair-accessible.*

Nook Farm is an old Hartford neighborhood that attracted a remarkable group of 19th-century writers and intellectuals connected by family ties and bonds of friendship. Among the distinguished company that settled here were women's rights activist Isabella Beecher Hooker, playwright and thespian William Gillette (see Gillette Castle, Trip F-13), Senator Joseph Hawley, and Charles Dudley Warner, editor of the *Hartford Courant* and coauthor with Mark Twain of *The Gilded Age.* Today most of Nook Farm has been torn down, but several of the original buildings remain, including the homes of its most famous residents, Twain and Harriet Beecher Stowe, and the carriage house that now serves as the visitor center.

Twain's house, designed by Edward Tuckerman Potter, is a colorful and idiosyncratic reflection of the author's personality, perhaps best appreciated by those who have read his works and know his humor. The south facade is modeled after a Mississippi River steamboat, the dressing room recreates a riverboat pilothouse, and the etched windows in the upstairs study, where Twain wrote *The Adventures of Tom Sawyer, The Adventures of Huckleberry Finn,* and five other books, memorialize his great passions in life—smoking, drinking, and billiards. Twain lived at Nook Farm with his wife and three daughters from 1874 to 1891, when financial difficulties forced him to sell the house and take to the lecture circuit.

A stone's throw from the Twain House is the much less flamboyant Victorian "cottage" of Harriet Beecher Stowe, who settled here in 1873 and remained until her death in 1896. This house, too, reflects the personal tastes of its owner: the design of the kitchen follows the specifications set forth in the book Stowe wrote with her sister, *The American Woman's Home;* some of her own paintings hang on the walls; there are mementos of her career as a writer and reformer, and many original items of furniture, including the tiny desk at which she penned her most important work, *Uncle Tom's Cabin* (1852), a book that aroused popular sentiment against slavery and sold 300,000 copies within a year— a staggering figure in those days.

State Capitol, 210 Capitol Ave., Hartford, CT 06106 (203-240-0222). *Open weekdays for tours (call for schedule); closed state holidays. Free. Wheelchair-accessible.*

Here is Hartford's most impressive building, seat of Connecticut government since 1879, housing the state executive offices and legislative chambers. A great gold-leaf dome presides over this eclectic architectural concoction by Richard Michell Upjohn. On our tour we'll see statues, murals, and historic displays featuring bullet-riddled flags, Lafayettte's camp bed, and other reminders of Connecticut's past, as well as a plaster model of the Genius of Connecticut, which adorned the capitol spire until it was melted down during World War II.

Raymond E. Baldwin Museum of Connecticut History, Connecticut State Library, 231 Capitol Ave., Hartford, CT 06106 (203-566-3056). *Open all year Mon-Fri 9-4:45, Sat 9-1; closed Sun and state holidays. Free. Wheelchair-accessible.*

This museum in the Connecticut State Library holds a range of exhibits depicting Connecticut history and industrial development. Of particular interest are the Connecticut-made clocks, the Selden auto, the portrait gallery of leading Connecticut citizens, the Colt collection of firearms, including a rare Wyatt Earp Buntline Special, and the original royal charter granted to the Connecticut colonists by Charles II in 1662 (see Travelers Tower, below). The library houses the official state archives and extensive law, social science, history, and genealogy collections.

Wadsworth Atheneum, 600 Main St., Hartford, CT 06103 (203-278-2670). *Open all year Tues-Sun 11-5, 1st-floor galleries Tues-Fri until 7; closed New Year's, Thanksgiving, Christmas. Adults $3, senior citizens and students $1.50, children under 13 free; free Thurs and 11-1 Sat. Film and lecture series, restaurant, museum shop. Tactile gallery; wheelchair access and wheelchair-accessible restroom at Avery entrance, also portable ramps for use throughout museum (call ahead so staff can make advance arrangements).*

One of the nation's oldest and best public art museums, the Wadsworth Atheneum has a well-deserved reputation for the excellence and breadth of its collections. More than 40,000 art objects, from ancient Egyptian artifacts to contemporary sculptures, are on display here in spacious galleries occupying five interconnected buildings. There's an extensive selection of paintings representing every major period and style since the 15th century, with some particularly fine works by Monet, Renoir, and other 19th-century French artists. Also noteworthy are the collections of American and English silver, Meissen porcelain, fur-

niture, and period costumes. One of the Wadsworth's most popular attractions is the Lions Gallery of the Senses, which was
originally conceived as a tactile exhibit area for the visually handicapped but soon proved an enjoyable and enlightening experience for all visitors.

Constitution Plaza. These 15 acres of elegant high-rises and landscaped promenades show the effects of urban renewal at its best.
Completed in 1964 at a cost of $40 million, the plaza combines
office space, shopping areas, and parking facilities, and is the setting for concerts, fashion shows, the annual and quite spectacular
Christmas Festival of Lights, and other special events. Among
the unique features of the plaza are the boat-shaped elliptical
headquarters of Phoenix Mutual Life, one of the few two-sided
buildings in the world, and the splashless fountain, designed to
resist the fiercest provocations from the plaza winds. Inside the
Connecticut Bank and Trust plaza entrance, in the commercial
banking room, is one of Alexander Calder's famous mobiles.

Travelers Tower, 1 Tower Square, Main St., Hartford, CT 06115
(203-277-2431). *Open for tours June thru Aug Sat-Sun 8:30-3:30,
Apr-May and Sept-Oct by reservation 24 hours in advance. Free.
Not wheelchair-accessible.*
　　When this famous tower was built in 1919, only six buildings in
America were taller. The highest point in Hartford, it rises 527
feet above sidewalk level, affording a splendid panoramic view of
Greater Hartford and the Connecticut River Valley. The tower
was built by the Travelers Insurance Company, a venerable Hartford institution that got its start in 1863 by insuring a Captain
James Bolter for $5,000 for a trip from his home to the post office
at a premium of two cents. Plenty of other travelers put in their
two cents' worth over the years, and the company grew to become one of the giants of the insurance field. There's an interesting exhibit on company history at the TRAVELERS MUSEUM (203-
277-5048) in Batterson Hall.
　　The Travelers Tower stands on the site once occupied by Sanford's Tavern, where in 1687 Sir Edmund Andros, James II's royal
governor of New England, demanded the surrender of the original charter granted to the Connecticut colonists by Charles II in
1662. While Andros was engaged in heated debate with the colo-

nists at Sanford's, Captain Joseph Wadsworth took the charter and squirreled it away in the hollow of an ancient white oak, where it remained safely hidden until the colonists succeeded in riding themselves of the autocratic Andros. The Charter Oak, thought to have been more than 1,000 years old, succumbed to a storm in 1856, but the 1662 charter is on display in the Baldwin Museum of Connecticut History (see above), and the family tree lives on in the white oak on the grounds of the Center Church, across from the Wadsworth Atheneum.

Old State House, 800 Main St., Hartford, CT 06103 (203-522-6766). *Open all year Tues-Sat 10-5, Sun 12-5; closed major holidays. Free. Visitor information center, gift shop; chamber concerts, outdoor summer concerts, farmers' market, special events. Some wheelchair-accessible facilities.*

This elegant Federal structure was the first public commission of Charles Bulfinch (1763-1844), one of America's best early architects. Bulfinch went on to design many other fine buildings, including the statehouse in Boston and Massachusetts General Hospital, but is perhaps best remembered for bringing the Capitol building in Washington, D.C., to completion in 1830. The Old State House served as Connecticut's state capitol from 1796 to 1878, and as Hartford's city hall from 1879 to 1915. Today it is a National Historic Landmark, museum, and cultural center. A rare Gilbert Stuart full-length portrait of George Washington hangs in the restored senate chamber.

Butler-McCook Homestead, 396 Main St., Hartford, CT 06103 (203-522-1806). *Open mid-May to mid-Oct, Tues, Wed, Thurs, and Sun 12-4; closed major holidays. Adults $1, senior citizens 75¢, children 25¢. Not wheelchair-accessible.*

This survivor of urban renewal stands in quaint contrast to the glittering office buildings of downtown Hartford. The oldest private home in the city (1782), it has been preserved as a museum of 18th- and 19th-century tastes in furnishings and decorative arts. On display are fine collections of silver, 19th-century American paintings, Chinese bronzes, Egyptian artifacts, toys, and dolls. The annual Victorian Christmas exhibit is a nice way to get into the spirit of the season.

FOR THE DRIVER: Take I-684 north to Brewster and pick up I-84 east through Danbury and Waterbury to Exit 43, Park Rd and West Hartford Center. After ramp, turn right on Park Rd, then left at next corner, Trout Brook Drive. Go ½ mi on Trout Brook to Science Museum of Connecticut, on right.

Before leaving West Hartford, abecedarians and admirers of the man who did so much to free American speech and spelling from the King's English will want to visit the NOAH WEBSTER HOUSE AND MUSEUM (203-521-5362), birthplace of the author of the groundbreaking *American Dictionary of the English Language* (1828). The Webster House is at 227 S Main St, right near Exit 41 off I-84; it can also be reached by turning left at Park Rd to Main St instead of right to Trout Brook Drive and Science Museum.

From Science Museum, turn right and continue on Trout Brook several blocks to Asylum Ave. Turn right on Asylum and watch for Elizabeth Park a short distance ahead on right.

Continue on Asylum Ave to end of park, cross Prospect Ave, and go 3 blocks to Elizabeth St. At this jct, on right, is Connecticut Historical Society, with a large Hartford fire alarm bell in front.

Go back on Asylum to Prospect Ave and turn left. Go a couple of blocks to Farmington Ave (CT 4), turn left, and proceed several blocks to Forest St. Turn right here to Nook Farm Visitor Center and Twain and Stowe Houses.

Go back to Farmington Ave, turn right, and continue towards downtown Hartford. Just before entrance to I-84, turn right on Broad St and proceed to stoplight at Capitol Ave. Turn left and watch for distinctive dome of State Capitol, shortly on left. At this point you may wish to park in a municipal lot and walk to the next attractions, all within a few blocks of one another.

Across street from Capitol is Baldwin House of Connecticut History and State Library. Behind Capitol is BUSHNELL PARK, the first land in the United States claimed for park purposes under eminent domain, laid out according to a natural landscape design influenced by the ideas of Hartford resident Frederick Law Olmsted. A popular spot for outdoor concerts and special events, the park is also the home of a RESTORED 1914 CAROUSEL, a real beauty transported here from Canton, Ohio. For a quarter you can ride one of the 48 brightly painted hand-carved horses and try for the brass ring. At the corner of Capitol Ave and Trinity St, which bisects Bushnell Park, is BUSHNELL MEMORIAL HALL (203-246-6807), a major performing arts center with a noteworthy art deco auditorium.

From Capitol, continue east on Capitol Ave several blocks to Main St. Turn left on Main, passing the impressive, highway-spanning HARTFORD PUBLIC LIBRARY and the ornate HARTFORD MUNICIPAL BUILDING. Just beyond is Wadsworth Atheneum. Between municipal building and Wadsworth is Burr Mall, a small park dominated by Alexander Calder's massive steel STEGOSAURUS. A little beyond Wadsworth on Main is Travelers Tower, and beyond that is the Old State House. Here turn right off Main St to Constitution Plaza.

Go back down Main St the way you came. On right, opposite Travelers Tower, is the ANCIENT BURYING GROUND, final resting place of some of Hartford's early settlers, with headstones dating back to 1640; look for the epitaph of Dr. Thomas Langrell, who "drowned in the glory of his years, and left his mate to drown herself in tears." Beyond cemetary, opposite Wadsworth Atheneum, is I. M. Pei's 1969 BUSHNELL TOWER and the neighboring CENTER CHURCH (1807), patterned after London's St. Martin's-in-the-Fields, with stained-glass windows by Louis Tiffany. The church stands on the site where the US Constitution was ratified by Connecticut in 1788. Continue on Main to intersection with Capitol Ave. Here, on left, is Butler-McCook Homestead.

Note that Hartford is only a few mi north of Wethersfield and the sites on Trip E-8, and about 14 mi north of Cromwell, home of the annual SAMMY DAVIS JR. GREATER HARTFORD OPEN (203-522-4171), usually held in late June.

The Good Old Days

TRIP E-10

OLD STURBRIDGE VILLAGE, Sturbridge, Massachusetts

DISTANCE: From GWB, about 155 mi. Fast speeds.

We'll really have to push ourselves to make it from New York City to Old Sturbridge Village and back in a day, but it deserves a mention because it's one of the most careful, informative, and enjoyable historical reconstructions in the country. Actually, we'll need the better part of a day to appreciate Old Sturbridge, so unless we're prepared to get a very early start and come back late, we'll want to save it for a weekend trip.

Old Sturbridge Village, Sturbridge, MA 01566 (617-347-3362). *Open all year late Mar to late Oct daily 9-5, Tues-Sun 10-4 rest of year;*

closed Christmas, New Year's. Adults $8.50, children 6-15 $4, under 6 free. Picnic facilities, dining at Bullard Tavern, gift shop. Annual July 4th, Thanksgiving, and other celebrations, special events all year. Leashed pets only on grounds, no pets in buildings unless carried (except seeing-eye dogs). Unpaved paths, steps and narrow entrances to many buildings, but some areas and activities manageable for wheelchairs.

Here is a marvelously restored New England village of the 1830s, complete with working historical farm, sawmill, carding mill, meetinghouse, general store, bank, lawyer's office, schoolhouse, blacksmith and tinsmith shops, cooperage, pottery, and other original buildings—more than 40 in all, some relocated from Vermont and Connecticut. Old Sturbridge moves to seasonal rhythms, with changing demonstrations of the various farm chores, arts, and crafts employed by our ancestors 150 years ago, at the dawning of the Industrial Revolution. Costumed interpreters playing the roles of villagers explain their work and way of life, giving us a remarkably vivid taste of the past. Everything here, down to the grass on the village common, has been carefully researched for authenticity (initially planted and mown like a modern lawn, the common was reseeded with a haylike grass and left to the ministrations of the village sheep, as it would have been in the 1830s). Old Sturbridge, which opened to the public in 1946 and has just celebrated its 40th anniversary, shows every sign of remaining untouched by the passage of time.

FOR THE DRIVER: Take I-684 north to Brewster. Here pick up I-84 east through Connecticut to Exit 3 in Massachusetts. Old Sturbridge Village is just off exit, on US 20 west.

Eastward Along Connecticut's Shore

• *Here we start just over the city line and move through parts of Westchester County into southern Connecticut, following the shoreline of Long Island Sound almost to where Rhode Island begins. This is beautiful country for sightseeing or recreation, with many historic port towns and the tang of saltwater and seafaring in the air.*

Exit Points
I-95, Hutchinson River Pkwy (HRP)

Main Roads
I-95 becoming New England Thruway becoming Connecticut Tpk, HRP becoming Merritt Pkwy/Wilbur Cross Pkwy in Connecticut

Connections
To reach I-95/New England Thruway, take
—Henry Hudson Pkwy, FDR Drive/Harlem River Drive, Major Deegan Expwy (I-87), or Bronx River Pkwy to Cross Bronx Expwy (I-95) and take I-95 north;
—Triborough Bridge to Bruckner Expwy to I-95 north;
—Bronx-Whitestone Bridge or Throgs Neck Bridge to I-95 north.
To reach HRP, take
—Henry Hudson Pkwy, FDR Drive/Harlem River Drive, Major Deegan Expwy (I-87), or Bronx River Pkwy to Cross Bronx Expwy (I-95) and take HRP exit instead of continuing on I-95 north;
—Triborough Bridge to Bruckner Expwy to HRP;
—Bronx-Whitestone Bridge or Throgs Neck Bridge to HRP.

Tolls
One-way highway tolls (collected in both directions) are given in "For the Driver" at the end of each trip and are calculated from the New York City line unless otherwise indicated. It is assumed that you cross the single barrier tolls on HRP (25¢ at Pelham), SMRP (25¢ at Yonkers), and New England Thruway (40¢ at New Rochelle), and all the barrier tolls on Merritt/Wilbur Cross from the Connecticut line to your destination (35¢ at Greenwich, Milford, Wallingford); if not, you don't pay. The Connecticut Turnpike no longer has any tolls.

For New York City bridge and tunnel tolls, see p. xvi; remember to add these to the highway tolls as appropriate, depending on your route.

Long Island Sound Crossings
There are two auto ferries linking Area F with Area G, Long Island. You may wish to combine trips in the two areas by taking a ferry.

Bridgeport-Port Jefferson Ferry (203-367-3043 or 516-473-0631), operating daily all year, $22 one way for car and driver, advance reservations required for car, crossing takes 1¼ hours; call for further information on fares and schedules.

New London-Orient Point Ferry (203-443-5035 or 516-323-2415), operating daily all year, $20 one way for car and driver, advance reservations required for car, crossing takes 1½ hours; call for further information on fares and schedules.

Fundamental Freedoms and Common Sense
TRIP F-1

ST. PAUL'S NATIONAL HISTORIC SITE AND BILL
OF RIGHTS MUSEUM, Mount Vernon
HUGUENOT-THOMAS PAINE HISTORICAL
ASSOCIATION, New Rochelle
SQUARE HOUSE, Rye

DISTANCE: From GWB to Rye, about 18 mi. Fast and average speeds.

On this and the next trip, we visit some sites in Westchester County
en route to Connecticut. For FURTHER INFORMATION, contact the
Westchester Tourism Council, 148 Martine Ave., White Plains,
NY 10601 (914-285-2941).

St. Paul's National Historic Site and Bill of Rights Museum, 897 S.
Columbus Ave., Mount Vernon, NY 10550 (914-667-4116). *Grounds
open all year daily, daylight hours; site open all year for guided
tours Tues-Fri 9-5 by appointment, Sat 12-4 with scheduled tours
at 12:30, 1:30, 2:30. Free. Museum shop, annual July 4th celebration, special events. Museum fully wheelchair-accessible; steps
into church, but interior manageable for wheelchairs.*

This handsome 1787 church is associated with the events leading to the arrest and trial of John Peter Zenger. A German-born
printer, Zenger emigrated to America in 1710 and in 1733 launched
his *Weekly Journal,* an opposition paper that attacked the policies
of the colonial government. In an election for Westchester assem-
blyman held that year on the church green, Quakers were denied
the right to vote because they refused to swear an oath on the
Bible affirming their status as landowners. Zenger took up their
cause in the first issue of his paper, denouncing the corrupt election, and broadening his attacks in subsequent issues. In 1734 he
was arrested for seditious libel, a loosely defined legal category
that embraced all criticism of the government, whether true or
false. At Zenger's trial in 1735, his lawyer, Andrew Hamilton,
won his client's acquittal on the grounds that the allegedly libel-
ous material in the *Weekly Journal,* including the article on the

1733 election, was true. This decision, recognizing truth as a defense in cases of libel, was a milestone in establishing freedom of the press, later enshrined in the First Amendment to the US Constitution.

The museum at St. Paul's commemorates these events in a series of dioramas and contains other informative exhibits on the freedoms of speech, press, religion, and assembly. Also here are exhibits on Westchester history, Revolutionary artifacts from the Battle of Pell's Point, and a working replica of Zenger's press. The original church served as a hospital during the Revolution, and the present structure is of considerable historical and architectural interest. The adjoining cemetery contains graves dating back more than three centuries.

Huguenot-Thomas Paine Historical Association, 983 North Ave., New Rochelle, NY 10804 (914-632-5376). *Open spring thru fall Fri-Sun 2-5 or by appointment. Suggested donation $1 adults, 25¢ children. Not wheelchair-accessible at present, but future alterations are planned; call in advance.*

The museum of the Huguenot-Paine Historical Association has an interesting collection of artifacts and documents relating to the early history of New Rochelle, originally home of the Siwanoy Indians, founded as a town by 30 Huguenot families in 1688. The association also maintains the nearby Thomas Paine Cottage on Sicard Ave. The great pamphleteer who wrote *Common Sense* and did so much in the cause of American freedom lived here only briefly. His Huguenot neighbors did not welcome his radical views, which had an enormous impact on public opinion during the American Revolution. Today the cottage is furnished much as it was during Paine's lifetime (1737-1809), but there are also some fine Victorian pieces.

Square House, 1 Purchase St., Rye, NY 10580 (914-967-7588). *Open all year Tues-Fri and Sun 2:30-4:30, and by appointment; closed major holidays. Free. Lectures, films, craft demonstrations, special events. Fully wheelchair-accessible.*

The Rye Historical Society has its headquarters in this restored 18th-century tavern where George Washington twice stopped in 1789, and which was visited by such notables as John Adams and

Lafayette. There are seven rooms with period furnishings and rotating historical exhibits.

FOR THE DRIVER: Take I-95 north to Conner St exit, turn left after ramp, go up 1 light and make another left. This road crosses US 1, Boston Post Rd, and becomes NY 22, Columbus Ave, taking you to St. Paul's National Historic Site, on right at 897 S Columbus.

Go back down 22 to jct with US 1, turn left, and go north about 3 mi to North Ave. Turn left and go a little under 2 mi to Thomas Paine Cottage, at far end of lake beyond statue. Just ahead on North Ave is Huguenot-Paine Historical Association museum.

Continue on North Ave to 2nd light. Turn left on street after light, to Webster Ave. Turn right on Webster and go to end, where it merges with HRP. Follow HRP north about 6 mi to jct with I-287, Cross Westchester Expwy, and take this east to Exit 11, US 1 south to Rye. Follow US 1 south several blocks to jct with NY 120, Purchase St. Here US 1 bears left and you bear right to Square House.

Rye Humor and Other Amusements

TRIP F-2

MUSEUM OF CARTOON ART, Rye Brook

PLAYLAND, Rye

DISTANCE: From GWB to Rye Brook, about 20 mi. Mainly fast speeds.

Museum of Cartoon Art, Comly Ave., Rye Brook, NY 10573 (914-939-0234). *Open all year Tues-Fri 10-4, Sun 1-5; closed major holidays. Adults $1.50, senior citizens and children under 12 75¢. Guest demonstrations, films. Not wheelchair-accessible, but will accommodate wheelchairs.*

Here, in a fanciful 5-story Victorian castle, are more than 60,000 original works by over 1,000 artists, along with extensive research and archival materials on the history of one of the world's liveliest art forms. The exhibits cover all types of cartoon art and animated films from 1899 to the present, and the greats of the field are enshrined in the Cartoonists' Hall of Fame. There's plenty of humor on display, from the slapstick to the sophisticated, as well as exhibits offering an education in the trenchant art of caricature and the political cartoon. Animated shorts and features are shown on weekdays to groups of 10 or more, and there are guest demonstrations by leading practitioners of cartoon art on the first Sunday of every month.

Playland, Rye, NY 10580 (914-921-0370). *Open daily early May to Labor Day, varied hours; call for schedule. Parking fee $5 per car weekends and holidays, $4 Fri evenings, $2.50 weekdays. Beach fee $2.25 adults, 50¢ children, senior citizens 50¢ on weekdays only; pool fee $3.50 adults, $1.50 children, senior citizens $1.50 on weekdays only. Picnicking, hiking, fishing, boat rentals (rowboats $4 per hr, 2-seater paddleboats $5 per hr, 4-seaters $8 per hr), ice skating, refreshment stand. Leashed pets only. Wheelchair-accessible parking and restrooms.*

This venerable amusement park on Long Island Sound has delighted generations of Westchester children while offering aid and comfort to their parents ("Eat your spinach and I'll take you to Playland"). The 40-acre park features 30 tried-and-true devices for producing exhilaration, plus game arcade, miniature golf, refreshment stands, boardwalk, lake, and Kiddy Land for the younger set. We can swim or sunbathe at the 1,200-foot-long beach, whet our blades at the 3-rink Ice Casino, fish from a rowboat on the lake, or lose ourselves in contemplation at the neighboring 170-acre Edith G. Read Natural Park and Wildlife Sanctuary.

FOR THE DRIVER: Take HRP north to Exit 30, marked "King St to Port Chester" (25¢). Turn right off ramp and go south on King St (NY 120A) about 1 mi to Comly Ave. Turn left on Comly, then take 1st left off Comly onto Magnolia Drive and park here for Museum of Cartoon Art. The museum was formerly in Port Chester; it's still in the same place, but that area of Port Chester was incorporated as the town of Rye Brook in 1982. Don't be dismayed if you can't find Rye Brook on the map—it isn't on the older ones and still hasn't made it onto many newer ones.

Go back to HRP and take it south to I-287, Cross Westchester Expwy. Take I-287 east to Port Chester and pick up I-95 south to Exit 11, Playland Pkwy. This takes you directly to Playland.

Nature, History, and Art in Greenwich

TRIP F-3

AUDUBON CENTER, Greenwich

BRUCE MUSEUM, Greenwich

PUTNAM COTTAGE, Greenwich

BUSH-HOLLEY HOUSE, Cos Cob

DISTANCE: From GWB to Greenwich via Audubon Center, about 35 mi. Fast and average speeds.

Audubon Center, 613 Riversville Rd., Greenwich, CT 06830 (203-869-5272). *Open all year Tues-Sun 9-5; closed major holidays. Adults $1, senior citizens and children 50¢, free to members of Audubon Society. Self-guided tours, gift and book shop. No picnicking or pets in nature study areas. Not wheelchair-accessible, but parking area is good for birdwatching.*

Here's the place to go for information on just about every phase of nature study. Established in 1942, this 485-acre wildlife sanctuary is home to about 90 species of birds, many types of small animals, and a profusion of wildflowers. There are 15 miles of hiking trails through varied habitats, and the visitor center has many excellent interpretive exhibits.

Bruce Museum, Museum Drive, Bruce Park, Greenwich, CT 06830 (203-869-0376). *Open all year Tues-Sat 10-5, Sun 2-5; closed major holidays. Adults $2, senior citizens $1.50, children $1. Gift shop. Ramp and 1 step into building; 1st floor manageable for wheelchairs.*

We might call this the "everything museum," for the range of exhibits here is unusually wide, covering fine arts, history, the natural sciences, and ethnology. Among other things, we can see wildlife dioramas, geological specimens, Indian relics, early American tools, and a nice selection of 19th-century American paintings. At the marine center we can meet a variety of animals that inhabit Long Island Sound, and deepen our acquaintance with some of them in the hands-on aquarium display.

Putnam Cottage, 243 E. Putnam Ave., Greenwich, CT 06830 (203-869-9697). *Open all year Mon, Wed, Fri 10-12 and 2-4. Adults $2, children under 12 free. Steps into building, difficult for wheelchairs.*

Known as Knapp's Tavern during the Revolutionary War, this small house was built around 1690 and is noteworthy for its rare scalloped shingles and huge fieldstone fireplaces. As a stagecoach station along the Boston Post Road, it was a convenient stopping place for Revolutionary leaders, among them General Israel Putnam. "Old Put" was a guest here in 1779 when he discovered a large number of British troops coming up the Post Road. Hurrying from the house, he urged his horse down the side of the cliff and made his escape. The local DAR chapter, which maintains the house as a museum, is responsible for the fine period furnishings and the lovely garden. There is also a restored barn on the grounds.

Bush-Holley House, 39 Strickland Rd., Cos Cob, CT 06807 (203-869-6899). *Open all year Tues-Sat 12-4; closed New Year's, Easter, July 4th, Thanksgiving, Christmas. Adults $2, senior citizens $1, children 50¢, preschoolers free. Not wheelchair-accessible.*

Originally a colonial saltbox built around 1685, today the headquarters of the Greenwich Historical Society, this beautiful house shows the architectural accretions and alterations of three centuries. It is furnished with authentic 18th- and 19th-century pieces and has many interesting features, including a room once used as a countinghouse and papered in an unusual design—a tax stamp from the time of King George II. Across from the enormous fireplace in the kitchen, a picture window looks out upon the herb garden. Children will enjoy the antique toy collection.

At the turn of the century, the Bush-Holley House was the residence of Elmer Livingston MacRae, one of the organizers of the historic 1913 Armory Show in New York City, which introduced modern art to the United States. Though outraged critics heaped vituperation on the 1,600 avant-garde paintings on display, denouncing the "degeneracy" of such works as Marcel Duchamp's *Nude Descending a Staircase,* the show helped to win an American public for modern art and revolutionized American painting. During MacRae's time, the Bush-Holley House became a magnet for artists and writers, attracting the likes of Willa Cather, Lincoln Steffens, and John Henry Twachtman. Paintings by MacRae, Twachtman, Childe Hassam, and other American impressionists adorn the walls of the house. On the grounds is a museum devoted to the works of sculptor John Rogers (1829-1904), who specialized in group studies of slaves, soldiers, and ordinary people. These "Rogers groups" became very popular during the Civil War and remain of interest as vivid records of their period.

FOR THE DRIVER: Take HRP north into Connecticut (25¢), where it becomes Merritt Pkwy. Continue to Exit 28, Round Hill Rd (35¢). After ramp, turn left on Round Hill and take it north a little over 1 mi to John St. Turn left and go about 1 mi west to Audubon Center, at corner of John St and Riversville Rd.

From Audubon Center, go south on Riversville Rd several mi to Glenville. Here turn left on Glenville Rd and follow it to end, at rotary. Take 1st right off rotary onto Deerfield Drive and follow this to end at US 1 (W Putnam Ave/Boston Post Rd), passing Greenwich Library on left. Turn left on US 1 and proceed to 2nd light, at Greenwich Ave. Turn right on Greenwich and go south through town, passing under railroad tracks and I-95. Continue on Greenwich, now Steamboat Rd, to next light, at water's edge. Here turn left onto Museum Drive and watch for stone pillars of Bruce Museum, driveway on left.

Go back to Steamboat Rd, turn right, and retrace your steps until you can't continue on Greenwich Ave, which is one way in the other direction. Turn right and go 1 block to Milbank Ave. Turn left on Milbank and proceed several blocks, continuing through traffic circle to jct with US 1 (E Putnam Ave). Turn right and go a short way to Putnam Cottage, red building on left.

From Putnam Cottage, turn left and go north on US 1. Shortly after sign for Cos Cob is a major intersection and stoplight at Strickland Rd. Here a small sign directs you to right; follow it to River Rd and Bush-Holley House, on right just before I-95 overpass.

Everything But the Kitchen Sink in Stamford

TRIP F-4

UNITED HOUSE WRECKING

WHITNEY MUSEUM OF AMERICAN ART

HOYT-BARNUM HOUSE

STAMFORD MUSEUM AND NATURE CENTER
BARTLETT ARBORETUM

DISTANCE: From GWB, about 40 mi. Mainly fast speeds.

Now we're in Stamford, a thriving industrial and research center with a population of 103,000 and a score of Fortune 500 companies, blessed with scenic beauty and an eclectic range of attractions that make it equally inviting as a place to live or visit. For FURTHER INFORMATION about the city, contact the Stamford Coliseum Authority, 429 Atlantic St., PO Box 10152, Stamford, CT 06904 (203-358-4184).

United House Wrecking, 328 Selleck St., Stamford, CT 06902 (203-348-5371). *Open all year Tues-Sat 9-5. No admission fee, free parking. Wide, level pathways; mostly manageable for wheelchairs.*

Here, spread over 6½ acres, is a mind-boggling, vocabulary-defying collection of whatnots, knickknacks, doohickeys, and thingamabobs. Need a weathervane, traffic light, church pew, life-size can-can girl, wooden Indian, birdbath, gargoyle, cherub, or New York subway A-train car? On the more practical side, how about some stained or beveled glass or a carved mantel or some antique furniture? Whatever you fancy, chances are you can buy it here, along with thousands of items you'd never have dreamed of looking for, much less finding—a simply unbelievable selection of architectural, agricultural, marine, commercial, and domestic treasures from yesteryear. If America were a great big house and Uncle Sam had decided to clean out the basement and the attic for the Bicentennial, say, you'd have to imagine that the result would look something like United House Wrecking, "the junkyard with a personality."

Whitney Museum of American Art, 1 Champion Plaza, Stamford, CT 06921 (203-358-7630 or -7652). *Open all year Tues-Sat 11-5; gallery talks 12:30 Tues, Thurs, Sat. Free admission; free parking in Champion garage. Wheelchair-accessible.*

A varied program of major exhibits awaits us at the Fairfield County branch of the prestigious Whitney Museum in New York City, founded in 1930 by Gertrude Vanderbilt Whitney to foster the development of American art. Carefully researched and beautifully mounted, the exhibits change every two or three months. Among the 1986 offerings were "American Art Since 1960," representing most of the major artistic trends of the last quarter-century through works assembled from private Connecticut collections; "Photographic Fictions," examining contemporary techniques of staged or arranged photography based on the manipulation of objects, images, and figures; and "Yesterday's Tomorrows: Past Images of the American Future," presenting an array of objects, drawings, photos, and films embodying the American perception of the future over the past 100 years.

Hoyt-Barnum House, 713 Bedford St., Stamford, CT 06903 (203-323-1975). *Open Apr thru Dec Tues-Thurs 11:30-2:30, Sat 12-4; closed major holidays. Adults $2, senior citizens $1, children 50¢. Not wheelchair-accessible.*

The Stamford Historical Society maintains this restored 1699 house, the oldest still standing in Stamford. Originally owned by a blacksmith, the house features four fireplaces, a commanding fieldstone chimney, and period furnishings reflecting life in Stamford over three centuries.

Stamford Museum and Nature Center, 39 Scofieldtown Rd., Stamford, CT 06903 (203-322-1646). *Open all year daily, Mon-Sat 9-5, Sun and holidays 1-5; closed New Year's, Thanksgiving, Christmas. Adults $2.50, senior citizens and children under 16 $1.50, under 5 free. Planetarium shows Sun 3:30 (fee), observatory Fri 8pm-10pm (fee). Nature trails, picnicking, gift shop; concerts, lectures, and special events all year. Mostly wheelchair-accessible.*

The fabulous mansion that once belonged to Henri Bendel today looks down upon a picturebook colonial New England farm, a small gem of a lake dotted with waterfowl, a pool of otters, and miles of trails. The working farm has a restored 1750 barn, grazing oxen, sheep, goats, and pigs, and an exhibit on early rural life. In the mansion are three galleries: an art gallery that mounts six to eight major exhibits a year, with a separate space devoted to works by experimental artists; a natural history gallery that shows us how the surrounding Connecticut landscape was formed by millions of years of geological activity; and an Indian gallery that introduces us to the "People of the Dawn." There are regularly scheduled shows at the Edgerton Memorial Planetarium, and an annual Astronomy Day highlighting the latest developments in the field. Other annual events include ice harvesting at Laurel Lake in January, maple sugaring from sap to syrup in March, Sheep-to-Shawl Day in May, craft demonstrations on Harvest Day in September, and cider making in the museum's antique press in October, followed closely by the Halloween jack-o'-lantern contest. At the Country Store gift shop we can choose calico, candles, condiments, candy, cookbooks, and a range of other old-fashioned, affordable souvenirs.

Bartlett Arboretum, University of Connecticut, 151 Brookdale Rd., Stamford, CT 06903 (203-322-6971). *Grounds open all year daily 8:30-sunset; office and library open all year Mon-Fri 9-4. Free. No picnicking, no pets. Difficult for wheelchairs.*

This 63-acre facility of the University of Connecticut College of Agriculture features cultivated gardens surrounded by natural woodlands with several ecology trails and a swamp walk. The arboretum specializes in collections of dwarf conifers, flowering trees and shrubs, and wildflowers. Many more varieties of plants thrive in the greenhouse, and there's a fine horticultural reference library.

FOR THE DRIVER: Take I-95 north (40¢) to Exit 6, Harvard Ave. After ramp, turn right on Harvard and go to end at Selleck St. Here is entrance to United House Wrecking.

Return to I-95 north briefly to Exit 8, Atlantic St. After ramp turn left on Atlantic, going under I-95, and proceed to Tresser Blvd. Turn right here to Champion garage and parking for Whitney Museum.

Go back on Tresser to Atlantic St and turn right. Almost immediately on left is the STAMFORD CENTER FOR THE ARTS (box office 203-323-2131; Chargit 800-223-0120 in CT, 212-944-9300 in NYC), home of the Stamford State Opera, the innovative Pilobolus Dance Theatre, and the Hartman Theatre, presenting first-rate classic and contemporary drama with top Broadway and international casts, designers, and directors. A few blocks further on Atlantic St, on left just before Broad St, is another performing arts center, the PALACE THEATRE (203-359-0009), with the Stamford Symphony Orchestra and the Connecticut Grand Opera in residence.

At intersection of Atlantic and Broad Sts, make a right on Broad and then a quick left on Bedford St. Go 2 blocks to Hoyt-Barnum House, on right at corner of Bedford and North Sts.

Continue on Bedford St, shortly passing the FIRST PRESBYTERIAN CHURCH (203-324-9522), a distinctive whale-shaped building (1958) designed by Wallace K. Harrison, with beautiful stained-glass windows by Frenchman Gabriel Loire. Proceed several blocks past church to jct of Bedford and High Ridge Rd (CT 137). Turn right, go north on High Ridge, cross Merritt Pkwy, and continue about ¾ mi to Scofieldtown Rd, passing STAMFORD HISTORICAL SOCIETY MUSEUM (203-329-1183) at 1508 High Ridge. Turn left on Scofieldtown to Stamford Museum and Nature Center.

Go back to High Ridge, turn left, and continue north briefly to Brookdale Rd. Turn left here to Bartlett Arboretum, shortly on right.

To return to New York City, go back down High Ridge to Merritt Pkwy and take it south (35¢), or go back into Stamford and pick up I-95 south (40¢).

Tradition and Innovation in Small-Town New England

TRIP F-5

NEW CANAAN HISTORICAL SOCIETY,
  New Canaan
SILVERMINE GUILD CENTER FOR THE ARTS,
  New Canaan
ALDRICH MUSEUM OF CONTEMPORARY ART,
  Ridgefield
KEELER TAVERN, Ridgefield

DISTANCE: From GWB to Ridgefield via New Canaan, about 60 mi. Fast and average speeds.

New Canaan Historical Society, 13 Oenoke Ridge, New Canaan, CT 06840 (203-966-1776). *Open all year Tues-Sat 9:30-12:30 and 2-4:30; museums open Wed, Thurs, Sun 2-4; summer hours may vary (call in advance). Adults $2, children under 19 free. Not wheelchair-accessible.*

Originally known as Canaan Parish, New Canaan was settled in 1731 on the high ridges north of Stamford. Its heritage has been preserved by the New Canaan Historical Society through a series of small, well-organized museums in the old buildings of the historic district. In the original Town House of Canaan Parish, we can visit a costume museum, a library of local history and genealogy, and the Cody Drug Store, a restoration of the town's first pharmacy (1845). Also on the grounds are the Georgian-style Hanford-Silliman House, a tool museum and print shop with working hand press, the 1799 Rock Schoolhouse, and the restored studio of sculptor John Rogers, with examples of his popular "Rogers groups" (see Bush-Holley House, Trip F-3).

Silvermine Guild Center for the Arts, 1037 Silvermine Rd., New Canaan, CT 06840 (203-966-5617 for galleries, -5618 for programs). *Open all year Tues-Sat 11-5, Sun 12-5; closed major holidays. Suggested donation $1-$2. Most facilities and restrooms wheelchair-accessible.*

This famous art center has a school and three galleries displaying the works of guild members. The center hosts the annual summer Art of Northeast USA exhibit, one of the nation's oldest juried competitions, and the biennial National Print Show. It also sponsors a summer chamber music festival and a month-long Christmas show and sale featuring an excellent selection of artwork and crafts in all price brackets.

Aldrich Museum of Contemporary Art, 258 Main St., Ridgefield, CT 06877 (203-438-4519). *Sculpture garden open all year daily; free. Museum open all year Tues-Fri 2:30-4:30, Sat-Sun 1-5; adults $1, senior citizens and children 50¢. Sculpture garden manageable for wheelchairs; low steps into museum, but most exhibits are upstairs.*

Here, in the unlikely setting of Ridgefield—settled in 1709 and still preserving the appearance of an 18th-century New England town—is a serious museum of contemporary art, with changing exhibits of modern and avant-garde works. The sculpture garden is an attractively landscaped outdoor installation of large-scale works by leading artists.

Keeler Tavern, 132 Main St., Ridgefield, CT 06877 (203-438-5485). *Open Feb thru Dec, 1-4 Wed, Sat-Sun, and Mon holidays. Adults $1.50, children 50¢. Guided tours, gift stop. Not wheelchair-accessible.*

Considerably more in keeping with Ridgefield's ambience than the Aldrich Museum, this 1733 tavern served as a stagecoach stop and patriot headquarters during the American Revolution and was later converted into a home. During the Battle of Ridgefield in 1777, a British cannonball took up permanent lodging in the wall. Among the subsequent residents was architect Cass Gilbert (1859-1934), designer of the Woolworth building in New York City, the Supreme Court building in Washington, D.C., and many other notable structures.

FOR THE DRIVER: Take HRP north into Connecticut (25¢), where it becomes Merritt Pkwy. Proceed to Exit 37 (35¢) and take CT 124 (Oenoke Ridge) north about 2½ mi to New Canaan Historical Society Town House, next to St. Michael's Lutheran Church, just beyond God's Acre. A little further up Oenoke Ridge is the NEW CANAAN NATURE CENTER (203-966-9577), 40 acres of woodland with nature trails, seasonal exhibits, a working solar greenhouse, and plants for sale.

Go back down CT 124 to jct with CT 106 to Wilton. Turn left and go northeast on 106, which shortly becomes Silvermine Rd. Continue to 3-way stop, where 106 goes left and Silvermine Rd goes right. Stay on Silvermine Rd for about 1 mi to Silvermine Guild Center for the Arts.

Continue northeast on 106 to jct with CT 33. Turn sharp left onto 33 and proceed several mi to Ridgefield. In town watch for CT 35 coming in from left. At this jct, on right, is Keeler Tavern, and just beyond, also on right, is Aldrich Museum of Contemporary Art.

Note that Ridgefield is not far from Danbury, Bethel, and the sites on Trip E-3. It is also near the New York line and some of the sites on Trips D-6 and D-7.

To return to New York City from Ridgefield, you can go north a few mi via CT 35 and US 7 to I-84 and take this west to I-684 south, or you can go south via CT 33 and US 7 back to Merritt Pkwy south (35¢) or I-95 south (40¢).

Castles by the Sand

TRIP F-6

LOCKWOOD-MATHEWS MANSION MUSEUM, Norwalk
NATURE CENTER FOR ENVIRONMENTAL
  ACTIVITIES, Westport
SHERWOOD ISLAND STATE PARK, Westport

DISTANCE: From GWB to Westport, about 45 mi. Mainly fast speeds.

Lockwood-Mathews Mansion Museum, 295 West Ave., Norwalk, CT 06850 (203-838-1434). *Open Mar to mid-Dec Tues-Fri 11-3, Sun 1-4; guided 1-hr tour, last tour starts 1 hr before closing. Adults $3, senior citizens and students $2, children under 12 free. Gift shop. Will accommodate wheelchairs.*

This Victorian palace was built between 1864 and 1868 by financier LeGrand Lockwood, who purchased the finest materials and imported artisans from Europe to create the rich hand-wrought detail found in each of the 50 rooms that surround the octagonal skylit rotunda. After Lockwood's death, the mansion was bought by Charles D. Mathews and remained in his family until 1938, when it was sold to the city of Norwalk. Plans to demolish it and erect a new city hall on the site were squelched by a band of concerned citizens who formed a corporation to undertake a major restoration effort and open the mansion as a museum. Today we can all be grateful for the preservation of this National Historic Landmark, of which Dr. William Murtagh, keeper of the National Register in Washington, D.C., has written, "The magnificent interior of the building has the best frescoed walls I have ever seen in this country, and the lavishness of the marble and wood inlay work almost defies description in the museum quality of its workmanship."

Nature Center for Environmental Activities, 10 Woodside Lane, Westport, CT 06880 (203-227-7253). *Open all year daily, Mon-Sat 9-5, Sun 1-4; closed major holidays. Adults $1, children under 12 50¢. Partially wheelchair-accessible; trails difficult for wheelchairs.*

This 62-acre wildlife sanctuary is an imaginatively designed showcase for natural history exhibits that include live animals of the area, an aquarium, fossils, shells, and some good dioramas. A small garden grows in the center courtyard, and several miles of marked nature trails lead from the building. A gift shop sells books on natural history and related subjects.

Sherwood Island State Park, Westport, CT 06880 (203-226-6983). *Open all year daily 8-sunset. Use fee Memorial Day to Labor Day*

$2 per car weekdays, $4 weekends and holidays; off-season $2 weekends. Picnicking, playing field, fishing, swimming, scuba diving, food concession. No pets. Wheelchair-accessible picnic area, toilets, and telephones.

This popular 243-acre park includes almost two miles of beach and two large picnic groves with fine views of neighboring Compo Cove and Long Island Sound. The waters here offer rich opportunities for fishermen and scuba divers, while the sands provide hours of pleasure for sunbathers and castle builders alike.

FOR THE DRIVER: Take I-95 north (40¢) to Exit 14 at Norwalk and follow exit road to West Ave. Turn left on West and go under I-95 to Lockwood-Mathews Mansion, shortly on right.

Return to I-95 and continue north to Westport. If you're interested in a cruise on Long Island Sound, take Exit 16 to Cove Marina, where the LADY JOAN (203-838-9003), a replica of a Mississippi paddlewheeler, makes daily excursions around the Norwalk Islands from July 1 to Labor Day. For Nature Center for Environmental Activities, remain on I-95 to Exit 17, turn left and go north on CT 33 to Sylvan Rd South, turn left, and continue across US 1 (State St), where it becomes Sylvan Rd North. At fork, Sylvan Rd goes left and you bear right on Stony Brook Rd to Woodside Lane. Turn left on Woodside Lane and go about ⅓ mi to nature center, on right.

Go back on Sylvan Rd to jct with US 1. Turn left and go northeast on US 1 across Saugatuck River to Westport. At jct with Sherwood Island Connector, turn right and follow it across I-95 into Sherwood Island State Park.

A Fair Day in Fairfield

TRIP F-7

FAIRFIELD HISTORICAL SOCIETY

CONNECTICUT AUDUBON SOCIETY BIRDCRAFT
  MUSEUM AND SANCTUARY

CONNECTICUT AUDUBON SOCIETY FAIRFIELD
  CENTER AND LARSEN SANCTUARY

DISTANCE: From GWB, about 50 mi. Mainly fast speeds.

Fairfield Historical Society, 636 Old Post Rd., Fairfield, CT 06430 (203-259-1598). *Open all year Mon-Fri 9:30-4:30, Sun 1-5; closed*

Sat and major holidays. Suggested donation $1 adults, 50¢ senior citizens and children. Steps into building, but wheelchairs can maneuver on 1st floor, which has many exhibits; ramp to be installed.

This museum has some fine exhibits, attractively displayed to depict local history since the Great Swamp Fight of 1637, when the Pequot Indians were vanquished by the English in the final battle of the Pequot War. The permanent collections include tools, ornaments, textiles, furniture, ceramics, silverware, paintings, dolls, toys, and maritime memorabilia, along with extensive documentary and genealogical holdings in the research library. The museum is a good place to inquire about sightseeing in Fairfield, which has three historic districts of particular interest: Greenfield Hill, the Old Post Road, and Southport Harbor, a thriving port of entry and shipping center until 1890.

Connecticut Audubon Society Birdcraft Museum and Sanctuary, 314 Unquowa Rd., Fairfield, CT 06430 (203-259-0416). *Grounds open all year daily; museum open all year Thurs, Sat, and Sun 12-5. Donation $1. No picnicking, no pets. Steps into building, but exhibits are on 1 level; trails difficult for wheelchairs.*

The first private songbird refuge in New England (1914), this sanctuary has become a refuge for featherless bipeds as well. From the pleasant walking trails and boardwalk observation area we can spot many different species of birds, along with the occasional government scientist (the sanctuary doubles as a federal banding station). The natural history museum displays dioramas of native and African wildlife, a taxidermy exhibit of animals and birds that died from natural causes and were mounted by one of the museum's early curators, and a set of deceptively lifelike decoys by the legendary Charles "Shang" Wheeler.

Connecticut Audubon Society Fairfield Center and Larsen Sanctuary, 2325 Burr St., Fairfield, CT 06430 (203-259-6305). *Building open all year Tues-Sat 9-4:30, also Sun 12-4:30 early Sept to Christmas; free. Sanctuary open all year daily dawn-dusk; trail fee $1 adults, 50¢ children. Building closed July 4th, last week of Dec, New Year's. No picnicking, no pets. Sensory trail for visually handicapped; gift shop wheelchair-accessible, some trails manageable for wheelchairs on dry days.*

The headquarters of the Connecticut Audubon Society features changing exhibits on state flora and fauna, solar energy applications, and a natural history library. In the adjoining Larsen Sanctuary, 6 miles of trails wind through 160 acres of woodlands, open fields, and marshes, home to more than 100 species of birds and animals, and an abundance of wildflowers, ferns, and trees. A special delight is the "singing and fragrance walk," designed for the visually handicapped but equally calculated to deepen an appreciation of the senses in those who have all five intact; soft paths with smooth wood handrails brush past prickly, fragrant evergreens across murmuring streams while birdsong fills the air.

FOR THE DRIVER: Take I-95 north (40¢) to Exit 22 and turn right on Beach Rd. After crossing US 1, go 1 block to Old Post Rd, turn right, and watch for Fairfield Historical Society on town green, 2nd building on right. You may want to continue down Old Post Rd through one of Fairfield's historic districts to Sasco Hill Rd, turn right briefly, and then go left across bridge onto Harbor Rd for a look at Southport Harbor.

From Fairfield Historical Society, go back on Old Post Rd to Beach Rd, turn left, and go back to US 1. Turn left and go south a short way to Unquowa Rd. Turn right here, cross railroad tracks, and watch for entrance to Birdcraft Museum and Sanctuary, on right.

To continue to Audubon Society Fairfield Center and Larsen Sanctuary, stay on Unquowa Rd and proceed under I-95 to Mill Plain Rd. Turn right and drive north about 4½ mi on Mill Plain, which becomes Burr St. Proceed past Merritt Pkwy underpass and watch for sanctuary, shortly on left.

If you're traveling to Fairfield in mid-May, be sure to attend the DOG-WOOD FESTIVAL (203-259-5596) at Greenfield Hills Congregational Church, Old Academy and Bronson Rds. For a week or so, this whole area turns into a fairyland of blossoms against a classic New England setting, and we can feast upon the visual delights of the dogwood while nibbling on home-baked goodies or browsing among the many antiques and crafts for sale. The dogwood also produces colorful foliage in the fall, though without the gustatory and acquisitive possibilities of the festival.

For return trip, go back on Burr St under Merritt and turn left on Congress St to entrance for Merritt back to New York City (35¢ plus 25¢ on HRP), or continue on Burr St/Mill Plain Rd back to I-95 south (40¢) in Fairfield.

To Bridgeport and to the Egress

TRIP F-8

HMS ROSE
P. T. BARNUM MUSEUM
MUSEUM OF ART, SCIENCE AND INDUSTRY
BEARDSLEY ZOOLOGICAL GARDENS

DISTANCE: From GWB, about 55 mi. Mainly fast speeds.

HMS Rose, Captain's Cove Marina, 1 Bostwick Ave., Bridgeport, CT 06605 (203-335-1433). *Open for ½-hr tours May thru Oct Tues-Sun 12-5. Adults $2, children under 12 $1. Fully wheelchair-accessible.*

Here is a replica of the flagship of Captain James Wallace, an officer of the British fleet stationed off the coast of New England in 1775 under the command of Admiral Samuel Graves. Fortunately for the Revolutionary cause, Graves was a singularly inept officer who made poor use of his forces. His half-hearted attempts to intimidate New England's seafaring towns inspired the colonists to take to their whalers and fishing boats and harass the British fleet. From such humble beginnings sprang the fledgling American navy, which had several early successes, including the capture of a tender from the *Rose*. On our tour of the *Rose* replica we learn more about colonial naval history and the workings of a British frigate. Afterwards we have an opportunity to visit several craft shops or dine at the restaurant and fish house on the premises.

P. T. Barnum Museum, 820 Main St., Bridgeport, CT 06604 (203-576-7320). *Closed for renovations until July 1988.*

You don't have to be one of those suckers born every minute to go for the P. T. Barnum Museum, packed with memorabilia of the career of Bridgeport's most famous resident. A master of hype, Phineas Taylor Barnum knew how to turn adjectives into superlatives and curiosity into cash. He spent the better part of the 19th century titillating America with such spectacles as the Fiji mermaid (part monkey, part stuffed fish), the Siamese twins Chang and Eng, and Bridgeport native Charles Sherwood Stratton, a.k.a. General Tom Thumb, the 2½-foot midget who entertained kings, queens, presidents, and about 20 million other folks under Barnum's skillful management. In 1850 Barnum promoted the American tour of coloratura soprano Jenny Lind, the "Swedish nightingale," and made her a tremendous success; in 1871 he opened his famous circus, with Jumbo the African elephant as the major (at 6½ tons) attraction; and in between he took time out to be mayor of Bridgeport. All this—plus more! more! more!—is recounted in the exhibits at the P. T. Barnum Museum. So step right up ladies and gents—but not right now; the museum is currently undergoing ambitious renovations and won't reopen until the summer of 1988. That may seem a long wait, but not for the Greatest Show on Earth.

Museum of Art, Science and Industry, 4450 Park Ave., Bridgeport, CT 06604 (203-372-3521). *Open all year Tues-Fri 11-5, Sat-Sun 12-5; closed major holidays. Adults $3.50, senior citizens and children 3-18 $2, under 3 free. Gift shop. Wheelchair-accessible entrance and restrooms, elevators to all floors.*

Whether our taste leans towards Indians, fine antiques, Renaissance or contemporary art, stargazing, or space travel, we'll find something to interest us here. The Sikorsky mock-up of a helicopter cockpit and rotor is a popular attraction, as are the hands-on science and technology exhibits. The children's museum bustles with activities designed to entertain and inform. The planetarium offers excellent programs suited to all ages from the second grade up, and the adjacent Du Pont-Wheeler Gallery of the Skies has a variety of heavenly displays. For those with a serious interest in circus history, there's a Barnum research collection of documents, photographs, and memorabilia. On the main floor are three art galleries with changing exhibits, and a citywide juried art show takes place here during the Barnum Festival every summer. The museum is located in a 90-acre park with an inviting nature trail.

Beardsley Zoological Gardens, Noble Ave., Bridgeport, CT 06610 (203-576-8082). *Open all year daily 9-4; closed Thanksgiving, Christmas, New Year's. Parking fee $5 per out-of-state car ($3 in-state, free to Bridgeport residents). Zoo admission $1 adults, 50¢ children 5-12; senior citizens, handicapped, and children un-*

der 5 free. Fees not collected during winter months, usually Dec thru Feb. Picnic area, snack bar, gift shop. No pets. Will accommodate wheelchairs.

More than 200 animals inhabit this 30-acre zoo, Connecticut's largest. Monkeys and birds have the run of a large building, sea lions cavort in an outdoor pool, and farmyard animals mingle with visitors in the children's zoo. Well-tended gardens make Beardsley especially attractive during blooming periods.

FOR THE DRIVER: Take I-95 north (40¢) to Exit 26. After ramp bear right on Wordin Ave to Bostwick Ave and turn left to HMS *Rose.*

Go back to I-95 and continue briefly to Exit 27. Here take CT 25 north to Exit 3. Shortly after ramp, on Main St across North Ave (US 1) is Barnum Museum.

Go back on Main to North Ave. Turn right here and go south briefly to Park Ave. Turn right on Park and follow it northwest about 2½ mi to Museum of Art, Science and Industry, in Ninety Acres Park.

Continue northwest on Park Ave to Merritt Pkwy and take it north to Exit 49S. Here take CT 25 south to Exit 5, Boston Ave. Bear right on Boston after ramp and go to 5th stoplight, at Noble Ave. Turn left on Noble and go about ¼ mi to Beardsley Zoological Gardens, entrance on left.

To Stratford-on-Housatonic

TRIP F-9

BOOTHE MEMORIAL PARK, Stratford

CAPTAIN DAVID JUDSON HOUSE AND CATHARINE
    B. MITCHELL MUSEUM, Stratford

AMERICAN SHAKESPEARE THEATRE, Stratford

ORONOQUE ORCHARDS, Stratford

INDIAN WELL STATE PARK, Shelton

DISTANCE: From GWB to Indian Well, about 70 mi. Mainly fast speeds.

Boothe Memorial Park, N. Main St., Stratford, CT 06497 (203-375-1233). *Grounds open all year daily 8-dusk; buildings open daily Easter to Thanksgiving Mon-Fri 11-1, Sat-Sun 1-4. Free. Picnic facilities, playground. Leashed pets only. Wheelchair-accessible* *restrooms in dining hall and outdoors; wide, level paths thru most of park.*

No one passes for the first time this group of strangely constructed buildings without doing a double-take. Built at random around the turn of the century by two eccentric brothers, the complex includes a newly renovated windmill, a large redwood structure full of baskets from all over the world, an enormous pipe organ in a building near a sunken garden, a blacksmith shop, a carriage museum, a clock-tower museum, and the old homestead building where the Boothe brothers lived. The park is situated on a hill affording some marvelous views of the whole area. A particular delight for flower fanciers and photographers is the beautiful Jackson and Perkins Trial Rose Garden.

Captain David Judson House and Catharine B. Mitchell Museum, 967 Academy Hill, Stratford, CT 06497 (203-378-0632). *Open mid-Apr thru Oct Wed, Sat, and Sun 11-4. Adults $2, senior citizens $1.50, students $1; or $5 per family. Guided tours. Not wheelchair-accessible.*

Built around 1750 on a foundation constructed over 100 years earlier, this well-preserved house is filled with typical furnishings from the 18th century. Of special interest are some of the architectural features—the hand-rived shingles on the east gable end of the house, the graceful curved pediment over the doorway, the traditional center stairway, the original wood paneling. Our tour takes us through various rooms steeped in an atmosphere of colonial living. The cellar holds a lower kitchen once used as a slave quarters, equipped with a huge fireplace and a display of period household implements and tools. Behind the Judson House is the Catharine Bunnell Mitchell Museum, with carefully researched exhibits tracing the history of Stratford from the period of Indian settlement to about 1830. Both the home and the museum are maintained by the Stratford Historical Society.

American Shakespeare Theatre, 1850 Elm St., Stratford, CT 06497 (office 203-378-7321; box office 203-375-5000 in CT, 212-966-3900 in NYC). *Grounds open all year daily 8-sunset. Theatre and costume museum open spring and summer during performances; call for schedule. No admission fee for park; tickets run about $7.*

Picnic area, marina. Leashed pets only, in picnic area only. Theatre, restrooms, and picnic area wheelchair-accessible.

This handsome replica of the renowned Globe Theatre in London is located in a scenic 12-acre state park on the banks of the Housatonic River. Some exceptional performances of Shakespeare have taken place here since the doors opened in 1955. During the season, there's a marina to accommodate boat-borne devotees of the bard, and though the play's the thing, we can still enjoy picnicking and sightseeing on the grounds in the off-season. The Globe is currently undergoing renovation and is scheduled to reopen in spring 1987.

Oronoque Orchards, 6911 Main St., Stratford, CT 06497 (203-378-7335). *Open all year daily.*

Posted at the driveway as we enter the lovely Oronoque grounds is the name of today's special home-baked pie. By the time we arrive at the counter, we've passed an enormous assortment of oven-fresh breads, muffins, cakes, turnovers. There are nearly 30 species of pie alone, plus candies, jams, gourmet foods, and a roomful of gifts for sale.

Indian Well State Park, Shelton, CT 06484 (203-735-7108). *Open all year daily 8-sunset. Use fee Memorial Day to Labor Day $1 per car weekdays, $2 weekends and holidays. Picnicking, playing field, hiking trails, swimming, fishing, boating, food concession. Leashed pets only, in picnic areas only. Picnic area, food concession, and phones wheelchair-accessible.*

Here's a lovely 153-acre park on the Housatonic River, perfect for picnicking or more active pursuits. The park takes its name from the Indian legends associated with the splash pool at the bottom of the scenic waterfall near the riverbank.

FOR THE DRIVER: Take HRP north into Connecticut (25¢), where it becomes Merritt Pkwy. Proceed to Exit 53S (35¢) and turn right after ramp onto CT 110 towards Stratford. Watch for 1st small road on right, Main St. Turn here and continue briefly to Boothe Memorial Park, on left.

Continue south on Main St, shortly rejoining CT 110. Proceed to jct with CT 113, bear right, and continue south on 113 (Main St), crossing US 1 (Barnum Ave) and passing under railroad tracks and I-95. Several blocks past I-95, just after Broad St, is Academy Hill, a small street on left. Turn here for Judson House and Mitchell Museum.

Continue on Academy Hill to next corner, Elm St. Turn right and proceed on Elm across Stratford Ave. Shortly watch for American Shakespeare Theatre, on left.

Just beyond theatre, turn right off Elm onto Wells Place and back to CT 113. Turn right and go north on 113, merging with CT 110 and continuing past Merritt Pkwy. Shortly watch for sign to Oronoque Orchards, on left at stoplight.

From orchards, turn left on 110 and continue north several mi, crossing CT 8. Soon after, watch for road on right to Indian Well State Park.

Eli for a Day

TRIP F-10

YALE UNIVERSITY, New Haven
  YALE UNIVERSITY ART GALLERY
  YALE CENTER FOR BRITISH ART
  BEINECKE RARE BOOK AND MANUSCRIPT
    LIBRARY
  PEABODY MUSEUM OF NATURAL HISTORY
  YALE COLLECTION OF MUSICAL INSTRUMENTS

DISTANCE: From GWB, about 75 mi. Mainly fast speeds.

On this trip we visit New Haven, established by Puritans in 1637-38 under a theocratic form of government that issued strict laws regulating public and private conduct—the original "blue laws," so named for the colored paper on which they were written. The town developed rapidly as a port of entry and industrial center, contributing many another first to American life, mostly in the field of manufacturing techniques and new products (among them two that would have horrified the promulgators of the blue laws: the corkscrew and the lollipop). Over the years, New Haven has had its fair share of famous citizens, including Noah Webster, Eli Whitney, and Charles Goodyear, not to mention a host of notable temporary residents passing through as students, from William Howard "Dollar Diplomacy" Taft to Jennifer "What a Feeling" Beals. Our trip focuses on New Haven's leading educational and cultural institution, Yale University, but there are many other attractions here besides—Revolutionary War fortifications, historic homes and museums, the renowned Long Wharf Theatre and Yale Repertory Theatre, fine municipal parks, cruises on Long Island Sound, and handsome buildings in a variety of architectural styles, from colonial, Georgian, and Federal to Urban Renewal. For FURTHER INFORMATION, contact the New Haven Convention and Visitors Bureau, 155 Church St., New Haven, CT 06510 (203-787-8367).

Yale University, New Haven, CT 06520 (203-432-2300). *Campus open all year daily for tours, Mon-Fri 10:30 and 2, Sat-Sun 1:30; no reservation required. Free. Most of campus wheelchair-accessible.*

Chartered in 1701, Yale occupied several different locations before settling in New Haven in 1716. It acquired its name in 1718 after a substantial donation from one Elihu Yale, an English merchant who prospered mightily from his somewhat dubious dealings as an official of the British East India Company. One of America's most prestigious universities, Yale became coeducational in 1969 and today has a student population of about 10,000. Our tour begins at Phelps Gateway on New Haven Green and takes in most of the campus buildings within walking distance, from the historic Old Campus and Connecticut Hall, where Revolutionary hero Nathan Hale once roomed, to the controversial abstract concrete Art and Architecture Building by Paul Rudolph.

Yale University Art Gallery, 1111 Chapel St., New Haven, CT 06520 (203-432-2600). *Open all year Tues-Sat 10-5, Sun 2-5, also Thurs 6pm-9pm mid-Sept to mid-May; closed New Year's, July 4th, Thanksgiving, Christmas. Free. Fully wheelchair-accessible.*

The nation's oldest college art museum has impressive collections of pre-Colombian, Oriental, and African art, European paintings from the Middle Ages to the 20th century, American decorative arts from colonial times to the present, 19th- and 20th-century American paintings, and modern sculpture. The museum has a pleasant, unhurried atmosphere, with enormous picture windows looking out on campus scenes.

Yale Center for British Art, 1080 Chapel St., New Haven, CT 06520 (203-432-2800). *Open all year Tues-Sat 10-5, Sun 2-5; closed*

New Year's, Memorial Day, July 4th, Labor Day, Thanksgiving, Christmas. Free. Tours and special programs (432-2858), museum shop. Fully wheelchair-accessible.

This outstanding public museum was established by Yale graduate Paul Mellon to preserve and display his collection of British art, the largest in the United States. The permanent and changing exhibits of paintings, sculpture, drawings, prints, and rare books trace aesthetic developments from the Elizabethan era to the mid-19th century, with special emphasis on the period between the birth of Hogarth in 1697 and the death of Turner in 1851, often considered the "golden age" of English art. In addition there are 13,000 reference volumes, an extensive photo archive, and a regular program of colloquia, lectures, concerts, and films to enhance our understanding of the artworks and their context. The museum building, a concrete, glass, and steel structure with interiors of travertine marble, white oak, and natural fibers, was the last design of American architect Louis I. Kahn. Fittingly, it stands across the street from his first major commission, the modern wing of the Yale Art Gallery.

Beinecke Rare Book and Manuscript Library, 121 Wall St., New Haven, CT 06520 (203-432-2977). *Open all year Mon-Fri 8:30-5, Sat 10-5; closed Sun, major holidays, and Sat in Aug. Free. Wheelchair-accessible.*

Some rare treasures await us here, including a Gutenberg Bible, original Audubon prints from *The Birds of America,* medieval illuminated manuscripts, and more or less opaque modern manuscripts left by Twain, Hemingway, and other great American writers. The unique windowless building filters light through translucent marble panels that protect the library's collections, if not its visitors, from the ravages of time.

Peabody Museum of Natural History, 170 Whitney Ave., New Haven, CT 06511 (203-432-5055). *Open all year daily, Mon-Sat 9-4:45, Sun and holidays 1-4:45; closed New Year's, July 4th, Thanksgiving, Christmas. Adults $2, senior citizens $1.50, children 5-15 $1, under 5 free; Tues free. Special programs and tours, weekend film series (Sept-Apr), gift shop. Fully wheelchair-accessible.*

The Peabody's admission fee is a small price to pay for a journey through 500 million years of geological and natural history.

Here Earth's story unfolds in a series of outstanding exhibits of meteorites, rocks and minerals, invertebrate life, insect specimens, birds, mammals, remains of the ancient cultures of Mexico and Peru, artifacts of the Plains and Connecticut Indians. Perhaps most dramatic is Dinosaur Hall, where huge fossil skeletons stand frozen against a vivid 110-foot-long mural, Rudolph F. Zallinger's Pulitzer Prize-winning *Age of Reptiles*. The Peabody, New England's largest natural history museum and one of the nation's best, offers us a world "big as a *Brontosaurus,* delicate as a butterfly's wing, varied as human lives."

Yale Collection of Musical Instruments, 15 Hillhouse Ave., New Haven, CT 06520 (203-432-0822). *Open Sep-July Mon-Wed 1-4, also Sun 2-5 Sept-May; closed Aug and during university recesses. Free. Annual concert series, lectures, demonstrations. Not wheelchair-accessible.*

Here are 850 beautifully wrought instruments spanning 4 centuries of musical history, representing the music-making traditions of North and South America, Europe, Africa, and Asia.

FOR THE DRIVER: Take I-95 north (40¢) to Exit 47 and follow Oak St Connector into downtown New Haven, crossing Church St and bearing right on N Frontage Rd to York St. Turn right here and proceed several blocks north on York to Elm St, turn right 2 blocks to College St, then right again to Phelps Gateway and NEW HAVEN GREEN. The green, dating from the 17th century, is surrounded by 3 impressive churches; football and Frisbee were born here, and many delightful events take place here each year, including the NEW HAVEN JAZZ FESTIVAL (203-669-1662), the NEW HAVEN SYMPHONY SUMMER MUSIC SERIES (203-776-1444), and the one and only BED RACE (203-787-8956 or -8367) in September.

Parking can be a problem in downtown New Haven, and Yale is best seen on foot in any case, so you may want to park in the commercial lot behind the Center for British Art, which you pass on your way to the green. It's at York and Crown Sts, 3 blocks up York after you turn off N Frontage. The following directions assume you're walking; if you're driving, some of the streets will be one way the wrong way, and you'll have to go around the block.

From Phelps Gateway, continue down College St to next corner, Chapel St. Turn right and go past next corner, High St, to Art Gallery, on right. Across street is Center for British Art.

Go back to High St, turn left, and go 2 blocks to Beinecke Library, at corner of High and Wall Sts.

Continue up High St to Grove St, turn right, go 3 blocks to Church St, and turn left. Proceed up Church St, bearing left across railroad tracks and Trumbull St, where Church becomes Whitney Ave. Shortly Temple St comes in from left, and at this jct is a good local history museum, the NEW HAVEN COLONY HISTORICAL SOCIETY (203-562-4183), at 114 Whitney. On next corner, Whitney and Sachem St, is Peabody Museum. For Collection of Musical Instruments, turn left on Sachem and go past museum to tiny Hillhouse Ave, then left again to 15 Hillhouse.

Clang, Clang, Clang Went the Trolley

TRIP F-11

SHORE LINE TROLLEY MUSEUM, East Haven

DISTANCE: From GWB, about 80 mi. Fast speeds.

Shore Line Trolley Museum, East Haven, CT 06512 (203-467-6927). *Operates Apr thru Nov: Apr and Nov Sun 11-5; May to Memorial Day and Labor Day thru Oct Sat-Sun and holidays 11-5; Memorial Day to Labor Day daily 11-5. Adults $3, senior citizens $2.50, children 5-11 $1.50, under 5 free; tickets good all day on date of sale. Picnic grove, gift shop. Inquire about schedule and rates for annual National Trolley Festival (June), Fall Foliage Special (Oct), Railfan Day (Columbus Day Sat), Santa Claus Special (Dec). Some facilities wheelchair-accessible.*

Remember those weather-filled mornings standing on the corner waiting for the trolley? Griping at paying our nickel for the crowded, jouncy ride? Then one day the trolley never came again.

Today we'll take a long drive just to visit some of these creatures from the past. We'll pay about 50 times the old fare. And chances are we'll love every minute. Our ride—a three-mile round trip along the shore—may be on the open "breezer" that once ran to the Yale Bowl, or on one of the other cars so carefully restored by the museum's craftsmen. Afterwards, or between rides (we can take more than one if we wish), our motorman will take us on a guided tour of the car barns and workshops. All told, there are more than 100 trolley, subway, and el cars on display, spanning the years between 1878 and 1945. We can deepen our knowledge of trolley history by visiting the Sprague building, named for Frank Julian Sprague, father of electric traction and developer of the first electric street railway (1887).

The Shore Line Trolley Museum is part of the Branford Electric Railway District, a National Historic Site. Apart from its educational aspects, the ride is a lot of fun, and a cheerful spirit prevails among the patrons, punctuated by an occasional twinge of nostalgia. Children tend to consider the trolleys about a half-step this side of the Conestoga wagon, while their elders wonder, "What happened? Where did they go?"

FOR THE DRIVER: Take I-95 north (40¢) to Exit 51, Frontage Rd (US 1). Proceed to traffic light at Forbes Place, turn right briefly, then left on Main St. Continue on Main to East Haven Green, then turn right on Hemingway Ave and left on River St, past green. Shortly watch for Shore Line Trolley Museum, on left.

Guilford's Historic Houses

TRIP F-12
   HYLAND HOUSE
   THOMAS GRISWOLD HOUSE
   HENRY WHITFIELD HOUSE

DISTANCE: From GWB, about 95 mi. Fast speeds.

Hyland House, 84 Boston St., Guilford, CT 06437 (203-453-9477 or -0579). *Open June-Sept Tues-Sun 10-4:30, Sept to mid-Oct Sat-Sun 10-4:30. Adults $1.50, senior citizens $1, children under 14 free. Not wheelchair-accessible.*

Here is a fine example of a colonial saltbox, built about 1660. The interior features some unusual woodwork, rare early furnishings, and three walk-in fireplaces equipped for 17th-century cooking. Upstairs we find sewing rooms, closets filled with period clothing, and wool and flax wheels.

Thomas Griswold House, 171 Boston St., Guilford, CT 06437 (203-453-3176). *Open mid-June to mid-Sept Tues-Sun 11-4, also Sat-Sun 11-4 to end of Sept. Adults $1.50, senior citizens $1, children 50¢, under 12 free. Not wheelchair-accessible.*

Another excellent example of a colonial saltbox, this 1774 house was once pictured on a commemorative stamp. It is now the headquarters of the Guilford Keeping Society, serving as a repository for documents, records, pictures, and artifacts dating back to 1735. We'll see the "borning room," the buttery, the "keeping room" where the fire was kept burning, a restored working blacksmith shop, a costume exhibit, and some fine local furniture. A barn museum outside holds a collection of antique farm tools.

Henry Whitfield House, Whitfield St., Guilford, CT 06437 (203-453-2457 or 566-3005). *Open mid-Jan to mid-Dec Wed-Sun 10-4 (10-5 Apr-Nov), also Mon of holiday weekends; closed Thanksgiving and mid-Dec to mid-Jan. Adults $1.25, senior citizens 75¢, children 50¢. Not wheelchair-accessible.*

This striking edifice, said to be the oldest stone house in New England, belonged to the founder of Guilford, the Reverend Henry Whitfield, who led a group of parishioners from England to America to avoid religious persecution. They arrived in 1639 and promptly set about building a typical English manor house, unaware of the rugged American winters that had taught their Pilgrim predecessors to construct smaller, more easily heated rooms; the Great Hall, 33 feet long and 15 feet wide, required a fireplace at either end and a partition to divide it into 2 rooms when more space was needed. Apparently the settlers were not unaware of other potential dangers of the New World, for they made the walls about 2 feet thick. Whitfield and his family lived in this stronghold, which was also used for church meetings. Today it is a museum of 17th- and 18th-century Guilford life.

FOR THE DRIVER: Take I-95 north (40¢) to Exit 58 and turn right on CT 77 to Guilford Green. Bear left around green to Boston St, turn left on Boston, and proceed a short distance to Hyland House. Continue briefly on Boston St to Griswold House, on right at Lovers' Lane. From here ask directions for back roads to Whitfield House.

Up the Connecticut River

TRIP F-13

PRATT HOUSE, Essex
STEAM TRAIN AND RIVERBOAT, Essex
GILLETTE CASTLE STATE PARK, Hadlyme
FLORENCE GRISWOLD MUSEUM, Old Lyme
NUT MUSEUM, Old Lyme

DISTANCE: From GWB, about 125 mi. Mainly fast speeds.

Pratt House, 19 West Ave., Essex, CT 06426 (203-767-8987). *Open June-Sept Fri-Sun 1-5. Adults $1.50, senior citizens $1, children under 12 free. Annual Christmas exhibit. Not wheelchair-accessible.*

This small center-chimney colonial house (1732), restored by the Society for the Preservation of New England Antiquities, is filled with furnishings from the 17th, 18th, and 19th centuries. There are fine collections of Connecticut redware and unusual Chinese "courting mirrors."

Steam Train and Riverboat, Valley Railroad Company, PO Box 452, Essex, CT 06426 (203-767-0103). *Operates early May to late Dec: Wed, Sat-Sun, and Memorial Day early May to early June; Wed-Thurs and Sat-Sun early to late June; daily late June thru Aug; Wed-Sun and Columbus Day early Sept to late Oct; Sun in Nov; weekends and some weekdays in Dec for Christmas special. Train ride $6.95 adults, $2.95 children 3-11; train ride and boat cruise $9.95 adults, $4.95 children 3-11; parlor car $1.95 extra per person; children under 3 free. Will accommodate wheelchairs.*

A vintage steam train uses 3,000 gallons of water and 3 tons of coal to take us on an hour-long journey into the past, whistling and chugging its way up the scenic Connecticut River from Essex to Deep River Landing. Here we have the option of transferring to a riverboat for an additional hour's voyage farther upriver, passing green hills dotted with fine old houses and landmarks like Gillette Castle (see below) and the GOODSPEED OPERA HOUSE (203-873-8668) in East Haddam, an ornate Victorian theater now devoted exclusively to the presentation and preservation of American musicals.

The train, powered by a classic steam-belching, bell-clanging locomotive, follows the route of the old Valley Railroad, which ran between Hartford and Old Saybrook from 1871 until it was gobbled up by J. P. Morgan's New York, New Haven & Hartford line. The living slice of history we get on our ride is supplemented by the antique cars on display at the Connecticut Valley Railroad Museum, including a rare self-propelled Brill car and a luxurious Pullman with revolving plush seats, rich carpeting, and leaded-glass partitions.

Gillette Castle State Park, 67 River Rd., Hadlyme, CT 06439 (203-526-2336). *Grounds open all year daily 8-sunset; free. Castle open Memorial Day to Columbus Day daily 10-5, Columbus Day to Christmas Sat-Sun 10-4; adults $1, children 50¢. Picnicking, hiking trails, fishing, canoe rentals and canoe camping (fees), food concession. Leashed pets only, in picnic areas only. Wheelchair-accessible picnic shelter; castle not wheelchair-accessible.*

High above the pastoral Connecticut River perches a dream castle built by the great turn-of-the-century actor and portrayer of Sherlock Holmes, William Gillette (1853-1937). A native of Hartford, Gillette chose this site because of the superb view. One of the first actors to hold that a characterization should be based on the performer's own strongest personality traits, he applied the same principle to his castle, which he designed himself and fitted out with many unique mechanical devices of his own invention. He lived here from 1919 to 1937 with a supporting cast of 15 felines to whom he was greatly attached; the 24-room castle contains, among other things, a large collection of cat curios, along with scrapbooks, clippings, and other memorabilia of Gillette's stage career. Today his ivy-covered fieldstone creation is the centerpiece of a beautiful 184-acre state park—a fact that reflects well on Connecticut in light of the stipulation in Gillette's will that his property should under no circumstances pass to "any blithering saphead who has no conception of where he is or with what surrounded."

Florence Griswold Museum, 96 Lyme St., Old Lyme, CT 06371 (203-434-5542). *Open all year: June-Oct Tues-Sat 10-5; Sun 1-5;*

Nov-May Wed-Sun 1-5. Adults $1, senior citizens 50¢, children free. Wheelchair-accessible.

This handsome late Georgian mansion (1817) was the hub of a turn-of-the-century art colony subsidized by Miss Florence Griswold, who lived here and took in such boarders as Childe Hassam, Henry Ward Ranger, and other American impressionists; when they were short on cash, the boarders did a little painting around the house to pay the rent. Some of their work, including these "house paintings," is now on display here, along with New England furnishings, decorative arts, and exhibits on local history. Next door and across the street, Miss Florence's tradition of supporting creativity lives on in the LYME ACADEMY OF FINE ARTS (203-434-5232), with year-round changing exhibits of paintings and sculpture, and the LYME ART ASSOCIATION (203-434-7802), founded by the members of the original Old Lyme art colony, now a noted gallery offering five major shows every summer.

Nut Museum, 303 Ferry Rd., Old Lyme, CT 06371 (203-434-7636). *Open May-Nov Wed and Sat-Sun 2-5. Admission 1 nut (any kind— you may qualify) plus $2 adults, $1 children 6-16. Not wheelchair-accessible.*

In a large room of her Victorian mansion, curator Elizabeth Tashjian invites us to behold an unparalleled display of nuts and nut artifacts from around the world: exotic nut novelties, nut jewelry, nut mini-furniture, paintings of nuts, and, on request, songs about nuts. Those who doubt the crucial role of nuts in history will have their eyes opened here.

FOR THE DRIVER: Take I-95 north (40¢) to Exit 69 at Old Saybrook and pick up CT 9 north to Exit 3 at Essex. Bear right after ramp and follow signs to Historic Essex Village and Pratt House. For Steam Train and Riverboat, go straight after ramp and follow signs.

The next stop, Gillette Castle, is on the east bank of the Connecticut River. If you take the combination train and riverboat ride from Essex, you'll see it from the water. If you want to visit it, you have two choices. Return to CT 9, continue north to Exit 6, and take CT 148 east to Chester, where you can get the CHESTER-HADLYME FERRY (Apr-Nov daily 7am-6:45pm; 75¢ per car and driver, 25¢ per passenger; capacity 8 cars), the second-oldest continuously operating ferry service in the United States. If the ferry is not operating or you prefer to drive, continue north on CT 9 to Exit 7 and take CT 82 across the river to East Haddam, where the first building you'll see is the Goodspeed Opera House; continue past it on 82, shortly bear sharp right, and head south a few mi to Gillette Castle State Park, following signs.

Essex and East Haddam are in the southern and eastern portions, respectively, of Middlesex County, a picturesque region stretching north along the Connecticut River. For FURTHER INFORMATION, contact the Connecticut Valley Tidewater Commission, 70 College St., Middletown, CT 06457 (203-347-6924).

From Gillette Castle, continue on CT 82 a few mi to jct with CT 156. Turn right and proceed south through Hamburg towards Old Lyme. Just before jct with I-95, turn left on CT 51 and go past shopping center to Florence Griswold House. Nearby, on Ferry Rd just off 156, is Nut Museum.

East of Old Lyme off I-95 are more historic coastal towns that can be reached on a day trip from New York City but are better visited when you have more time to spare: NEW LONDON and environs, with an array of historic houses, parks and beaches, and marine attractions, including day-long whale-watching excursions to Montauk Point; GROTON, where the *USS Nautilus,* the world's first nuclear submarine (1954), was built and is now preserved as a memorial and museum; and MYSTIC, with its famous restored seaport and living maritime museum, also a departure point for windjammer cruises on Long Island Sound. For FURTHER INFORMATION about this area of Connecticut, contact the Southeastern Connecticut Tourism District, Olde Towne Mill, 8 Mill St., New London, CT 06320 (203-444-2206), and Mystic Seaport, Mystic, CT 06355 (203-572-0711); a 90-minute self-guided auto tape tour with mile-by-mile narration and background material (both historical and musical) is available at the Tourist Information Center, Building 1D, Olde Mistick Village, Mystic, CT 06355 (203-536-1641), or from CC Inc., PO Box 385, Scarsdale, NY 10583 (914-472-5133).

Touring on Long Island

• *Our next trips take us to that famous 120-mile-long fish-shaped piece of glacial deposit called Long Island, with its innumerable bays, coves, and inlets on Long Island Sound to the north and its beautiful ocean beaches to the south—"that slender riotous island which extends itself due east of New York," as F. Scott Fitzgerald called it, "the old island here that flowered once for Dutch sailors' eyes—a fresh, green breast of the new world."*

To judge by the way the city empties out and the LIE fills up on weekends, many New Yorkers already have their favorite retreats on the island. This section outlines four long drives that take us to all the familiar haunts and suggest some possibilities for exploration off the beaten track. We'll be traveling in a more or less straight line out to the fishtail tip of Long Island, first along the North Shore and North Fork, where historic New England-type towns flourish, then along the South Shore and South Fork, with miles of beaches that apparently come and go at the will of the Atlantic Ocean.

Exit Points
There are many highways and combinations of highways that will take you from the city to Long Island. Choose the one most convenient for you, depending on your point of departure and traffic conditions. Some possibilities:
  —from Manhattan, take Queens-Midtown Tunnel to Long Island Expwy (LIE);
  —from upper Manhattan or the Bronx, take Cross Bronx Expwy to Bronx-Whitestone Bridge or Throgs Neck Bridge, then take Cross Island Expwy or Clearview Expwy to LIE, Northern State Pkwy, or (from Cross Island Expwy) Southern State Pkwy;
  —from Verrazano Bridge, Brooklyn, or Queens, take Brooklyn-Queens Expwy to LIE, or take Interborough Pkwy becoming Grand Central Expwy becoming Northern State Pkwy, or take Shore Pkwy becoming Southern Belt Pkwy becoming Sunrise Hwy, with a connection from Southern Belt to Southern State Pkwy via Laurelton Expwy.

Main Roads
The main roads across Long Island are the LIE (I-495), Northern State Pkwy, Southern State Pkwy, and Sunrise Hwy (NY 27). With the exception of Sunrise Hwy, these are not the roads used as reference points for the drives in this area, but because the island is narrow and has many connecting north-south roads, you can get almost anywhere from any route you choose.

Tolls
There are no highway tolls on Long Island, and only the occasional bridge toll (given in text). For New York City bridge and tunnel tolls, see p. xvi.

Long Island Sound Crossings
For auto ferries linking Area G with Area F (Connecticut shore), see "Traveling to Area F," pp. 259–60.

Gold Coast Mansions and Historic Ports

TRIP G-1

NORTH SHORE

DISTANCE: From GWB to farthest point, Riverhead, about 80 mi. Average speeds.

Long Island, occupied on the west by the two New York City boroughs of Brooklyn and Queens, stretches east across Nassau and Suffolk Counties, encompassing populous suburbs, thriving seaport towns, quaint villages, and some of the finest beaches anywhere to be found. It is rich in Indian lore and colonial history, studded with fine architecture, blessed with fertile farmlands and almost limitless recreational opportunities. Most of the island's shore towns have public beaches but require permits or parking stickers for nonresidents; if you're planning a beach outing, check with the nearest municipality first.

For FURTHER INFORMATION about Long Island, contact the Long Island Tourism and Convention Commission, Administrative Headquarters, 213 Carleton Ave., Central Islip, NY 11722 (516-234-4959), the Long Island Association of Commerce and Industry, 80 Hauppauge Rd., Commack, NY 11725 (516-499-4400), the Long Island State Park Region, PO Box 247, Babylon, NY 11702 (516-669-1000), the Nassau Convention Office, Long Island Tourism Commission, Nassau Veterans Memorial Coliseum, Uniondale, NY 11553 (516-794-4222), the Nassau County Department of Commerce and Industry, 1550 Franklin Ave., Mineola, NY 11501 (516-535-4160), and the Suffolk County Office of Economic Development, 4175 Veterans Memorial Highway, Ronkonkoma, NY 11779 (516-588-1000).

North Shore. On this drive, we'll go east on NY 25A (Northern Blvd. in Queens), noting the attractions along our route and to the north and south. For FURTHER INFORMATION, see the sources listed in the above headnote; for specific areas covered on this trip, contact the Great Neck Chamber of Commerce, 1 Great Neck Rd., Great Neck, NY 11201 (516-487-2000), the Glen Cove Chamber of Commerce, 128 Village Square, Glen Cove, NY 11542 (516-

676-6666), the Huntington Township Chamber of Commerce, 151 West Carver St., Huntington, NY 11743 (516-423-6100), the Port Jefferson Chamber of Commerce, W. Broadway, Port Jefferson, NY 11777 (516-473-1414), and the Riverhead Chamber of Commerce, Box 291, Riverhead, NY 11901 (516-727-7600).

Just over the Nassau County line from Queens, to our left off 25A in the Great Neck area, is the US MERCHANT MARINE ACADEMY (516-482-8200) at Kings Point, where we can visit the Memorial Chapel honoring the service's war dead and see exhibits on shipping history in the American Merchant Marine Museum. On most Saturdays in spring and fall, regimental reviews are held on the grounds. The academy is very attractively located, and its main administrative center, Wiley Hall, was once the country home of automobile magnate Walter P. Chrysler. On our way to the academy, we pass the turnoff for the SADDLE ROCK GRIST MILL (516-420-5288), a 1700 stone mill powered by the tides (currently closed for renovations).

Continuing east on 25A, we come to MANHASSET VALLEY PARK (516-365-8585), a lovely small park with a restored schoolhouse where we can brush up on the Three R's. Built in 1806 at a cost of about $400, the Manhasset Valley School features old-time desks with inkwells, early textbooks, and painstaking examples of penmanship as it was taught in the good old days.

North of Manhasset is SANDS POINT PARK AND PRESERVE (516-883-1612), former Gold Coast estate of Daniel Guggenheim and his son Harry, founder of *Newsday*. On the grounds are the English Tudor-style Hempstead House, the Irish-influenced Castlegould, and the Normandy-style manor house Falaise, which is open for guided tours (no children under 12). The very, very rich have a knack for picking beautiful spots, and Sands Point is no exception. It has a great view of Long Island Sound and looks across Hempstead Harbor to Glen Cove and Garvies Point, our next stop. Here, at GARVIES POINT MUSEUM AND PRESERVE (516-671-0300), we can see exhibits on the geological formation of the region and its history of Indian settlement as revealed by archeological findings. We can also follow 5 miles of nature trails through 62 acres of forests, meadows, and high bluffs overlooking boulder-strewn beaches.

Now we're ready to charge up Sagamore Hill for a visit to the beloved summer retreat of America's 26th president, Theodore

Roosevelt. The centerpiece of the SAGAMORE HILL NATIONAL HISTORIC SITE (516-922-4447) in Oyster Bay is TR's family home, restored to the period of his presidency (1901-1909). Completed in 1885, this fine old Victorian structure incorporates many of Roosevelt's personal desires, including a large piazza with rocking chairs where the family could sit and watch the setting sun, a bay window with a southern view, and enormous fireplaces. We'll see objects collected on his trips around the world, gifts from the famous, family heirlooms, trophies, and personal mementoes such as the "Clara-doll" in the playroom and the Teddy bears named after him. "Nothing," said Roosevelt, "can take the place of family life." Near the house is the Old Orchard Museum, offering historical exhibits, documents, photographs, and hourly showings of a stirring documentary on the highlights of TR's life.

On the way to Sagamore Hill, we pass several other sites well worth visiting. Some of the finest collections of plantings in the East are to be found at the 400-acre PLANTING FIELDS ARBORETUM (516-922-9200), with its superb specimens of trees, shrubs, and flowers, particularly lavish displays of rhododendrons and azaleas, and a Synoptic Shrub Collection presenting an A-to-Z sampler of species and varieties best as ornamentals. On the grounds is a 75-room Elizabethan-Tudor mansion, originally the estate of marine insurance magnate William Robertson Coe. South of Planting Fields, just across 25A, is MUTTONTOWN NATURE CENTER (516-922-3123) in East Norwich, where we can hike along some lovely nature trails and inspect the displays in the nature study building.

The town of Oyster Bay has several buildings of historic interest. RAYNHAM HALL (516-922-6808), on Main St., is a 1740 clapboard saltbox with a Victorian addition. Home of the Samuel Townsend family, it served as headquarters for the Queen's Rangers after Long Island was taken by the British during the American Revolution. WIGHTMAN HOUSE (516-922-5032), on Summit St., is an even older colonial saltbox, built around 1720. It now contains historical exhibits, town memorabilia, and the collections of the Oyster Bay Historical Society.

On the way to or from Sagamore Hill, we may also want to stop off at the THEODORE ROOSEVELT MEMORIAL SANCTUARY AND TRAILSIDE MUSEUM (516-922-3200), 11 acres of woodland maintained by the National Audubon Society as a refuge for wild birds and a tribute to TR's record as an early and ardent conservationist.

Before continuing along the North Shore, we'll go back and investigate a few of the attractions south of our route. Just over the Nassau County line from Queens, between NY 25 and NY 24, is the famous BELMONT PARK RACE TRACK (718-641-4700 or 516-488-6000), with thoroughbred racing spring through fall. A good way to start off a day's excursion on Long Island is "Breakfast at Belmont," which gives us an opportunity to watch the horses work out while we dine at the trackside cafe.

A few miles east of Belmont, on Herrick's Rd. off Shelter Rock Rd., is the MATHEMATICS MUSEUM (516-496-8295), with audiovisual displays and hands-on exhibits that make numerical relationships come alive. This is a great place for kids with math anxiety, and possibly for adults seeking to improve their odds at Belmont.

Still south of 25A and a little further east, we come to two attractions sure to delight horticulturists and lovers of beauty. The CLARK GARDEN (516-621-7568) in Albertson, an affiliate of the Brooklyn Botanic Garden, boasts a magnificent Hunnewell Rose Garden, along with gardens of ferns, herbs, and flowers of every variety, all in an exceptionally beautiful setting of ponds, streams, and stands of pine and hemlock. Nearby is OLD WESTBURY GARDENS (516-333-0048), the former estate of financier John S. Phipps, a 100-acre park containing 8 formal gardens, including the Boxwood Garden, with its ancient giant boxwood and reflecting pool, the Walled Garden, with 2 acres of herbaceous borders and brilliant seasonal flower displays, and the charming Cottage Garden, once the playground of the Phipps children, with a small thatched cottage surrounded by a miniature garden and a fairyland of flowering shrubs. Westbury House, a fine Stuart-style mansion built early in this century, contains many priceless antiques and paintings by Gainsborough, Sargent, Reynolds, and other noted English artists. Both house and grounds are patterned after an English country estate of the 18th century.

Westbury is also the site of ROOSEVELT RACEWAY (516-222-2000), offering night harness racing on an alternate schedule with Yonkers Raceway (see Trip D-1), and the year-round WESTBURY MUSIC FAIR (516-333-0533), with a varied program of theater, musicals, concerts, and special shows. Both attractions are only minutes away from Eisenhower Park and the MUSEUM IN THE PARK (516-292-4162), housing exhibits and a reference library devoted to Nassau County and Long Island history.

Now we resume our journey along the North Shore, going from Oyster Bay to nearby Cold Spring Harbor, just over the Suffolk County line. As befits an old whaling town, Cold Spring Harbor has a WHALING MUSEUM (516-367-3418) with a completely outfitted whaling boat, many tools of the trade, and other artifacts of this bygone era, including a scrimshaw collection of over 400 pieces. A considerably less gargantuan fisherman's target is the focus of attention at the 100-year-old COLD SPRING HARBOR FISH HATCHERY (516-692-6768), where we can observe trout in various stages of maturation and see exhibits on fish and amphibians native to New York.

Our next stop is Huntington, today known chiefly as a commuter suburb and center of precision manufacturing, but a town that still preserves many reminders of its past. The HUNTINGTON HISTORICAL SOCIETY (516-427-7045) maintains the David Conklin Farmhouse (c. 1750), with period furnishings and displays on local history, the Powell-Jarvis House (1795), a favorite with antique buffs, and the Huntington Trade School (1905), with local history exhibits and research collections. Huntington's Hecksher Park, a popular spot for picnicking and outdoor concerts, contains the noted HECKSHER MUSEUM (516-351-3250), with a fine permanent collection of paintings and sculpture from the 1500s to the present.

North of town nature beckons at TARGET ROCK NATIONAL WILDLIFE REFUGE (516-286-0485), another of those beautiful former estates of wealthy former New Yorkers (in this case banker Ferdinand Eberstadt), with the inevitable mansion and formal gardens, acres of hardwood forest, and a lovely beach; it's now a serious center for nature study and environmental education, with no picnicking, swimming, or pets allowed. On the way to Target Rock, in Lloyd Harbor, we pass the gracious JOSEPH LLOYD MANOR HOUSE (516-941-9444), a large colonial home with period furnishings and an 18th-century garden.

South of Huntington, on New York Ave. near West Hills Park, is the WALT WHITMAN BIRTHPLACE STATE HISTORIC SITE (516-427-5240), where the "good gray poet" was born in 1819. Whitman spent his boyhood in this small shingled farmhouse, which has been restored as a museum honoring America's first major poet. The lower floor contains period furnishings; upstairs are documents, pictures, some of Whitman's manuscripts, and various exhibits. As a young man, Whitman returned to Huntington to teach school and edit the weekly *Long Islander;* not far south of his birthplace, in Melville, is the headquarters of another Long Island paper, NEWSDAY (516-454-2179), which recently launched a New York City edition. *Newsday* is open to the public for tours by advance arrangement (no children under 10).

A few miles east of Huntington is Centerport, and here, at the tip of Little Neck Point, is an attraction not to be missed: the VANDERBILT MUSEUM (516-261-5656), housed in a mansion built by William K. Vanderbilt II, a great-grandson of the legendary Commodore Cornelius Vanderbilt. Known as Eagle's Nest, this opulent 24-room Spanish Revival edifice was a simple 6-room country dwelling before it fell under the transforming spell of the Vanderbilt fortune. William K. was an enthusiastic naturalist, sportsman, and collector. Today the exotic art treasures he gathered in his world travels fill the dining room, bedrooms, library, and sitting room. There are several enormous hobby collections and a natural history display of over 17,000 marine and wildlife specimens, many of them quite rare. Outside we see panoramic vistas through columns of marble from the ruins of Carthage, Spanish-Moroccan buildings with belltower and bells dating from 1715, courtyards and mosaic-bordered walks, landscaped gardens overlooking Northport Bay. Also on the grounds is the VANDERBILT PLANETARIUM (516-757-7500), an excellent facility with year-round shows on weekends and holidays, and an expanded summer schedule.

Continuing east, we come to Northport, settled by English Puritans in 1656 on land purchased from the Matinecock Indians. The town has an excellent harbor, and its rich seafaring past is unfolded in the exhibits at the NORTHPORT HISTORICAL MUSEUM (516-757-9859), located in the Carnegie Library. On the tip of a spit of land jutting out into Long Island Sound is EATON'S NECK LIGHTHOUSE, built in 1798 and still casting its warning beacon almost 18 miles out to sea.

A little east of Northport, just off 25A, is SUNKEN MEADOW STATE PARK (516-269-4333), with a nice beach for swimming in the generally placid waters of the Sound. Sunken Meadow also has picnicking, hiking trails, year-round fishing, winter sports, and three 9-hole golf courses. While we're in the area, we may want to zip down the Sunken Meadow State Parkway to check out the action at the LONG ISLAND ARENA (516-499-0800) in Commack, where there's a nonstop flea market and a variety of scheduled events, from boxing to rock concerts.

If we continue east on 25A from Sunken Meadow, we shortly arrive in Smithtown, where we'll see the famous BULL STATUE in a small park in the center of town. The statue commemorates the exploits of one of the early town fathers, Richard Smith, who made a bet with the Indians about how far a man could travel on a bull in a day. Impressed with his demonstration, the Indians granted him all the land he and his mount covered. Researchers are still attempting to determine whether the bull went further in those days. There are a number of historic buildings in Smithtown, including the CALEB SMITH HOUSE (516-265-6768), where the local historical society makes its headquarters.

Moving right along, we head towards Stony Brook on 25A, passing a sign for the SAINT JAMES GENERAL STORE (516-862-8333), built by a descendant of the man who rode the bull, and due to celebrate its 130th anniversary of continuous operation in 1987. Much of the original flavor still remains, with old-fashioned foods, candies, spices, preserves, and many other accessories of 19th-century life.

Now we come to Stony Brook, an old harbor town where we can easily spend a day. The entire village is a bit of a museum piece, having been restored to the Federal period through the generosity of philanthropist Ward Melville in the early 1940s. It's a pleasant place to shop, dine, stroll, or explore the MUSEUMS AT STONY BROOK (516-751-0066), a remarkable historical and cultural complex housing collections of art and artifacts from centuries past. In the History Museum we find wonderful exhibits of costumes, dolls, toys, textiles, and housewares, and permanent displays of finely crafted decoys and miniature period rooms. The Art Museum offers changing exhibits of 19th-century paintings, with emphasis on the works of American genre painter William Sydney Mount (1807-1868), a Stony Brook resident and one of the first artists to portray blacks sympathetically, if stereotypically. A new Carriage Museum, scheduled to open late in 1986, is currently being constructed to house a renowned collection of 250

American and European horse-drawn carriages, among them fringed surreys, stately Victorias, Wells Fargo coaches, a Russian sleigh, a Conestoga wagon, and a colorful gypsy caravan. Also part of the museum complex are several period buildings, including a smithy, a one-room schoolhouse, and a working 1751 gristmill. In addition to the museums, Stony Brook is the site of a branch of the STATE UNIVERSITY OF NEW YORK (516-689-6000), with many events and facilities open to the public, notably the MUSEUM OF LONG ISLAND NATURAL SCIENCES (516-632-8230) and the FINE ARTS CENTER (516-632-7230).

Leaving Stony Brook, we continue east on 25A to Port Jefferson, another attractive harbor town, where the PORT JEFFERSON FERRY (516-473-0631) docks on its four daily round trips to Bridgeport, Connecticut (see Trip F-8), from mid-May to mid-October. On our way, in Setauket, we pass the THOMPSON HOUSE (516-941-9444), a colonial saltbox built around 1700, once the home of Long Island historian Benjamin F. Thompson, and the 1729 CAROLINE CHURCH OF BROOKHAVEN (516-941-4245), with its distinctive Union Jack weathervane. In East Setauket we find another colonial saltbox, the SHERWOOD-JAYNE HOUSE (516-941-9444). In and around Port Jefferson are many other historic sites to explore, as well as an array of shops, restaurants, beaches, and yacht clubs.

About 9 miles east of Port Jefferson is the William Floyd Parkway, taking us south to BROOKHAVEN NATIONAL LABORATORY (516-282-2123), a major research complex with the first nuclear reactor built to investigate peaceful uses of atomic energy. The lab offers a 2½-hour tour and show on weekends during summer. Long Islanders, among others, are having their doubts about even the peaceful uses of nuclear energy these days—*vide* the controversy over the SHOREHAM NUCLEAR POWER PLANT (516-929-6700) and the LILCO takeover; if we want to visit the *casus belli,* Shoreham's north of 25A just before the turnoff for the William Floyd Parkway. From the lab, the parkway continues south all the way to Fire Island (Trip G-3). A little southeast of the lab off the LIE, near Manorville, is the LONG ISLAND GAME FARM AND ZOOLOGICAL PARK (516-727-7443), with a collection of exotic and native animals and a talented cast of sea lion performers on the bill at the Oceanarium Sea School Theater.

A little over 5 miles from the William Floyd Parkway turnoff,

NY 25A merges with NY 25. From here we continue east on 25 to Riverhead, last stop on our North Shore drive. Another historic town with fine beaches, boating facilities, and deep-sea fishing, Riverhead is the home of the SUFFOLK HISTORICAL MUSEUM (516-727-2881), depicting the history of the county and its people in a series of exhibits highlighting early crafts, transportation, whaling, and the Long Island Indian legacy. Also in Riverhead is the EAST END ARTS CENTER'S CARRIAGE HOUSE (516-727-0900), where artists in residence give demonstrations and conduct workshops on their various skills.

Fertile Fields, Welcoming Waters

TRIP G-2

NORTH FORK

DISTANCE: From GWB to farthest point, Orient Point, about 110 mi. Average speeds.

On this drive, we pick up where we left off on the North Shore, following NY 25 east. For FURTHER INFORMATION, see the Long Island and Suffolk County sources listed in the headnote to Trip G-1; for specific areas covered on this trip, contact the Greenport-Southold Chamber of Commerce, Box 66, Greenport, NY 11944 (516-477-1383), and the Shelter Island Chamber of Commerce, 17 Grand Ave., Shelter Island, NY 11964 (516-749-0399). If you visit a municipal beach, remember to inquire about nonresident permits or parking stickers.

North Fork. We begin our drive east of Riverhead, through acres of rolling farmland and fields of potato plants, berry vines, vegetables, and fruit trees. Soon we come to Mattituck, with a fine harbor and several buildings of historic interest. If we're passing through in mid-June, we'll want to watch for the annual LIONS CLUB STRAWBERRY FESTIVAL AND COUNTRY FAIR.

About 3 miles east of Mattituck is Cutchogue, where we find the OLD HOUSE, the OLD SCHOOLHOUSE MUSEUM, and the WICKHAM FARMHOUSE (516-298-8353) clustered around the historic village green. The Old House, built in 1649, is a particularly good example of English Tudor architecture and is furnished with authentic period pieces, as is the Wickham Farmhouse, dating from the early 1700s. The Old Schoolhouse Museum (1840), Cutchogue's first district school, takes us back to the basics of 19th-century education. Cutchogue is also the home of the HAR-GRAVE VINEYARD (516-734-5111), one of Long Island's oldest and best-known wineries.

From Cutchogue, we continue east to Southold, passing another fine winery, PINDAR VINEYARDS (516-734-6200) in Peconic. Southold, too, is a historic town proud of its past. Its ARCHAEO-LOGICAL MUSEUM (516-765-3029) has one of the largest and best collections of Indian artifacts on Long Island, and its restored VILLAGE GREEN COMPLEX (516-765-5500), administered by the local historical society, gives us a vivid slice of 18th-century life through its displays of clothing, furniture, tools, and housewares. The Southold Historical Society also maintains the HORTON'S POINT LIGHTHOUSE MARINE MUSEUM on Long Island Sound.

Not far east of Southold is Greenport, an old whaling town often described as "New England on Long Island." Here, in addition to fine beaches, great fishing, and some outstanding seafood restaurants, we'll find a variety of attractions: the RACHEL AND EBE-NEZER (516-765-1249), a graceful replica of a 19th-century "tall ship," available for day trips or longer excursions; the charming MUSEUM OF CHILDHOOD (516-477-0720), with a hand-carved model Swiss village, a miniature ferris wheel, antique dolls and doll furniture, and an array of other toys; and the STIRLING HISTORICAL SOCIETY (516-477-0099), a restored 1831 homestead museum.

Greenport is also the docking point for the FERRY TO SHELTER ISLAND (516-749-0139), one of Long Island's loveliest and least "touristy" spots. This aptly named patch of land, 7 miles long and 6 miles wide, was settled in 1652 by New England Quakers fleeing Puritan persecution and is still a peaceful haven today. Situated between the North and South Forks, it has a highly irregular coastline pierced by inlets and caressed by coves, with miles of pristine beaches and acres of gently rolling hills. It is also accessible by ferry from Sag Harbor (Trip G-4).

Our next stop is Orient, near the eastern tip of the North Fork. Here ORIENT BEACH STATE PARK (516-323-2440) spreads over a 357-acre peninsula on Gardiners Bay, offering excellent swimming and fishing. In town, on Village Lane, is the OYSTERPONDS HISTORICAL SOCIETY (516-323-2480), a complex of seven museum buildings that has been designated a National Historic District.

Nearby is the THEATRE IN THE WORKS (516-323-3602), a tiny play-house offering summer entertainment in the unlikely setting of a 1926 ice cream parlor.

From Orient it's a short hop to Orient Point, which is as far east as we can go on the North Fork unless we want to board the ORIENT POINT FERRY (516-323-2415 or 203-443-5035) for a 1½-hour trip to New London, Connecticut. (There's a smallish island east of Orient Point, Plum Island, but it's used by the government for "animal disease" experiments and is off limits to the public—no doubt for good reason.) The ferry service operates daily except Christmas and requires advance reservations if we want to take our car along.

By the Sea, by the Beautiful Sea

TRIP G-3

SOUTH SHORE

DISTANCE: From GWB to farthest point, Hampton Bays, about 90 mi. Average speeds.

On this drive we use NY 27 and NY 27A as our main routes and reference points. For FURTHER INFORMATION, see the sources listed in the headnote to Trip G-1; for specific areas covered on this trip, contact the Long Beach Chamber of Commerce, 100 W. Park Ave., Long Beach, NY 11561 (516-432-6000), the Hemp-stead Chamber of Commerce, 1776 Nichols Court, Hempstead, NY 11550 (516-483-2000), the Garden City Chamber of Com-merce, 114 7th St., Garden City, NY 11530 (516-746-7724), the Village of Freeport, 46 N. Ocean Ave., Freeport, NY 11520 (516-378-4000), the Hicksville Chamber of Commerce, 358-B Mid Is-land Plaza, Hicksville, NY 11801 (516-931-7170), the Amityville Chamber of Commerce, 253 Countyline Rd., Amityville, NY 11701 (516-789-3557), the Village of Lindenhurst, 430 S. Wellwood Ave., Lindenhurst, NY 11757 (516-957-5700), the Patchogue Chamber of Commerce, 15 N. Ocean Ave., Patchogue, NY 11772 (516-475-0121), the Hampton Bays Chamber of Commerce, Box 64, Hamp-ton Bays, NY 11946 (516-728-2211), and the Greater Westhamp-ton Chamber of Commerce, 25 Riverhead Rd., Westhampton Beach, NY 11978 (516-288-3337). If you visit a municipal beach, remember to inquire about nonresident permits or parking stickers.

South Shore. We cross into Nassau County on NY 27 (Southern Belt Parkway), which becomes Sunrise Highway paralleling NY 27A, Montauk Highway, until the two merge near Southampton on the South Fork (Trip G-4). A few miles southwest of Valley Stream, the first major town we come to, is Lawrence, where we can visit ROCK HALL (516-239-1157), a Georgian colonial manor filled with artwork and antiques. From here we may want to continue south across the Atlantic Beach Bridge (50¢ each way) onto LONG BEACH, a popular resort island with 5 miles of beach, a 3-mile boardwalk, fishing piers, and other recreational facilities.

Continuing east from Valley Stream, we shortly come to Lynbrook, and just south of here in East Rockaway's Memorial Park is the GRIST MILL MUSEUM (516-599-2278), with two floors of East Rockaway memorabilia and exhibits on Indian and maritime history. North of Lynbrook are several attractions we may want to investigate before proceeding along the shore. In Hempstead, on North Franklin St., we find the AFRICAN AMERICAN MUSEUM (516-485-0471), with exhibits exploring the history and cultural heritage of Afro-American Long Islanders. Also in the Hempstead area are the NASSAU VETERANS MEMORIAL COLISEUM (516-794-9300), home of the New York Islanders hockey team, and HOFSTRA UNIVERSITY (516-560-6700), with many sporting events, performances, and galleries open to the public. In Garden City, at the US Army Air Corps base at Mitchel Field, is the CRADLE OF AVIATION MUSEUM (516-222-1190), tracing the history of air travel from the Wright Brothers to the Space Age. Nearby ADELPHI UNIVERSITY (516-663-1120 or 212-347-9460) offers a range of cultural, theatrical, and sports events.

Back on NY 27, we continue east to Freeport, a fishing and boating center with the famous "Nautical Mile" of WOODCLEFT CANAL, a great place to dine on seafood, shop for fresh fish, charter a boat, take a canal excursion, or watch the Great Canoe Races held annually in July. Freeport is also the gateway to one of the most popular parks in the Greater New York City area, JONES BEACH STATE PARK (516-785-1600), a 2,413-acre playground with 5 miles of oceanfront beach, additional swimming at Zach's Bay and in the saltwater and freshwater pools, boat dock and rentals, fishing, nature and bike trails, and a host of other activities. The JONES BEACH OUTDOOR THEATRE (516-221-1000) seats over 8,000 for concerts by name pop, country, and rock entertainers. Jones Beach attracts enormous crowds but by and large knows how to handle them. Getting there is another matter; try to go early on a weekday to avoid the automotive holding pattern on the approach roads on weekends. On the way to Jones Beach from Freeport via Meadowbrook State Parkway, we pass a junction with the Loop Parkway, which takes us to several parks and beaches on the east end of Long Beach Island (see above).

A little east of Freeport on 27 is Merrick, settled in 1643 and named for its original inhabitants, the Merokian Indians, commemorated by the town's 18-foot TOTEM POLE. About 2 miles beyond Merrick is Wantagh, another access point for Jones Beach State Park, via the Wantagh State Parkway. From Wantagh, we may want to detour north several miles to Hicksville to look at the magnificent doors of TRINITY EVANGELICAL LUTHERAN CHURCH (516-931-2225), exact replicas of the bronze doors executed over a quarter-century by Florentine sculptor Lorenzo Ghiberti for the east portal of the Baptistery of the Duomo of San Giovanni Battista. Ghiberti's fellow Florentines were so impressed with the doors, whose gold-leaf-embellished panels depict scenes from the Old Testament, that they named them the "Gates of Paradise." Also in Hicksville, in the Old Heitz Place courthouse and jail, is the HICKSVILLE GREGORY MUSEUM (516-822-7505), an outstanding geology museum with over 4,000 rock and mineral specimens, including a fluorescent display, as well as fossils, seashells, Indian and local history artifacts, and a large Lepidoptera collection.

Just east of Wantagh, on Washington Ave. in Seaford, is another good place to study natural history, the TACKAPAUSHA MUSEUM AND PRESERVE (516-785-2802), with exhibits on the flora, fauna, and geological formation of Long Island. Several miles of nature trails wind through the preserve's 80-acre glacial outwash plain, where many species of birds nest.

From Seaford, it's a short hop north to Bethpage, site of the year-round NASSAU FARMER'S MARKET (516-931-8400) on Route 107, open Friday and Saturday for shopping in 300 indoor booths. Nearby, off Bethpage Parkway, is BETHPAGE STATE PARK (516-249-0700), a beautifully groomed facility of almost 1,500 acres, with tennis courts, a regulation baseball diamond, hiking and biking trails, a ski tow, and a golfer's paradise of five 18-hole golf courses. North of the park, on Round Swamp Rd., is the OLD BETHPAGE VILLAGE RESTORATION (516-420-5280), a living history museum with 30 restored antebellum buildings, a working farm, and costumed interpreters reenacting life on rural Long Island from 1830 to 1850, when the Industrial Revolution was beginning to make itself felt.

Returning to NY 27, we continue east through Massapequa across the Suffolk County line to Amityville, with many charming restored homes and antique shops. For an interesting slice of local history, we'll stop in at the Amityville Historical Society's LAUDER MUSEUM (516-598-1486), where we can inquire about a walking tour of the historic village center. Just east of Amityville is Lindenhurst, where the local historical society operates two more fine repositories of South Shore history, the OLD VILLAGE HALL MUSEUM (516-957-4385) and the 1901 RESTORED DEPOT AND FREIGHT HOUSE (516-226-1254), with railroad memorabilia and an old-time working telegraph system.

Continuing east a few miles on 27, we come to the Robert Moses Causeway, which takes us across Great South Bay to CAPTREE STATE PARK (516-669-0449), on the eastern tip of the same offshore bar as Jones Beach (see above), and linked to it by Ocean Parkway. Captree is an ideal spot for fishermen, who can try their luck off the piers or rent a fishing boat at the dock. Also at the dock is Captree Excursions, offering boat tours of Great South Bay and Fire Island.

Proceeding south across Fire Island Inlet on the Robert Moses Causeway, we come to ROBERT MOSES STATE PARK (516-669-0449), a 1,000-acre stretch of shore with fine beaches, windswept sand dunes, and excellent swimming and fishing areas. The park occupies the western tip of Fire Island, the famous 32-mile-long barrier beach and resort colony. FIRE ISLAND NATIONAL SEASHORE (516-289-4810) comprises almost 20,000 acres of the island and has three areas open to the public: Sailors Haven, with marina, swimming beach, snack bar, visitor center, and nature and interpretive activities; Watch Hill, with comparable facilities plus a 26-site campground; and Smith Point West, with visitor center, interpretive activities, and a wheelchair-accessible boardwalk. The extraordinary Sunken Forest, a unique ecosystem trapped in a depression behind the dunes at Sailors Haven, displays many unusual plant adaptations and is shrouded in an air of primeval mystery.

The Robert Moses Causeway is one of only two auto routes to Fire Island; the other is William Floyd Parkway/Smith Point Bridge at the eastern end. However, no roads run the length of the island, and the only way to reach the points in between is to walk or take one of several passenger ferries that run from the South Shore to various points on the island: FIRE ISLAND FERRY SERVICE (516-665-3600 or 666-3600) from Bay Shore, serving Saltaire, Kismet, Fair Harbor, Dunewood, and Ocean Beach, with charter trips to Sunken Forest and additional service (516-665-2115) to Ocean Bay Park and Seaview; SAYVILLE FERRY SERVICE (516-589-0810) from Sayville, serving Fire Island Pines, Cherry Grove, and Barrett Beach; SUNKEN FOREST FERRY COMPANY (516-589-8980), also from Sayville, serving Sunken Forest/Sailors Haven; and DAVIS PARK FERRY COMPANY (516-475-1665) from Patchogue, serving Davis Park and Watch Hill.

From the Robert Moses Causeway, we'll pick up NY 27A, Montauk Highway, and continue east to Bay Shore, one of the ferry terminals serving Fire Island. On the way, we pass SAGTIKOS MANOR (516-665-0093), a colonial mansion dating from the 1690s, home of an aristocratic family, headquarters of British general Henry Clinton during the Revolutionary War, proud recipient of an overnight stay by George Washington in 1790. A short way east, in Islip, is THE GRANGE (516-567-8798), a recreated Long Island farm village complete with working windmill.

Continuing east briefly on 27A, we come to the junction with Southern State Parkway, which takes us south to HECKSHER STATE PARK (516-581-4433), some 1,600 scenic acres facing Great South Bay, with 3 miles of waterfront, a nature preserve, and a range of recreational facilities. Just beyond the Southern State junction on 27A is the BAYARD CUTTING ARBORETUM (516-581-1002), under cultivation since 1887, with a magnificent collection of trees that includes some of the original plantings. The lovely Connetquot River flows by, attracting flocks of aquatic birds, and there are marked nature trails (some of them wheelchair-accessible) through the pinetum, the swamp cypresses, the rhododendron plantings, the wildflower section, and other beautiful areas of this 609-acre horticultural center. Just north of the arboretum is CONNETQUOT

RIVER STATE PARK PRESERVE (516-581-1005), almost 3,500 acres crisscrossed by hiking trails and bridle paths, with an old gristmill and a fish hatchery on the grounds.

Still eastbound on 27A, we come to the SUFFOLK MARINE MUSEUM (516-567-1733) in West Sayville, where we can see some fascinating exhibits on Long Island maritime history, including a turn-of-the-century boatshop, a 1907 restored oyster cull house, the oyster schooner *Priscilla* (1888) and sloop *Modesty* (1923), and a collection of equipment used in lieu of the poetic gifts of Lewis Carroll's Walrus to pry oysters from their beds. Nearby Sayville is a terminal for ferries to Fire Island (see above), as is Patchogue, another few miles east on 27A.

About 3 miles east of Patchogue is a turnoff for Bellport, an interesting Great South Bay village listed on the National Register of Historic Places. Here we find the BELLPORT-BROOKHAVEN HISTORICAL SOCIETY MUSEUM (516-286-8773), a multi-building complex that includes a blacksmith shop, a milk house, the Post Crowell House, the Underhill Studio Museum of Early American Decoration, and the nearby Barn Museum, with an eclectic range of exhibits including marine and nautical displays, gyroscopic instruments designed by the noted American inventor Elmer A. Sperry, Indian artifacts, toys, and more. In the neighboring shore community of Brookhaven, where the Carmans River empties into Bellport Bay, is WERTHEIM NATIONAL WILDLIFE REFUGE (516-286-0485), established in 1947 to preserve one of the last natural estuarine environments on Long Island. Because of its fragile ecology, the refuge is open to the public only along the Indian Landing Nature Trail, an excellent walk for birdwatchers and naturalists.

Returning to 27A, we continue east a few miles to the turnoff for Mastic Beach, passing the William Floyd Parkway, which leads across Smith Point Bridge to Fire Island (see above). In Mastic Beach, at 20 Washington Ave., is the WILLIAM FLOYD ESTATE (516-399-2030), the 250-year-old homestead of Brookhaven-born William Floyd, Long Island's only signer of the Declaration of Independence.

Our next stops, about 14 miles east of Mastic Beach, are quaint Quogue and fashionable Westhampton Beach, the former hugging an inlet of Moriches Bay, the latter completely surrounded by water, both popular shore resort and recreation areas. In Quogue is the OLD SCHOOLHOUSE MUSEUM (516-653-4111), with artifacts and exhibits on local history.

About 8 miles further east on 27A, where the Shinnecock Canal links Great Peconic Bay and Shinnecock Bay, is the last stop on our South Shore drive, Hampton Bays, an appealing place for family outings, fishing expeditions, swimming, and sailing.

Through the Hamptons to Montauk

TRIP G-4

SOUTH FORK

DISTANCE: From GWB to farthest point, Montauk Point, about 130 mi. Average speeds.

Here we continue from our last stop on the South Shore, Hampton Bays, following NY 27A/27, Montauk Highway. For FURTHER INFORMATION, see the Long Island and Suffolk County sources listed in the headnote to Trip G-1; for specific areas covered on this trip, contact the Southampton Chamber of Commerce, 76 Main St., Southampton, NY 11968 (516-283-0402), the East Hampton Chamber of Commerce, 74 Park Place, East Hampton, NY 11937 (516-324-0362), the Sag Harbor Chamber of Commerce, Box 116D, Sag Harbor, NY 11963 (516-725-0011), and the Montauk Chamber of Commerce, Box CC, Montauk, NY 11954 (516-668-2428). If you visit a municipal beach, remember to inquire about nonresident permits or parking stickers.

The **South Fork** means the Hamptons, and the Hamptons mean different things to different people. Reams have been written about this string of towns, which have been variously praised as *the* place to be on Long Island and criticized as too "trendy." Whether our tastes run to celebrity watching or birdwatching, the fact remains that the Hamptons are beautiful and stately old towns, if a bit hectic at times. We may want to be in the thick of the fast-paced social scene, or we may want to visit during the week or in the off-season, but whenever we go, we'll soon see why so many of the famous and not-so-famous have succumbed to the Hamptons' charms.

We'll begin by following NY 27A across the Shinnecock Canal

to Southampton, passing the SHINNECOCK INDIAN RESERVATION, site of the colorful Powwow held every year on Labor Day weekend. A prime shopping district, Southampton also offers many cultural and historical attractions. The PARRISH ART MUSEUM (516-283-2118) in the center of town has a fine permanent collection of paintings and sculptures, including many works by William Merritt Chase, and sponsors an ambitious program of changing exhibits, concerts, lectures, films, and theatrical productions. Southampton was settled in 1640, and its long history is traced in the Indian, colonial, and whaling exhibits at the SOUTHAMPTON HISTORICAL SOCIETY MUSEUM (516-283-2494) on Meeting House Lane, a lovely, sprawling frame house with restored outbuildings. The HALSEY HOMESTEAD (516-283-3527) on S. Main St. is the oldest colonial saltbox in New York State.

East of Southampton, shortly after NY 27A merges with NY 27, is Water Mill, originally 40 acres of land granted by the town of Southampton to one Edward Howell in 1644, on condition that "sayd Edward Howell doth promise to build for himself to supply the necessities of the towne, a sufficient mill at Mecoxe." Over the years Howell's mill changed hands many times and provided power for grinding grain, spinning cloth, and manufacturing paper. Today it has been restored as the WATER MILL MUSEUM (516-726-9685) and once again grinds grain as it did over three centuries ago. Also here are several innovative exhibits on the history of milling and other vanished arts of the preindustrial era, all designed to encourage visitor participation.

Continuing east on 27, we come to Bridgehampton, sometime hangout of the literati and stop on the social circuit. At the BRIDGEHAMPTON HISTORICAL MUSEUM (516-537-1088), we can visit the 1775 Corwith Homestead, a blacksmith shop, and an old engine house. A few miles northwest of town, near Noyack, is the BRIDGEHAMPTON RACE CIRCUIT (516-537-3770), with auto and motorcycle racing weekends from spring to fall.

From Bridgehampton we'll head north on the Sag Harbor Turnpike (NY 79), passing the BRIDGEHAMPTON WINERY (516-537-3155), open for guided tours on weekends from May to September. In the picturesque and pleasantly low-key town of Sag Harbor, once the fourth-largest whaling port in the world, we find many reminders of the colonial and seafaring past. The SAG HARBOR WHALING MUSEUM (516-725-0770), a Greek Revival mansion (1845) with roof ornamentation of carved blubber spades and harpoons, and a right whale jawbone arching over the doorway, has several rooms devoted to local history, in addition to a large collection of whaling tools and memorabilia. The restored 1789 CUSTOMS HOUSE (516-941-9444) recalls the days when Sag Harbor was Long Island's principal port of entry. In the late 19th century, after the whaling industry declined, Sag Harbor was the site of a watch-casing factory that employed many Jewish workers. TEMPLE ADAS ISRAEL (516-725-1770), a white frame building with striking stained-glass windows, was built in 1898 to serve them and is Long Island's oldest Jewish temple. Above Sag Harbor is North Haven peninsula, where we can board a FERRY (516-749-1200) to Shelter Island (Trip G-2). Across from the peninsula, on a spit of land between Noyack and Little Peconic Bays, is the ELIZABETH MORTON NATIONAL WILDLIFE REFUGE (516-725-2270).

The Sag Harbor-East Hampton Turnpike (NY 114) takes us to our next stop, perhaps the most beautiful town on Long Island, as rich in history and architecture as it is in society-page functions and designer labels. East Hampton is best seen on a walking tour, provided we can find a place to park. A good starting point is HOME, SWEET HOME (516-324-0713), inspiration for the 1820s song of that title and boyhood home of its author, actor and playwright John Howard Payne. Built in the late 17th century, it houses fine collections of American furnishings, a gallery with changing exhibits, and Payne memorabilia. The Pantigo Windmill (1771) and a period herb garden are on the grounds. Next door is MULFORD FARM MUSEUM (516-324-6869), a restored farmhouse built around 1680, now a museum of architectural history maintained by the East Hampton Historical Society. The society has its headquarters at the nearby OSBORN-JACKSON HOUSE (516-324-6850), a 1725 colonial saltbox with later additions, and also maintains the 1784 CLINTON ACADEMY (516-324-1850), New York's first preparatory school. There's another historic windmill in East Hampton, the handsome and fully equipped HOOK MILL (516-324-0713), built as a gristmill in 1806 and still up to the old grind.

The center of East Hampton cultural life is the GUILD HALL (516-324-0806), with changing art exhibits and an interesting program of poetry readings and workshops. Guild Hall's JOHN DREW THEATER (516-324-4050) offers year-round entertainment and a particularly fine summer menu of theatrical productions, concerts, and films. Finally, like the other towns along the South Fork, East Hampton (village and town—note that the town includes East Hampton, Amagansett, and Montauk) offers a full range of facilities for fishing, boating, swimming, and other water sports.

Nearby Amagansett, just east of East Hampton, is a lovely small town with another good museum of local seafaring history, the TOWN MARINE MUSEUM (516-267-6544). In addition to whaling exhibits, shipwrecks, and a fascinating installation on underwater archeology, there are several displays on methods of commercial and sport fishing.

Our last stop, on the easternmost tip of Long Island far from the madding crowds, is Montauk, justly renowned for its excellent fishing—27 world-record catches have been hauled from its waters—and striking windswept scenery. In the past, Montauk has survived a couple of major development attempts (in one of the few happy results of the Depression, plans to turn it into a northern Miami Beach crashed along with the stock market, though the tower built by the would-be developer still stands rather incongruously in the heart of town), and despite recent encroachments, it remains relatively unscathed by the real-estate boom and social whirl of the Hamptons.

Montauk was settled in 1655 on land purchased from the Montaukett Indians, and danged if the cowboys didn't follow soon after, turning the place into a big ranch whose major social event was the annual cattle drive from Patchogue. We can learn more about this fascinating history at the SECOND HOUSE MUSEUM (516-668-5440). There's a lot of wilderness left at several parks in the area, including HITHER HILLS STATE PARK (516-668-2554) and starkly beautiful MONTAUK POINT STATE PARK (516-668-2461), site of the historic Montauk Point Lighthouse, erected by order of George Washington in 1795.

We don't usually think about cowboys and Indians when we think of New York, much less about eons-old geological processes, but here at Montauk Point, gazing out into the vast gray Atlantic Ocean, we can almost imagine the birth of a continent and the discovery of a New World.

Your Own Backyard

• *Now that we've spent a few hundred pages escaping New York City for the charms of upstate New York and neighboring states, we'll take a moment to remind ourselves of what's right here under our noses waiting to be discovered or enjoyed anew. Manhattan spends so much time in the glare of the spotlight and has elicited so many words per square inch of territory that we're going to skip it altogether and concentrate on the less-publicized attractions of the oft-neglected Other Four Boroughs.*

There's No Place Like Home . . .
TRIP H
STATEN ISLAND
THE BRONX
QUEENS
BROOKLYN

If you live in New York City, chances are you know very little about your own borough and even less about the other four. You've probably seen some of Manhattan's world-famous sights, but there's more to Manhattan than those (see the shelfful of guides at your local library or bookstore), and there's more to New York City than Manhattan (see below). For FURTHER INFORMATION about all five boroughs, contact the New York Convention and Visitors Bureau, 2 Columbus Circle, New York, NY 10019 (212-397-8222).

Staten Island was sighted in 1524 by Giovanni da Verrazano, the Italian explorer for whom the bridge linking it with Brooklyn is named. Henry Hudson, sailing for the Dutch East India Company, visited it in 1609 and gave it the name that stuck, Staaten Eyelandt. The British soon followed the Dutch, and the island became Richmond County, after the Duke of Richmond. During the Revolutionary War, Staten Island was the site of a large British base. Today it is the least urban and least populous of New York City's boroughs, with many attractive neighborhoods, fine parks and beaches, and unspoiled stretches of great natural beauty. It is accessible by car from the Verrazano Bridge and by water via the famous STATEN ISLAND FERRY (212-806-6940 or 718-390-5253), a 5-mile trip from South Ferry in Manhattan to the Saint George terminal, offering magnificent views of the Manhattan skyline, the Statue of Liberty, and the bustling harbor and bay. A ferry museum at the terminal gives us a fascinating glimpse of the history of this enjoyable and efficient form of transportation.

The rich history of Staten Island can be explored at several fine museums and restorations. SNUG HARBOR CULTURAL CENTER (718-448-2500), at 914 Richmond Terrace in New Brighton, is a complex of 26 historic buildings centered around Sailors Snug Harbor, America's first home for retired sailors, and an outstanding example of Greek Revival architecture. This National Historic Landmark overlooking the Kill Van Kull today serves as a major center of the fine and performing arts. On the grounds are many 19th-century and modern sculptures and the lovely Staten Island Botanical Garden.

The STATEN ISLAND MUSEUM (718-727-1135), at 75 Stuyvesant Place near the ferry, has natural history exhibits, a genealogical and research library, and changing exhibits highlighting the work of local artists. The CONFERENCE HOUSE (718-984-2086), at the foot of Hylan Boulevard in Tottenville, is a 1670s stone manor house with period furnishings, a working kitchen, and cooking and craft demonstrations on the first Sunday of each month. Also known as Billopp House, it was the site of the only peace conference of the American Revolution, held in 1776 between Admiral Howe, commander of the British fleet in North America, and members of the Continental Congress, including Benjamin Franklin and John Adams. The negotiations failed and the Revolutionary War continued, with results that are well known.

The most ambitious historical project on the island is the RICHMONDTOWN RESTORATION (718-351-1611), in the Greenbelt area, the only restored village in New York City. Here we can visit 25 buildings (11 on their original sites) dating from the 17th to the 19th centuries, including the oldest standing elementary schoolhouse in the United States, the Voorlezer's House (1695). Regional history comes vividly alive at Richmondtown as we visit the various houses, shops, and exhibits, learning about early trades and crafts, modes of transportation, local material culture, and the techniques by which the village has been restored.

In 1850, after his defeat by Napoleon III, the great Italian patriot Giuseppi Garibaldi took refuge on Staten Island in Rosebank, sharing a simple farmhouse with his countryman and friend Antonio Meucci, whose experiments with the telephone predated those of Alexander Graham Bell by some years. Today the farmhouse has been restored and the memory of those expatriate years has been preserved in the GARIBALDI-MEUCCI MUSEUM (718-987-6643) at 420 Tomkins Ave.

Staten Island also has several museums devoted to specialized interests. The lively STATEN ISLAND CHILDREN'S MUSEUM (718-273-2060) at 15 Beach St. in Stapleton has rotating participatory exhibits on various topics in the arts, humanities, and sciences. Those fascinated by Oriental philosophy, history, and art will find untold treasures at the highly respected JACQUES MARCHAIS CENTER OF TIBETAN ART (718-987-3478) at 338 Lighthouse Ave. in Richmond, housed in two stone buildings patterned after a Tibetan monastery. The MUSEUM OF ARCHAEOLOGY AT STATEN ISLAND (718-273-3300), located in the main hall of Wagner College in Grymes Hill, takes us back to early history and prehistory through its collections from Egypt, the Near and Far East, Greece, Italy, Europe, Africa, Oceania, and the Americas, with one gallery devoted to New York City's Indian heritage.

Nature lovers will also find much to delight them on Staten Island. On the western shore in New Springville is the WILLIAM T. DAVIS WILDLIFE REFUGE (718-727-1135), 260 acres of marshland and forest habitat sheltering a range of plant and animal life. In the middle of the island is HIGH ROCK PARK CONSERVATION CENTER (718-987-6233), a National Environmental Education Landmark, offering an informative selection of tours and interpretive exhibits. The STATEN ISLAND ZOO (718-442-3100) is a small but well-maintained facility with a variety of mammals and birds, some good marine displays, and an extensive collection of reptiles, including the most species of rattlesnakes to be found anywhere under a single roof. Finally, the National Park Service administers 26,000 acres of shoreline and parkland as the STATEN ISLAND UNIT (718-351-8700) of Gateway National Recreation Area. Two areas south of the Verrazano Bridge off Hylan Boulevard are open to the public: Great Kills Park, with excellent swimming and fishing, and Miller Field, an early hangar complex built just after World War I, with tennis courts, a roller rink, and playing fields to add to its historic interest.

The Bronx, the only New York City borough permanently attached to the North American continent and the definite article, was settled by Jonas Bronck in 1639 on land purchased from the Dutch. Though the South Bronx has become a nationwide symbol of urban blight, there is much to recommend the rest of the borough. In addition to its two best-known attractions—the world-renowned BRONX ZOO (212-367-1010) and YANKEE STADIUM (212-293-6000), home of the famous Bombers and birthplace of the famous cheer—the Bronx has its own Little Italy, Belmont, with the bustling ARTHUR AVENUE MARKET offering a panoply of palate-tempting Italian treats, and its own little chunk of New England in Long Island Sound, CITY ISLAND, with its fine seafood restaurants, picturesque old houses, and proud shipyards where master builders have crafted many sleek and graceful America's Cup yachts over the years. We can learn more about these largely undiscovered corners of New York at the ENRICO FERMI CENTER/BELMONT LIBRARY (212-933-6410), one of the largest Italo-American research collections in the country, and the CITY ISLAND HISTORICAL AND NAUTICAL MUSEUM (212-885-0794).

Did you know that the Bronx was an important colonial settlement where Revolutionary War battles once raged? These and other facts about the borough's past are preserved at the VALENTINE-VARIAN HOUSE AND MUSEUM OF BRONX HISTORY (212-881-8900), on Bainbridge Ave. and 208th St., a fieldstone farmhouse built in 1758, later the boyhood home of New York City mayor Isaac Varian; at the beautiful VAN CORTLANDT MANSION (212-543-3344), at 246th St. and Broadway in Van Cortlandt Park, the 1748 estate of one of New York's leading families, which served as headquarters of both British and American troops during the Revolution and sheltered George Washington many times; and in Van Cortlandt Park itself, originally part of a Dutch land grant, now a 2-square-mile recreational area with facilities for swimming, horseback riding, picnicking, handball, and tennis, and the intriguing spectacle of weekend cricket matches played by Bronx residents from the West Indies.

Speaking of residents from foreign shores, the Bronx is home to the MUSEUM OF MIGRATING PEOPLES (212-320-2300) in Truman High School, at Baychester Ave. and Donizetti Place, where artifacts, photographs, and documents trace the waves of immigration and intramigration that have shaped our city and our country. And speaking of parks, you'll probably be surprised to learn that 23% of the Bronx's 42 square miles is parkland. Indeed, the city's largest park and one of its finest beaches are located in the northeast corner of the Bronx, across from City Island: PELHAM BAY PARK, over 2,000 acres with a range of recreational facilities, a marine zoology and geology sanctuary, a wildlife refuge, beautiful ORCHARD BEACH (212-885-1828), and the historic BARTOW-PELL MANSION (212-885-1461), a handsome specimen of Greek Revival architecture with Empire furnishings. The Bronx also boasts two outstanding botanical gardens: the NEW YORK BOTANICAL GARDEN (212-220-8700), on Southern Boulevard in Bronx Park, 250 acres of flowering trees and shrubs, rose, rock and herb gardens, pine and hemlock forests, the lovely Bronx River waterfall, and the landmark Crystal Palace, where we can wander through nonurban jungles, arid deserts, and other exotic environments; and WAVE HILL (212-549-2055), at 249th St. and Independence Ave., a beautifully situated former Hudson River estate, now home to some remarkable plant life, both wild and cultivated.

The Bronx also has its share of cultural attractions, most notably the borough's answer to Lincoln Center, LEHMANN COLLEGE CENTER FOR THE PERFORMING ARTS (212-960-8833), a modern complex including a concert hall, two theaters, and a recital hall, with an impressive roster of dance, concerts, and theatrical performances. The BRONX MUSEUM OF THE ARTS (212-681-6001), at Grand Concourse and 161st St., is a showcase for modern and contemporary painting, sculpture, graphics, and photography. More remote in time but in some ways just as modern in sensibility are the exhibits at the EDGAR ALLAN POE COTTAGE (212-881-8900), on Grand Concourse and Kingsbridge Rd., where the brooding poet and father of the detective mystery spent his last years and wrote "Annabel Lee" and "The Bells," among other works.

Geographically New York's largest borough, **Queens** is the land of arrivals and departures, where the skies are cloudy all day with planes taking off from John F. Kennedy International Airport and La Guardia Airport. The center of attraction in Queens is FLUSHING MEADOW-CORONA PARK, 1,258 acres located between the Grand Central and Van Wyck Expressways, site of the World's Fairs of 1939-40 and 1964-65, and present home of the USTA NATIONAL TENNIS CENTER (718-271-5100) and the annual US Open, and of SHEA STADIUM (718-509-8499), which witnesses the yearly vicissitudes of the New York Mets, winners of the 1986 World Series. Also here are the QUEENS ZOO AND CHILDREN'S FARM ZOO (718-699-7239), the lovely QUEENS BOTANICAL GARDEN (718-886-3800), Broadway hits at the QUEENS THEATRE IN THE PARK (718-592-5700), and two fine museums: the recently refurbished

NEW YORK HALL OF SCIENCE (718-699-0005), with a dazzling array of hands-on state-of-the-art exhibits on chemistry, physics, biology, oceanography, space technology, and more; and the QUEENS MUSEUM (718-592-5555), with an innovative program of interdisciplinary fine arts presentations, changing exhibits, and a permanent collection that includes the 9,000-square-foot *Panorama*, a detail-perfect architectural model of the five boroughs.

Queens was settled by the Dutch in 1635 and occupied by the British during the Revolutionary War. In between, a substantial number of Quakers arrived and made their mark on the borough. BOWNE HOUSE (718-359-0528), at 37-01 Bowne St., was built in 1661 by John Bowne, a Quaker who led an important struggle for freedom of worship under Dutch rule. It is the oldest New York City house open to the public. The nearby OLD QUAKER MEETINGHOUSE (718-358-9636), at 137-16 Northern Boulevard near Main St., dates from the late 17th century and is still in use.

Just over the Queensboro bridge from Manhattan, at 34-31 35th St., is the ASTORIA MOTION PICTURE AND TELEVISION FOUNDATION (718-784-4520), which has played a major role in New York's renaissance as a movie and video production center. Astoria has a long and distinguished moviemaking history. Between 1921 and 1932 the original studio produced 110 silent films and 35 "talkies," starring such luminaries as Rudolph Valentino, the Barrymores, Claudette Colbert, W. C. Fields, and the Marx Brothers. In the late 1930s, with Hollywood in its Golden Age, Astoria declined, but during World War II it was reborn as the Army Pictorial Center, producing about 30 propaganda and educational films a year until it shut down in 1970. Astoria reopened its doors as a commercial operation in 1975-76, and today we can visit the studio and see a fascinating exhibit, "Making Movies in New York: 1896-1982," tracing the history of the motion picture industry and the vital role of New York in the development of this indigenous American art form.

Queens is also the home of the largest thoroughbred racetrack in the United States, AQUEDUCT (718-641-4700), and includes two sections of Gateway National Recreation Area: JAMAICA BAY WILDLIFE REFUGE (718-474-0613), which teems with birdlife during the spring nesting season and the fall migrations along the Atlantic Flyway; and the BREEZY POINT UNIT (718-474-4600) on the western tip of Rockaway peninsula, where old Fort Tilden, one of New York City's shore defenses on and off since the War of 1812, now serves as a center for environmental education and a starting point for exploration of the dunes and the marine life of the ocean and bay beaches.

As befits the city's most populous borough, **Brooklyn** holds a range of attractions to suit every taste, from the all-American pastimes of a day on Coney Island to cultural institutions that compete with Manhattan's in sophistication.

Brooklyn's Gowanus and Wallabout Bays attracted Dutch settlers as early as 1636, and about 10 years later the Dutch established the farming community of Breuckelen near what is now the BROOKLYN HEIGHTS HISTORIC DISTRICT, just over the Brooklyn Bridge. This 50-block area holds many superb examples of the brownstone architecture for which the borough is famous, and the promenade along the East River offers some of the best views of the bridge and the Manhattan skyline to be found anywhere in the city. Also in Brooklyn Heights, at 120 Pierpont St., is the LONG ISLAND HISTORICAL SOCIETY (718-624-0890), housing an excellent research collection and library of local history. Not far away, appropriately located in an old subway station on Schermerhorn St. at Boerum Place approaching the Brooklyn Bridge, is the NEW YORK CITY TRANSIT EXHIBIT (718-330-3060), featuring antique cars, equipment, and memorabilia dating back to 1903—a testimonial to the city's grandly conceived and executed rapid transit system, now so sadly in decline.

In the Fort Greene section of Brooklyn, off Flatbush Ave. at 30 Lafayette Ave., is one of New York's most distinguished cultural centers, the BROOKLYN ACADEMY OF MUSIC (718-636-4100), popularly known as BAM. Founded in 1859, it is among the oldest performing arts centers in America and is noted for its annual Next Wave Festival of vanguard dance, musical, and theatrical presentations, in addition to a varied program of more traditional performances.

Up Flatbush Ave. from BAM is the imposing Soldiers and Sailors Memorial Arch at Grand Army Plaza, one of the entry points to 526-acre PROSPECT PARK (718-788-0055), whose designers, Frederick Law Olmsted and Calvert Vaux, preferred it to their better-known creation in Manhattan, Central Park. Site of many outdoor concerts in summer, the park includes a skating rink, boating lakes, and—unfortunately—a lamentable little zoo in bad need of improvement; renovations are planned over the next few years, but in the meantime visitors may wish to register a complaint with the New York City Department of Parks and Recreation, 95 Prospect Park West, Brooklyn, NY 11215 (718-965-6511).

Across from Prospect Park and adjacent to each other on Eastern Parkway are two prime Brooklyn attractions. The 50-acre BROOKLYN BOTANIC GARDEN (718-622-4433) is justly renowned for its many beautiful plantings—among them a rose garden, a children's garden, an herb garden, a fragrance and Braille garden, and a collection of flowering cherry trees—and especially for its three Japanese gardens and bonsai collection. The BROOKLYN MUSEUM (718-638-5000) is one of the leading art museums in the country and has particularly fine Egyptian and primitive collections. Further down off Eastern Parkway, at 145 Brooklyn Ave., is the BROOKLYN CHILDREN'S MUSEUM (718-735-4432), founded in 1899 as the first museum in the world planned specifically for children, and carrying on its fine tradition with displays of over 40,000 natural history, ethnological, and technological artifacts designed to encourage participation and understanding.

At the southern end of Brooklyn is the hurly-burly world-unto-itself of CONEY ISLAND (718-266-1234), with its legendary amusement park, boardwalk, beach, and hotdog-downing, cotton-candy-consuming throngs. Also here is the NEW YORK AQUARIUM (718-266-8711), with a large and varied collection of marine life, from invertebrate forms to whales, and aquatic shows by performing sea lions and dolphins. Separating the east end of Coney Island from "mainland" Brooklyn is SHEEPSHEAD BAY, an attractive shore community with delights for active and passive seafood lovers alike. Boats depart from its piers regularly for deep-sea fishing expeditions, and there are many fine restaurants and clam bars in the area. Nearby, between Sheepshead Bay and Jamaica Bay, is the headquarters and Brooklyn section of GATEWAY NATIONAL RECREACTION AREA (718-338-3338), with a variety of environmental education programs centered at Floyd Bennett Field, which witnessed plenty of aviation history in its previous life as New York's first municipal airport.

Index

329